ENGLISH SYNTAX

ENGLISH SYNTAX

second edition

C. L. Baker

The MIT Press
Cambridge, Massachusetts
London, England

This book was set in Times Roman by Asco Trade Typesetting Ltd., Hong Kong and was printed and bound in the United States of America.

Library of Congress Cataloging-in-Publication Data

Baker, C. L. (Carl Lee)
    English syntax / C. L. Baker.—2nd ed.
      p. cm.
    Includes bibliographical references and index.
    ISBN 0-262-02385-7 (hc).—ISBN 0-262-52198-9 (pb)
    1. English language—Syntax. 2. English language—Grammar, Generative. I. Title.
PE1361.B35   1995
425—dc20   94-48244
                                               CIP

For Andrew and Catherine

Contents

ix   Contents

As was the case with the first edition, this new edition is designed to be used as a textbook in a basic course in English syntax at either the undergraduate level or the beginning graduate level. My intention at the time I was preparing the first edition was to come as close as possible to writing a work that would be self-contained and thus would be as successful as possible with students who lacked prior coursework in English syntax or in syntactic theory. In using the first edition as a textbook in my own classes, I noticed many respects in which the material could be augmented and reformulated so as to render it more accessible to such an audience. My major goal in preparing this new edition has been to carry out as many such "accessibility" improvements as possible, with the hope of making the work useful and effective for a significantly larger fraction of its intended readership. In pursuit of this goal, I have made a great many minor revisions and also a significant number of major revisions and additions. Before describing the most important changes, I would like to repeat from the preface to the first edition a few observations concerning the general orientation of the book.

The approach to English syntax that is followed in this book has its roots in the discipline of linguistics. As with linguistic work in general, the main goal is not so much prescriptive as descriptive. Thus, unlike many traditional school grammars, this book is not primarily concerned with defining proper English usage. Instead, it takes the English language as it is used today and attempts to describe the way in which its sentences are formed. As a consequence of this orientation, virtually no attention is given to sentences like *Bob was setting on his bed* or *John and me fed the pigeons,* where the usages of individual speakers do not always agree. By contrast, a great deal of time is spent on trying to understand the structure of uncontroversially acceptable sentences like *Joe asked Martha to tell him where to put the chair* and *There seems to be a flaw in this proof.*

The fact that this book has a descriptive rather than prescriptive orientation is enough to give it a strongly linguistic character. More narrowly, it falls within the spirit of a particular approach to linguistics known as the *generative* approach. This approach, which was pioneered by Noam Chomsky of the Massachusetts Institute of Technology in the middle and late 1950s, has become far and away the most widely followed method for the study of syntax. The central underlying premise is that a person's fluency in a given language rests on largely unconscious knowledge of a vast system of rules that define the well-formed structures of the language. It is then the business of the linguist who is studying this language to try to determine what these unconscious rules are. Applied to the syntax of English, the generative approach has given rise to an enormous explosion of new research and new ideas. The result of nearly four decades of scholarly work is an increasingly deep and comprehensive idea of what it is that a person knows when he or she knows English.

Although this book follows the generative approach, it does not conform in detail to any of the particular generative theories of syntax that have been developed in recent years—theories such as Transformational Grammar, the Extended Standard Theory, Relational Grammar, Lexical-Functional Grammar, Generalized Phrase-Structure Grammar, Government-Binding Theory, or Head-Driven Phrase-Structure Grammar. Readers who have some knowledge of these theories may detect their influence at various points in the text. Those readers who wish to study one or more of these theories, either during their reading of this book or afterward, can take many of the basic descriptive ideas about English syntax presented here and reformulate them in terms of the particular theories in which they are interested.

As a result of studying this book, readers should come to understand the most important syntactic rules of English and how they interact in the formation of individual sentences. This understanding should be sufficiently detailed and concrete to enable them to analyze mildly complicated English sentences with a certain degree of confidence and comfort. The following sentence provides an illustration:

The man and woman whose children wanted to help them decide which design to adopt have already realized that the new kitchen will be much more difficult to keep clean than the old one was.

Before working through this book, many students (especially native speakers of English) will consciously perceive this sentence as little more than a sequence of individual words that somehow make sense together. By the end of the book, the same readers should be able to identify a variety of structural units, including the following:

- the relative clause introduced by *whose children*
- the infinitival indirect question introduced by *which design,* with the missing direct object of *adopt*
- the clausal complement introduced by *that*
- the infinitival complement of *difficult,* with the missing object of *keep*
- the comparative construction associated with this adjective phrase

Beyond this, they should have an idea of the rules that create these individual structures, those that license their use in the larger contexts in which they occur, and those that account for certain basic properties of their interpretation.

For those readers who want to achieve this level of mastery, doing the exercises is essential. In addition to making new material more familiar, they provide a constant review of material introduced earlier. Their overall effect is to ensure an understanding of English rules and English structure that is active and concrete rather than passive and vague.

As suggested in the opening paragraph, the vast majority of the changes in this edition have been made with the intent of rendering the book more effective for its intended audience. The most important of these changes are the following:

- The imaginary dialogue in chapter 1, the purpose of which is to introduce the general method used to uncover unconscious syntactic rules, has been supplemented with extensive running commentary on the logical significance of what is being said at each step of the way.
- The discussion of the distinction between complements and modifiers at the beginning of chapter 3 has been made more explicit and has been supported with specific examples.
- The discussion of complement configurations in chapter 3 has been augmented by the addition of a new subsection ("Simple Complement Rules in Complicated Sentences"). This subsection illustrates the manner in which a lengthy, complicated phrase arises not from a single lengthy and complicated rule, but instead from the interaction of several short and simple rules.

- Chapter 4 includes a new subsection ("Practical Interlude: More on the Relation between Rules and Trees"). The purpose of this subsection is to illustrate the precise way in which success in constructing tree diagrams for complex sentences requires constant reference to specific syntactic rules as well as to the individual words that make up the sentences.
- Section 5.3, which concerns the interpretation of the definite article, has been revised extensively, with less emphasis on the universal implication that often accompanies the article's use and much more emphasis on the question of how a certain entity or set of entities meets the requirement of being "established" or "registered" in a discourse.
- A new section ("A More Sophisticated View of Missing-Phrase Constructions") has been added at the end of chapter 9. Beyond the fact that the nature of missing-phrase constructions is of interest in its own right, this section serves the practical purpose of building a foundation for the discussion in chapter 10 of the difference between *that* clauses and relative clauses.
- The description of comparative clauses in chapter 12 has been completely reworked; the new treatment affords a more systematic approach to understanding the structures of individual examples.
- In chapter 15, the section devoted to scope has been augmented by the addition of a preparatory discussion concerning the basic nature of this essential concept, in anticipation of examining how the concept figures in the behavior of negative and nonassertive elements in English.
- A new subsection ("Practical Strategies for Dealing with Conjoined Structures") has been added in chapter 16.
- An appendix ("The Context of English Syntax: Epilogue with References") is provided for those readers who are curious about how the subject matter that they have seen in this textbook fits into the broader enterprise of generative syntactic theory.
- Another appendix ("Summary of Basic Syntactic Structures") has been added at the end of the book. This appendix gathers in one place, for easy reference, all of the "tree pieces" that have been proposed in the text.

One additional type of change will be apparent at many places in the book. Where possible, I have developed new exercises whose intent is to draw the reader's attention to historical and dialectal variation, and also to actually attested samples of current English. The general aim of this effort is to give readers an initial idea of the interesting syntactic problems that can be found in the English of books from various periods and also in the English of newspapers and everyday communications.

In preparing this new edition, I have had the help of a great many people. First of all, my students in several different syntax classes at the University of Texas at Austin have politely but persistently prodded me for greater clarity or completeness on a variety of specific points. In addition, several colleagues—in particular, Ileana Comorovski, Manfred Krifka, Richard Meier, Gil Rappaport, Carlota Smith, Bob Wall, and Steve Wechsler—have given me comments based on their experiences in using the first edition in the classroom, or else have looked at tentative versions of new material prepared for the second edition. I am also grateful for the comments and suggestions contained in published reviews of the first edition by D. J. Allerton, Rodney Huddleston, and Hermann Wekker. In a different vein altogether, I would like to thank George Hastings for making available to me the excellent syllabus that he developed for his English syntax course at the State University of New York at Albany. Seeing in detail how creatively the first edition could be used in the hands of a committed teacher was a significant source of inspiration for me during my work on the second edition.

I would like to conclude by adding a word of thanks to several people at MIT Press. For this edition as for the previous one, Larry Cohen provided invaluable help and encouragement at every step of the way and was an unfailing source of sound judgment on a great many matters both large and small. Anne Mark, who carried out the copyediting in her customary stellar fashion, substantially improved the readability of the text and used her remarkable grasp of the overall structure and intent of the work to get the right solutions to literally hundreds of problems of editorial detail. Finally, I am grateful to Larry and Anne, and also to Amy Pierce, for taking the time to read and comment on a preliminary draft of appendix A.

PART I

INTRODUCTION

Chapter 1

The Field of English Syntax

The central purpose of this chapter is to give a preliminary idea of what we will be doing in this book. In section 1.1, we will see what the field of English syntax is concerned with and how we can proceed to study it. In section 1.2, we will see how the study of English syntax fits within the general context of modern linguistics. In section 1.3, we will consider how best to understand the different varieties of English that we hear around us. This discussion will provide helpful background ideas for section 1.4, where we will compare the approach taken here with the approach taken in traditional school textbooks on English grammar.

1.1 THE SUBJECT MATTER OF ENGLISH SYNTAX

By the *syntax* of a language, we mean the body of rules that speakers of the language follow when they combine words into sentences. Thus, when we investigate *English* syntax, we will be trying to determine the rules that dictate how *English* speakers combine words to make sentences.

At first glance, it may not be clear how much there is to be said about English rules. In particular, those who have grown up with English as their native language often take it for granted that no special rules are required for success in using English. For example, in an appropriate situation they might utter a sentence such as (1).

(1) Martha lives in the house that John sold to her.

In producing this sentence, they would typically have the impression that they were not following any rules at all but merely letting the thought to be expressed dictate the choice of words and their arrangement in the sentence. These speakers, then, might find it hard to believe that any special rules of English sentence formation played a role in shaping this utterance. Thus, we need to start our discussion by looking at some reasons for believing that rules of English syntax really exist.

1.1.1   Evidence for Rules of Syntax

We get a first piece of evidence that English sentence formation follows rules when we look at how the thought expressed in (1) might be expressed by a speaker of Japanese. Let us imagine a person whose only knowledge about English consists of some information about English words and their meanings obtained from a Japanese-to-English dictionary. The most likely result of this person's effort to express this thought would be the sentence given in (2), which corresponds word by word to the sentence that would convey the same thought in Japanese.

(2) Martha John her to sold house in lives.

Even though this imaginary Japanese speaker has a coherent thought to express and knows the necessary English words, he or she clearly does not have the means to construct a successful English sentence. The striking difference in acceptability between (1) and (2) suggests that a person who sets out to construct an acceptable English sentence must also use some rules that dictate allowable English *word order*. (It should be obvious that an English speaker who tried to construct a Japanese sentence without knowing any rules for Japanese word order would have just as serious a problem in making a sentence that was acceptable to fluent Japanese speakers.)

   More evidence that knowing some words and having a thought to express are not enough is provided by the following pairs of sentences:

(3) a. The mayor gave John some good advices.
   b. The mayor gave John some good advice.

(4) a. This man going to the station.
   b. This man is going to the station.

(5) a. Jack read the book that Marsha bought it for him.
   b. Jack read the book that Marsha bought for him.

(6) a. Anyone didn't see the accident.
   b. No one saw the accident.

When asked to say which sentence in each of these pairs is the more acceptable one, fluent speakers of English would invariably pick the (b) sentences. They might describe the (a) sentences as "funny-sounding" or "not normal" or "the wrong way to say it," even though they would find it easy to tell what thought the sentences were supposed to communicate. All the (a) sentences are of types that occasionally occur in the speech and writing of students who are in the early stages of learning English as a foreign language. Here again, we can see that a knowledge of English words and their meanings is not enough to guarantee that a person with a thought to convey will be able to express it in a sentence that English speakers will consider acceptable.

We thus have some initial evidence to suggest that English speakers follow rules of some kind when they put sentences together. One curious aspect of these rules requires mention right away: people who have learned English in early childhood as their native language and speak it fluently as adults are typically unable to say exactly what rules determine the correct word order in (1), or dictate the choice of the (b) sentences in preference to the (a) sentences in (3)–(6). In addition, when they create sentences or when they decide which of two sentences sounds better, they are usually not even aware that they are following any rules. Thus, if we are to believe that English speakers follow syntactic rules, we must hold that these rules are *unconscious*. The view we get, then, can be depicted as in (7).

(7)

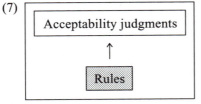

The arrow from the lower box to the upper one indicates that what is in the lower box determines what is in the upper one—in this case, that rules determine acceptability judgments. The contrast between the absence of shading in the top box and the presence of shading in the bottom one is designed to mark the difference between what is conscious and what is not. The acceptability judgments that we made in (3)–(6) are "accessible to our introspection": in effect, we can look inside our minds and observe our differing reactions to the sentences in each pair. By contrast, the rules that determine these judgments are "inaccessible to our introspection": we cannot look into our minds and see what the rules are, just as we cannot watch them operating when we are making individual judgments.

Some native speakers of English might find it difficult to believe in the existence of mental rules of which they have no conscious awareness.

They might prefer an alternative view, which could be expressed as follows: "I really don't think that I followed any rules when I picked out the (b) sentences in (3)–(6) as the good ones. Any speaker of English would pick the (b) sentences simply because they are similar to sentences that he or she would have heard before." This view is pictured in (8).

(8)

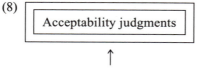

At first glance, this position might seem to be much more natural than the one diagrammed in (7), which required us to believe in unconscious mental rules. After all, the clearest, most indisputable fact about human language development is that the utterances a person hears in early childhood play an indispensable role in determining what sentences the same person will accept and use at a later stage of life. This fact forces us to acknowledge in some way or other the contribution of previously heard utterances. The immediate question, though, is whether diagram (8) gives us a reasonable picture of this contribution.

The most important claim that this diagram makes is that previously heard sentences determine judgments *directly,* without the help of mental rules. Before we look at the problems with this view, we need to note that if speakers are to use utterances heard in their past experience to judge sentences offered to them in the present, then they must have some mental record of the past sentences. So we need at least to exchange the diagram in (8) for the slightly more complex one in (9).

(9)

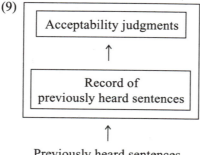

One more change needs to be made in our diagram. Even people who claim that judgments are made on the basis of previous sentences rather than on the basis of rules must admit that they do not consciously remember any significant number of previously heard sentences and that they have no awareness of actually using them in judging pairs of sentences like those in (3)–(6). Thus, for the same reason that we shaded the *rules* in diagram (7), we must now shade the *record of previously heard sentences* in diagram (9). The new picture that emerges is (10).

(10)

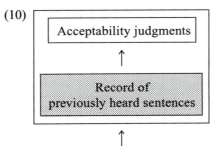

Previously heard sentences

Thus, the basic choice between these two views comes down to a choice between believing in an unconscious set of mental rules and believing in an equally unconscious record of previously heard sentences.

Two basic arguments favor the "rules" view over the "previous sentences" view. The first is that keeping a sufficient record of previously heard utterances would require an immense amount of mental storage. Because of the "mental search" time that would have to be spent in looking for "similar sentences," we would expect acceptability judgments to take much more time than they actually take. The second consideration is that there is a serious problem in saying how the record of earlier utterances would actually be used to judge new ones. The problem hinges on the question of what counts as "similarity." More specifically, we need to know when a sentence heard now and a sentence heard in the past qualify as being "similar." For instance, imagine a person who had a mental list of sentences that included (11a). He or she might well conclude that sentence (11b) is "similar" enough to be acceptable.

(11) a. The mayor gave Joe some good suggestions.
b. The mayor gave Joe some good advices.

Thus, if we really judged the acceptability of new sentences by their degree of "similarity" to sentences heard previously, we would almost certainly accept many sentences that in fact we reject.

For these reasons, we will put aside the view represented in (10) and go back to the one represented in (7), in which our judgments are determined by rules. How, though, can we recognize the undeniable connection between sentences heard in childhood and sentences accepted in maturity? The answer is that there is an *indirect* connection: the sentences heard in childhood determine our mental rules, and these rules in turn determine the sentences that we accept in adulthood. This can be pictured as in (12), an expanded version of (7).

(12)

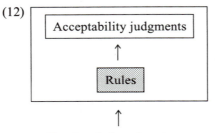

Previously heard sentences

1.1.2   How We Discover the Rules

Suppose that we accept the idea pictured in (12). We then need to consider how we find out exactly what the rules are. As was noted above, we cannot look inside our minds and observe them directly. What we can observe, though, are some of the *effects* of these rules. In particular, we can look at judgments of acceptability, of the sort that we have seen several times already. We can then take these observations as hints or clues concerning the nature of the invisible rules. A concrete illustration of this kind of detective work is given below in the form of a dialogue between a graduate student from France and his American friend. The central project is to determine exactly what rule of English is broken in sentence (3a) (the *good advices* example).

Day 1

Pierre: Yesterday I wrote the sentence The mayor gave John some good advices, *and today it came back corrected.*

David: You should have said, The Mayor gave John some good advice.

Pierre: Yes, that's what the teacher wrote on the paper, but I still don't see what rule I violated with the original sentence.

When Pierre tells David about his latest misfortune with the English language, David just offers "first aid" for the ill-formed sentence, by suggesting how it might be changed so as to be acceptable, normal English. But for Pierre, first aid is not enough. He wants a diagnosis, some hypothesis about what rule he has broken.

David: I don't know that there's any rule, except that sentences like that just don't sound very good.

Here David is simply restating the problem, without solving it at all. Pierre wants something better.

Pierre: I know that already. Couldn't you give me a rule that would help me to avoid making the same kind of mistake in the future?
David: Let's just say that the word advice *is permitted but the word* advices *is not.*
Pierre: That looks like the right idea. It would allow me to say some good advice *but not* some good advices.

David offers a tentative rule (a particular prohibition associated with the word *advice*). Pierre goes away satisfied, at least for the time being.

Day 2
Pierre: I'm still having trouble with the word advice. *The rule you gave me yesterday says that you can't use it in the plural, so I thought it would be OK to write* The president was hoping for a good advice. *But this sentence came back marked wrong, too. So it's not enough just to say that you can't use* advices.
David: I guess that advice *follows two rules. One is the rule that prohibits using it in the plural, and the other is a rule that says it can't be used with* a *or* an.
Pierre: Thanks. That's a help.

David helps out with another tentative rule, but Pierre is starting to wonder how much he is going to have to learn and remember about just the single word *advice*.

Day 3
Pierre: Just when I thought things were going better, I had another problem. I've seen sentences where one *is used as a replacement for a repeated*

word. For instance, I'm sure that I've seen sentences like The car that Bill bought was smaller than the one that Martha bought. *Does that sound OK to you?*

David: It's perfect.

Pierre: Then what's wrong with this sentence: The advice that Jones got was more helpful than the one that Smith got? *I was corrected on that sentence today.*

David: I agree that it sounds terrible. Let's just say that the word one *can't be used in place of* advice.

Pierre: We now have three separate rules just for advice. *I hope I don't have to learn this many rules every time I learn a new English word.*

David: Don't worry. I doubt very seriously that there are any others as bad as this one.

Pierre is becoming apprehensive. He has already encountered three separate rules just for the single word *advice*.

(13) a. *Advice* can't be used in the plural.
      b. *Advice* can't be preceded by *a* or *an*.
      c. *Advice* can't be replaced by *one*.

He is beginning to fear that he will have to learn a number of small, specific rules like this for every English word. David, on the other hand, sees nothing to be alarmed about: his unconscious command of English still leaves him with the impression that English is quite easy. Because of his comfortable position as a native speaker, he hasn't yet seen fit to involve his intellect in trying to get to the bottom of Pierre's problems.

Day 4

Pierre: Do you think you could help me again? This time I'm having trouble with the word furniture. *In fact, I made two mistakes in the same composition. I wrote* We had hoped to get three new furnitures every month, but we only had enough money to get a furniture every two weeks.

David: Maybe you ought to make a list of rules for furniture, *just like we did for* advice.

Pierre: It looks as if you can't say furnitures, *and you can't use* furniture *with* a *or* an. *As a matter of fact,* furniture *is starting to look a lot like* advice.

The parallels that Pierre has established already are apparent in the following two pairs of rules:

(14) a. *Advice* can't be used in the plural.
    b. *Furniture* can't be used in the plural.

(15) a. *Advice* can't be preceded by *a* or *an*.
    b. *Furniture* can't be preceded by *a* or *an*.

Pierre: While we're at it, we might see if the third of our restrictions on advice *is matched by a corresponding rule for* furniture.

Pierre now wants to find out whether the word *furniture* shares a third property with *advice*, so he constructs an experimental sentence and presents it to David, thus pressing him into service as his "native informant."

Pierre: How does this sentence sound to you: The furniture we bought last year was more expensive than the one we bought this year?
David: Terrible! You definitely can't use the word one *as a replacement for* furniture.
Pierre: This is really odd. I don't see why advice *and* furniture *should follow the same rules. Can you think of any other words that behave this way?*

Pierre is struck by what appears to be a puzzling coincidence. He is inviting his native informant to play a more active role.

David: Let's try a couple of words that are related in meaning to advice *and* furniture. *How about* suggestion *and* armchair? *Let's see. We can talk about* suggestions *and* armchairs. *Also, it's OK to say* a suggestion *and* an armchair. *Finally, we can use* one *as a replacement for these words:* the first suggestion and the second one; this armchair and that one. *So these two words are completely different from* advice *and* furniture.

The native speaker constructs some experimental examples of his own and then serves as his own informant. He discovers that *suggestion* and *armchair* behave completely differently from *advice* and *furniture*.

Pierre: I think maybe I have another word that's like advice *and* furniture. *How do these sentences sound:* We discovered some new evidences, *or* We need an evidence, *or* The evidence that you provided is more interesting than the one that I provided?
David: They're all pretty hopeless.

David's response to Pierre's experimental sentences confirms that *evidence* is like *advice* and *furniture*.

Pierre: Let's see what happens if you try clue *instead of* evidence: We discovered some new clues, *or* We need a clue, *or* The clue that you provided is more interesting than the one that I provided.
David: They all sound perfectly normal.

Again, Pierre presents some experimental examples to his native informant, and the informant renders a judgment. The result: *clue* turns out to be like *suggestion* and *armchair*. Pierre now stops to take stock of the situation.

Pierre: Each word we've tried is either like advice *or like* suggestion. *Maybe the simplest thing to do would be to make a list of words like* advice *and a list of words like* suggestion. *Let's call them "group 1 words" and "group 2 words." Then maybe I can replace all of these tiny little rules by some general rules.*

In effect, Pierre has rediscovered the traditional grammatical distinction between "mass nouns" and "count nouns." So far, his word lists look like this:

(16) *Group 1 (mass nouns)*   *Group 2 (count nouns)*
    advice   suggestion
    furniture   armchair
    evidence   clue

David: What are your rules going to say?
Pierre: I think they'll be pretty simple, something like this: (1) only group 2 words can be plural; (2) only group 2 words can go with a *or* an; *(3) only group 2 words can be replaced by* one.

At this point, Pierre has arrived at a more sophisticated idea of what the rules of English are like. Instead of assuming the existence of three special rules that mention the particular word *advice*, he now assumes the existence of three general rules, each of which refers to a large class of nouns —the traditional class of count nouns.

David: So you don't have to say anything at all about advice *itself?*
Pierre: I do have to say something, but not very much. I just have to say that it's a group 1 word, not a group 2 word.

Although Pierre agrees that *advice* cannot occur in the plural, he now no longer believes that there is a specific rule of English to this effect. Instead, he believes that this fact is deducible from the following rules:

(17) Only count nouns can occur in the plural.

(18) *Advice* is not a count noun.

David: Just out of curiosity, is there anything special that only your group 1 words can do?

Pierre: I don't know offhand. Can you think of any place where advice *would work but* suggestion *wouldn't?*

David: How about after much? *I can say* too much advice, *but* too much suggestion *and* too much suggestions *both sound bad. Also,* much furniture *and* much evidence *sound OK, but* much armchair *and* much clue *don't.*

Once again, David constructs some experimental examples himself. The questions he wants to answer are as follows:

(19) a. Does *much* allow following mass nouns?
      b. Does *much* allow following count nouns?

In constructing experimental examples to answer these questions, he has made implicit use of something that he has already learned, namely, the class membership of several particular nouns.

Pierre: So there's at least one rule that allows group 1 words to do something: Only a group 1 word can occur with much.

The idea here is similar to what we saw earlier.

(20) What English speakers unconsciously know:
      a. Only mass nouns can occur with *much.*
      b. *Suggestion* is not a mass noun.
      c. *Advice* is a mass noun.

(21) What is deducible from what they know:
      a. *Suggestion* cannot occur with *much.*
      b. *Advice* can occur with *much.*

Pierre: What happens with bean? *Could you say* We had some beans for supper, *or* Let me have a bean, *or* The bean on his plate is bigger than the one on my plate?

David: The ideas conveyed by the last two sentences are a little silly, but all three of them sound like perfectly normal English.

Pierre: So I guess bean *is a group 2 word. What about* radish?

David: Hmm . . . radishes, a radish, a big radish and a little one. *They all seem to work OK.*

Pierre: It looks as if there's a general rule here.
David: What's that?
Pierre: If a noun designates a vegetable, then it will be a count noun.

Pierre is perfectly reasonable in searching for some general rules that would dictate which English nouns are mass nouns and which are count nouns. Trying to find general rules is always a good idea. As it happens here, some counterexamples turn up.

David: Wait a minute. What about broccoli? *I bought a broccoli doesn't sound very good to me. A* spinach *doesn't sound very good either. And nobody would get away with saying* George ate some corns.
Pierre: OK. So I guess the rule I suggested isn't really an English rule.

David tries using several more names of vegetables in ways that work for count nouns, but the results are bad. Under pressure from these counter-examples, Pierre backs off. Although the particular general rule that he proposed proves to be untenable, it is worth emphasizing again that Pierre was absolutely right to want to look for a general rule.

David: Wait a minute. I just thought of something else. What are you going to do with a word like cake? *You could perfectly well say* cakes, a cake, *or* this cake and that one, *all of which seems to put it in group 2. But you can also say* too much cake, *which means that it ought to go in group 1. It looks as if there's a contradiction here.*
Pierre: I don't know any reason why we couldn't just put it in both groups. Then in some examples it would behave like advice *and in other examples it would behave like* suggestion. *So if someone said* too much cake, *I would know it was a group 1 word in that example, but if they said* a cake, *I would know it was a group 2 word.*

The two friends have just discovered that some nouns may be used either as mass nouns or as count nouns.

(22) *Group 1 (mass nouns)*   *Group 2 (count nouns)*
    advice   suggestion
    furniture   armchair
    evidence   clue
    cake   cake

When we just look at such a word in isolation from the rest of a sentence in which it appears, we cannot tell which use is involved.

(23)   cake   (ambiguous)

However, we can often tell whether *cake* has been taken from the mass noun list or the count noun list when we see the sentence as a whole.

(24) | Fred baked a cake for Martha. | (unambiguous)

Here the word *a* that appears before it leads us to deduce that it is a count noun in this sentence. In later chapters, we will see many situations where the same logic applies to sequences of words as well as to individual words.

David: Would it be a group 1 word or a group 2 word in an example like George put the cake on the table?
Pierre: That all depends on what kinds of words can follow the word the, *and we haven't yet said anything about that.*
David: Let's see. I can say the advice he gave me, *but I can also say* the suggestion he gave me. *So I guess that* the *allows both group 1 words and group 2 words.*
Pierre: Wouldn't it follow, then, that George *put the cake on the table could have either of two separate interpretations?*
David: Now that you mention it, it does have two interpretations. I can see a picture in my mind of either a piece of cake or a whole cake being put on the table. In the first mental picture, it's "some cake," and in the second, it's "a cake."

Another discovery: there are instances in which a word that is ambiguous in isolation from the rest of the sentence in which it appears remains ambiguous when we see the sentence as a whole.

(25)   cake   (ambiguous)
    | George put the cake on the table. | (still ambiguous)

We will also encounter many situations of this second sort in later chapters, both with individual words and with sequences of words.

Pierre: Thanks for the help. I've also got a question about adverbs. I don't understand why my instructor didn't like it when I wrote I eat often cake. *But I think I'll pester you about that tomorrow.*
David: Always glad to be of service.

At this point, the syntactic dialogue ends temporarily. It has clearly had a happy conclusion: as a result of their unusual persistence and intelligence, Pierre and David have succeeded in rediscovering the traditional grammatical classes of *mass nouns* (their group 1) and *count nouns* (their group 2). In addition, they have found some general rules applying to words in these classes. These simple rules are typical in two major respects of most of those that we will be discussing in the remainder of this book. In the first place, native speakers of English show complete agreement in making the judgments that these rules dictate. In the second place, they are by and large totally unaware that these rules exist or that they use them in their everyday speech and writing. We have thus discovered some specific examples of the kind of hidden, unconscious rules of English shown in the shaded part of diagram (12).

Even though the "research" that Pierre and David did was conducted in a casual, unsystematic way, their efforts illustrate several aspects of serious syntactic study. The entire project started with a puzzle, the question of why a certain sentence was not acceptable in English. A first guess was made (the proposal that *advices* was not a legitimate English word), but later clues showed that this guess was too limited in the facts that it accounted for. The investigators did not know at the beginning what the critical clues were going to be; some of them they stumbled onto by accident and others they found by doing little "experiments" that they thought of along the way. At several points, they were able to use what they had already learned as the basis for constructing experiments that allowed them to learn something further. When they added to their rules or modified them, they did so for one of two quite different reasons. Sometimes it was from a desire to account for more of the clues that they had found; at other times, it was to create a simpler, neater system. Both of these desires played a role in their eventual success, and both of these desires guide syntacticians in their efforts to arrive at a conscious understanding of the unconscious rules of the English language.

Exercises

1. In the course of studying English, Pierre has seen many examples of the word *every* occurring with count nouns: sequences like *every student, every building,* and *every book.* A few days after the end of the dialogue recorded above, he finds himself wondering whether *every* can also occur with mass nouns. He raises the question with David, who takes the word *cake* from the mass noun list and con-

structs the experimental sentence *Martha bought every cake.* Since this sentence is acceptable, David concludes that *every* can occur with mass nouns as well as with count nouns. Pierre, however, is suspicious. He takes the word *furniture* from the mass noun list and constructs the experimental sentence *Dan sold every furniture,* which David as native informant promptly rejects. Pierre then concludes that *every* occurs only with count nouns. Explain as clearly as you can what it is that makes Pierre's deduction sounder than David's.

2. Pierre wants to find out whether *lamp* belongs on the list of count nouns. Which of the following experimental sentences provides him with useful evidence for a positive answer?

    a. Clarence bought a lamp.
    b. He gave the lamp to Martha.

Explain your answer briefly but clearly.

3. For each of the following nouns, answer two separate questions:

    A. Can it be a count noun?
    B. Can it be a mass noun?

For each yes or no answer, provide an acceptable or unacceptable experimental example that justifies it. Prefix with an asterisk every example that you consider unacceptable (e.g., *every furniture*).

    a. parsley
    b. vehicle
    c. traffic
    d. paper
    e. thing
    f. stuff
    g. watermelon
    h. noodle
    i. spaghetti
    j. hair
    k. wheat
    l. discussion
    m. luggage
    n. suitcase
    o. turkey
    p. activity
    q. light
    r. lightning

4. For each of the following words, answer three questions:

    A. Does it occur with singular count nouns?
    B. Does it occur with plural count nouns?
    C. Does it occur with mass nouns?

Support each yes or no answer with an experimental sentence.

   a. each
   b. this
   c. most

1.2 ENGLISH SYNTAX AS A SUBFIELD OF LINGUISTICS

The approach that we will be taking in this book has its roots in the larger field of linguistics. In order to become fully comfortable with this approach, let us look briefly at the history of this relatively new discipline and identify its most basic ideas.

1.2.1 The Development of Modern Linguistics

Although human thinkers had for many centuries been interested in the phenomenon of human language in general and also in particular human languages, the beginning of the nineteenth century saw an explosion of interest in what came to be called *historical and comparative linguistics.* The original fuel for this interest was provided by a small number of European scholars, who in the space of only a few years at the beginning of the nineteenth century accumulated evidence for an astonishing idea: that a vast array of superficially dissimilar European and Asian languages were actually descended from a common prehistoric parent language. This family of languages, which included languages as far separated as Irish on the west and Persian and Sanskrit on the east, became known as the *Indo-European* family. Scholars were concerned for the remainder of the century with the enormous project of charting all of the relationships among languages in this group and determining the historical changes that had occurred in various branches. Beyond this, especially in the latter part of the nineteenth century and on into the twentieth, they were concerned with a broader project: an attempt to understand the nature of language change in general.

Early in this period of linguistics, one particular fact became overwhelmingly clear, namely, that all languages are constantly changing. Even Classical Latin, which earlier scholars had wanted to consider pure and timeless, was now seen to be the result of a sequence of historical changes whose starting point was not even remotely visible. Applied to English, this basic insight implies that the present-day language, by its very nature as a human language, must even now be undergoing a substantial number of changes, and that it would be futile and pointless for anyone to try to freeze it in its present state.

Alongside this interest in language history and language change, increasing attention was given in the early decades of this century to studying the structure of individual languages, and the movement known as *structural linguistics* arose. For many European countries, the native languages in their colonial possessions invited serious study; in the United States and Canada, a multitude of Native American languages offered similar opportunities. In addition to the great wealth of detailed information that was obtained from these projects, both about the individual languages studied and about the workings of human language in general, two very simple but basic truths became apparent. The first was that, contrary to what was widely believed at the time, there are no "primitive" languages. The languages of tribes that by European standards are quite primitive technologically have proved to be just as complex as the major European languages, and just as rich in their expressive possibilities. Even though many of these languages had never been written down and had never been the subject of grammar books, they proved to be governed by coherent systems of rules in exactly the same way that the better-known written languages are. The second basic truth learned in this period was that different languages are much more widely diverse than had been suspected earlier. The practical consequence was that language scholars abandoned the earlier practice of trying to fit the description of every newly encountered language into the mold provided by the rule systems of Latin and Greek. Instead, they increasingly adopted the view that each language deserved to be described in its own terms.

In the middle and late 1950s, a new movement arose within linguistics; it came to be called *generative grammar*. In many ways this movement represented a natural development out of the structural linguistics of the preceding decades. However, in several respects it was quite revolutionary. The most striking change was its strong psychological orientation, centered around the conviction that the study of language is essentially a study of one aspect of the human mind. The discussion in section 1.1 reflects this idea clearly: what we try to discover when we investigate English syntax is a system of rules that lies hidden in the minds of fluent speakers of the language.

Besides inquiring about the unconscious rules of particular languages, generative grammar has been concerned with an even deeper psychological problem, that of discovering what aspects of human language capacity are determined by our common human genetic endowment rather than by our differing early language environments. The basic idea is that part of what we know about our language is *innate,* that is, present by virtue of the nature of the human organism rather than by virtue of our early experience with our language. In particular, though all human children clearly require help from their language environment in order to learn the rules of their language, there is now much evidence that their minds are provided ahead of time with unconscious principles that dictate what general *kinds* of rules are to be expected. The contribution of these innate principles is shown in diagram (26), an expanded version of (12).

(26)

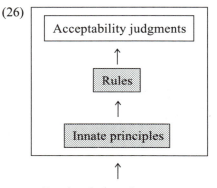

Previously heard sentences

Although the major focus of this book is on English rules rather than on innate principles, particular principles will occasionally be mentioned. In a few cases, we will even use them in our conscious search for the rules of English, just as human children use them in their unconscious search for the rules of their language.

Generative grammar thus consists of two related enterprises. One of these is concerned with discovering the rules of particular languages, for instance, English, Chinese, and Arabic. The other is concerned with uncovering the genetically determined principles that make their effects felt in all languages. Just as we speak of English grammar, Chinese grammar, and Arabic grammar when we are talking about the rules of these individual languages, so we can use the term *universal grammar* when we are talking about the genetically determined principles.

1.2.2   Other Areas of English Grammar

Syntactic rules make up only one of several major systems in a fluent speaker's total knowledge of English. In addition to these rules that govern sentence formation, a speaker knows rules of several other kinds.

(27) a. *Morphological rules*—rules that regulate the formation of words
   b. *Semantic rules*—rules that determine interpretations of words and sentences
   c. *Phonological rules*—rules that determine allowable patterns of sounds
   d. *Phonetic rules*—rules that determine the actual pronunciation of words and sentences

For each of these distinct sets of rules for an individual language like English, there is a corresponding component of universal grammar, that is, a distinct system of innate principles that provide a language learner with unconscious ideas in advance concerning the exact types of rules to expect in the language to which he or she is exposed.

In the course of exploring these various rule systems individually, generative linguists have discovered a number of interesting respects in which these systems are interdependent. Of special importance for syntax has been the exploration of the ways in which syntax is related to semantics.

The most basic connection between syntax and semantics resides in the fact that many of the semantic rules that provide interpretations for sentences make reference to the structures that are determined by the syntactic rules. To take just one example, sentence (28) exhibits a special English construction that we will study in detail in chapter 9.

(28) Martha finds John *easy to understand.*

In addition to agreeing on the acceptability of this sentence, fluent speakers of English agree in viewing *John* as the "understood object" of the word *understand*, rather than the "understood subject." Even if they do not use these traditional terms to describe their intuition, they can tell that (28) implies (29a) but does not imply (29b).

(29) a. It is easy for Martha to understand John.
   b. It is easy for John to understand Martha.

Several interpretive rules play a significant role in obtaining this result. One of these rules makes reference to the special syntactic construction. In describing this construction, then, we will want to go beyond matters that are narrowly syntactic and to offer a brief description of its interpretation. The inclusion of discussions on such interpretive topics follows a long-standing practice of syntacticians, one that is reflected in a wide variety of syntactic works ranging from very traditional studies to the most recent generative studies.

At several points in this book, we will also observe another kind of connection between semantics and syntax, involving cases in which words with similar interpretations have similar syntactic properties as well. To take just one example, we will see in chapter 3 that words belonging to the semantic class of "personal-care verbs"—words such as *dress, wash,* and *shave*—all may appear in a particular syntactic configuration and are given a special semantic interpretation when they do so. In this and other cases like it, we will identify the semantic class in question and also the special syntactic behavior that its members share.

1.3 DIFFERENT VARIETIES OF ENGLISH

In regard to examples (3)–(6), it was noted that we would find almost total agreement if we were to ask many different English speakers for their judgments. Sometimes, though, we find clear cases in which different speakers do not agree.

1.3.1 Geographical Varieties

The following are four sentences that might well give rise to conflicting judgments:

(30) I'm not sure that Joe loved Alice, but he might have done.

(31) This car needs washed.

(32) You might should get a new muffler.

(33) Joe thinks the Celtics will win tonight, and so don't I.

Although virtually all American speakers would find (30) quite strange, a great many British speakers would find it completely normal. With (31), we would find a clear difference of opinion within the United States: residents of the Ohio-Pennsylvania border area would find (31) perfectly normal, but almost everyone else would find it somewhat strange. In similar fashion, (32) would be accepted principally in the south central states (Texas in particular), and (33) would find its strongest support in Boston and adjacent areas of New England.

In discussing differences of this sort, we often speak of *geographical varieties* or *geographical dialects* of English. We can even imagine that what customarily goes under the name "the English language" is actually a loose family of more or less closely related sublanguages. If we picked out the dialects of two particular areas—for example, Boston and Pittsburgh—and set out to write down all the rules of each dialect, we would discover that most of the rules we found were shared by the two dialects, only a small number of rules serving to differentiate them.

If we ask ourselves how differences of these sorts are maintained over several generations, the answer is immediately obvious: there are some small differences between the English heard by Pittsburgh children and the English heard by Boston children. Pittsburgh children are exposed to sentences that exhibit the "needs washed" construction, and they form unconscious rules that allow for it; correspondingly, Boston children hear "so don't I" examples and form their unconscious rules accordingly. This situation is represented in (34).

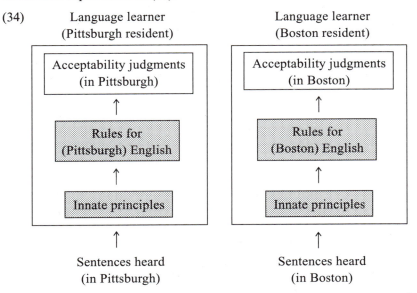

The differences found in the speech of adult Pittsburgh and Boston residents are most plausibly traced to differences in the speech they were exposed to in childhood.

1.3.2   Standard versus Nonstandard English

Let us turn now to another group of examples that give rise to conflicting reactions among speakers.

(35) a. Joe isn't here.
      b. Joe ain't here.

(36) a. He doesn't live here now.
      b. He don't live here now.

(37) a. They did it themselves.
      b. They did it theirselves.

(38) a. We told him to take those old boards away.
      b. We told him to take them old boards away.

Many English speakers use the (a) sentences consistently; many others, though, show a definite tendency to use the (b) sentences, at least in their everyday speech. Both groups of speakers, however, often agree in classifying the (a) sentences as more "correct" than the (b) sentences. The type of contrast shown here is often referred to as a contrast between *standard* and *nonstandard* (or "substandard") English.

In subsection 1.3.1, it was maintained that all persons exposed to a language in childhood succeed in learning a uniform set of unconscious rules for their language. But the conflicting preferences in (35)–(38) are sometimes seen as supporting just the opposite view, namely, that some children are much more successful than others in the degree to which they master their native language. On this view, a strong and consistent preference for the "correct" (a) examples would indicate successful language learning, whereas a preference for the "incorrect" (b) examples would be taken as a symptom of unsuccessful language learning.

What could be the source of inaccurate learning of a native language? One initially plausible possibility would be to say that some individuals are simply less gifted as language learners; perhaps for genetic reasons, their innate principles are either defective or incomplete. This overall idea can be diagrammed as in (39).

(39)   Successful language learner   Unsuccessful language learner
              (talented)   (untalented)

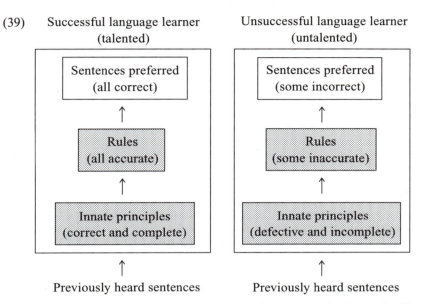

                Previously heard sentences   Previously heard sentences

Although this idea might seem natural at first, it overlooks a significant fact. What is overlooked becomes clear as soon as we compare in more detail the personal history of a "successful" learner with that of an "unsuccessful" learner. If we had to guess whether the two learners were exposed to the same kinds of utterances in childhood, we would guess right away that they were not, basing this guess on our everyday experience with different kinds of English speech and different individual speakers. Adults who feel completely natural with *Joe isn't here* have almost certainly grown up hearing *isn't* in their immediate social surroundings. By contrast, adults who feel more comfortable with *ain't* have almost certainly grown up hearing *ain't* from family members and friends. Looking at this fact, we might think of a second interpretation of the contrasts shown in (35)–(38): perhaps the "successful" learner and the "unsuccessful" learner have the same inherent equipment for language learning, and the difference in what they learn should be traced back to differences in the utterances that they heard as children. We are thus moving toward an environmental explanation for the differences in (35)–(38), instead of a genetic explanation.

One possibility is that the first learner has heard sentences that follow rules strictly, whereas the second has heard sentences that do not follow any set rules. Then we might expect the first learner to have a much better chance than the second of arriving at the rules of the language. This idea is pictured in (40).

(40)   Successful language learner   Unsuccessful language learner
          (good language environment)   (poor language environment)

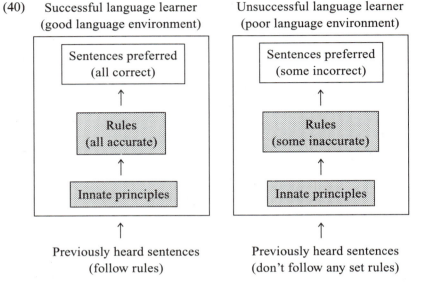

          Previously heard sentences   Previously heard sentences
                (follow rules)   (don't follow any set rules)

This diagram, like (39), implies that some language learners are more successful than others in learning the rules of their native language. What is new in this diagram is the implication that the deficiencies of the non-standard speaker are to be attributed to an inferior language environment rather than to an inferior talent for language learning.

But now we need to give some critical scrutiny to the basic assumption that diagrams (39) and (40) share. Is it really true, as they imply, that the speech of some English speakers is not governed by rules to the same extent as the speech of other speakers? With this question in mind, let us look again at one of the pairs of sentences with which we started this discussion.

(41) a. He doesn't live here now.
     b. He don't live here now.

For the person who says (41a), the unconscious rule might well be that *doesn't* is a possible alternative way of saying *does not*. For the person who says (41b), a similar rule could be given: *don't* is a possible alternative way of saying *does not*. The second statement looks just as much like a rule as the first statement does. (The two speakers would share a rule saying that *don't* is an alternative way of saying *do not*.)

Let us also consider another of the sentence pairs presented earlier.

(42) a. They did it themselves.
     b. They did it theirselves.

To see what the difference in the rules is here, it will be helpful to make lists of all of the so-called *reflexive* pronouns for the two varieties of English that we are considering.

(43) *Standard*   *Nonstandard*

myself	ourselves	myself	ourselves
yourself	yourselves	yourself	yourselves
himself	themselves	hisself	theirselves
herself		herself	
itself		itsself	

The first two rows of this chart are the same for both varieties. For these forms, we can state the following rule:

(44) To make a reflexive pronoun, use the appropriate possessive form and attach it to -*self* (singular) or -*selves* (plural).

Below the first two rows, the two sides of the chart no longer agree. The right side continues with the same rule: *his, her, its,* and *their* are all possessives. The left side, by contrast, switches to the so-called objective forms (*him, her, it, them*). Thus, whereas the nonstandard reflexives are accounted for entirely by the simple and general rule in (44), the standard reflexives must be accounted for by the decidedly more complicated two-part rule in (45).

(45) a. To make a first- or second-person reflexive pronoun, use the appropriate possessive form and attach it to -*self* (singular) or -*selves* (plural).
     b. To make a third-person reflexive pronoun, use the appropriate objective form and attach it to -*self* (singular) or -*selves* (plural).

Thus, we see that speakers who say *theirselves* are definitely following a rule, the one given in (44). Moreover, they are following a more regular, general rule than speakers who say *themselves*.

Careful consideration of these examples, then, suggests that it is a mistake to believe that some English speakers follow rules in their speech and others do not. Instead, it now appears that *all* English speakers are successful language learners: they all follow unconscious rules derived from their early language environment, and the small differences in the sentences that they prefer are best understood as coming from small differences in these rules. Diagram (46) shows the new picture that emerges.

(46)   Language learner   Language learner
              (standard English)   (nonstandard English)

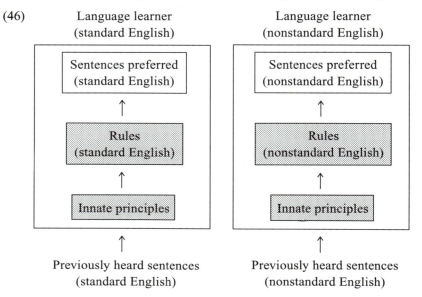

           Previously heard sentences   Previously heard sentences
               (standard English)   (nonstandard English)

We now have a picture of the differences between a standard speaker and a nonstandard speaker that is completely parallel to the picture given in (34) of the difference between a Pittsburgh speaker and a Boston speaker. Exposure to slightly different kinds of examples in early childhood leads to slightly differing sets of unconscious rules, which in turn lead to slightly different preferred sentences. The differences of the sort that we are looking at here follow lines of social class and ethnic group rather than geographical lines. Thus, we can speak of *social varieties* or *social dialects*.

We still need to consider why the (a) forms in (35)–(38) are felt by so many speakers of English to be "better." No linguistic findings of the past century provide any basis for selecting one rule system as inherently superior to another. In fact, it is highly unlikely that a linguist who was given sets of rules for two different varieties of a language could decide just by looking at the rules which one was the variety thought better by speakers of the language.

If what is widely felt as the superiority of standard English over other varieties is not to be found in any characteristics of the rule system, then what could its source possibly be? The answer turns out to be quite simple:

a certain variety of speech is often felt to be superior to others because the people who happen to speak it have a high degree of power and prestige for reasons having nothing to do with language. When we look for the group in our society to whom the preferred speech we have been talking about is most completely native, it turns out to be roughly the urban educated white middle class. As a large group with a high degree of prestige in this society, they have had the good fortune to have their own particular native variety of English enshrined as "standard American English."

If this standard American English is not inherently better than other varieties of American English, then why should we insist on teaching it in schools, colleges, and universities? The answer again is simple: the nonstandard constructions of the sort we have been discussing are *stigmatized;* that is, the person who writes them or utters them in educated middle-class settings runs the risk of being considered ignorant, uneducated, or even stupid. Thus, especially for those members of American society who plan to spend their lives in middle-class occupations or the professions, being able to use standard English is at the very minimum a matter of sheer self-defense.

Exercises

1. Suppose that Alfred and Beth are two speakers of American English whose speech patterns differ in the way indicated in (i) and (ii).

(i)   Alfred: He don't know what he's talking about.

(ii) Beth: He doesn't know what he's talking about.

In the text, this difference was accounted for by means of the following contrasting unconscious rules for the two varieties:

(iii) Alfred's unconscious grammar: The contracted form of *does not* is *don't.*

(iv) Beth's unconscious grammar: The contracted form of *does not* is *doesn't.*

Just on the basis of the contrast between (i) and (ii), an alternative hypothesis might be proposed, namely, that the difference between the two speakers is actually to be accounted for by the differing rules in (v) and (vi).

(v)   Alfred's unconscious grammar: The form *do* goes with both singular and plural subjects.

(vi) Beth's unconscious grammar: The form *do* goes with plural subjects, the form *does* with singular subjects.

Which of these two accounts of the difference between Alfred and Beth is favored if we find that the two speakers agree in using the following additional examples? What would we have expected from the other account?

(vii)   How long do George's brothers want to keep that car?

(viii) What does Alice want for lunch?

Explain your answer briefly but clearly.

2. Observation of the speech of Ruth and Fred turns up the following difference between them:

(i)   Ruth: We come to Austin three times last month.

(ii) Fred: We came to Austin three times last month.

Two different ideas might be proposed about how this difference should be accounted for.

(iii)   Unlike Fred, Ruth does not make any distinction between "present-tense" verb forms and "past-tense" verb forms.

(iv)   Ruth uses *come* as the past-tense form of *come,* whereas Fred uses *came.*

If you were asked to determine which of these two ideas was correct, what additional evidence would you want to take into consideration, and what might you conclude from it?

1.4   SCHOOL GRAMMAR AND MODERN SYNTAX

In this concluding section, we will look at the relationship between the way in which English syntax is studied in traditional school grammars and the way in which it will be studied in this book. It will be useful to begin by discussing the central goal of school grammar. Reduced to essentials, it is to provide native English speakers with the rules that they need to know if they are to speak and write "the best English possible." To a certain extent, "the best English possible" means English conforming to the rules of the most prestigious dialect. Thus, for instance, many school grammars contain rules having the effect of prohibiting *ain't,* or prohibiting *don't* as a contracted version of *does not.*

In some cases, school grammars also offer arguments purporting to show the inherent superiority of certain rules found in the prestige dialect. One such argument is often given in connection with the contrasting examples in (47).

(47) a. I didn't tell anybody.
     b. I didn't tell nobody.

Sentences like (47a) are often described as being more "logical" than sentences like (47b). The alleged illogic of (47b) as it is used by nonstandard speakers resides in the fact that it contains two negative words to express an intended meaning that involves just a single logical negation. Such arguments for the superiority of the rules of the prestige dialect always prove to have a fragile foundation. By the argument given above, for instance, we would have to insist that many of the important standard languages of the world, languages such as French and Spanish, are logically deficient and in need of correction. The fact that this charge is never made against French and Spanish suggests that there is no reason to lodge it against nonstandard English. The point to be remembered is that in discussing the rules of standard English, we will be content to try to discover what the rules are and will refrain from trying to give arguments for their superiority over the corresponding nonstandard rules, in cases where differences exist.

There has traditionally been a second source of rules for "the best English possible." Among these rules are the ones that label the (a) sentences in (48)–(51) as correct and the (b) sentences as incorrect.

(48) a. It is I.
     b. It is me.

(49) a. Father and I went down to camp.
     b. Father and me went down to camp.

(50) a. Whom did you see?
     b. Who did you see?

(51) a. John is taller than I.
     b. John is taller than me.

These rules owe their place in school grammars to a project that began in the English Renaissance. At that time, it was felt that the best of all possible languages would be one in which the grammatical rules of the language could be identified with the rules of reasoning that humans everywhere use. Classical Greek and Latin appeared to Renaissance thinkers to be the languages that most clearly embodied this ideal. Thus, to the extent that the rules of English as it was then spoken deviated from the rules of these ancient languages, it seemed desirable to change the English rules in order to make English a more "reasonable" language. None of the four rules needed to get the "correct" (a) sentences above were originally native to English. Instead, they were all borrowed from Latin and imposed on English by scholars who felt that they were improving the language by doing this.

The assumptions on which this project was based have been completely abandoned in modern language scholarship. In particular, Latin and Greek are now seen as neither more nor less logical than any of the thousands of other languages that have been spoken during the history of the human species. In addition, as scholars have increased their knowledge of the way in which individual languages work, the general idea that one language can be improved by borrowing rules from another has fallen into disrepute. Nevertheless, the rules borrowed from Latin live on in traditional school textbooks. What makes this fact unfortunate is that Classical Latin and Early Modern English had markedly different systems of syntactic rules, and the rules that fit quite easily into the Latin system have always constituted an unnatural appendage on the English system. Unlike the vast majority of English syntactic rules, which are learned unconsciously in childhood, these rules are not learned by native speakers without the expenditure of a great deal of labor and explicit instruction.

To a large extent, then, school grammars for native English speakers have the aim of "improving" their speech and writing, eliminating or modifying any rules that differ from those found in the prestigious "standard" dialect or that differ from the small collection of rules borrowed from Latin several centuries ago.

The present book has a different aim. Instead of trying to modify the unconscious rules that speakers of English learn in childhood, we will be trying to discover what these rules actually are, following the strategy illustrated in subsection 1.1.2. We will assume that in an overwhelming majority of cases, English speakers know which sentences are good and which are not, and we will try to devise rules that conform to their judgments. In contrast to what is assumed in school grammars, we will assume that any conflicts we find between rules and judgments call for a reassessment of the rules, rather than a change in the judgments.

One more point needs to be made about the difference between school grammar and the type of grammar we will be pursuing here. Because of their basic aim, school grammars typically cover only a small fraction of English syntactic rules. The reason for this narrowness is that most of the syntactic rules for the standard variety of English are shared with virtually all other varieties of the language. We have already seen two simple examples of rules that are the common property of English speakers everywhere: one is the rule that restricts *much* to mass nouns, and the other is the rule that requires a noun replaced by *one* to be a count noun. These rules are not discussed in school grammars simply because every speaker of English uses them correctly without any special instruction.

The result of this exclusive attention to points at which different dialects come in conflict is that the major outlines of English syntax are hardly ever hinted at. In this book, the primary focus will be on just these broad outlines. As a result, we will be giving most of our attention to rules that many readers will not have heard of before. Although many of these rules will seem strange at first, we will find as we proceed that they fit together in a very tight, systematic way to tell us exactly what sequences of words count as good English sentences, and what structures these sentences have.

Although traditional school grammar and the kind of grammar that we will be doing differ markedly in their general aims and assumptions, there is one area in which they have much in common. In addition to teaching rules of syntax from the prestige dialect of English and from Latin, school grammars provide a general framework of grammatical concepts. These concepts include "parts of speech" (e.g., nouns, verbs, adjectives), grammatical categories (e.g., singular, plural, first person, feminine gender), and grammatical relations (subject, direct object, indirect object, predicate). The major reason for including these concepts in school grammars is to make it possible for students to understand the rules given to them, many of which refer to one or more of the concepts. For instance, at least some English-speaking children learn in school about the contrast between mass nouns and count nouns. At least one rule found in many school grammars refers to these concepts: it is the rule that states that *less* should be used only with mass nouns, and not with plural count nouns. The inclusion of this rule in school grammars arises from a minor dialect difference among speakers of English: in addition to allowing *less* in sentence (52a), some speakers would allow it in (52b), in place of the standard (52c).

(52) a. Joe has less furniture (mass noun) than Fred has.
     b. Joe has less books (plural count noun) than Fred has.
     c. Joe has fewer books (plural count noun) than Fred has.

In order to use this rule about *less,* it is clearly necessary to be able to distinguish mass nouns from plural count nouns.

In the syntactic investigations that we will pursue in later chapters, we will use many of the same concepts. To an even greater extent than in school grammars, we will find justification for these concepts in the general rules of English syntax that they allow us to state easily. Just as we have already seen several rules that require a distinction between count nouns and mass nouns, so we will also find several very basic rules that require a distinction between nouns and verbs, between common nouns and proper nouns, between singular and plural, and so on. The end result of looking carefully at the rules in which these traditional concepts play a role will be a fuller appreciation of their genuine usefulness.

PART II

THE SYNTAX OF PHRASES:
HEADS, COMPLEMENTS, AND SUBJECTS

Chapter 2

Major English Phrase Types

The goal of part II of this book, which spans chapters 2–9, is to develop some detailed ideas about English *phrase structure*—about the way in which English sentences are organized into successively smaller units. Chapter 2 is intended to serve two major functions within this larger scheme. The first function, which is the burden of section 2.1, is to offer a preliminary view of what it means to talk about phrase structure, and what kinds of questions arise in studying it. The second function, which is served by the remaining sections of the chapter, is to give a brief overview of a few basic types of English phrases, those that have the most important roles to play in the construction of larger, more inclusive phrases.

2.1 PRELIMINARY REMARKS ON PHRASE STRUCTURE

We can get a rough initial idea of what it means to talk about the phrase structure of a sentence by looking at (1).

(1) The puppy keeps putting my slippers behind the couch.

To the conscious perception of a fluent speaker of English who casually listened to this sentence, it would sound like nothing more than a sequence of individual words following one after another. Yet a traditional grammarian of English would offer something like the following as a guess about how this speaker unconsciously perceived this sentence:

(2) a. The word *the* joins with the word *puppy* to make the phrase *the puppy*.
   b. The word *the* joins with the word *couch* to make the phrase *the couch*.
   c. The word *behind* joins with the phrase *the couch* to make the phrase *behind the couch*.

d. The word *my* joins with the word *slippers* to make the phrase *my slippers.*

e. The word *putting* joins with the phrase *my slippers* and the phrase *behind the couch* to make the phrase *putting my slippers behind the couch.*

f. The word *keeps* joins with the phrase *putting my slippers behind the couch* to make the phrase *keeps putting my slippers behind the couch.*

g. The phrase *the puppy* joins with the phrase *keeps putting my slippers behind the couch* to make the sentence *The puppy keeps putting my slippers behind the couch.*

Diagram (3) is a graphic representation of this structure.

(3)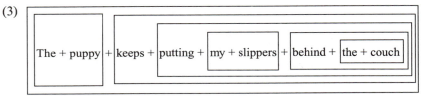

In discussing the syntax of a particular phrase, we will find it useful to consider two separate matters. The first concerns the "external syntax" of the phrase, the central question being how the phrase can be used in larger constructions. The second concerns the "internal syntax" of the phrase, the question being how the phrase itself is constructed. For example, if we were studying the phrase *putting my slippers behind the couch* as it is used in sentence (1), a consideration of its external syntax would lead us to ask what rules of English allow it to be used in the position where it appears in (1), and not in other imaginable positions such as those in (4), where the asterisks indicate that the sentences are judged unacceptable.

(4) a. *The puppy [putting my slippers behind the couch].
    b. *The puppy wants [putting my slippers behind the couch].

By contrast, if we want to understand the internal syntax of this phrase, we must ask what rules allow us to combine the word *putting* with the two phrases that follow it (*my slippers* and *behind the couch*) to make the phrase in question, but not with either phrase alone or with phrases of types other than these.

(5) a. *The puppy kept [putting my slippers].
    b. *The puppy kept [putting behind the couch].

    c. *The puppy kept [putting my slippers safe].
    d. *The puppy kept [putting my slippers to be behind the couch].

As noted above, the remaining sections of this chapter are concerned with giving a brief view of some of the most basic English phrase types. This discussion is intended as preparation for the task of saying how various types of larger phrases are formed. Because of this focus, we will be dividing individual phrases into groups primarily on the basis of properties that affect their external syntax, that is, their capacity to fit into larger structures. To take a concrete example, the phrase in (6a) shares one property with (6b) and shares a different property with (6c).

(6) a. approves of his brother
    b. fond of his brother
    c. seems quiet

The phrases (6a) and (6b) are alike in both ending with *of his brother,* whereas (6a) and (6c) are alike in beginning with the same kind of word (what we will call, following traditional English grammar, a *present-tense verb*). Although both kinds of shared properties need to be recognized in a complete grammar of English, only the property that (6a) shares with (6c) will be important in this chapter, because only this kind of shared property carries with it a similarity in external behavior.

In the course of this discussion, we will observe some initial examples of the kinds of roles that are played in English syntax by certain traditional part-of-speech distinctions. One possible by-product of this discussion will be a greater understanding of the basis for particular part-of-speech classifications, for instance, for the standard dictionary classification of *approve* as a verb and *fond* as an adjective. We will also come to an initial understanding of why it is useful to distinguish various *verbal inflections* such as past tense, past participle, and present participle.

2.2 PHRASES THAT SERVE AS SENTENCE PREDICATES

A first example of an important class of phrases comes to light as soon as we look closely at the following rule of traditional English grammar:

(7) A sentence consists of a subject and a predicate.

The usual school grammar definition of *subject* is "the thing talked about," whereas *predicate* is often defined as "the thing said about the subject." Thus, in a sentence like *Irma fed the crocodile, Irma* comes out as the subject and *fed the crocodile* comes out as the predicate.

A natural question to ask is what class of phrases can serve as predicates, for the purposes of rule (7). We can see immediately that not every kind of phrase can qualify. One pair of phrases that differ in this regard is given in (8).

(8) a. want to leave the meeting
    b. eager to leave the meeting

Each of these phrases is well formed in its own right. In addition, the two are quite close in meaning. But when we try to join them with a suitable subject such as *the senators,* only the first resulting sentence is acceptable.

(9) a.   The senators want to leave the meeting.
    b. *The senators eager to leave the meeting.

This difference in acceptability clearly resides in some difference between *want* and *eager,* since, apart from these two words, the phrases are the same. We find similar contrasts in acceptability with other pairs of phrases that differ from each other only in a single word.

(10) a.   The senators *approve of their spokesperson.*
     b. *The senators *fond of their spokesperson.*

(11) a.   The senators *know that the president is telling the truth.*
     b. *The senators *certain that the president is telling the truth.*

Evidently the words *want, approve,* and *know* play a central role in determining that the phrases containing them are allowed as predicates of sentences. By the same token, the words *eager, fond,* and *certain* have some property that makes the phrases containing them unsuitable for use as sentence predicates. These examples raise an obvious question: what is it about *want, approve,* and *know* that makes their phrases better as sentence predicates than the corresponding phrases built around *eager, fond,* and *certain*?

A similar question arises when we try to use the following phrases as sentence predicates:

(12) a. practice medicine
     b. doctors of medicine

(13) a. run for office
     b. candidates for office

(14) a. oppose the mayor
   b. opponents of the mayor

Only the first phrase in each pair gives good results.

(15) a.   The men *practice medicine.*
   b.   *The men *doctors of medicine.*

(16) a.   Joe's sisters *run for office.*
   b.   *Joe's sisters *candidates for office.*

(17) a.   The firefighters *oppose the mayor.*
   b.   *The firefighters *opponents of the mayor.*

Thus, the same kind of question arises again: what is it about the (a) phrases in (12)–(14) that makes them better sentence predicates than the (b) phrases? The twelve words that seem to be of central importance in the examples considered so far can be sorted into two groups.

(18) a. want, approve, know, practice, run, oppose
      (acceptable as first word of sentence predicate)
   b. eager, fond, certain, doctor, candidate, opponent
      (unacceptable as first word of sentence predicate)

We get a clear hint concerning the words in (18a) and those in (18b) as soon as we ask how these twelve words would be classified in an English dictionary. If we look up these words, we will find that those in (18a) are classified as *verbs,* whereas the first three of those in (18b) are classified as *adjectives* and the last three as *nouns.* Let us now adopt the term *head of a phrase* to refer to the single word in the phrase that determines how the phrase as a whole can be used. Then we can summarize our findings in the following simple statement:

(19) Only a *verb phrase* is permissible as the predicate of a sentence.

Note that the term *verb phrase* as used here and throughout the remainder of this book means "phrase headed by a verb," rather than "phrase consisting of verbs." (The term is sometimes used with the latter interpretation in traditional works on English grammar.)

This first example of a group of phrases that are relevant for the operation of a grammatical rule has brought out two general points. The first is that whether a phrase qualifies for a certain use depends at least in part on some single key word in the phrase, which we have called the *head.* The second is that one property of the head that is important in this regard is its part-of-speech classification. In the present instance, it is critically important to know that the head word is a *verb*.

2.3   PHRASES THAT HELP TO BUILD SUBJECTS

We find occasion to refer to another traditional part of speech when we examine phrases that can join with the word *the,* to make larger phrases that can function as subjects of sentences. Here are some examples:

(20) a. the *king of Spain*
     b. the *leader of our army*
     c. the *heir to this throne*
     d. the *governor of Texas*
     e. the *members of a committee*

If we look up the part-of-speech classification of the five words that directly follow the word *the,* we find that all of them are *common nouns.* Some simple experiments show that this is not just a coincidence. When we try to combine the word *the* with phrases headed by words that are not common nouns, the results are unacceptable.

(21) a. *the *leads our army*   (*leads* is a verb)
     b. *the *ran this club*   (*ran* is a verb)
     c. *the *fond of your king*   (*fond* is an adjective)
     d. *the *angry at those judges*   (*angry* is an adjective)
     e. *the *serve on a committee*   (*serve* is a verb)
     f. *the *Joe Smith*   (*Joe Smith* is a proper noun)

Our result, then, can be expressed roughly as follows:

(22) The word *the* can be combined with a *common-noun phrase* (a phrase headed by a *common noun*).

We thus have another instance in which the part-of-speech classification of the head of a phrase plays a central role in determining whether the phrase is acceptable in a certain context. Here it has been important to know whether the head word is a *common noun.*

2.4   PHRASES HEADED BY ADJECTIVES

So far, we have seen one rule that calls for phrases with verbs as heads and another that calls for phrases with common nouns as heads. Let us now look at a situation in which phrases headed by adjectives are singled out. The following sentences exemplify one such situation:

(23) a. *Joan seems *want to leave the meeting.*
     b. Joan seems *eager to leave the meeting.*

(24) a. *The delegates seem *approve of their leader.*
     b. The delegates seem *fond of their leader.*

(25) a. *The contestants seem *know the rules.*
     b. The contestants seem *certain of the rules.*

After *seem,* we can apparently have phrases headed by adjectives but not phrases headed by verbs.

Phrases headed by common nouns also give worse results in this situation than those headed by adjectives.

(26) a. Vera seems [*fond* of chess].
     b. *Vera seems [*lover* of chess].

(27) a. Fred seems [*foolish* about money].
     b. *Fred seems [*fool* about money].

Thus, when we want to describe the kind of phrase that can follow *seem,* we need to refer to *adjective phrases* (i.e., phrases headed by *adjectives*).

2.5 PHRASES CONSISTING OF A SINGLE WORD

So far, every phrase we have studied consists of the head word plus other words. Is it ever possible for a phrase to consist just of the head word by itself? We can get an answer by examining the following new examples, keeping in mind the rules developed above:

(28) a. The soldiers *snore.*
     b. the *desk*
     c. The merchants seem *despondent.*

The word *snore* is definitely a verb. If we can also consider *snore* in (28a) to be a phrase headed by a verb, then this sentence satisfies rule (19), which requires that sentence predicates be verb phrases. In similar fashion, the word *desk* is certainly a common noun. If we can also view it in (28b) as a phrase headed by a common noun, then this sequence satisfies rule (22), which identifies the phrases that can be combined with the word *the*. Finally, the word *despondent* is an adjective, and if we can view it in (28c) as a phrase headed by an adjective, then our rule for what can follow *seem* is satisfied. Thus, if we want the rules developed above to cover as many situations as possible, we have good reason to allow our concept of *phrase* to include at least some sequences that consist of only a single word.

Exercises

1. Below are listed several phrases; with each phrase are some example sentences in which the phrase appears. Some of these sentences are acceptable; others are not. Using the given sentences as your evidence, answer the following three questions:

    A. Could this phrase be a verb phrase?
    B. Could this phrase be an adjective phrase?
    C. Could this phrase be a common-noun phrase?

In interpreting the evidence, you will need to think about the rough rules developed in the preceding discussion.

    a.   *search for money*
        They *search for money*.
        *They seem *search for money*.
        The *search for money* was successful.

    b.   *lecture on warfare*
        The politicians *lecture on warfare*.
        *The politicians seem *lecture on warfare*.
        The *lecture on warfare* was hilarious.

    c.   *approach the runway*
        The planes *approach the runway*.
        *The planes seem *approach the runway*.
        *The *approach the runway* was carried out smoothly.

    d.   *safe*
        *They *safe*.
        The ladders seem *safe*.
        The *safe* was open.

    e.   *list of the passengers*
        *They *list of the passengers*.
        *They seem *list of the passengers*.
        The *list of the passengers* was long.

2. Below are listed a number of phrases, in each of which the head word is italicized. For each one, devise simple experiments to answer the following three questions:

A. Can the phrase be a verb phrase?
B. Can the phrase be an adjective phrase?
C. Can the phrase be a common-noun phrase?

Base these experiments on the rules developed in this section. Be sure to mark with an asterisk examples that seem to you to be unacceptable. Note: Some of the heads may qualify for more than one part-of-speech classification. The first is done as an example.

a. *walk* in the park
   Answer:
   The students walk in the park.   (Yes, it can be a verb phrase.)
   *John seems walk in the park.   (No, it cannot be an adjective phrase.)
   the walk in the park   (Yes, it can be a common-noun phrase.)
b. *cross* at the sign
c. *appear* in court
d. *thought* that all cows eat grass
e. *revision* of the manuscript
f. *sailor*
g. *grief*
h. *grieve*
i. *run*
j. *talk* with their friends
k. *tired* of the conversation

2.6   DISTINCTIONS AMONG VERB FORMS

In the previous section, we gave as a general rule that only a phrase headed by a verb can serve as the predicate of a sentence. This rule has the virtue of accounting for contrasts such as the following:

(29) a.   The senators [*know* that the president is telling the truth].
     b.   *The senators [*certain* that the president is telling the truth].

Nevertheless, a consideration of a broader range of examples shows that it is still too permissive.

2.6.1   Present Tense and Past Tense

Although all of the sentences given in (30) have predicates whose head words are verbs, only the first two sentences are acceptable.

(30) a.   The students [*know* the answers].
     b.   The students [*knew* the answers].
     c.   *The students [*knowing* the answers].
     d.   *The students [*known* the answers].

These examples show clearly that our rules need to distinguish among different *inflectional forms* of the same verb. Here we adopt some traditional terminology for English verb inflections and label the four verb forms used above as follows:

(31) a. *know*   present tense
     b. *knew*   past tense
     c. *knowing*   present participle
     d. *known*   past participle

We can now replace our original statement (19) about sentence predicates by the more precise statement in (32).

(32) Only a phrase headed by a *present-tense* or *past-tense* verb can serve as the predicate of a sentence.

One more kind of restriction still needs to be added, as the following examples show:

(33) a. *The student [*know* the answers].
     b. The student [*knows* the answers].

(34) a. The students [*know* the answers].
     b. *The students [*knows* the answers].

The unacceptability of *know* in (33a) and *knows* in (34b) clearly rests on the fact that the verb phrase is joined with *the student* in the first case and with *the students* in the second. We see a similar contrast in the following pairs of examples:

(35) a. *He [*know* the answer].
     b. I [*know* the answer].

(36) a. He [*knows* the answer].
     b. *I [*knows* the answer].

The rule needed here is one traditionally referred to as a rule of "agreement" between the subject and the verb that heads the predicate.

(37) A verb must agree with its subject in number and person.

For number, English provides two choices.

(38) a. *Singular:* The subject refers to a single individual or is headed by a mass noun.
     b. *Plural:* The subject refers to two or more individuals.

For person, three possibilities are distinguished in English.

(39) a. *First person:* The subject refers to a group of one or more individuals that includes the speaker.

b. *Second person:* The subject refers to a group of one or more individuals that includes the person or persons being addressed but does not include the speaker.

c. *Third person:* The subject refers to a group of one or more individuals that includes neither the speaker nor the person(s) being addressed.

By these definitions, the following are examples of subjects from each of the six possible person-number categories:

(40) a. First person singular: *I*
b. First person plural: *we, John and I, three of us*
c. Second person singular: *you*
d. Second person plural: *you, both of you, you three guys, you and Bill*
e. Third person singular: *he, she, it, the woman, Joan, one of the students*
f. Third person plural: *they, Alice and Fred, many of them, the students*

We can now say how the forms of *know* depend on the number and person of the subject. All of the subjects from the above list go well with *knew,* the past-tense form. Those in the third-person singular group require the form *knows* as their present-tense form. Subjects from the remaining five person-number groups take *know* instead.

The different forms of *know* are typical in the way in which they agree with their subjects. For English verbs in general, there is one past-tense form that agrees with subjects of all person-number combinations. In the present tense, there is a special form with *-s* for third-person singular subjects, and a form without *-s* for subjects from all five of the other groups. The only verb that shows a greater number of forms than this is the verb *be,* where distinctions for person and number are made in the past tense (*was* versus *were*) as well as in the present tense (*is* versus *are*), and where there is a separate form for the first person singular of the present tense (*am* instead of *are*).

With all of these details as background, we can restate the rule for the kinds of phrases that may be used as sentence predicates.

(41) The predicate of a sentence must be a phrase headed by a present- or past-tense verb.

When used along with the rule in (37) that requires verbs to agree with their subjects, this rule gives the right results for all of the examples considered so far. This rule still needs one more modification, though, which will be made in subsection 2.6.5.

2.6.2   Nontensed Verb Forms

We have seen that present-participial and past-participial verb forms cannot be used as predicates of independent sentences. Let us now look briefly at how they can be used. The examples in (42) illustrate the possibilities for the present participle.

(42) a. The actors kept [*forgetting* their lines].
  b. We caught them [*eating* the chocolates].

In each of these examples, replacing the present participle by another form of the verb gives bad results.

(43) a. *The actors kept [$\begin{Bmatrix} forgot \\ forget \\ forgotten \end{Bmatrix}$ their lines].

  b. *We caught them [$\begin{Bmatrix} ate \\ eat \\ eaten \end{Bmatrix}$ the chocolates].

Thus, we have found two situations that require a phrase whose head is not just any verb form, but specifically a present participle. In chapter 3 we will look at other situations in which phrases headed by present participles occur and also at the nature of the rules that dictate their use. For now, we will simply observe that a present participle seems to be the only acceptable verb form after *kept* and also after *caught them*.

Turning now to phrases headed by past participles, we find them used in situations of the sort illustrated in (44).

(44) The guests have [*eaten* the shrimp].

This is the only inflectional form allowed in this context, as we can see by substituting other forms of *eat*.

(45) *The guests have [$\begin{Bmatrix} ate \\ eat \\ eating \end{Bmatrix}$ the shrimp].

For now, we will just say that the context after *have* calls for a phrase headed specifically by a past participle.

Exercise

1. Below are listed several sets of verb forms. Using the statement made in the final sentence of the preceding text, devise some simple experimental sentences to determine which of the forms is the past participle. As in earlier exercises, put asterisks on sentences that you judge unacceptable.

- a. sang, sung, sing
- b. watch, watched
- c. come, came
- d. bring, brought
- e. hang, hung
- f. wrote, write, written
- g. say, said
- h. do, did, done
- i. has, had, have
- j. been, be, is, was

2.6.3 The Bare-Stem Form

Another English verb form must be mentioned here, one that is less often discussed than other forms in school grammars. This form is illustrated in (46).

(46) a. Joe will [*watch* the patient].
  b. Martha will make him [*drink* the medicine].

As before, replacing *watch* and *drink* with other inflectional forms gives bad results.

(47) a. *Joe will [$\left\{ \begin{array}{l} \textit{watches} \\ \textit{watching} \\ \textit{watched} \end{array} \right\}$ the patient].

  b. *Martha will make him [$\left\{ \begin{array}{l} \textit{drank} \\ \textit{drinking} \\ \textit{drunk} \end{array} \right\}$ the medicine].

At first glance, the verbs *watch* and *drink* in (46) look like nothing more than present-tense forms. In particular, phrases that look exactly like them appear as the predicates of independent sentences.

(48) a. Joe and Martha [*watch* the patients].
  b. The patients [*drink* the medicine].

Yet we have two good reasons for wanting to say that the verbs *watch* and *drink* in (46) are not present plural forms. The first reason is that, unlike the true present-tense forms, they show no agreement with the subject. Even though *Joe* is singular in (46a) and *him* is singular in (46b), a verb form with *-s* would be impossible.

(49) a. *Joe will [*watches* the patient].
     b. *Martha will make him [*takes* the medicine].

The second reason for believing that the verb forms in (46) are not present plurals is that there is one particular English verb, *be,* that shows two different forms. Whereas the present plural form is *are,* the form used in the situations we are looking at now is *be.*

(50) a. *The dog will [*are* quiet].
     b. The dog will [*be* quiet].

(51) a. *Fred will make him [*are* quiet].
     b. Fred will make him [*be* quiet].

For these two reasons, then, we will distinguish a *bare-stem* form, one that looks exactly like the present plural except for the one verb *be.* We have just seen two situations in which phrases headed by bare stems are called for: after *will* and after *make him.*

Exercises

1. Assuming the truth of the rule that says that *will* requires a phrase headed by a bare stem, construct experiments that show which of the two words given in the pairs below is the bare-stem form. (Mark with asterisks any examples that you feel are unacceptable.) The first is done as an example.

    a. came, come
       Answer:
       Experimental sentences:
       *Fred will came to the meeting.
       Fred will come to the meeting.
       Conclusion: *Come* is a bare stem, *came* is not.
    b. do, did
    c. has, have
    d. go, gone
    e. got, get

2. The sentences given below show verb phrases used as parts of larger constructions that have not yet been discussed. For each of the sentences, determine whether the italicized phrase has a present plural or a bare stem as head. Do this

by replacing the phrase with some phrase headed by *are* and the same phrase headed by *be*, and see which one sounds more acceptable. The first is done as an example.

a. We saw them *take the money*.
   Answer:
   Experimental sentences:
   *We saw them are rude.
   We saw them be rude.
   Conclusion: This is a context that requires a phrase headed by a bare stem rather than a phrase headed by a present tense.
b. Do not *pester the animals*.
c. We know the witnesses *seem eager to cooperate*.
d. Jane isn't sure where the students *keep the books*.
e. Why not *try to catch the minnows*?

2.6.4 Infinitival Phrases

The bare-stem form of the verb is actually used in the formation of a slightly more complex type of phrase exemplified in (52).

(52). a. Joe intends to pay the fine.
     b. Jacob forgot to lock the cage.
     c. It is fun to be noisy.

We will call phrases of this type *infinitival phrases;* they are formed by adding the special infinitival marker *to* to a bare-stem verb phrase. Sentence (52c), in which *to* is followed by *be*, provides clear evidence that the verb phrase after *to* is headed by a bare stem. The following examples show that no other form is possible:

$$(53) \quad \text{*It is fun to} \left\{ \begin{array}{l} am \\ are \\ is \\ was \\ were \\ been \\ being \end{array} \right\} \text{noisy.}$$

2.6.5 "Defective" Verbs: Modals

There is one special group of verbs in English that do not have the variety of inflectional forms that most verbs have. These are traditionally called *modals;* this class is made up of the words *can, could, will, would, shall, should, may, might,* and *must.* As the following examples show, these verbs resemble past- and present-tense verbs, in that the phrases they head can serve as sentence predicates:

(54) a. The students [*can* resolve this problem].
    b. The patients [*may* be staying in their rooms].
    c. Fred and Harry [*must* have forgotten the beer].

Unlike ordinary present-tense verbs, however, modals do not show a distinct singular form in *-s*. Instead, the form that was used in (54) with plural subjects is also used with singular subjects.

(55) a. The student [$\left\{\begin{array}{l} can \\ *cans \end{array}\right\}$ resolve this problem].
    b. The patient [$\left\{\begin{array}{l} may \\ *mays \end{array}\right\}$ be staying in his room].
    c. Fred [$\left\{\begin{array}{l} must \\ *musts \end{array}\right\}$ have forgotten the beer].

Also, modals do not have past-participial, present-participial, or bare-stem forms. We can see this by comparing *can stand on his head* with *be able to stand on his head*. Although the two phrases have similar meanings, they do not have the same inflectional possibilities. *Be able to stand on his head* has the full range of inflectional forms; these allow it to appear in situations in which *can stand on his head* is impossible.

(56) a. John has [been able to stand on his head].
    b. *John has [can (could) stand on his head].

(57) a. John will [be able to stand on his head].
    b. *John will [can stand on his head].

(58) a. [Being able to stand on his head] is important to him.
    b. *[Canning stand on his head] is important to him.

The one inflectional distinction that several of the modals make is the distinction between present tense and past tense. To take the clearest example, in some circumstances it makes sense to view *could* as a past-tense form and *can* as the corresponding present-tense form.

(59) a. Last year, Sandra *could* whistle the national anthem.
    b. This year, Sandra *can* whistle the national anthem.

We will see additional reasons for such a view in chapter 17, when we discuss the rules involved in assigning time interpretations to sentences.

However, there are many respects in which the modals do not behave like regular combinations of a verb stem plus a tense but instead act like single units with special meanings. For this reason, we will analyze them for the time being as single linguistic units.

In view of the fact that modals can head phrases that serve as sentence predicates, we need to revise our earlier rule concerning such predicates. As a preliminary step, let us give the following definition:

(60) A verb is *finite* if it is a present-tense verb, a past-tense verb, or a modal. It is *nonfinite* otherwise. Correspondingly, the phrase headed by the verb will itself be finite or nonfinite.

The rule for sentence predicates can now be stated as follows:

(61) The predicate of a sentence must be a finite verb phrase.

2.7   OTHER PARTS OF SPEECH AS HEADS

So far in this chapter, we have seen several examples in which phrases that share the same external behavior have head words belonging to a single part-of-speech class. As a result, several of the rules that we have devised have been of the following form:

(62) Any phrase whose head belongs to part of speech (and possibly inflectional class) *x* can be used in such-and-such a way to form a larger construction.

The traditional parts of speech that have been mentioned so far are verb, adjective, and noun. A natural question to ask here is whether the other traditional parts of speech are referred to in rules of this type. The remaining parts of speech are often assumed to be those given in (63), where several examples of each are given in parentheses.

(63) a. Prepositions (*in, on, about, to, around*)
     b. Pronouns
        • Definite pronouns (*I, you, him, them*)
        • Indefinite pronouns (*something, anyone*)
     c. Conjunctions
        • Coordinating conjunctions (*and, or, nor, but*)
        • Subordinating conjunctions (*that, because, when, what, before, after*)
     d. Articles (*the, a, an, this, those*)

e. Adverbs
  • Manner adverbs (*slowly, wistfully, courageously*)
  • Degree adverbs (*very, extremely, rather, quite*)
  • Locative adverbs (*here, there, everywhere*)
  • Frequency adverbs (*often, occasionally, frequently, never*)

By and large, the answer to our question is that only the prepositions (along with some related adverbs and subordinating conjunctions) seem to be phrasal heads that play a major role in determining the external syntax of the phrases in which they occur. To take two specific examples, the external behavior of the three-word phrase *into the house* is largely determined by the preposition *into,* and the external behavior of a "clause" like *because he lost his checkbook* is determined by the subordinating conjunction *because.* Even here, though, we must note a difference between prepositions, on the one hand, and common nouns, adjectives, and verbs, on the other. With prepositions, we find no rules that allow the class of prepositions as a whole to head phrases that are called for by heads of larger constructions. Instead, we find rules of this type that refer to subclasses of prepositions (e.g., *locative prepositions* and *motion prepositions*) or to individual prepositions such as *of* and *to*. In later discussions of relative clauses and questions, we will see a small number of rules that refer to the class of prepositions as a whole, but they are rules of a different kind from the ones that we are considering here. Some of the other parts of speech listed above (or some of their subclasses) will also prove their usefulness by being mentioned in particular syntactic rules of English, but, as with the prepositional rule just mentioned, these rules are different from the ones discussed earlier in this chapter.

Exercise

1. As noted in this section, prepositions play a major role in determining the external syntax of the phrases in which they occur. As it happens, though, we cannot invariably tell everything about the way in which a prepositional phrase is used just by looking at the preposition alone. For example, the following sentences show three quite different types of phrases, all of which are headed by the preposition *in:*

  a. Sarah drank the tea *in the morning*.   (time phrase)
  b. Sarah drank the tea *in the kitchen*.   (locative phrase)
  c. Sarah drank the tea *in ten minutes*.   (duration phrase)

In order to understand the intended function of these phrases correctly, what other information must English speakers use in addition to the information that *in* is the head of the phrase?

2.8   ADDITIONAL TYPES OF PHRASES

We have now accumulated a list of several different phrase types, each one exhibiting a distinctive external behavior. In each of the examples studied so far, the behavior of the phrase is determined by the part-of-speech membership and (in the case of verbs) the inflectional form of the head word. In preparation for the work of the next chapter, we will discuss three additional types of phrases, each of which can be defined on the basis of a shared external behavior. These three types differ in one significant respect from those discussed already: it is harder to define them by referring to a single kind of head word.

2.8.1   Noun Phrases

Roughly speaking, the class of noun phrases consists of those sequences that can serve as subjects of sentences and also can fulfill some other functions. Following a standard but somewhat misleading usage, we will refer to these phrases as *noun phrases*. The following sentences give examples of a few of the most frequent types of noun phrases, where the phrases serving as subjects are italicized:

(64) (These consist of *the* plus a common-noun phrase.)

$$\left.\begin{array}{l} \textit{The} + \textit{king of Spain} \\ \textit{The} + \textit{chairman of the committee} \\ \textit{The} + \textit{sheriff} \end{array}\right\} \text{expelled his opponents.}$$

(65) (These consist of *pronouns*.)

$$\left.\begin{array}{l} \textit{I} \\ \textit{She} \\ \textit{You} \end{array}\right\} \text{should know the answer.}$$

(66) (These consist of *proper nouns*.)

$$\left.\begin{array}{l} \textit{John} \\ \textit{Shirley} \\ \textit{Alice} \end{array}\right\} \text{lost the money.}$$

(67) (These consist of noun phrases in possessive form plus common-noun phrases.)

$$\left\{ \begin{array}{l} \textit{The woman's} + \textit{brother} \\ \textit{My} + \textit{donkey} \\ \textit{Alice's} + \textit{picture of Joe} \\ \textit{Joe's} + \textit{beer} \end{array} \right\} \text{ has disappeared.}$$

With this large class of phrases identified, we can state a more specific rule for independent sentences.

(68) A sentence can consist of a noun phrase and a finite verb phrase.

With one exception, the noun phrases that are used as subjects can also be used in other ways, several of which we will discuss in chapter 3. The exception concerns pronouns: subject pronouns must be *nominative* (*I, you, he,* etc.), whereas nonsubject pronouns must be *accusative* (*me, her, you,* etc.). The general category of noun phrases exhibits a great many other internal patterns, which will be discussed in more detail in chapter 5.

Exercise

1. Listed below are a variety of sequences that can appear in English sentences, in particular, after English verbs. For each sequence, determine experimentally whether it qualifies as a possible noun phrase. Do this by constructing an experimental sentence in which you try to use the sequence in accordance with rule (68), and then judge the acceptability of the sentence, marking with asterisks any sentences that you think are unacceptable. The first is done as an example.

    a. the dog in the cage
       Answer:
       Experimental sentence: *The dog in the cage* belongs to Rhoda.
       Judgment: This sentence is acceptable.
       Conclusion: Yes, this sequence qualifies as a possible noun phrase.
    b. the baby to the hospital
    c. the man drunk
    d. the letter to Fred
    e. the man that Martha hired Fred
    f. the man that Martha hired
    g. Fred to the library

2.8.2 Locative Phrases

Locative phrases are used to indicate stationary location, as in the following examples:

(69) a. Joe stayed *at the cemetery.*
   b. Jane found the turtle *over there.*
   c. The keys are *right up here on the counter.*

As these examples show, phrases in this group take a variety of different forms, and (as with noun phrases) it is sometimes hard to identify one particular kind of word that serves as head. For the time being, we will chiefly make use of locative phrases consisting just of a locative prepositional phrase—that is, phrases of the sort exemplified in (69a).

2.8.3 Motion Phrases

Motion phrases typically indicate some kind of movement in a certain direction or toward a certain location. Here are some examples:

(70) a. The tomato fell *into the soup.*
   b. The chairman walked *back up here onto the stage.*
   c. The lion moved *toward the hyena.*
   d. Jones took the lawnmower *around the house.*

Motion phrases are often quite similar in form (or even identical) to locative phrases, so that the interpretation of a sequence of such words frequently depends on the context in which it is found. The examples in (71) contain a locative phrase and an identical motion phrase.

(71) a. Jane kept her textbook *over there.*   (locative phrase)
   b. Jane took her textbook *over there.*   (motion phrase)

Here is how we can tell that these classifications are correct. We need to pick out a phrase that could only be a motion phrase, and substitute it in both of these sentences. For instance, a phrase introduced by *to* is reliably a motion phrase but not a locative phrase. We then construct the following examples:

(72) a. *Jane kept her textbook *to the lecture.*
   b. Jane took her textbook *to the lecture.*

These examples show that *kept* calls for a locative phrase, whereas *took* calls for a motion phrase.

Exercise

1. As noted above, the phrase *over there* can be either a locative phrase or a motion phrase, depending on the context. Below are six sentences containing this

phrase. For each one, decide which of these two phrase types the context requires. Do this by constructing experimental sentences like the ones in (72).

a. Joe placed the chair *over there*.
b. He should have brought it *over there*.
c. Jane left the paper *over there*.
d. Joe arrived *over there* at ten o'clock.
e. Greta is *over there*.
f. Jerry rolled the cart *over there*.

Chapter 3

Phrase-Internal Syntax: Heads and Their Complements

3.1 COMPLEMENTS, MINIMAL PHRASES, AND MODIFIERS

In section 2.1, we saw that some phrases contain key words that are traditionally referred to as *heads,* and that certain properties of the heads (their part-of-speech classification and in some instances their inflectional form) play a key role in determining whether the phrases can be used in the formation of larger structures. For instance, we saw that the phrase *eaten the shrimp* can join with the verb *have* to make a larger phrase (*have eaten the shrimp*), by virtue of the fact that the head word of the smaller phrase (*eaten*) is a past-participial verb.

In the present chapter, we will adopt the opposite perspective, shifting our attention to the way in which head words dictate the *internal* structure of their phrases. One idea that will be important throughout this chapter is that individual head words may choose certain types of phrases to function as their *complements,* and that the head and its complements, if any, are joined closely to form a *minimal phrase.* When the head is a verb, this minimal phrase typically represents a basic action, process, or state. An additional assumption about the internal structure of phrases (one that will be less important in this chapter than later in the book) is that a minimal phrase may be augmented by the addition of one or more phrases serving as *modifiers,* the result being a larger phrase. For reasons that will be discussed in the next several paragraphs, these concepts impose an analysis along the lines shown in (1b) for the verb phrase of the sentence in (1a).

(1) a. Martha put some money in the bank on Friday.

b.

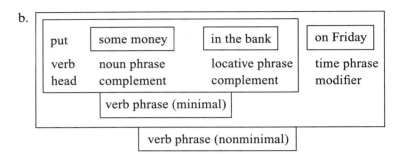

According to the picture in (1b), the verb *put* serves as a head. It goes together with two complements (the noun phrase *some money* and the locative phrase *in the bank*) to make the phrase *put some money in the bank*, the minimal verb phrase in this sentence. To this minimal phrase is joined a modifier (the time phrase *on Friday*). The result is a slightly larger (nonminimal) verb phrase, also headed by the same word *put*.

What grounds do we have for distinguishing complements from modifiers? Although a detailed discussion of this question would take us quite far afield, it may be illuminating here to look briefly at two respects in which the head-complement relation and the head-modifier relation differ.

One difference is that individual head words vary quite markedly in the complements that they allow, but show a much smaller tendency to require or prohibit specific modifiers. This individuality in the choice of complements is shown in (2)–(7), for the verbs *put, keep,* and *stay.*

(2) Two complements: noun phrase + locative phrase
  a.   Martha put Fido behind the garage.
  b.   Martha kept Fido behind the garage.
  c.   *Martha stayed Fido behind the garage.

(3) Two complements: noun phrase + adjective phrase
  a.   *George put Fido busy.
  b.   George kept Fido busy.
  c.   *George stayed Fido busy.

(4) One complement: noun phrase
  a.   *Karen put Fido.
  b.   Karen kept Fido.
  c.   *Karen stayed Fido.

(5) One complement: locative phrase
    a.   *Oscar put behind the counter.
    b.   *?Oscar kept behind the counter.
    c.   Oscar stayed behind the counter.

(6) One complement: adjective phrase
    a.   *Jane put busy.
    b.   Jane kept busy.
    c.   Jane stayed busy.

(7) No complements
    a.   *Harry put.
    b.   *Harry kept.
    c.   Harry stayed.

We find an entirely different situation with a modifier such as the time phrase *on Friday*. As the sentences in (8)–(10) show, the phrases that the same three verbs head are equally acceptable with the modifier or without it.

(8) a. Martha put some money in the bank on Friday.
     b. Martha put some money in the bank.

(9) a. Jane kept busy on Friday.
     b. Jane kept busy.

(10) a. Oscar stayed behind the counter on Friday.
     b. Oscar stayed behind the counter.

Thus, one basic difference between complements and modifiers is that the former appear in verb phrases only on the strength of invitations from specific heads, whereas the latter are generally free to appear or not appear, without regard to what the specific head happens to be.

The necessity of distinguishing between complements and modifiers is also suggested by a construction that English speakers commonly use in order to avoid repeating material—namely, the verb phrase *do the same thing*. The use of this construction is illustrated in (11).

(11) Martha *put some money in the bank on Friday*.
    And Shirley $\begin{Bmatrix} \textit{put some money in the bank on Friday} \\ \textit{did the same thing} \end{Bmatrix}$.

Here the whole verb phrase of the second sentence is identical with the whole verb phrase of the first sentence. As a result, it is possible to replace the second verb phrase in its entirety with *did the same thing*.

Now let us see what happens in a situation where the verb phrases are identical only up to the modifying time phrase, with the two time phrases being different.

(12) Martha *put some money in the bank* on Friday.

And Shirley $\begin{Bmatrix} put\ some\ money\ in\ the\ bank \\ did\ the\ same\ thing \end{Bmatrix}$ on Monday.

As (12) shows, it is completely acceptable to leave a modifier behind when we replace the second of two identical sequences with *did the same thing*. Now, what happens when we try to do this kind of replacement in a situation where we have different complements instead of different modifiers?

(13) Martha *put some money* in the bank.

And Shirley $\begin{Bmatrix} put\ some\ money \\ *did\ the\ same\ thing \end{Bmatrix}$ in her wall safe.

Here we have tried (unsuccessfully) to replace just the head verb and the noun-phrase complement, leaving behind the locative-phrase complement. The unacceptability of the result is explained immediately if we make three simple assumptions.

- The complements of a head are included in the head's minimal phrase.
- The locative phrase that occurs with *put* is a complement of *put* and thus is included in its minimal verb phrase.
- *Did the same thing* cannot replace a sequence that is less than a minimal verb phrase.

Exactly the same kind of experimental technique can be extended to the problem of distinguishing between complements and modifiers of common nouns. It turns out that substitution by the word *one* or *ones* is sensitive to what constitutes a minimal common-noun phrase (i.e., a minimal phrase headed by a common noun).

At first glance, it might appear that *one(s)* only replaces common nouns, as in (14).

(14) a. The big *dog* chased the small $\begin{Bmatrix} dog \\ one \end{Bmatrix}$.

b. This *town* is larger than that $\begin{Bmatrix} town \\ one \end{Bmatrix}$.

However, other examples show clearly that more than just a common noun by itself can be replaced.

(15) a. This *picture of Fred* is more flattering than that
$\left\{ \begin{array}{l} \textit{picture of Fred} \\ \textit{one} \end{array} \right\}$.

b. This *student of chemistry* is more industrious than that
$\left\{ \begin{array}{l} \textit{student of chemistry} \\ \textit{one} \end{array} \right\}$.

c. This *book from France* is more valuable than that
$\left\{ \begin{array}{l} \textit{book from France} \\ \textit{one} \end{array} \right\}$.

These additional examples suggest that the basic rule about *one(s)* is that it replaces a common-noun *phrase*, rather than just a common noun.

It is also possible in some cases to leave a phrase behind, that is, to replace less than all of the material that follows the noun.

(16) a. The [*king* from France] is taller than the [$\left\{ \begin{array}{l} \textit{king} \\ \textit{one} \end{array} \right\}$ from Spain].

b. The [*book* that I reviewed] is longer than the [$\left\{ \begin{array}{l} \textit{book} \\ \textit{one} \end{array} \right\}$ that you reviewed].

c. The [*student of physics* with long hair] is more intelligent than the [$\left\{ \begin{array}{l} \textit{student of physics} \\ \textit{one} \end{array} \right\}$ with short hair].

We can infer from these examples that sometimes the minimal common-noun phrase does not include all of the material that follows the noun. Thus, the situations we see in (16) can be represented as in (17), where the minimal common-noun phrases are indicated by brackets.

(17) a. [*king*] from France
b. [*book*] that I reviewed
c. [*student of physics*] with long hair

In other examples, though, leaving something behind leads to unacceptability.

(18) a. *The *student* of physics is taller than the $\left\{ \begin{array}{l} \textit{student} \\ \textit{*one} \end{array} \right\}$ of chemistry.

b. *The *king* of England is taller than the $\left\{ \begin{array}{l} \textit{king} \\ \textit{*one} \end{array} \right\}$ of Spain.

Here it appears that we have tried to get away with replacing less than the minimal common-noun phrase. Thus, the situations we see in (18) can be represented as in (19), where again the minimal common-noun phrases are indicated by brackets.

(19) a. [*student* of physics]
  b. [*king* of England]

We can make sense of all of this if we say that (a) certain of the phrases that follow a noun are complements of the noun and fall within the minimal phrase headed by the noun; (b) certain other phrases are modifiers and fall outside the minimal phrase headed by the noun. We have relied for this result on a process that is very much analogous to the process that replaces verb phrases by *do the same thing*. Just as *do the same thing* can't replace less than a minimal verb phrase, so *one* can't replace less than a minimal common-noun phrase. In both instances, the particular substitution rule gives us a technique for distinguishing complements from modifiers. The result of all of these observations about common-noun phrases can be seen by looking at (20a) and the associated diagram in (20b).

(20) a. student of physics from France
  b.

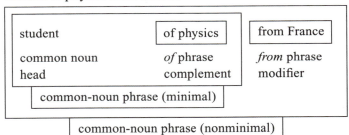

The overall structure of this common-noun phrase is thus very close to that proposed for the verb phrase in (1). The only difference is that the particular verb that we saw in (1) had two complements in its minimal phrase, whereas the common noun *student* has only one.

For the remainder of this chapter, we will concentrate on the ways in which head words combine with complements to build minimal phrases, postponing a detailed discussion of modifiers until chapters 10, 11, and 12. The greater part of the discussion in this chapter will be devoted to verbs and their complements, followed by brief discussions of complementation with adjectives and nouns. The chapter will conclude with a description of the graphic system that will be used throughout the remainder of the book for representing basic structural properties of English sentences.

Exercise

1. At first glance, the following two sentences appear to share the same structure:

(i) Fritz locked Fido *in the garage.*

(ii) Fritz bathed Fido *in the garage.*

However, if we try to replace everything up to the locative phrase by *do the same thing,* we find that the results are not the same.

(iii) George *locked Fido* in the kitchen, and then Fritz $\left\{ \begin{array}{l} locked\ Fido \\ *did\ the\ same\ thing \end{array} \right\}$ in the garage.

(iv) George *bathed Fido* in the kitchen, and then Fritz $\left\{ \begin{array}{l} bathed\ Fido \\ did\ the\ same\ thing \end{array} \right\}$ in the garage.

What do (iii) and (iv) suggest about the locative phrase *in the garage*? Is it a complement in both (i) and (ii), a modifier in both (i) and (ii), or a complement in one and a modifier in the other? Explain your answer briefly.

3.2   PARADIGM SETS AND COMPLEMENT CHOICE

As preparation for discussing verbs and their complements, it will be helpful to consider what properties of individual words are relevant for complement choice. Let us take as an example the word *gone*. This word can serve as the head of a phrase such as *gone to the picnic*. One important fact about *gone* is that it is a past participle. It is this fact that allows the phrase it heads to be joined with the word *have,* as noted in subsection 2.6.2.

(21)   The workers have [*gone* to the picnic].

What property of the word *gone* is responsible for allowing it to join with the motion phrase *to the picnic*? The past-participial property seems to be irrelevant here, as the following ungrammatical sentences show:

(22)   *The workers have $\left\{ \begin{array}{l} [\textit{carried}\ to\ the\ picnic] \\ [\textit{forgotten}\ to\ the\ picnic] \\ [\textit{fastened}\ to\ the\ picnic] \end{array} \right\}$.

On the other hand, all of the other inflectional forms of *go* do share this capacity to combine with a motion phrase.

(23) a. The workers are [*going* to the picnic].   (present participle)
     b. The workers [*went* to the picnic].   (past tense)
     c. The workers [*go* the the picnic].   (present plural)
     d. The workers will [*go* to the picnic].   (bare stem)

We will use the expression *GO* to refer to this set of related verb forms as a whole. (We will refer to this set and others like it as *paradigm sets*.) Then the fact that the word *gone* is the past-participial form from the paradigm set GO can be represented as follows:

(24) gone
     [GO]
     [PastPart]

The differing contributions of the [GO] property and the [PastPart] property are shown in the following diagram:

(25) have

The [GO] property (i.e., the fact that *gone* is a particular form from the set {*go, went, gone, goes, going, go*}) is important inside the boxed phrase, allowing the word *gone* to be joined with a motion phrase like *to the picnic*. By contrast, the [PastPart] property is important outside the phrase, allowing the phrase as a whole to be accepted by the verb *have*.

What is true for *gone* is true for other verbs as well. The paradigm set to which the verb belongs (GO, PUT, THINK, etc.) is important for determining the particular complements that the verb takes inside its own minimal phrase. By contrast, the inflectional form of the verb (present, past, past participle, etc.) determines how the phrase as a whole fits into larger constructions.

In what follows, the term *verb* will be used in two slightly different ways. In some cases, it will refer to a paradigm set (e.g., "the verb GO"), and in other cases, it will refer to an individual word (e.g., "the verb *gone*"). The context will generally make clear which meaning is intended.

3.3   A WAY OF EXPRESSING COMPLEMENT POSSIBILITIES

One part of the syntactic knowledge that English speakers have consists of a vast number of small rules concerning the complement-taking properties of individual words. We have already stated one such rule informally, when we observed that the verb GO can join with a following motion phrase. Such rules concerning what complements are taken by each individual head word can be expressed as in (26), which gives the rule that is needed for GO.

(26) [GO MotP]

We will refer to rules of this type as *complement rules*. This rule expresses the idea that a member of the paradigm set GO can combine with a motion phrase to make a minimal phrase of its own. Paradigm sets whose members cannot occur with motion phrases will not be found in this particular configuration. Thus, for example, the unacceptability of (27) can be accounted for by noting that CARRY cannot join with a motion phrase by itself.

(27) *John carried to the picnic.

Another way to make the same point is to say that the expression in (28) is not an actual rule of English.

(28) [CARRY MotP]

3.4 TWO FUNCTIONS OF NOUN PHRASES AS COMPLEMENTS

We are almost ready to see how complements are chosen by individual verbs. But before we turn to this project, one last preliminary matter requires attention.

In chapter 2, we identified a group of phrases that could serve as subjects of sentences; we referred to this group by the standard (but somewhat arbitrary) term *noun phrases*. These phrases can also serve as complements to verbs, but with different verbs they serve in two fundamentally different ways. In many instances (actually in the vast majority of cases), noun phrases serve as *arguments:* they identify the person or thing playing a certain role. In other instances, though, they serve as *predicates,* providing information about someone or something mentioned earlier in the sentence. The following two examples illustrate this difference:

(29) a. Jesse sued a contractor.
     b. Jesse became a contractor.

In (29a), the verb *sued* requires that two roles be filled, the role of plaintiff and the role of defendant. The noun phrase *a contractor* describes the person filling the second of these roles, but it indicates nothing at all about Jesse. In (29b), by contrast, *a contractor* does not identify the person filling a second role in the sentence, but instead provides a description of Jesse. In (29a), then, the noun phrase *a contractor* serves as an argument, whereas in (29b) it serves as a predicate. Clearly, some difference between *sued* and *became* is responsible for this difference in the interpretation of the noun phrase in question. In general, the particular verb with which a noun-phrase complement occurs will dictate whether it is an argument or a predicate. Because argument noun phrases are so much the more common, we will often use the term "noun phrases" to refer to them instead of the more cumbersome term "argument noun phrases."

3.5   SOME VERB + COMPLEMENT COMBINATIONS

We are now ready to see what kinds of complement configurations occur in English, and which configurations are chosen by particular verbs. Below is a list of some of the common possibilities. We will make a traditional distinction here, dividing this list of verb phrases into *intransitive* and *transitive*. The intransitive list will consist of phrases in which there is no *direct object,* that is, no argument noun phrase called for directly by the verb itself. The transitive list will be made up of phrases in which such a direct object is present.

3.5.1   Intransitive Complement Configurations

(30) Some verbs can occur in the configuration [—], that is, without any complements at all.
a. John [disappeared].
   [DISAPPEAR]
b. The bottle [broke].
   [BREAK]

(31) Some verbs can appear in the configuration [— NP_{Pred}], that is, with a predicate noun phrase.
a. Jane [became   *a surgeon*].
   [BECOME NP_{Pred}]
b. Fred [is   *a swindler*].
   [BE NP_{Pred}]

(32) Some verbs can appear in the configuration [— AdjP], that is, with an adjective phrase.

    a. Alice [is   *intelligent*].
      [BE AdjP]
    b. Ben [seems   *eager to read the book*].
      [SEEM AdjP]
    c. Fred [became   *fond of Ruth*].
      [BECOME AdjP]

(33) Some verbs can appear in the configuration [— LocP], that is, with a locative phrase.
    a. Martha [stayed   *at the hospital*].
      [STAY LocP]
    b. Fred [resides   *in Chicago*].
      [RESIDE LocP]

(34) Some verbs can appear in the configuration [— MotP], that is, with a motion phrase.
    a. Robert [went   *to the hospital*].
      [GO MotP]
    b. Alice [moved   *into the room*].
      [MOVE MotP]

(35) Some verbs can appear in the configuration [— $VP_{PresPart}$], that is, with a present-participial verb phrase.
    a. Joseph [is   *stealing cookies*].
      [BE $VP_{PresPart}$]
    b. Jean [keeps   *asking questions*].
      [KEEP $VP_{PresPart}$]

(36) One verb can appear in the configuration [— $VP_{PastPart}$], that is, with a past-participial verb phrase.
    a. Carolyn [has   *taken the money*].
      [HAVE $VP_{PastPart}$]

(37) Some verbs (specifically, the modals) can appear in the configuration [— VP_{Stem}], that is, with a bare-stem verb phrase.
    a. John [must   *be happy*].
      [MUST VP_{Stem}]
    b. Jill [may   *be sick*].
      [MAY VP_{Stem}]

(38) Some verbs can appear in the configuration [— InfP], that is, with an infinitival phrase.

a. Kathy will [try *to write a letter*].
   [TRY InfP]
b. Jeff [hopes *to get a job*].
   [HOPE InfP]

3.5.2 Transitive Complement Configurations

(39) Some verbs can appear in the configuration [— NP], that is, with a noun phrase.
a. Joe [saw *Fred*].
   [SEE NP]
b. Alice [broke *the bottle*].
   [BREAK NP]
c. Kate [made *a birdhouse*].
   [MAKE NP]
d. John [paid *the plumber*].
   [PAY NP]
e. Polly [ate *the cracker*].
   [EAT NP]

(40) Some verbs can appear in the configuration [— NP NP$_{Pred}$], that is, with a noun phrase and a predicate noun phrase.
a. Jane [considers *Bill a good friend*].
   [CONSIDER NP NP$_{Pred}$]
b. Alex [called *his brother a liar*].
   [CALL NP NP$_{Pred}$]

(41) Some verbs can appear in the configuration [— NP AdjP], that is, with a noun phrase and an adjective phrase.
a. Joe [kept *it cold*].
   [KEEP NP AdjP]
b. Fido [made *Alice quite angry*].
   [MAKE NP AdjP]

(42) Some verbs can appear in the configuration [— NP LocP], that is, with a noun phrase and a locative phrase.
a. Joe [kept *it in the garage*].
   [KEEP NP LocP]
b. Martha [placed *them on the counter*].
   [PLACE NP LocP]
c. Alice [put *Felix in the play pen*].
   [PUT NP LocP]

(43) Some verbs can appear in the configuration [— NP MotP], that is, with a noun phrase and a motion phrase.

    a. We [moved   *it   into the room*].
      [MOVE NP MotP]

    b. Fred [took   *Alice   to the hospital*].
      [TAKE NP MotP]

(44) Some verbs can appear in the configuration [— NP VP$_{PresPart}$], that is, with a noun phrase and a present-participial verb phrase.

    a. Joe [heard   *Fred   asking questions*].
      [HEAR NP VP$_{PresPart}$]

    b. The police [caught   *John   stealing hubcaps*].
      [CATCH NP VP$_{PresPart}$]

(45) Some verbs can appear in the configuration [— NP VP$_{Stem}$], that is, with a noun phrase and a bare-stem verb phrase.

    a. We [made   *George   be quiet*].
      [MAKE NP VP$_{Stem}$]

    b. Martha [watched   *David   open the letters*].
      [WATCH NP VP$_{Stem}$]

    c. Nathan [let   *the dog   eat the biscuit*].
      [LET NP VP$_{Stem}$]

(46) Some verbs can appear in the configuration [— NP InfP], that is, with a noun phrase and an infinitival phrase.

    a. We [persuaded   *John   to keep the money*].
      [PERSUADE NP InfP]

    b. Martha [asked   *Alice   to open the door*].
      [ASK NP InfP]

3.5.3   Ditransitive Complement Configurations

One more transitive complement configuration, [— NP NP], requires mention. This configuration is illustrated in (47).

(47) a. John [sent   *Martha   a check*].
    b. We [gave   *Fred   a wastebasket*].

In each of these sentences, the verb is followed by two noun phrases. Unlike the last noun phrase in the examples with CONSIDER and CALL, however, which serves as a predicate, the last noun phrase in each of these examples serves as an argument. Instead of describing some noun phrase mentioned earlier in the sentence, it identifies the object conveyed to the person identified by the noun phrase before it. In traditional grammar, the second of these argument noun phrases is analyzed as the direct object, corresponding to the direct objects in (39)–(46), and the noun phrase that precedes it is called the *indirect object*. Thus, in the sentences in (47), *a check* and *a wastebasket* are direct objects, and *Martha* and *Fred* are indirect objects. For these two verbs, we need the following complement rules:

(48) a. [SEND NP NP]
      b. [GIVE NP NP]

3.5.4   Simple Complement Rules in Complicated Sentences

In the preceding three subsections, we have observed a variety of different complement configurations in which individual English verbs can appear. Most of these configurations have been illustrated with example sentences that have fairly simple structures. Thus, it may not be clear at this point that the complement rules offered above will work for longer, more complicated examples. For instance, we might ask whether these complement rules would account for the example in (49).

(49) Martha has made Alice let the baby eat the pudding.

This sentence has a predicate verb phrase in which the head *has* is accompanied by a total of three verbs (*made, let,* and *eat*) and three noun phrases (*Alice, the baby,* and *the pudding*). None of the rules given above make any direct provision for three verbs or three noun phrases. Thus, this example might appear to force us to adopt the following extremely complicated complement rule for HAVE:

(50) [HAVE $V_{PastPart}$ NP V_{Stem} NP V_{Stem} NP]

When we work our way carefully through the predicate verb phrase in (49), though, we find that every aspect of its structure can be accounted for with simple complement rules. We can think of each verb along the way as forming its phrase by issuing invitations to one or more smaller phrases, in ways dictated by one of its complement rules. We begin by considering the invitation issued by *has*.

(51) a. The verb *has* is one of the forms of HAVE.
      b. HAVE figures in the complement rule [HAVE $VP_{PastPart}$]. Thus, *has* can invite a past-participial verb phrase into the phrase that it heads.

   c. *Made* qualifies as a past participle, so that *made Alice let the baby eat the pudding* will qualify as a past-participial verb phrase, provided it has a legitimate internal structure itself.
   d. Therefore, *has made Alice let the baby eat the pudding* has a legitimate internal structure, so far as its head word *has* is concerned.

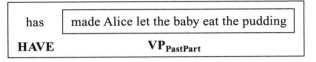

At this point, HAVE has finished its regulatory work. Thus, it is now appropriate to consider the invitations that *made* can issue.

(52) a. The verb *made* is one of the forms of MAKE.
   b. MAKE figures in the complement rule [MAKE NP VP$_{Stem}$]. Thus, *made* can invite a noun phrase and a bare-stem verb phrase into the phrase that it heads.
   c. *Alice* qualifies as a noun phrase.
   d. *Let* qualifies as a bare stem, so that *let the baby eat the pudding* will qualify as a bare-stem verb phrase, provided it has a legitimate internal structure itself.
   e. Therefore, *made Alice let the baby eat the pudding* has a legitimate internal structure, so far as its head word *made* is concerned.

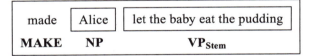

Having finished with *made,* we turn now to *let,* which issues the same sort of invitation that *made* issued.

(53) a. The verb *let* is one of the forms of LET.
   b. LET figures in the complement rule [LET NP VP$_{Stem}$]. Thus, *let* can invite a noun phrase and a bare-stem verb phrase into the phrase that it heads.
   c. *The baby* qualifies as a noun phrase.
   d. *Eat* qualifies as a bare stem, so that *eat the pudding* will qualify as a bare stem verb phrase, provided it has a legitimate internal structure itself.

e. Therefore, *let the baby eat the pudding* has a legitimate internal structure, so far as its head word *let* is concerned.

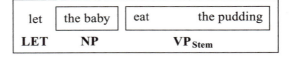

Finally, we consider the verb *eat*.

(54) a. The verb *eat* is one of the forms of EAT.
   b. EAT figures in the complement rule [EAT NP]. Thus, *eat* can invite a noun phrase into the phrase that it heads.
   c. *The pudding* qualifies as a noun phrase.
   d. Therefore, *eat the pudding* has a legitimate internal structure.

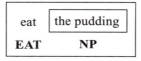

A composite view of the manner in which various requirements are satisfied is provided by the diagram given in (55).

(55)

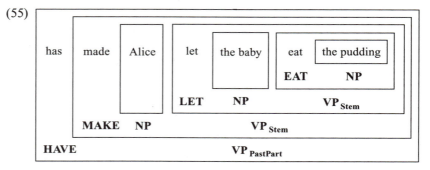

The general idea that this diagram illustrates is an extremely important one. The structural details of this large and rather complex phrase do not result from a pattern of "centralized regulation" from the head verb *has* but instead exhibit a clear pattern of "decentralized regulation." Thus, what is required to account for sentence (49) is not the single very complicated rule given in (56), but the set of four simple rules given in (57).

(56) [HAVE $V_{PastPart}$ NP V_{Stem} NP V_{Stem} NP]   [=(50)]

(57) a. [HAVE VP$_{PastPart}$]
    b. [MAKE NP VP$_{Stem}$]
    c. [LET NP VP$_{Stem}$]
    d. [EAT NP]

Another important general idea is worth mentioning here, one that is likely to seem strange at first glance to many native English speakers, for whom speaking and writing generally proceed without any conscious awareness of syntactic rules. This idea is that, in any given well-formed English sentence that we say or write, each word or phrase in that sentence has a legitimate place only by virtue of some highly specific invitation, based on one or more particular rules of the language. The point can be illustrated with the relatively simple sentence in (58).

(58) Martha asked John to pay the plumber.

The rules that are responsible for the invitations in this sentence are those given in (59), all of which we have seen previously.

(59) a. A noun phrase can consist of a proper noun alone.
    b. A noun phrase can consist of *the* plus a common-noun phrase.
    c. A sentence consists of a noun phrase and a finite verb phrase. (A *finite verb* is a present tense form, a past-tense form, or a modal.)
    d. Any form of ASK can head a phrase in which it occurs with a noun phrase followed by an infinitival phrase (in short, [ASK NP InfP]).
    e. An infinitival phrase consists of *to* plus a bare-stem verb phrase.
    f. Any form of PAY can appear in a phrase in which it occurs with a noun phrase (in short, [PAY NP]).

Because of (59a), *Martha* and *John* both qualify as noun phrases and thus are entitled to accept noun-phrase invitations. A similar conclusion holds for the phrase *the plumber,* because of (59b). Rule (59c) issues an invitation for a noun phrase, which is accepted here by *Martha.* The same rule also issues an invitation for a finite verb phrase, for which the phrase headed by the past-tense verb *asked* is suitable. *John* accepts the noun-phrase invitation issued by ASK in (59d), and the remaining sequence of words has a place in the sentence on the strength of the infinitival-phrase invitation issued by ASK in the same rule. Rule (59e) regulates the formation of this infinitival phrase: it calls for the word *to* and also issues an invitation for a bare-stem verb phrase, for which the phrase headed by *pay* qualifies. Finally, *the plumber* accepts the noun-phrase invitation issued by PAY, as specified in (59f).

Exercises

1. Below are sentences that illustrate the complement-taking properties of some intransitive verbs. For each sentence, give the complement rule that allows that verb to appear in the particular configuration in which it appears in that sentence. The rules that you write should involve the following intransitive configurations:

[—]	[— VP$_{PresPart}$]
[— NP$_{Pred}$]	[— VP$_{PastPart}$]
[— AdjP]	[— VP$_{Stem}$]
[— LocP]	[— InfP]
[— MotP]	

The first one is done as an example.

a. The officers [*should* release the prisoner].
   Answer: [SHOULD VP$_{Stem}$]
b. Geraldine [*stood* on the platform].
c. Fred [*started* asking Phil to check the batteries].
d. Alice [*became* the president of the senate].
e. The peach [*tasted* sweet].
f. Joe [*sneezed*].
g. The refugees [*long* to return to their homeland].
h. Jerry's car [*rolled* into the kitchen].
i. Robert [*has* disowned his children].
j. Karen [*will* find an answer].

2. Below are sentences that illustrate the complement-taking possibilities of some transitive verbs. For each sentence, give the complement rule that allows that verb to appear in the particular verb phrase in which it appears in that sentence. The rules that you write should involve the following transitive configurations:

[— NP]	[— NP VP$_{PresPart}$]
[— NP NP$_{Pred}$]	[— NP VP$_{Stem}$]
[— NP AdjP]	[— NP InfP]
[— NP LocP]	[— NP NP]
[— NP MotP]	

The task essentially involves looking at what comes after the verb and breaking it into a noun phrase plus one of the other phrase types.

a. Joe [*let* Martha's cat eat the liver].
b. Sarah [*asked* me to let Harry keep the painting].
c. Brenda [*allowed* the children to cross the road].
d. Louis [*heard* the chairman of the committee ask Fred to open a window].

    e. Jane [*left* her picture of Tom in the lounge].
    f. Arnie [*brought* his nephew to the concert].
    g. We [*saw* the leader of the group writing a note].
    h. Joe should [*have* the children put the gerbils in the basement].
    i. Bonnie [*borrowed* your typewriter].
    j. George [*mailed* the attorney his photograph of the accident].
    k. Hard work [*made* Horatio the president of the company].

3. The sentences in the following list contain a mixture of transitive and intransitive verbs. As in the two preceding exercises, for each sentence, give the complement rule that allows the italicized verb to appear in the particular verb phrase in which it appears in that example. In each case, your rule should involve a configuration from one of the two groups of configurations given in the preceding exercises.

    a. Carol [*hid* the manuscript in the cupboard].
    b. The counselors [*made* the campers run around the lake].
    c. Joseph [*found* the mayor's keys].
    d. Fred [*hired* Sharon to change the oil].
    e. Martha [*found* John an overcoat].
    f. They [*pushed* the prisoners into the truck].
    g. Fran [*hopes* to persuade Harry to make the cook wash the dishes].
    h. The lecture [*ended*].

4. In each of the following sentences, a verb is italicized and its inflectional form is identified. For each such verb form, identify the rule that legitimizes that particular form in that particular context in the sentence. The first two are done as examples.

    a. Martha may *buy* the typewriter.   (bare stem)
       Answer: MAY takes a phrase headed by a bare stem verb (i.e., [MAY VP$_{Stem}$]).
    b. The students *live* in Austin.   (present tense)
       Answer: A sentence consists of a noun phrase and a finite verb phrase (and present tense counts as finite).
    c. Fred seems to *have* been sleeping.   (bare stem)
    d. Sharon has *been* eager to finish the book.   (past participle)
    e. Gordon *tried* to open the jar.   (past tense)
    f. Jason caught Albert *stealing* apples.   (present participle)
    g. Fred should let Jane's mother *read* the letter.   (bare stem)
    h. Trisha keeps *asking* Karen's sister to buy the car.   (present participle)

5. There are several verbs in English that show no outward difference between past tense, past participle, and bare stem. Three such verbs are *hit, let,* and *cut.* The following sentences contain several italicized occurrences of these words. For each such occurrence, decide whether it is a past tense, a past participle, or a bare stem. Justify your answer by giving a rule from those discussed so far that requires the use of one or the other inflectional form, just as you did in your answers to

exercise 4. In some of the examples, the relevant rule will be a complement rule; in other examples, it will be one of the rules from chapter 2. The first answer is provided as an illustration.

> a. Joe intends to make Bill *cut* the log.
>   Answer: One of the complement rules for MAKE is [MAKE NP VP$_{Stem}$]. Therefore, *cut* must be a bare-stem verb in this sentence.
> b. Janet *let* George open the letter.
> c. Harry must have *cut* the wire.
> d. You may *let* the children divide the strawberries.
> e. The ball *hit* the ceiling.
> f. We watched the ball *hit* the ceiling.
> g. Martha asked Harry to *cut* the wire.

3.5.4   *Do* + Plus Bare Stem: A Special Tensed Construction

One more type of English verb phrase deserves attention here, a type of finite phrase that plays a special role in English syntax. Phrases of this kind are formed when a tensed DO combines with a bare stem verb phrase. These phrases are sufficiently different from ordinary verb phrases to merit a separate discussion.

We can get an initial look at verb phrases of this new type by examining their use in one variety of emphatic sentence. The pairs of sentences in (60)–(62) show the contrast between the ordinary finite verb phrases used in nonemphatic sentences and the new type of verb phrase used in their emphatic counterparts. (Small uppercase letters indicate emphatic stress.)

(60) a. I went to the post office.
   b. I DID go to the post office.

(61) a. Sheila likes apples.
   b. Sheila DOES like apples.

(62) a. They live in Boston.
   b. They DO live in Boston.

The difference between each (a) sentence and its corresponding (b) sentence can be described as follows: where the (a) sentence contains a phrase headed by an ordinary tensed verb, the (b) sentence contains a corresponding phrase headed by a bare-stem form, this phrase serving as a complement of some tensed form of DO. This contrast can be seen more clearly in the following display, where the left column contains ordinary tensed verb phrases and the right column contains the special verb phrases headed by DO:

(63) *Ordinary verb phrases*   *Verb phrases headed by DO*

a. went to the post office	DID go to the post office
(past-tense verb phrase)	(past DO + bare-stem verb phrase)
b. likes apples	DOES like apples
(pres sg verb phrase)	(pres sg DO + bare-stem verb phrase)
c. live in Boston	DO live in Boston
(pres pl verb phrase)	(pres pl DO + bare-stem verb phrase)

Let us refer to the verb phrases found in the (a) sentences as *general-purpose finites* and to those in the (b) sentences as *special-purpose finites*.

We can provide for verb phrases of this new type by giving a special complement rule for the verb DO.

(64) [DO VP$_{Stem}$]

This rule, which is similar to the ones given earlier for the modals, allows DO to take a bare-stem verb phrase as a complement. Thus, it allows the formation of all of the special-purpose phrases given in the right column of (63).

In addition to saying how special-purpose phrases are formed, we also need rules to spell out how they are used. By the end of this book, we will have accumulated a variety of such rules. Right now we are in a position to state our first rule, one that accounts for emphatic sentences.

(65) To form an emphatic affirmative sentence:
    a. use a special-purpose verb phrase;
    b. put extra stress on the finite verb.

Taken together, the rules in (64) and (65) allow us to account for a broad range of emphatic sentences. However, some further examples of this construction are not accounted for. In each of the three sets of sentences given in (66)–(68), the (a) sentence is an unemphatic sentence, the (b) sentence is the emphatic counterpart predicted by rules (64) and (65), and the (c) sentence is the actual emphatic counterpart.

(66) a.   John has gone to the library.
    b.   *John DID have gone to the library.
    c.   John HAS gone to the library.

(67) a.   We are trying to solve the puzzle.
    b.   *We DO be trying to solve the puzzle.
    c.   We ARE trying to solve the puzzle.

(68) a.   Jack can play the fiddle.
  b.   *Jack DOES can play the fiddle.
  c.   Jack CAN play the fiddle.

Although these additional examples might appear to pose a problem for rule (65), they can actually be accounted for without complicating the rule at all. We simply need to say that for a handful of exceptional verbs, the special-purpose structures are identical to the corresponding general-purpose structures. These exceptional verbs include tensed forms of BE, tensed forms of perfect HAVE, and all of the modals (CAN, COULD, MAY, MIGHT, SHALL, SHOULD, WILL, WOULD, and MUST). As we will see in later chapters, this same small group of verbs is exceptional in exactly the same way in all of the other situations in which special-purpose finite phrases are required.

Exercise

1. The rules given above yield (ii) as an emphatic counterpart for (i).

(i)   Jason sold his motorcycle.

(ii)   Jason DID sell his motorcycle.

In addition, though, it is possible to retain the general-purpose structure and place emphatic stress on *sold*.

(iii)   Jason SOLD his motorcycle.

Think about the differences between the contexts in which it would be natural to say (ii) or (iii). Describe these differences as clearly as you can.

3.6   MULTIPLE COMPLEMENT RULES

As is indicated by the examples presented above, many verbs occur in more than one environment. Thus, for instance, BREAK occurs alone, as well as with an object noun phrase. The relevant examples are repeated here.

(69) a. The bottle [broke].   [BREAK]
  b. Alice [broke   *the bottle*]. [BREAK NP]

Likewise, the verb MAKE occurs in three of the configurations listed above.

(70) a. Kate [made   *a birdhouse*].   [MAKE NP]
  b. Fido [made   *Alice   quite angry*]. [MAKE NP AdjP]
  c. We [made   *George   be quiet*].   [MAKE NP VP$_{\text{Stem}}$]

Many other verbs are like these two in that they appear in more than one complement configuration. In many instances, such multiple environments do not follow any general pattern. For instance, the possibilities for MAKE illustrated in (70) have to be learned as three separate facts about this verb. In other instances, though, pairs of environments for a verb are related by rules with some degree of regularity. BREAK, for example, is just one of several "change-of-state" verbs that have intransitive and transitive pairs related to each other in the same way. Three more examples are given here.

(71) a. The music [changed].   [CHANGE]
     b. Alice [changed *the music*].   [CHANGE NP]

(72) a. The door [closed].   [CLOSE]
     b. Joe [closed *the door*].   [CLOSE NP]

(73) a. The ice [melted].   [MELT]
     b. The sun [melted *the ice*].   [MELT NP]

Verbs expressing movement display a similar relation.

(74) a. The house [moved].   [MOVE]
     b. The men [moved *the house*].   [MOVE NP]

(75) a. The cart [rolled *into the garage*].   [ROLL MotP]
     b. Amy [rolled *the cart into the garage*].   [ROLL NP MotP]

(76) a. The box [slid *onto the lawn*].   [SLIDE MotP]
     b. Joe [slid *the box onto the lawn*].   [SLIDE NP MotP]

In each of the pairs of sentences in these two groups, the relation in meaning between the intransitive and the transitive sentence can be described by the rule given in (77).

(77) If a certain verb can occur as an intransitive verb expressing change of state or motion, then the same verb can be used as a transitive verb expressing the *causation* of the state of affairs expressed by the intransitive verb.

A different regular relation between intransitive and transitive uses of the same verb is shown in the following examples:

(78) a. Joe [shaved].   [SHAVE]
     b. Joe [shaved *Fred*].   [SHAVE NP]

(79) a. Fred [dressed].   [DRESS]
      b. Fred [dressed *the baby*].   [DRESS NP]

Here the transitive verb is more basic, and the intransitive use is understood as expressing an idea that could have been expressed by a transitive sentence with a reflexive pronoun as the object of the verb. Thus, for example, *Joe shaved* has the same meaning as *Joe shaved himself.* This possibility exists for a large class of verbs that might be called *personal-care verbs,* some of which have particles associated with them (SHAVE, DRESS, BATHE, CLEAN *up,* WASH *up*). We can state the following rough rule:

(80) If a certain verb can be used as a transitive verb denoting personal care, then the same verb can be used as an intransitive verb, with an understood reflexive pronoun as object.

3.7 COMPLEMENT RULES MENTIONING PARTICULAR WORDS

Thus far, we have looked at many examples of verbs that call for broad, general categories such as noun phrases, adjective phrases, motion phrases, and so forth. For some verbs, however, specific individual words need to be mentioned in stating complement possibilities. One such word is GIVE, as it occurs in the following example:

(81) Joe [gave *the presents to the children*].

At first glance, *to the children* might appear to be just a motion phrase. Yet when we try to construct sentences in which GIVE appears with motion phrases headed by other prepositions, the results are unacceptable.

(82) *Joe [gave *the presents* $\begin{Bmatrix} \textit{into the room} \\ \textit{onto the wagon} \\ \textit{up the stairs} \end{Bmatrix}$].

In contrast to GIVE, the verb TAKE allows the full range of motion phrases.

(83) Joe [took *the presents* $\begin{Bmatrix} \textit{to the children} \\ \textit{into the room} \\ \textit{onto the wagon} \\ \textit{up the stairs} \end{Bmatrix}$].

Thus, *to* appears to be the only preposition that goes well with GIVE. The rule that we must state for GIVE, then, is that it can be joined with a noun phrase and a "*to* phrase" (a phrase headed by the particular preposition *to*). Thus, the appearance of GIVE in this configuration is allowed by the following complement rule:

(84) [GIVE NP *To*-P]

The verb DEPEND displays similar behavior.

(85) We can [depend   *on his cooperation*].

The preposition *on* is often used as a locative preposition, as in sentences like *Sam stayed on the porch.* Yet the prepositional phrase in (85) does not seem to have a locative meaning. Furthermore, DEPEND does not permit other locative prepositions.

(86) *We can [depend $\left\{\begin{array}{l} \textit{in good weather} \\ \textit{at his cooperation} \\ \textit{above the truth of his testimony} \end{array}\right\}$].

In this respect, DEPEND is different from a verb like STAY, which allows a full range of locative phrases.

(87) We can [stay $\left\{\begin{array}{l} \textit{on this street} \\ \textit{in this county} \\ \textit{at his house} \\ \textit{above the laundromat} \end{array}\right\}$].

Thus, it appears that the verb DEPEND can only accept a phrase headed by the particular preposition *on*. This "*on* phrase" is mentioned in the following complement rule:

(88) [DEPEND *On*-P]

This formulation of a complement rule for DEPEND should not be taken as suggesting that *on his cooperation* in (85) is not a prepositional phrase. Indeed, this sequence is simultaneously a prepositional phrase (a phrase headed by a preposition) and an *on* phrase (a phrase headed by *on*). For the purposes of serving as a complement to DEPEND, though, it is the latter property that is important.

The individual words that are mentioned as such in complement rules are for the most part taken from the class of prepositions, and also from the related class of words called *particles,* which will be discussed in detail in chapter 6.

Exercise

1. Each of the sentences given below contains a bracketed verb phrase and is followed by two possible complement rules, one mentioning a general class of phrases and the other mentioning phrases headed by a specific word. Decide which rule is correct for the verb. Justify your answer by giving additional sentences and noting whether they are acceptable or unacceptable.

    a. John [blamed the accident on his brakes].
        i. [— NP LocP]
        ii. [— NP *On*-P]
    b. Jane [left the book on the table].
        i. [— NP LocP]
        ii. [— NP *On*-P]
    c. Martha [moved it to the kitchen].
        i. [— NP MotP]
        ii. [— NP *To*-P]
    d. Fred [proved it to the police].
        i. [— NP MotP]
        ii. [— NP *To*-P]

3.8   POSSIBLE AND IMPOSSIBLE COMPLEMENT RULES

In the complement rules given so far, two kinds of units have been mentioned. The first kind consists of general phrase types such as NP, MotP, LocP, and AdjP. The second kind consists of phrases headed by specific words, phrases with names like *To*-P and *On*-P. A natural question to ask now is this: are there any verbs that appear in complement rules that refer to types of individual words rather than to types of phrases? For example, are there any verbs that are best described as taking a bare-stem *verb* as a complement, rather than a bare-stem *verb phrase*?

At first glance, it might seem that there would be nothing wrong with mentioning word types rather than phrase types. Consider again the complement rule that permits LET to appear in (89).

(89) Alice [let Fido chew the rawhide].

This verb phrase is clearly permitted by the rule [LET NP VP$_{Stem}$], the complement rule for LET given in (45c). But in this situation, it might appear that we could have done just as well with [LET NP V$_{Stem}$ NP]. This second possibility certainly seems reasonable as long as we are looking only at sentence (89). But a difficulty arises as soon as we look at additional examples. Here are just a few:

(90) a. Alice [let Fido sleep].
   b. Alice [let Fido go into the kitchen].
   c. Alice [let Fido try to swallow the pill].

The original rule, which mentioned the general phrase type VP$_{Stem}$, accounts for these new examples immediately, since *sleep, go into the kitchen,* and *try to swallow the pill* all count as bare-stem verb phrases. By contrast, the alternative rule for (89) in terms of the word type V$_{Stem}$ does not cover the three new examples at all. Just for the three extra sentences given in (90), the following added rules would be necessary:

(91) a. [LET NP V$_{Stem}$]
   b. [LET NP V$_{Stem}$ MotP]
   c. [LET NP V$_{Stem}$ InfP]

We thus have good reason to think that the original rule in terms of phrase types was correct. We find additional reason in the fact that no complement rules are known, in English or any other language, that mention word types such as V$_{Stem}$ rather than phrase types such as VP$_{Stem}$. In the remainder of this book, then, we will assume that all such complement rules must be stated completely in terms of general phrase types or phrases headed by particular individual words.

Exercise

1. Below is a list of verb phrases. With each example, two complement rules are given, both of which allow that particular verb phrase. The first rule in each pair obeys the restriction proposed above, whereas the second does not. For each such pair, show that the second rule is too narrow. Do this by constructing an acceptable sentence that is accounted for by the permitted complement rule but not by the illegal one.

   a. Jane [saw him walking into the parlor].
      [SEE NP VP$_{PresPart}$]   (permitted)
      [SEE NP V$_{PresPart}$ MotP]   (not permitted)
   b. Fred [considers us competent].
      [CONSIDER NP AdjP]
      [CONSIDER Pronoun Adj]
   c. Jane [has tried to revise the article].
      [HAVE VP$_{PastPart}$]
      [HAVE V$_{PastPart}$ InfP]

3.9 COMPLEMENTS OF ADJECTIVES AND COMMON NOUNS

In chapter 2, we saw several examples of phrases headed by adjectives and common nouns. The adjective phrases shared with each other the external property of going well with the verb SEEM; the common-noun phrases could combine with the word *the* or possessive words to make noun phrases. These earlier discussions, then, were concerned with the external environments in which adjective phrases and common-noun phrases appeared. In the next two subsections, we examine the kinds of complement rules associated with particular adjectives and common nouns.

3.9.1 Adjectives and Their Complements

In several of the examples considered in chapter 2, and in many other examples, the phrase that an adjective heads consists of the adjective alone.

(92) a. Milton seems [*despondent*].
     b. The suitcases seem [*light*].
     c. Joanna seems [*intelligent*].
     d. The barometer seems [*unreliable*].
     e. The porter seems [*tired*].
     f. Alice seems [*angry*].

In other examples, the adjective is followed by a phrase that serves as its complement.

(93) a. The reporters seem [*eager* to leave the meeting].
     b. The hounds seem [*fond* of the hunters].
     c. The sociologists seem [*compatible* with the historians].
     d. These bottles seem [*similar* to those bottles].
     e. Your friends seem [*tired* of the conversation].
     f. The inmates seem [*angry* at the warden].

These examples suggest that there are rules of English that specify the complement possibilities for each individual adjective, just as there are rules that do the same thing for individual verbs. The examples given above provide evidence for the following complement rules:

(94) a. [DESPONDENT]
     b. [LIGHT]
     c. [INTELLIGENT]
     d. [UNRELIABLE]

    e. [TIRED]
    f. [ANGRY]
    g. [EAGER InfP]
    h. [FOND *Of*-P]
    i. [COMPATIBLE *With*-P]
    j. [SIMILAR *To*-P]
    k. [TIRED *Of*-P]
    l. [ANGRY *At*-P]

As we might guess from these examples, the complement combinations found with adjectives are much less varied than those found with verbs. The most common complement rules for adjectives call either for no complements at all or else for single complements of various sorts. There are no adjectives that can take two complements, in the way that verbs such as PERSUADE and MAKE can.

Exercise

1. Among the complement rules mentioned in the preceding discussion are the following:

(i) [BECOME AdjP]

(ii) [ANGRY *At*-P]

These rules imply that the adjective *angry* rather than the verb *became* is responsible for inviting an *at* phrase into a sentence like *Jonah became angry at Gordon*. Suppose that we now consider an alternative analysis, namely, that it is the verb *became* that is responsible for the presence of the *at* phrase. Under this analysis, the relevant complement rules are the following:

(iii) [BECOME AdjP *At*-P]

(iv) [ANGRY]

See if you can think of other sentences, grammatical or ungrammatical, that provide evidence in favor of the first analysis of this sentence as against the alternative.

3.9.2 Common Nouns and Their Complements

With common nouns, we find almost the same complement configurations that we found with adjectives. By far the most frequent configuration is the one in which the noun has no complements.

(95) a. the [*plan*]   [PLAN]
     b. Joe's [*book*]   [BOOK]
     c. the [*beer*]   [BEER]

However, there are also a fair number of common nouns that take phrases headed by particular prepositions, and also some that take infinitival phrases.

(96) a. their [*proximity* to their neighbors]   [PROXIMITY *To*-P]
     b. Bill's [*faith* in Fred's sister]   [FAITH *In*-P]
     c. the [*king* of England]   [KING *Of*-P]
     d. the [*bottom* of the barrel]   [BOTTOM *Of*-P]
     e. the [*effort* to find a vaccine]   [EFFORT InfP]
     f. Jack's [*desire* to become famous]   [DESIRE InfP]

Exercise

1. Among the complement rules mentioned in the preceding discussion are the following:

(i) [BREAK NP]

(ii) [BOTTOM *Of*-P]

These rules imply that the common noun *bottom* rather than the verb *broke* is responsible for inviting an *of* phrase into a sentence like *Marvin broke the bottom of the barrel.* Suppose that we now consider an alternative analysis, namely, that it is the verb *broke* that is responsible for the presence of the *of* phrase. Under this analysis, the relevant complement rules are the following:

(iii) [BREAK NP *Of*-P]

(iv) [BOTTOM]

See if you can think of other sentences, grammatical or ungrammatical, that provide evidence in favor of the first analysis of this sentence as against the alternative.

3.10 A METHOD OF REPRESENTING PHRASE STRUCTURE

We have already discovered a large number of rules about how phrases of different types are constructed, and about how these phrases are used to build larger constructions. Moreover, we now know enough to start analyzing particular individual sentences, such as (97).

(97) The judge made Smith pay the fines.

In this section, we will discuss *tree diagrams,* a widely used method for representing the structure of phrases and sentences graphically.

    The most important hint we have concerning the structure of this sentence is provided by the rule given in (98a), which can be represented graphically by the diagram in (98b).

(98) a. A sentence consists of a noun phrase and a finite verb phrase.

b.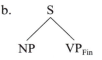

This rule leads us immediately to look for a way of dividing sentence (97) into a noun phrase and a finite verb phrase, where once again, a finite verb is a present-tense form, a past-tense form, or a modal. *The judge* is a possible noun phrase, and the remainder of the sentence (*made Smith pay the fines*) is headed by a past-tense verb and thus qualifies as a finite verb phrase. We thus arrive at the statement in (99a), which conforms to rule (98a) and which can be represented graphically as in (99b).

(99) a. The sentence *The judge made Smith pay the fines* consists of two parts: a noun phrase (*the judge*) and a past-tense verb phrase (*made Smith pay the fines*).

b.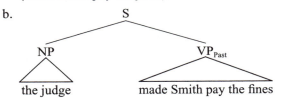

In place of the marking *Fin* that was used in the general diagram in (98b), the VP in (99b) carries the marking *Past,* indicating the specific variety of finite verb that we find in this example.

We might now want to analyze this verb phrase in more detail. The head verb is *made,* the past-tense form of MAKE. Each of the three complement rules that we verified for MAKE in subsection 3.5.2 is given in (100), along with a translation into English and a translation into tree form (the latter providing the additional information that MAKE is a verb).

(100) a. [MAKE NP]

(A form of MAKE can head a phrase in which it has a noun phrase as its complement.)

b. [MAKE NP AdjP]

(A form of MAKE can head a phrase in which it has a noun phrase and an adjective phrase as its complements.)

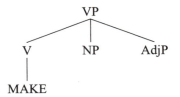

c. [MAKE NP VP_{Stem}]

(A form of MAKE can head a phrase in which it has a noun phrase and a bare-stem verb phrase as its complements.)

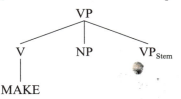

The last of these is the one called for here: *Smith* is a possible noun phrase, and *pay the fines* qualifies as a bare-stem verb phrase. (The reason for not selecting the structure in (100a) is the topic of exercise 1 at the end of this section.) Thus, we get the additional statement in (101a), which can be represented graphically by the diagram in (101b).

(101) a. The past-tense verb phrase *made Smith pay the fines* consists of three parts: the head verb *made,* a noun phrase (*Smith*), and a bare-stem verb phrase (*pay the fines*).

b.

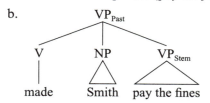

Although the tree diagram in (101b) is consistent with the overall form of (100c), it is more detailed in three respects: (a) it indicates the presence of the particular noun phrase *Smith* and the particular bare-stem verb phrase *pay the fines*; (b) it contains the specific past-tense form *made* in place of the unspecified MAKE; (c) it has the subscript *Past* on the top VP, reflecting the inflectional form of *made*.

Let us look finally at the phrase *pay the fines*. In subsection 3.5.2, we established the following complement rule for PAY:

(102) [PAY NP]

(A form of PAY can head a verb phrase in which it has a noun phrase as its complement.)

Applying this complement rule to this verb phrase, we get the statement in (103a) and the corresponding tree diagram in (103b).

(103) a. The bare-stem verb phrase *pay the fines* consists of two parts: the head verb *pay* and a noun phrase (*the fines*).

b.

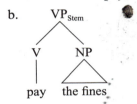

We have now made three statements about sentence (97), and we have three diagrams that express the content of these statements graphically. If we wanted to, we could keep these three diagrams separate, as we have done up to now. On the other hand, if we want to get a comprehensive view of the organization of the entire sentence, we can combine the three smaller diagrams into a single large one. The result is the detailed diagram (104) for the sentence as a whole.

(104)

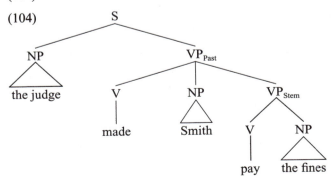

This single diagram expresses simultaneously all three of our original statements about the way in which this sentence is formed.

Tree diagrams are used quite widely in scholarly works and textbooks. Their major justification is that they provide quick and efficient representations of some important organizational properties of individual sentences. It is much quicker to draw the tree in (104) than it is to write out all of the individual statements that the tree expresses.

There are other systems that provide exactly the same kind of information about sentence structure. One is the *labeled bracketing* illustrated in (105).

(105) [$_S$[$_{NP}$ the judge] [$_{VP\_Past}$[$_V$ made] [$_{NP}$ Smith] [$_{VP\_Stem}$[$_V$ pay] [$_{NP}$ the fines]]]]

Our choice of tree diagrams over labeled bracketing and other equivalent systems rests mainly on two considerations. The first is that the system of tree diagrams is relatively easy to learn and use. The second is that this system has been adopted more widely in recent years than any other system, so that familiarity with it will be helpful to those readers who go on to other works on syntax.

Exercises

1. In discussing sentence (97), we analyzed *Smith pay the fines* as a sequence consisting of two phrases (a noun phrase and a bare-stem verb phrase). Why would it not have been just as legitimate to analyze it as a noun phrase and represent it with the following tree diagram?

(i)

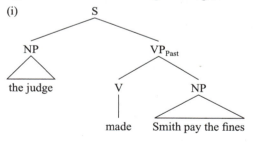

As noted in (100a), MAKE can in fact appear in a verb-phrase configuration in which it has just a noun-phrase complement. Hint: Use the experimental tactic called for in the exercise at the end of subsection 2.8.1 to see whether it is appropriate to classify *Smith pay the fines* as a noun phrase.

2. We have seen many examples of complement rules in this chapter, each of which has the effect of allowing a particular verb in a certain complement configuration. To take a single example, one of our rules was the following:

(i) [MAKE NP VP$_{Stem}$]

Translated into plain English, this rule says that any form of MAKE can head a phrase in which it is accompanied by two complements: a noun phrase and a bare-stem verb phrase. As noted in the preceding discussion, there is another way to express the content of this rule, along with the additional information that MAKE is a verb.

(ii)

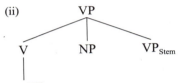

MAKE

Below are some of the other complement rules presented in the text for individual verbs. For each one, give the alternative version of the rule in tree form.

    a. [HEAR NP VP$_{PresPart}$]
    b. [MOVE MotP]
    c. [KEEP NP AdjP]
    d. [DISAPPEAR]
    e. [BECOME NP$_{Pred}$]
    f. [BREAK NP]
    g. [PERSUADE NP InfP]
    h. [KEEP NP LocP]
    i. [GO MotP]
    j. [BE VP$_{PresPart}$]
    k. [DO VP$_{Stem}$]

3. Study the following tree, and then follow the instructions below it:

(i)

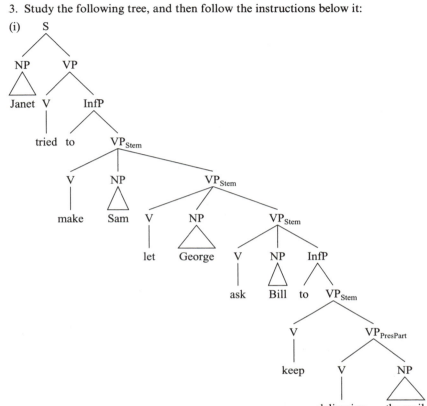

A. Express in tree form the complement rule that allows *make* to head the phrase in which it appears.

B. Express in tree form the complement rule that allows *keep* to head the phrase in which it appears.

C. Express in ordinary English the rule for the formation of infinitival phrases that is implied by this tree structure. Note: If you want to check your answer to this question, review subsection 2.6.4.

D. Write out the entire sequence of words constituting the verb phrase of which *tried* is the head.

E. Write out the entire sequence of words constituting the verb phrase of which *let* is the head.

4. Below are two different trees for the sentence *Bob put the baby in the stroller.*

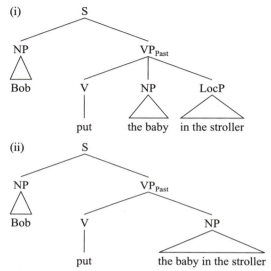

Which of these two trees is consistent with the rules that we have discussed so far, including the complement rule offered for PUT in subsection 3.5.2? Do you think that we should add another complement rule for PUT to allow the alternative structure? Hint: Review the observations about *put* that were made in section 3.1.

5. Draw tree diagrams for the sentences listed below. Since very little has been said about the internal structure of noun phrases, adjective phrases, locative phrases, and motion phrases, do not try to draw a detailed structure for any phrases of these kinds. Just draw triangles instead. Be sure to check that any division of a verb phrase that is shown in your tree is one that is allowed by the complement rules in this chapter and that anything you analyze as a noun phrase is indeed a legitimate noun phrase (see exercise 1). Also, for each verb phrase, indicate its inflectional form (Stem, PresPart, etc.).

    a. The chairman of the committee kept Bill in the kitchen.
    b. Sarah tried to keep the tiles clean.
    c. Joe may hear Martha playing her harmonica.
    d. The soldiers must ask Bill to make the baby be quiet.
    e. The pollution DOES seem to make the water unsafe.

Chapter 4

Clauses as Complements and Subjects

In chapter 2, *noun phrases* were introduced as a special class of phrases that could serve as subjects of sentences. In chapter 3, it was noted that noun phrases could also serve as complements of verbs and objects of prepositions.

In this chapter, we will examine structures of a different sort that can serve as complements and also as subjects. What distinguishes these new structures from noun phrases is that one of their essential parts is a construction that is either identical to an ordinary sentence or else very similar to one. We will refer to these structures as *clauses*. In section 4.1, we will examine the internal structure of three basic types of clauses. In subsequent sections, we will discuss the external syntax of clauses of these types, that is, the ways in which they can be used in the formation of still larger structures.

4.1 THE INTERNAL STRUCTURE OF CLAUSES

4.1.1 *That* Clauses

A first type of clause is illustrated in (1).

(1) a. Harry believes [that Jane's attorney is honest].
    b. Beth told Bill [that the cow left the pasture].

In each of these examples, the bracketed structure can be broken down into two main parts. The first part is just the word *that*; the second is a sequence that could qualify as a well-formed independent sentence.

(2) a. Jane's attorney is honest.
    b. The cow left the pasture.

Let us refer to the bracketed structures in (1) as "*that* clauses." Then the following simple rule spells out their structure:

(3) A *that* clause can consist of the word *that* plus a sentence.

In tree form, the same rule can be expressed as follows:

(4)   *That*-C

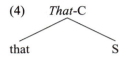

This rule assigns the structures in (5) to the *that* clauses in (1).

(5)   *That*-C   *That*-C

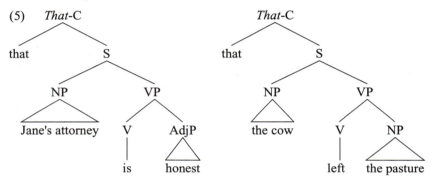

Each of the *that* clauses in (1) consists of the word *that* joined to a sequence of words that qualifies as a sentence, as shown in (2). English also allows another variety of *that* clause.

(6) a. I insist [that he guard the paintings].
    b. The rules require that [the executives be polite].

At first glance, these clauses might look just like those considered already. However, taking away *that* from the bracketed sequences in (6) gives sequences that cannot stand alone as independent sentences.

(7) a. *He guard the paintings.
    b. *The executives be polite.

Despite their unacceptability, the sequences in (7) show a clear similarity to ordinary sentences. In particular, they have exactly the same subject-predicate division, and nominative pronouns like *he* are used as subjects. The only difference is that the main verb of the sequences in (7) is a bare stem instead of a finite verb: *guard* in (6a), instead of the present-tense singular verb *guards*, and *be* in (6b), instead of the present-tense plural verb *are*.

Our problem now is to find a way of describing *that* clauses of this second type that reveals both their similarity to ordinary *that* clauses and their one significant difference. As the first step toward a solution, we make two new assumptions.

(8) a. Sentences can have predicates headed by words other than finite verbs.
　　b. Sentences as well as verb phrases can be classified according to the inflectional form of the head verb.

Thus, for example, *he guards the paintings* would be a present-tense sentence, since the head verb of its predicate is the present-tense verb *guards*. By contrast, *he guard the paintings* would be a bare-stem sentence, since the head verb of its predicate is the bare-stem verb *guard*. This analysis would dictate the tree diagrams in (9) for these sentences.

(9) a.　　　　　　　　　　　　b.

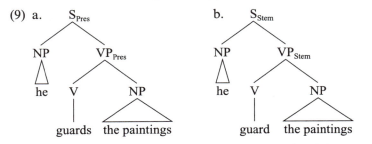

We now allow *that* clauses to be formed from either of these two types of sentences, and we mark the resulting clause according to the inflectional form of the sentence that it contains.

(10) A *that* clause consists of the word *that* plus either (i) a finite sentence (present or past or modal) or (ii) a bare-stem sentence.

(11) A *that* clause is classified according to the inflectional form of the head verb of its sentence.

These rules allow us to use the sentence structures in (9) to create the *that* clauses in (12).

(12) a. *That*-C$_{Pres}$ b. *That*-C$_{Stem}$

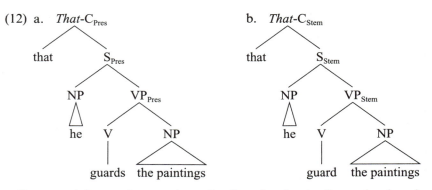

One remaining matter requires attention. In chapter 2, we developed the following rules for the formation of sentences:

(13) A verb phrase is finite if it is headed by a present-tense verb, a past-tense verb, or a modal.

(14) The predicate of a sentence must be finite.

As rule (14) is stated, it is violated by the structure in (12b), which contains a sentence whose head verb is not finite. Thus, (14) needs to be replaced by the following rule, which singles out *independent* sentences, those that are acceptable as free-standing utterances:

(15) Independent sentences must be finite.

This rule will allow independent sentences like (16a) but will prevent those like (16b).

(16) a. Your brother is at the meeting.
     b. *Your brother be at the meeting.

At the same time, it will say nothing about the nonindependent sentences that are found in *that* clauses, thus allowing the two distinct types of *that* clauses that actually occur.

(17) a. that your brother is at the meeting   (finite *that* clause)
     b. that your brother be at the meeting   (bare-stem *that* clause)

In section 4.2, we will examine the external syntax of these two constructions, that is, the way in which each is used in the formation of larger structures.

4.1.2 Infinitival Clauses

Another type of structure that deserves to be included in a discussion of English clauses is illustrated in (18).

(18) a. Fred intends [for Sam to review that book].
    b. Sally would prefer [for the children to finish the porridge].

In each of these two examples, the bracketed construction consists of the word *for*, a noun phrase, and an infinitival phrase. The decision to regard these constructions as clauses may seem strange, in view of the fact that (as illustrated in (19)) the sequences following the word *for* are even farther from being independent sentences than were the bare-stem sentences discussed in the previous subsection.

(19) a. *Sam to review that book.
    b. *The children to finish the porridge.

Nevertheless, we will refer to structures of this sort as *infinitival clauses*. The justification for viewing them in this way will become apparent later in this chapter, when we consider similarities between their external behavior and the external behavior of *that* clauses.

In order to have a complete view of the structure of infinitival clauses, we need to get ahead of our story for a moment and consider their external syntax. The infinitival clauses in (18) occur as complements of the verbs INTEND and PREFER. As it happens, each of these verbs also allows a complement consisting of an infinitival phrase alone.

(20) a. Fred intends [to review that book].
    b. Sally would prefer [to finish the porridge].

In fact, the parallel examples in (18) and (20) illustrate a perfectly general regularity of English: in every situation in which a clause introduced by *for* can be used, it is possible to have an infinitival phrase by itself. We thus have reason to believe that the infinitival phrases in (20) are serving there as abridged versions of the longer constructions introduced by *for*. We will thus regard the bracketed constructions in (20) as infinitival clauses, along with those in (18). The following two rules state how this type of clause can be formed:

(21) a. An infinitival clause can consist of a *for* phrase plus a noun phrase plus an infinitival phrase.
    b. An infinitival clause can consist of an infinitival phrase alone.

These rules can be given in tree form as follows:

(22) a.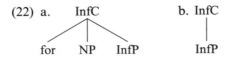

The structures of the bracketed portions of (18a) and (20a) will be as shown in (23).

(23) a.

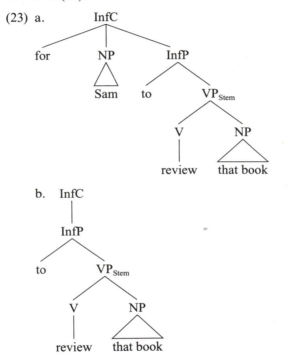

Exercises

1. For each of the following sentences, draw a tree diagram of the bracketed portion:

   a. John says [that Larry uses the code].
   b. The company requires [that Larry use the code].
   c. Thomas would like [for Larry to use the code].
   d. Thomas would like [to use the code].

2. The following clause is ambiguous in isolation:

[that the officers use the code]

Explain what the two different structures are, or, if you prefer, indicate the difference by drawing two tree diagrams.

4.1.3 Indirect Questions

An even more complex type of clause is illustrated in the sentences in (24).

(24) a. John knows [whose books Shirley located].
　　 b. Dr. Smith has forgotten [which customer George was shouting at].
　　 c. Janet told me [how many employees Karen introduced to the visitors].

The bracketed sequences in these sentences look similar to the following independent structures that we commonly refer to as *questions*:

(25) a. Whose books did Shirley locate?
　　 b. Which customer was George shouting at?
　　 c. How many employees did Karen introduce to the visitors?

In what follows, we will assume that the bracketed structures in (24) deserve to be called questions, too. One suggestive piece of evidence for this view is that John knows whose books Shirley located just in case he knows the answer to the question "Whose books did Shirley locate?" In order to distinguish between these two constructions, we will refer to the bracketed subsequences in (24) as *indirect questions* and to the sequences in (25) as *direct questions*. The only significant difference between them, the difference in verbal structure and word order, will be discussed in chapter 14.

　　The first thing we notice about the indirect questions in (24) is that they all begin with phrases that contain what we can call "*wh* words." (This terminology is loose; the word *how* actually begins with *h* instead of *wh*.) In all three of these indirect questions, the initial phrases happen to be noun phrases.

(26) a. [$_{NP}$ whose books]
　　 b. [$_{NP}$ which customer]
　　 c. [$_{NP}$ how many employees]

We will call such noun phrases *questioned noun phrases;* the abbreviation for such noun phrases will be NP_Q. We should note in passing here that *who, whom,* and *what* can be single-word questioned noun phrases.

(27) a. John knows [[_NP_ *what*] Shirley located].
  b. Dr. Smith has forgotten [[_NP_ *who*] George was shouting at].
    (informal)
  c. Janet told me [[_NP_ *whom*] Karen introduced to the visitors].
    (formal)

In each of the indirect questions in (24), the second major part is a sequence that follows the questioned noun phrase. In the examples under consideration, these sequences are exactly like incomplete sentences.

(28) a. Shirley located.
  b. George was shouting at.
  c. Karen introduced to the visitors.

All three of the incomplete sentences in (28) contain particular words (*located, at,* and *introduced,* respectively) that ordinarily require noun-phrase objects. Thus, what we seem to have here are sentences in which one particular noun phrase is "missing." We can get a clearer picture of these sequences if we write them with blanks to indicate the position of the missing noun phrase.

(29) a. Shirley located ____
  b. George was shouting at ____
  c. Karen introduced ____ to the visitors

We will refer to such structures as *sentences with missing noun phrases,* which we will abbreviate as *S/NP* in tree diagrams.

We are now ready to state a tentative rule for forming indirect questions of the type illustrated in (24). This rule is given in (30), both in words and in a diagram.

(30) An indirect question (IQ) can consist of a questioned noun phrase (NP$_Q$), followed by a sentence with a missing noun phrase (S/NP).

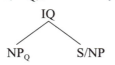

The tree structures for the particular indirect questions that we have been discussing are shown in (31).

(31) a.

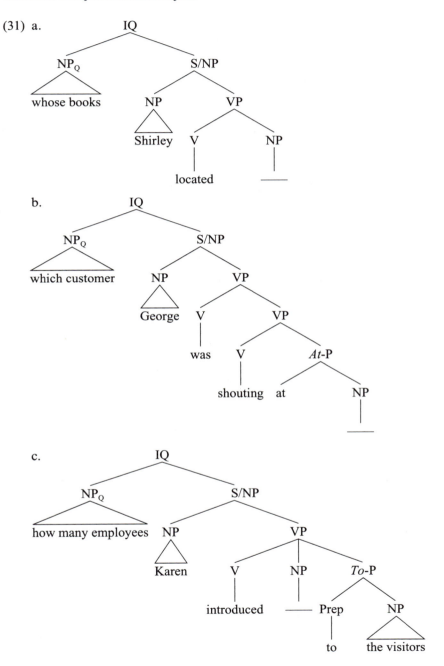

Now that we have made a start at describing the syntax of indirect questions, let us consider their interpretation. The most basic matter concerns the missing noun phrase. In independent sentences, such missing noun phrases are unacceptable.

(32) a. *Shirley located ____.
     b. *George was shouting at ____.
     c. *Karen introduced ____ to the visitors.

LOCATE, AT, and INTRODUCE all must have objects provided for them in some manner. The usual way to identify an object is to put an actual noun phrase in the normal position for the object, as in the following simple sentences:

(33) a. Shirley located *Robert's books*.
     b. George was shouting at *Mr. Norris*.
     c. Karen introduced *ten employees* to the visitors.

However, the indirect questions that we are now examining illustrate an additional way in which objects in a phrase may be identified: they may be identified by some outside noun phrase. As we can tell intuitively, in each indirect question it is the questioned noun phrase that identifies the missing object. We can think of the questioned noun phrase as being linked to the missing noun phrase in two steps. First, the questioned noun phrase is coupled with the following sequence, that is, to the sentence with the missing noun phrase, as in (34).

(34)

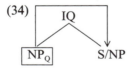

Then this identification is passed on to the missing noun phrase itself, as in (35).

(35) S/NP

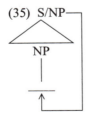

Putting these two processes together, we get the complex identification process represented in (36).

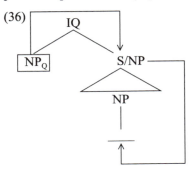

The questioned noun phrase has donated its meaning to a particular kind of incomplete sentence, and this incomplete sentence has used this donated meaning to provide an identification for its missing noun phrase.

For our original set of indirect questions, we now obtain the diagrams in (37), which contain information both about the structures involved and about the way in which these structures are interpreted.

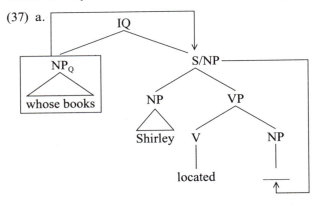

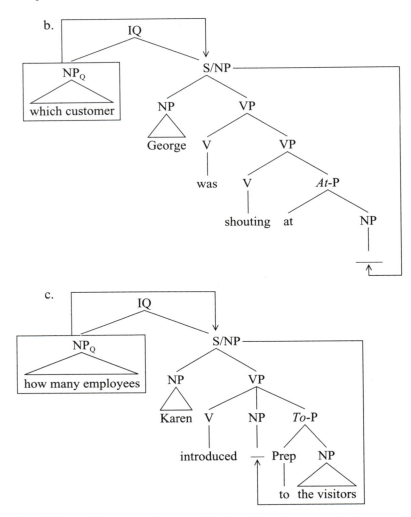

In all three of the examples considered so far, the questioned noun phrase has donated its meaning to a missing noun phrase somewhere inside the verb phrase. Not surprisingly, there are also indirect questions in which the questioned noun phrase provides an interpretation for the subject. A typical example is given in (38).

(38) Smith knows [*which clerk* opened the letter].

The analysis that we developed with the earlier three examples in mind can be extended easily to this new one. The bracketed sequence can be divided into an interrogative noun phrase (*which clerk*) followed by a sentence with a missing noun phrase (____ *opened the letter*). In this case, of course, the missing noun phrase is just the subject. The tree diagram for this type of indirect question is given in (39).

(39)

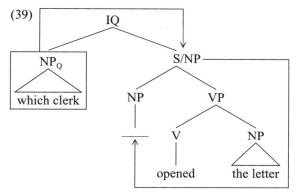

In the situation where objects of prepositions are questioned, we actually have two ways of forming an indirect question. The one we have seen already is shown in (40a); the other is shown in (40b).

(40) a. Dr. Smith has forgotten [*which room* George stayed *in* ____].
     b. Dr. Smith has forgotten [*in which room* George stayed ____].

The first of these questions is introduced by the questioned noun phrase, and the preposition appears in its normal position in the verb phrase. By contrast, the second question is introduced by the entire prepositional phrase, and we find an unoccupied prepositional-phrase position in the verb phrase instead of an unoccupied noun-phrase position. Let us define a *questioned prepositional phrase* (*PrepP$_Q$*) as a prepositional phrase whose noun phrase is a questioned noun phrase. This is illustrated in tree form in (41).

(41) PrepP$_Q$

Prep   NP$_Q$

Then we need the following additional rule:

(42) An indirect question can consist of a questioned prepositional phrase (PrepP$_Q$), followed by a sentence with an empty prepositional phrase (S/PrepP).

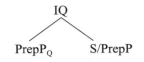

For the indirect question in (40b), the tree diagram in (43) is appropriate.

(43)

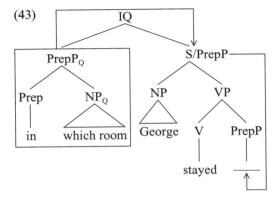

One question must be addressed concerning the labeling of the phrases in (43). In chapter 2, we classified sequences like *in this room* and *at the theater* as locative phrases. Why, then, is the sequence *in which room* called a prepositional phrase in (43) instead of being called a locative phrase? The answer is that *in which room* (like *in this room* and *at the theater*) is both a prepositional phrase and a locative phrase. We used the prepositional-phrase label in (43) because the prepositional property is the one that is important in determining the possibility of using the phrase to introduce an indirect question. As the following examples show, virtually all kinds of prepositional phrases can be fronted in indirect questions:

(44)

Dr. Smith has forgotten

⎧ *into which room* the patient went _____
⎪ *with which surgeon* the patient consulted _____
⎨ *on which nurse* the patient depended _____
⎪ *for whom* the orderly made the bed _____
⎩ *to whom* the patient sent the money _____ ⎭ .

What particular kind a given prepositional phrase happens to be is of no importance for its capacity to introduce indirect questions.

In addition to indirect questions that begin with questioned noun phrases and prepositional phrases, we also find indirect questions that begin with questioned phrases of other types. In each such question, there is an empty phrase of the same type in the accompanying sentence. Several examples are given in (45), each one accompanied by a normal declarative sentence that shows the usual position of a phrase of the type being questioned.

(45) a. Laura told me [*how fond of your aunt* the children are ＿＿]. (adjective phrase)
(The children are *very fond of your aunt*.)
   b. Matthew knows [*when* the concert will begin ＿＿].   (time phrase)
(The concert will begin *at eight o'clock*.)
   c. Fred told us [*where* his horse is ＿＿].   (locative phrase)
(His horse is *in the barn*.)

In (45a), the indirect question is introduced by an interrogative adjective phrase (*how fond of your aunt*), which is followed by a sentence with an empty adjective phrase (*the children are* ＿＿). In (45b), the initial interrogative phrase is a time phrase (*when*), which is followed by a sentence with an empty time phrase (*the concert will begin* ＿＿). Finally, in (45c), the interrogative phrase is a locative phrase (*where*), which is followed by a sentence with an empty locative phrase (*his horse is* ＿＿). Each indirect question is thus divided into two parts as shown in (46).

(46)
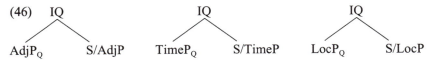

When the associations between questioned phrases and empty phrases are added, the diagrams shown in (47) result.

(47)
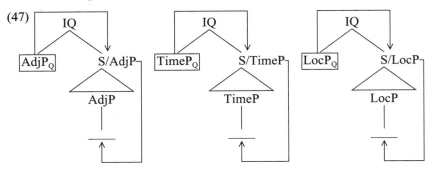

As general rules for all of the indirect questions considered so far, we can give the following statements:

(48) a. An indirect question can consist of a questioned phrase of any sort (an XP_Q) plus a sentence containing an empty phrase of the same sort (an S/XP).

b. The initial questioned phrase is donated to the incomplete sentence, which then uses it to identify its missing phrase.

The structures that (48a) creates are represented schematically in (49a). Adding the interpretive information in (48b) gives the diagram in (49b).

(49) a.

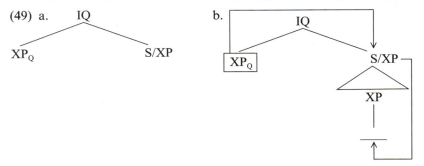

In addition to questions of the type discussed so far, there is a group of indirect questions that do not contain missing phrases. These questions are introduced by *whether* and *if*. Some of them correspond to direct questions that call for yes-or-no answers.

(50) a. Joseph will tell you [*whether* Martha is leaving].
b. Joseph will tell you [*if* Martha is leaving].
c. Is Martha leaving?

Others correspond to direct questions that call for a choice between alternatives.

(51) a. We want to know [*whether* John sued Karen or Karen sued John].
b. We want to know [*if* John sued Karen or Karen sued John].
c. Did John sue Karen or did Karen sue John?

For the yes-no indirect questions, we can add the simple rule in (52).

(52) An indirect question may consist of the word *whether* or *if* plus a finite sentence.

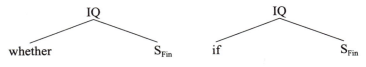

The structure for the indirect question in (50a) is then as shown in (53).

(53)

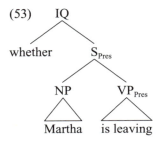

For the indirect questions that give alternatives, the necessary rules will be discussed in chapter 16, in the course of a systematic treatment of conjoined structures.

In all of the indirect questions considered so far, what follows the initial phrase is a finite sentence, with or without an empty phrase. English also allows indirect questions based on infinitival phrases.

(54) a. Fred knows [*which politician* to vote for].
     b. Karen asked [*where* to put the chairs].

This construction specifically makes use of infinitival phrases rather than infinitival clauses, as can be seen by the unacceptability of the sentences in (55).

(55) a. *Fred knows [which politician for Kenneth to vote for].
     b. *Karen asked [where for Harold to put the chairs].

The structures in (54), like similar ones based on finite sentences, contain empty phrases. Specifically, the preposition *for* ordinarily requires a noun-phrase object, and the verb *put* ordinarily requires a locative phrase. For these structures, then, we need the following rule:

(56) a. An indirect question can consist of a questioned phrase (XP_Q) followed by an infinitival phrase that contains an empty phrase of the same sort ($InfP/XP$).
     b. The initial questioned phrase is donated to the incomplete infinitival phrase, which then uses it to identify its missing phrase.

The structures that (56a) creates are represented schematically in (57a); the identifications created by (56b) are represented in (57b).

(57) a.

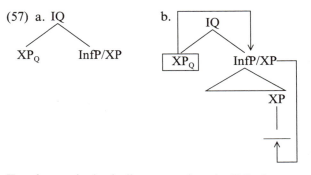

For the particular indirect questions in (54), the structures in (58) result.

(58) a.

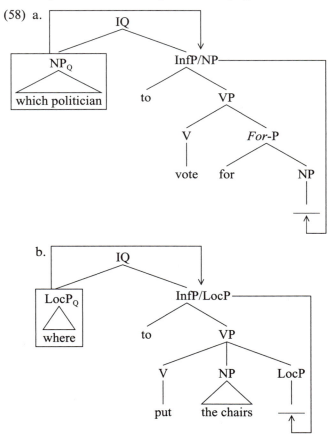

In addition, as with questions based on finite sentences, infinitival indirect questions can be introduced by *whether*.

(59) Marcos needs to decide [*whether* to capture Joe's queen].

In this case, once again, the infinitival phrase does not contain an empty phrase, and the rule we need is thus just the following:

(60) An indirect question can consist of *whether* plus an infinitival phrase.

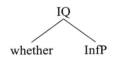

For the particular indirect question in (59), this gives the tree in (61).

(61)

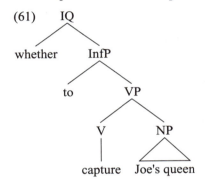

Before leaving this section, let us summarize the rules that we have developed. Indirect questions can be based on either of two structures: finite sentences or infinitival phrases. One variety consists of *whether* or *if* plus a complete structure. The other variety consists of a questioned phrase of some sort (an XP_Q) plus a structure with a corresponding missing phrase.

The indirect question construction is the first "missing-phrase" construction that we have seen so far. In later chapters, we will encounter many other such constructions. In each of them, a corresponding phrase from outside will provide an identification for this empty phrase. All of these constructions will thus look in part like the structure in (62).

(62)

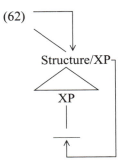

Structure/XP

XP

Exercises

1. Each of the sentences below contains an indirect question. Begin by dividing each indirect question into its two basic parts: (a) the questioned phrase; (b) the structure containing the empty phrase. Indicate the position of the empty phrase by inserting a dash. Finally, say what type of construction each of the two parts is. The first sentence is done as an illustration.

    a. We have forgotten [which dog we wanted to buy].
       Answer:
       Questioned phrase: which dog (an NP_Q)
       Structure containing empty phrase: we wanted to buy ____ (an S_{Fin}/NP)
    b. Joseph has forgotten [how many matches he has won].
    c. Caroline will remember [how much money to send to the bank].
    d. Noah knows [where to keep the ledgers].
    e. Jack asked Nora [which policeman had given her a ticket].
    f. Brenda wanted to know [how dull the meeting was likely to be].
    g. Jasper wonders [which book he should attempt to persuade his students to buy].
    h. The committee knows [whose efforts to achieve peace the world should honor].

2. Using the preliminary work that you have done in the previous exercise, draw a tree diagram for each of the indirect questions. You do not need to provide detailed structures for the questioned phrases themselves; just use triangles for these.

4.2   THE EXTERNAL SYNTAX OF CLAUSES

Now that the four basic types of English clauses have been described, we will examine their external behavior, focusing on the rules that dictate the way in which these structures figure in the formation of larger constructions. We will look first at their use as verb complements and then at their use as complements of adjectives, prepositions, and nouns. Next we will study their use as subjects and examine a rather surprising construction in which they are understood as subjects even though they give the appearance of being complements.

4.2.1 Clauses Used as Verb Complements

All four types of clauses discussed in section 4.1 can be used as verbal complements. In particular, all of them can occur alone with certain head verbs.

(63) a. Jane *knows* [that George hates olives].   (finite *that* clause)
   b. Mark *insists* [that Debby keep the change].   (bare-stem *that* clause)
   c. Nancy would *prefer* [for Freddy to stay in the nursery]. (infinitival clause)
   d. George will *know* [which dog chased White-Paws].   (indirect question)

The complement configurations illustrated in these examples are given in (64).

(64)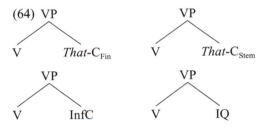

In addition, some verbs head phrases in which a finite *that* clause or an indirect question is preceded by a noun phrase.

(65) a. Richard *told* Martha [that Edward stole the cookies].   (finite *that* clause)
   b. Dana *taught* Orville [where to find snails].   (indirect question)

The configurations illustrated here are given in (66).

(66)

As with all of the previous verb-phrase configurations that we have considered, individual verbs vary a great deal with respect to which of these new configurations they appear in. For each of the four clause types in turn, we will look briefly at the verbs that take them as complements.

4.2.1.1   Verbs Taking Finite *That* Clauses   The verbs that allow finite *that* clauses make up a sizable class of English verbs. We begin with the examples in (67) and (68), divided between those in which the clause is the only complement and those in which the clause follows a noun phrase.

(67) a. We *believe* [that the war has ended].
   b. Carla *knows* [that her friends have arrived].
   c. Norman *realizes* [that your brother wants his job].
   d. Smith *claims* [that Jones wrecked Fred's truck].
   e. Jones *says* [that Smith is a liar].
   f. Anna *guessed* [that Jerry would get the job].
   g. We *assume* [that these sentences are acceptable].

(68) a. Joe *warned* the class [that the exam would be difficult].
   b. We *told* Marsha [that she should consult an accountant].
   c. Carol *convinced* me [that the argument was sound].
   d. The teachers *taught* the children [that mathematics was tedious].

Roughly speaking, these verbs include all of those that involve knowing, believing, and saying. For each one of these verbs, we need a complement specification that allows it to occur with a finite *that* clause. For instance, BELIEVE will figure in the rule in (69a), and WARN will figure in the rule in (69b).

(69) a. [BELIEVE *That*-C$_{Fin}$]
   b. [WARN NP *That*-C$_{Fin}$]

These two specifications can be given in tree form as in (70).

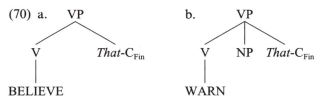

We will of course have corresponding rules for the other verbs illustrated in (67) and (68). A complete tree diagram for a sentence containing an object *that* clause is shown in (71).

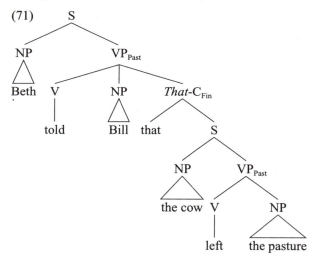

As this diagram shows, the rule for forming *that* clauses has the effect of allowing us to use a small sentence (*the cow left the pasture*) as a part of a larger one. Actually, this larger sentence can itself be used in a *that* clause, which can serve as the object of an even larger sentence, (72a), whose tree diagram is given in (72b).

(72) a. You may know [that Beth told Bill [that the cow left the pasture]].

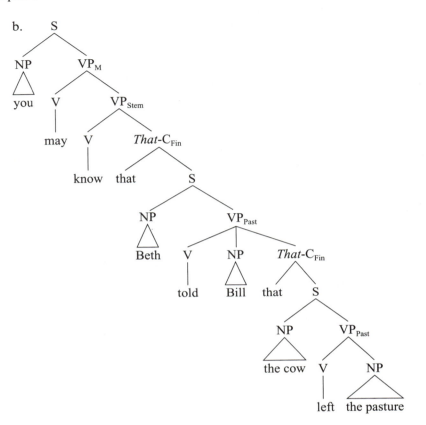

Exercises

1. For each of the verbs given below, construct experimental sentences to answer two questions:

    A. Does it appear in the configuration [— *That*-C$_{Fin}$]?
    B. Does it appear in the configuration [— NP *That*-C$_{Fin}$]?

With each yes answer, provide an acceptable sentence; with each no answer, provide an unacceptable sentence. In testing for the [— NP *That*-C$_{Fin}$] possibility, use pronouns or proper nouns in the NP position, in order to avoid confusion with similar-looking sequences of a kind that we will study in chapter 10.

    a. WANT
    b. HOPE
    c. SAY
    d. TELL
    e. PERSUADE

    f. MAINTAIN
    g. TRY
    h. REPLY

2. Draw a tree diagram for each of the following sentences:
    a. Fred will warn Martha that she should claim that her brother is patriotic.
    b. Doris said that the king of France told the nobles that he would save them.

4.2.1.2 Verbs Taking Bare-Stem *That* Clauses The bare-stem *that* clause, like its finite cousin, can serve as the complement of a verb. As noted earlier, this clause appears in only one verb-phrase configuration, the one in which it is the only complement.

(73)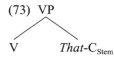

The verbs that allow this type of clause are quite limited in number. INSIST and REQUIRE are clear examples.

(74) a. I *insist* [that the defendant leave the courtroom].
     b. The rules *require* [that the executives be polite].

For these verbs, then, the following specifications are needed:

(75) a. [INSIST *That*-C$_{Stem}$]
     b. [REQUIRE *That*-C$_{Stem}$]

The same specifications in tree form are given in (76).

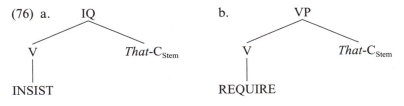

Exercise

1. Each of the following sentences contains a *that* clause. Each of these clauses contains a verb that in isolation could be either a finite verb (a present plural) or a bare stem. For each example, construct an experimental sentence that will enable you to decide whether the italicized verb is one that calls for a finite *that* clause or a bare-stem *that* clause.

    a. We *hope* [that the members of the jury understand the law].
    b. Sharon has *requested* [that the candidates stay in the hall].
    c. Joe *suspects* [that the agents open his mail].
    d. Ellen *asked* [that you read her letters].

4.2.1.3 Verbs Taking Infinitival Clauses Verbs taking infinitival clauses are much less common than those taking *that* clauses. This class of verbs includes WANT, PREFER, and LIKE.

(77) a. Karen *wants* [for Bill to get a diploma].
        Complement rule: [WANT InfC]
    b. Charles would *prefer* [for the butler to open the bottle].
        Complement rule: [PREFER InfC]
    c. Curt *likes* [for the poodle to stay under the porch].
        Complement rule: [LIKE InfC]

The same rules may be expressed in tree form as in (78).

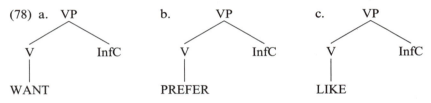

One matter deserves special attention at this point. The rules for infinitival clauses in (21) and the corresponding tree diagrams in (22), both of which are repeated here, allowed two different versions of infinitival clauses.

(21) a. An infinitival clause can consist of a *for* phrase plus a noun phrase plus an infinitival phrase.
    b. An infinitival clause can consist of an infinitival phrase alone.

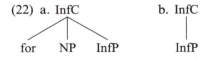

Because of this dual possibility for infinitival clauses, the verb INTEND would need to figure in only a single complement rule, [INTEND InfC]. This one rule would allow for the appearance of INTEND in both of the sentences in (79).

(79) a. Maxine intends [for Harry to buy a car].
     b. Maxine intends [to buy a car].

A natural question to ask now can be put as follows. Are all of the verbs we are concerned with just like INTEND, calling for infinitival *clauses*? Or are there some verbs that should be specified as requiring infinitival *phrases*, as was originally suggested in chapter 3 for verbs like TRY and HOPE? The answer is provided by the pairs of examples in (80)–(83).

(80) a. Beth tried to ask a question.
     b. *Beth tried for Bill to ask a question.

(81) a. Joe hoped to find a solution.
     b. *Joe hoped for Beth to find a solution.

(82) a. George tends to avoid confrontations.
     b. *George tends for Marsha to avoid confrontations.

(83) a. Jane persuaded Bill to finish the book.
     b. *Jane persuaded Bill for Joan to finish the book.

Our complement rules for these four verbs and for others that do not allow the *for* construction will just mention infinitival *phrases:* [TRY InfP], [HOPE InfP], [TEND InfP], [PERSUADE NP InfP]. However, for verbs like INTEND, WANT, and LIKE, we will use rules that mention infinitival *clauses,* in recognition of the fact that they can take both kinds of infinitival constructions, the one that has a *for* + noun phrase and the one that does not.

Exercises

1. For each of the following sentences, decide whether the italicized verb should be given the specification [— InfC] or the specification [— InfP]. Justify your decisions by devising experimental sentences in which the verbs are accompanied by infinitival clauses introduced by *for* and indicating whether they are grammatical or ungrammatical.

   a. John *decided* to keep the money.
   b. Fred *needs* to wash the dishes.
   c. Carol *seems* to enjoy calculus.
   d. Marsha *attempted* to unlock the door.
   e. Jerry *longed* to return to Iowa.

2. Draw a tree diagram for each of the following sentences:

   a. Carlton would like for Enid to play a sonata.
   b. Ned prefers to stay in Boston.

4.2.1.4 Indirect Questions as Complements Like *that* clauses, indirect questions occur as complements of a large number of English verbs. The examples in (84) and (85) illustrate the two basic configurations in which they occur.

(84) a. John *knows* [whose boat sank].
   b. Geraldine *wondered* [which car George wanted to sell].

(85) a. Janet *asked* me [how many forks to give to the customer].
   b. Charles *told* us [how tall his brother's wife was].

With KNOW and WONDER, the indirect question is the only complement. Thus, these verbs appear in the rules [KNOW IQ] and [WONDER IQ]. With ASK and TELL, on the other hand, the indirect question is preceded by a noun phrase. For these two, then, we need the rules [ASK NP IQ] and [TELL NP IQ]. In tree form, we can express these complement rules as in (86).

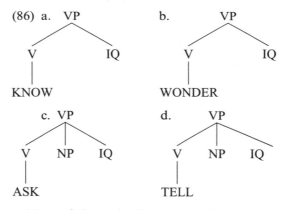

(86) a. VP   b.   VP
       V   IQ   V   IQ
       KNOW   WONDER

   c. VP   d.   VP
      V NP IQ   V NP IQ
      ASK   TELL

Most of the verbs that take indirect questions also take *that* clauses, WONDER and INQUIRE being the main exceptions. We might at first be tempted to think that the reverse holds true as well, in other words, that all verbs allowing *that* clauses also allow indirect questions. But the following pairs of examples show that such a view would be false:

(87) a. Harvey *denied* [that he had been reading that article].
   b. *Harvey *denied* [which book he had been reading].

(88) a. Henrietta *thinks* [that your dog was irresponsible].
   b. *Henrietta *thinks* [whose dog was irresponsible].

(89) a. Carol *claimed* [that she had spent five thousand dollars].
   b. *Carol *claimed* [how much money she had spent].

These examples show that we cannot predict that a certain verb will allow indirect questions merely by knowing that it allows *that* clauses. Many verbs (e.g., KNOW) allow both constructions, but many others (e.g., DENY) allow only *that* clauses.

Is there some other way of guessing which verbs will take indirect questions? A careful inspection shows that certain "meaning classes" of verbs seem to favor them. One small class consists of "interrogative verbs." This class includes ASK, WONDER, and INQUIRE.

(90) John $\begin{Bmatrix} asked \\ wondered \\ inquired \end{Bmatrix}$ [which book he should read]. $\begin{Bmatrix} [\text{ASK IQ}] \\ [\text{WONDER IQ}] \\ [\text{INQUIRE IQ}] \end{Bmatrix}$

Another class, a much larger one, consists of "verbs of knowledge," including verbs such as KNOW, LEARN, and FORGET, which involve an increase or decrease in knowledge.

(91) Karen $\begin{Bmatrix} knew \\ learned \\ forgot \end{Bmatrix}$ [which drawer contained the money]. $\begin{Bmatrix} [\text{KNOW IQ}] \\ [\text{LEARN IQ}] \\ [\text{FORGET IQ}] \end{Bmatrix}$

This class also includes verbs that take indirect objects, where the subject of the verb causes an increase in knowledge on the part of the indirect object.

(92) Pete $\begin{Bmatrix} taught \\ told \\ informed \end{Bmatrix}$ Fred [which plants were edible]. $\begin{Bmatrix} [\text{TEACH NP IQ}] \\ [\text{TELL NP IQ}] \\ [\text{INFORM NP IQ}] \end{Bmatrix}$

Other smaller verb classes whose members allow indirect questions include "decision verbs" and "verbs of concern."

(93) Marsha will *decide* [which book Carol should review].
     [DECIDE IQ]

(94) Bill never seems to *care* [how many errors he has overlooked].
     [CARE IQ]

Exercise

1. All of the verbs listed below allow *that* clauses as complements. Construct experimental sentences to determine which ones also allow indirect questions and which ones do not. One word of warning on this exercise. Constructions that start with *what, when,* and *where* do not give reliable results here, since they sometimes represent a construction of an entirely different type that will be discussed in chapter 7. Better results can be obtained with *why, whose* plus a noun, or *how much.*

a. GUESS
b. REPLY
c. OBJECT
d. FEEL
e. MAINTAIN
f. NOTICE
g. SPECIFY
h. CONFESS

4.2.2 Clauses Used as Complements of Adjectives, Prepositions, and Nouns

In the previous subsection, we examined the use of clauses as complements of verbs. Many of these clause types also occur as complements of certain adjectives, as the following examples show:

(95) Jerry is *confident* [that the farmers respect him].
[CONFIDENT *That*-C$_{Fin}$]

(96) George is *insistent* [that the witnesses be truthful].
[INSISTENT *That*-C$_{Stem}$]

(97) a. Cornelia seems *eager* [for her brother to catch a cold].
b. Cornelia seems *eager* [to catch a cold].
[EAGER InfC]

(98) Carol is *uncertain* [which articles you read].
[UNCERTAIN IQ]

These specifications have the diagram form shown in (99).

(99)

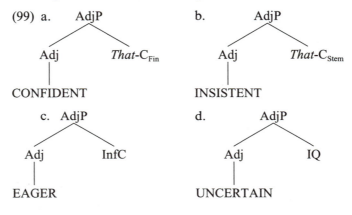

Clauses are much more restricted in their occurrence with prepositions. As a matter of fact, neither *that* clauses nor infinitival clauses may occur as objects of prepositions.

(100) *Alan is thinking *about* [that his students are eager to learn English].

(101) a. *We are counting *on* [for Nathan to make an announcement].
      b. *Fred is talking *about* [to stay in Laredo].

The only clauses that work well as prepositional objects are indirect questions.

(102) a. The outcome depends *on* [how many candidates participate in the election].
      b. Fred is thinking *about* [whether he should stay in Laredo].

Clausal complements also occur with many nouns. The noun phrases in (103), for example, show that the noun EAGERNESS can take an infinitival clause as its complement.

(103) a. John's *eagerness* [for Harriet to win the election]
      b. John's *eagerness* [to win the election]
         [EAGERNESS InfC]

Here the relation in meaning between the noun EAGERNESS and the following infinitival clauses is very much the same as that between the adjective EAGER and the same clauses.

(104) a. John is *eager* [for Harriet to win the election].
      b. John is *eager* [to win the election].

At first glance, the noun phrases in (105) might seem to show that *that* clauses have a similar capacity to occur as complements of nouns.

(105) a. the *allegation* [that Fred signed the check]
      b. the *belief* [that the directors were present]

The relation between noun and clause here might appear to be the same as that between verb and clause in (106).

(106) a. Bill *alleged* [that Fred signed the check].
      b. We *believed* [that the directors were present].

Yet the noun phrases in (105) do not stand for acts of alleging and believing, respectively. Instead, they describe the propositions denoted by the two *that* clauses. The preceding noun in (105a) characterizes the associated *that* clause as an allegation, and the preceding noun in (105b) characterizes its *that* clause as a belief.

The noun phrases in (105) thus show interesting similarities to another group of noun phrases in English. This second group is illustrated by the left-hand examples in (107).

(107) a. the number seven   seven
       b. the verb *create*   *create*
       c. my friend Elmer   Elmer

The noun phrases on the left refer to the same entities as the corresponding ones on the right. The major difference is that the left-hand noun phrases provide extra characterizations of these entities: seven is characterized as a number, *create* is characterized as a verb, and Elmer is characterized as my friend.

In view of these observations, we will analyze these examples as being divided into a definite noun phrase and either a *that* clause or a proper noun. This analysis yields tree structures like those in (108), where *PN* stands for "proper noun."

(108)

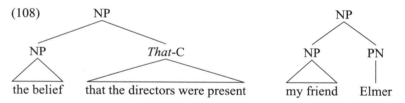

A significant number of other nouns are also appropriate for this construction. Examples of such nouns are given in (109); by contrast, (110) exhibits several nouns that cannot occur in this context.

(109) a. Columbus's *conviction* [that the earth is round]
       b. Bertram's *claim* [that the earth is flat]
       c. the *idea* [that James can play the flute]
       d. the *view* [that Martha knows how to bake croissants]

(110) a. *Columbus's *attention* [that the earth is round]
       b. *Bertram's *article* [that the earth is flat]
       c. *the *ignorance* [that James can play the flute]
       d. *the *expertise* [that Martha knows how to bake croissants]

Exercise

1. Construct experimental sentences to determine which of the following nouns take *that* clauses. As your sample *that* clause, use either *that all cows eat grass* or *that John stayed in Denver*. These sequences are unambiguously *that* clauses. In particular, neither one is a relative-clause structure of the sort that will be discussed in chapter 10.

    a. FEAR
    b. REMORSE
    c. ENJOYMENT
    d. THEORY
    e. THOUGHT
    f. PROPOSITION
    g. BOOK
    h. REFUSAL

4.2.3   Clauses Used as Subjects

4.2.3.1   Some Initial Examples   In the preceding subsection, we examined four different clause structures that could be used as complements of various sorts of English words. In this new subsection, we will look at the possibilities for using these structures as subjects.

We begin by considering a single example.

(111) [That Jane sold her car] surprised Bill.

The first five words of this sentence clearly make up a finite *that* clause. The remaining two words (*surprised Bill*) make up a past-tense verb phrase. Thus, the structure of the sentence as a whole is as shown in (112).

(112)

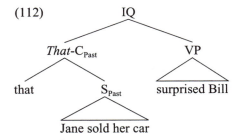

To account for this example, we need the following new rule:

(113) A sentence can consist of a *that* clause plus a verb phrase.

We also find sentences in which other kinds of clauses are used as subjects.

(114) a. *For Alice to hire an assistant* would be desirable.
         (infinitival clause)
     b. *That the king be present at the wedding* is mandatory.
         (bare-stem *that* clause)
     c. *Which theory you should adopt* is unclear.   (indirect question)

For these examples, we need to revise the rule in (113) so as to allow for
additional clause types as subjects. We can do this by simply referring to
clauses in general in the rule.

(115) A sentence can consist of a clause plus a verb phrase.

For the examples in (114), we can draw the tree diagrams in (116).

(116) a.

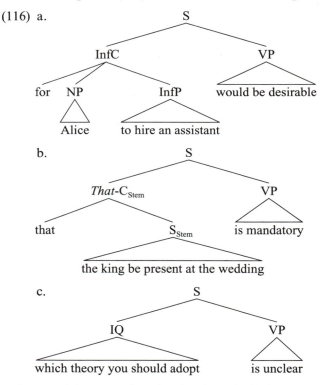

One special assumption that has been implicit in the foregoing discussion deserves some explicit attention. In all of the examples considered in
this subsection, the clauses that served as subjects were not analyzed as
noun phrases. At first glance, it might seem perfectly natural to analyze
them as noun phrases, given the earlier definition of the noun-phrase class

as including constructions that could serve as subjects, objects, objects of prepositions, and so on. We have already seen that two of the three clause types cannot serve as objects of prepositions, a restriction that immediately sets them apart from ordinary noun phrases. In subsection 4.2.5, we will see that there are situations in which clauses cannot even appear as subjects. In view of their special behavior, then, clauses will not be granted the status of noun phrases.

Exercise

1. Divide each of the following sentences into a clause plus a verb phrase, and identify the clause type. The first is done as an example.
  a. That Cora burned her textbooks made her teachers suspicious.
     Answer: The sequence *that Cora burned her textbooks* is a finite *that* clause; the sequence *made her teachers suspicious* is the verb phrase that it joins with.
  b. How many goldfish Harry bought seems to be unclear.
  c. Which books Holmes will put on the reading list remains a mystery.
  d. That George intends to let Bob make a speech made Susan despondent.
  e. For Iris to move to Chicago would break Arthur's heart.
  f. That Bill tried to discover which drawer Alice put the money in made us realize that we should have left him in Albuquerque.
  g. For Willie to tell the teacher that the dog had eaten his homework was inexcusable.

4.2.3.2 Restrictions on Subjects At this point, we face the same kind of problem with regard to subjects that we faced in earlier sections of this chapter with regard to objects. We saw then that verbs can differ with respect to whether they allow clausal objects.

(117) a.   Jane told Bill [that the story was true].
       b.   *Jane gave Bill [that the story was true].

We can now construct examples that show the same kind of differences with respect to subjects.

(118) a.   [The explosion] surprised Fred.
       b.   [That the firecracker exploded] surprised Fred.

(119) a.   [The delegates] selected Bill.
       b.   *[That Roger was unpopular] selected Bill.

These examples indicate clearly that although SURPRISE allows both noun phrases and *that* clauses as subjects, SELECT allows only noun phrases.

Our earlier rules for individual verbs mentioned allowable complements but did not say anything about allowable subjects. Let us now replace this old kind of rule by a new kind, one that identifies subjects as well as complements. Examples of this new kind of rule, which can be referred to as *subject/complement rules,* are given in (120).

(120) a. NP [SURPRISE NP]
          That-C$_{Fin}$ [SURPRISE NP]
      b. NP [SELECT NP]

These rules, like the complement rules employed earlier, indicate that both SURPRISE and SELECT take ordinary noun phrases as complements. However, they also provide information on allowable subjects, this information being given by the items to the left of the bracketed material. The two rules for SURPRISE indicate that it allows both ordinary noun phrases and finite *that* clauses as subjects, whereas the single rule for SELECT limits its possible subjects to just ordinary noun phrases.

We need to provide the same kind of additional information in the rules for individual adjectives. We have already seen many examples of adjectives that take various kinds of complements. We have also seen some sentences in which clauses serve as subjects of verb phrases that contain adjectives; a representative set of examples is given in (121).

(121) a. [That Dorothy missed the lecture] was regrettable.   (finite *that* clause)
      b. [For Jacob to remove the motor] is unnecessary.   (infinitival clause)
      c. [That Carol sign the deed] is mandatory.   (bare-stem *that* clause)
      d. [How much money Gordon spent] is unclear.   (indirect question)

Even though the main predicates of these sentences are headed by BE, the allowable subjects are determined not by BE, but by the four adjectives. We can convince ourselves of this fact by leaving the occurrences of BE in place and changing the adjectives. It is not hard to find new adjectives that make the sentences unacceptable.

(122) a. *[*That* Dorothy missed the lecture] was *enjoyable*.   (finite *that* clause)
      b. *[For Jacob to remove the motor] is *undeniable*.   (infinitival clause)

    c. *[That Carol sign the deed] is *obvious*.   (bare-stem *that* clause)

    d. *[How much money Gordon spent] is *true*.   (indirect question)

Thus, we have good reason to think of various adjectives as requiring this or that kind of subject, even though the subject does not join directly with the adjective phrase, but instead joins with a verb phrase. The adjectives in (121), then, require the following rules:

(123) a. *That*-C_{Fin} [REGRETTABLE]

      b. InfC [UNNECESSARY]

      c. *That*-C_{Stem} [MANDATORY]

      d. IQ [UNCLEAR]

Chapter 8 will provide a more general treatment of how subject requirements are satisfied. Among other things, we will see why it makes sense to let the adjectives select the subjects, even though the phrases that actually join with the subjects are headed by verbs.

    In the remainder of this book, we will encounter many situations in which the main question of interest concerns the complements that a certain word takes, rather than the subjects that appear with it. In situations of this type, free use will be made of complement rules, rather than of the slightly more cumbersome subject/complement rules.

Exercise

1. All of the adjectives listed below allow *that* clauses as subjects. Construct experimental sentences to determine which ones also allow indirect questions as subjects, and which ones do not.

    a. TRUE

    b. EVIDENT

    c. POSSIBLE

    d. APPARENT

    e. UNCERTAIN

    f. UNLIKELY

4.2.4 The Clausal Substitute *It* and Pseudocomplements

We have now seen several sentences in which clauses function as subjects. Despite being acceptable, these sentences often strike speakers of English as somewhat awkward, and not completely natural for ordinary writing and conversation. At least some of the awkwardness seems to be due to the relative "heaviness" of the clause as a left-hand element in the sentence.

As it happens, the rules of English provide an alternative method for expressing the same thoughts, one that avoids a heavy initial structure. This alternative is illustrated in (124)–(127). The (a) examples are of the type that we have already studied, and the (b) examples show the new structure.

(124) a. [That Jane sold her car] surprised Bill.
      b. *It* surprised Bill [that Jane sold her car].

(125) a. [For Martha to keep the money] would be desirable.
      b. *It* would be desirable [for Martha to keep the money].

(126) a. [To postpone the project] would be inadvisable.
      b. *It* would be inadvisable [to postpone the project].

(127) a. [Which theory you should adopt] is unclear.
      b. *It* is unclear [which theory you should adopt].

In the (b) sentences, the pronoun *it* replaces the clause in the position of the subject, and the clause is shifted to the right. In particular, we will assume that the clause becomes the rightmost part of the verb phrase with which the word *it* is linked. This assumption gives (128) as the structure of (124b).

(128)

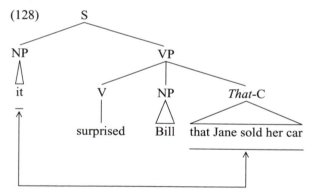

We will refer to the word *it* used in this way as a *clausal substitute,* and to the clause in its new position as a *pseudocomplement.* By this last name we mean that the clause is not understood as a complement, but nevertheless occupies a position that is appropriate for a complement.

The fact that a *that* clause can occur as a pseudocomplement in (124b) is clearly related to the fact that it can occur as a subject in (124a). For this reason, it would be desirable to have the rule in (129) cover two distinct cases.

(129) *That*-C [SURPRISE NP]

The first is the situation in which the *that* clause itself is found in subject position; the second is the situation in which subject position is occupied by the substitute *it*. The following principle gives the desired result:

(130) In a situation in which a clause would have some use as a subject, it is possible to employ in its place the clausal substitute *it* linked to a pseudocomplement clause of the same type.

For example, we know from our earlier discussion that the verb SURPRISE permits a *that* clause as subject. Now principle (130) tells us that SURPRISE can also have *it* as subject, linked to a *that*-clause pseudocomplement. Thus, both of the structures in (131) will satisfy the rule in (129).

(131) a.   b.

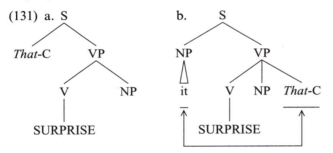

Similarly, the rule allowing a *that* clause as subject of the adjective CLEAR would be satisfied by both of the structures in (132).

(132) a.   b.

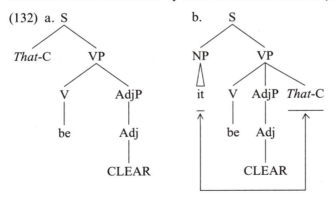

A similar situation in which the clausal substitute *it* appears arises with verbs such as MAKE and CONSIDER. As we saw in chapter 3, these verbs occur in the configuration depicted in (133).

(133)

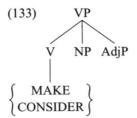

The following sentences exemplify this structure, when ordinary noun phrases occupy the object position:

(134) a. Martha made the test difficult.
　　　b. Joe considered the payment insufficient.

In (134a), *the test* not only satisfies the object requirement of MAKE; it also satisfies the subject requirement of DIFFICULT, just as it does in the simple sentence *The test was difficult*. The noun phrase *the payment* fulfills the same dual role in (134b). Of interest in the present discussion is that the substitute *it* can be used as the object of MAKE and CONSIDER, with a *that* clause appearing as a pseudocomplement of the adjective.

(135) a. Joe made *it* clear [that the money had vanished].
　　　b. Dorothy considers *it* unlikely [that the problem is solvable].

In these examples, we will assume that the pseudocomplement is the rightmost part of the adjective phrase that accompanies the *it*, since the adjective phrase is the phrase most directly joined with *it*. Thus, the tree diagram in (136) is appropriate for the first of these sentences.

(136)

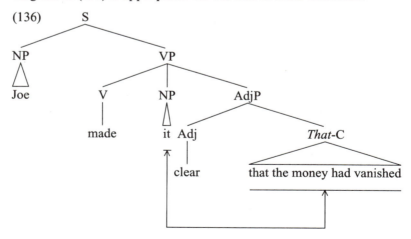

There are a few English verbs that allow only the configuration with *it* and a pseudocomplement, excluding sentences in which the clauses occur in ordinary subject position. Two examples are SEEM and APPEAR.

(137) a. *It* seems that John has identified the problem.
b. *[That John has identified the problem] seems.

(138) a. *It* appears [that Brenda has dictated a letter].
b. *[That Brenda has dictated a letter] appears.

Thus, for these two verbs, and also for a few other verbs and adjectives, the configuration in (139a) is incorrect, since it would allow sentences in which *that* clauses occurred in normal subject position with these verbs. As a result, we must assign the configuration in (139b) to these verbs directly, rather than deriving the desired configuration from (139a) by using principle (130).

(139) a. *That*-C [—]
b. *it* [— *That*-C]

Thus, the rules required for these two verbs will include those in (140).

(140) a. *it* [SEEM *That*-C]
b. *it* [APPEAR *That*-C]

4.2.5   Practical Interlude: More on the Relation between Rules and Trees

At this stage, the structures that we are studying are getting somewhat complicated. It is thus worth reemphasizing a point that was made at the end of chapter 3, when tree diagrams were introduced—namely, that when we want to draw a diagram for a given sentence, it is essential to ask ourselves what the relevant rules are for the sentence. In situations where we manage to get a clear idea of the rules, the correct tree structures will follow almost automatically.

To illustrate the value of "throwing ourselves on the mercy of the rules," let us try to develop a structure for the following sequence:

(141) That John admires Alice seems clear.

Starting from the top down, the first question to ask is what this sequence is. The first few words might suggest that it is a *that* clause, so that the top line of the tree should contain just the symbol given in (142).

(142) *That*-C

However, reading the entire sequence leaves us with the intuitive sense that it is a sentence. Thus, a better initial guess about what belongs at the top of the tree is given in (143).

(143) S

In order to proceed further, we need to think about the various rules that we have seen for sentences. (In the interests of simplifying the discussion, we will omit mention of finiteness.) The entire collection is given in (144).

(144) a. A sentence can consist of a noun phrase and a verb phrase.
   b. A sentence can consist of a *that* clause and a verb phrase.
   c. A sentence can consist of an infinitival clause and a verb phrase.
   d. A sentence can consist of an indirect question and a verb phrase.

A quick look at the first few words of (141) gives us a clue that it starts with a *that* clause and thus that (144b) is the rule we want. This rule, translated into tree form, gives the structure shown in (145).

(145) S
   /\
That-C VP

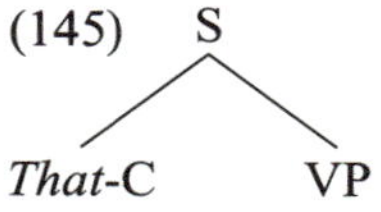

Seeing the word *John* coming immediately after *that,* we might be tempted to say that this *that* clause has the structure shown in (146).

(146) *That*-C
   /\
 that NP

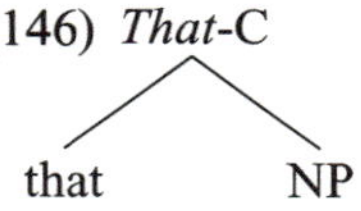

However, if we think about rules rather than about words, we realize that we do not have any rule that allows a *that* clause to consist of *that* plus a noun phrase. As a matter of fact, if we concentrate on rules, we can now take several further steps in developing this structure without even looking at the words in the sentence. In the first place, we have the following rule for *that* clauses:

(147) A *that* clause consists of the word *that* followed by a sentence.

Applied to expand the tree in (145), this rule gives (148).

(148)

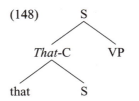

Now we have a smaller sentence. *John* (the word immediately after *that*) must be the first word of this sentence, and it looks like a good candidate for being a noun phrase. Therefore, it is reasonable to guess that the relevant rule for building this sentence is the one given in (144a), which translates into the tree in (149).

(149) S

Applied to the tree diagram we are developing, this gives the still more expanded structure in (150).

(150)

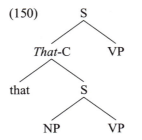

We have now succeeded in uncovering all of the essential architecture that we need. Getting this far was the really difficult part of drawing a tree diagram for this sentence. The remaining work of filling in the rest of the details is quite straightforward; it yields the tree in (151).

(151)

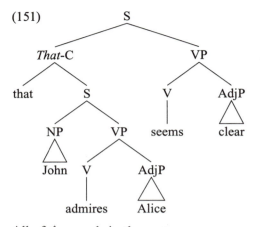

All of the words in the sentence are now accounted for, and every aspect of this structure is consistent with the rules that we have developed.

Let us next try to develop a slightly different sort of complex structure, the one required for the sentence in (152).

(152) That it is doubtful that Bill knows that Martha will get the job
       seems clear.

Once again, we begin by asking what kind of sequence this is. Although it is definitely rather complex, it still feels intuitively like a sentence, an intuition that we can expect the rules to confirm. Thus, we want to start with a rule that builds a sentence structure. Once again, rule (144b) is the one that is clearly called for.

(153)   S

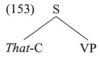

That-C   VP

Again, we can develop a great deal of basic architecture without knowing any more than that the sequence is a sentence whose subject is a *that* clause. We immediately get (154), identical to (150).

(154)

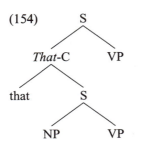

All we did to make these two additions was to apply the rule for *that* clauses and the first of our rules for sentences.

Now let us try to determine the structure of the lower sentence. The subject noun phrase is pretty clearly the word *it*. One possibility to consider immediately is that this *it* is acting as a substitute subject, standing in for some clause at the end of the sentence. In the present instance, this possibility is confirmed when we look at what follows. After the adjective *doubtful*, we find a *that* clause. So the verb phrase after *it* will consist of the verb *is*, the adjective phrase *doubtful*, and the *that* clause. We can also immediately add an indication of the basic structure of the *that* clause, together with the sentence inside it. Putting in this additional structure thus gives the nearly completed diagram in (155).

(155)

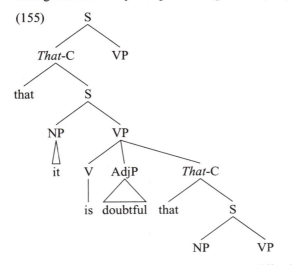

The structure of the lowest sentence is not difficult to determine, as we can see by considering this sentence in isolation.

(156) Bill knows that Martha will get the job.

Here the verb phrase will be headed by *know* and will contain one last *that* clause, which in turn will contain the very simple sentence *Martha will get the job*.

(157)

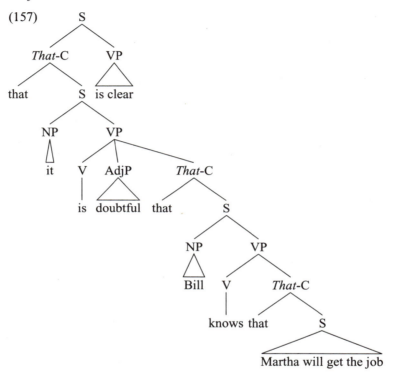

Thus, even a sentence as long and complicated as this one yields its structure when we force ourselves to be as steady and consistent as possible in making our tentative structures correspond to what is required by the rules that we have studied.

Exercise

1. Draw a tree diagram for each of the following sentences:
   a. It amazed Pete that the ants survived the drought.
   b. It surprised Bill that it was unclear that George deserved a trophy.
   c. That it was possible that John would forget to feed the goldfish bothered Susan.

4.2.6   More Noun-Phrase Positions Where Clauses Are Unacceptable

In this chapter, we have seen several examples of noun-phrase positions in which clauses are allowed. To begin with, we observed clauses serving as complements of transitive verbs such as KNOW and BELIEVE. We also observed sentences in which clauses appeared in subject position. We did note, though, that *that* clauses and infinitival clauses do not work well as objects of prepositions. We now need to look at several other situations in which a clause cannot be used in a normal noun-phrase position. These examples will provide the additional evidence alluded to earlier for not analyzing clauses as genuine noun phrases. In the situations to be examined here, speakers of English typically rely heavily on the *it* + pseudocomplement strategy.

Let us begin by looking again at clauses serving as first complements of MAKE and CONSIDER. In this situation, only the clausal substitute *it* can appear in the normal position of the object. When we try to put the clause itself there, the results are unacceptable.

(158) a. *Joe made *that the money had vanished* clear.
      b. *Dorothy considers *that the problem is solvable* unlikely.

A clue about how we should view the unacceptability of these sentences is provided by additional examples in which clauses are unacceptable as subjects. To begin with, there is a sharp difference between the declarative in (159a) and the corresponding question in (159b).

(159) a. *That the money had vanished* was obvious.
      b. *Was *that the money had vanished* obvious?

With the substitute *it* used instead, both declarative and question are equally acceptable.

(160) a. *It* was obvious *that the money had vanished.*
      b. Was *it* obvious *that the money had vanished*?

In addition, there is a clear difference between a clause as a main clause subject and the same clause used as the subject of a complement clause.

(161) a. *That the money had vanished* was obvious.
      b. *Sarah wonders whether *that the money had vanished* was obvious.

Again, these examples should be compared with the corresponding examples in which the clausal substitute is used.

(162) a. *It* was obvious *that the money had vanished.*

     b. Sarah wonders whether *it* was obvious *that the money had vanished.*

Although the actual mental rules or principles that give these results are not well understood, the observations offered above can be summarized as follows. Regarding occurrence as a subject, a *that* clause is acceptable only in an independent sentence, and then only when nothing occurs to its left. Regarding its use as a complement, a *that* clause is acceptable as a single complement, and also as a second complement. It cannot occur as the object of a verb when another complement follows. Parallel restrictions hold for the other types of clauses studied in this chapter.

4.3 THE OMISSION OF *THAT* AND *FOR*

Both *that* clauses and infinitival clauses sometimes appear in a slightly abbreviated form. In addition to the (a) examples in (163) and (164), which we have already discussed, the rules of English also allow the (b) examples.

(163) a. Karen thinks *that Fred is feeding her rabbit.*

     b. Karen thinks *Fred is feeding her rabbit.*

(164) a. Barney would like *for you to hear his story.*

     b. Barney would like *you to hear his story.*

In the second example in each pair, the word that introduces the clause has been omitted.

The omission of the clause-introducing word is allowed only under certain restricted circumstances. It is impossible when the clause is serving as a subject.

(165) a. *That Fred is feeding her rabbit* annoys Karen.

     b. **Fred is feeding her rabbit* annoys Karen.

(166) a. *For Bill to leave the room* would be desirable.

     b. **Bill to leave the room* would be desirable.

In addition, the clause cannot be separated from the verb by an adverbial expression.

(167) a. Marshall believes very strongly *that he should be the candidate.*

     b. *Marshall believes very strongly *he should be the candidate.*

(168) a.   Theresa would like very much *for you to attend the recital.
      b.   *Theresa would like very much *you to attend the recital.*

Finally, the omission is completely acceptable with some verbs and adjectives but is relatively less acceptable with others, depending to a degree on the speaker's dialect. We have already seen sentences containing words that clearly allow the omission. In the following pairs of sentences, by contrast, the particular verbs and adjectives are less hospitable to the omission:

(169) a.   Bob replied that he needed to eat a hamburger.
      b.   ?Bob replied he needed to eat a hamburger.

(170) a.   Nona exclaimed that Bill's nose was frozen.
      b.   ?Nona exclaimed Bill's nose was frozen.

(171) a.   We would prefer for you to stay here.
      b.   ?We would prefer you to stay here.

Taking all of these observations into consideration, we can state an optional rule for omitting *that* and *for* as follows:

(172) Certain verbs and adjectives permit the optional omission of
       the clause-introducing words *that* and *for* in their clausal
       complements, when the clause is not separated from the verb or
       adjective.

The requirement that the clauses be complements prevents the rule from applying to subject clauses, thus preventing the unacceptable examples in (165b) and (166b). The omission of *that* and *for* can be indicated in tree diagrams by parenthesizing the omitted elements, as illustrated in (173).

(173) a.

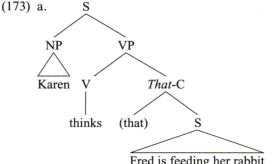

b.

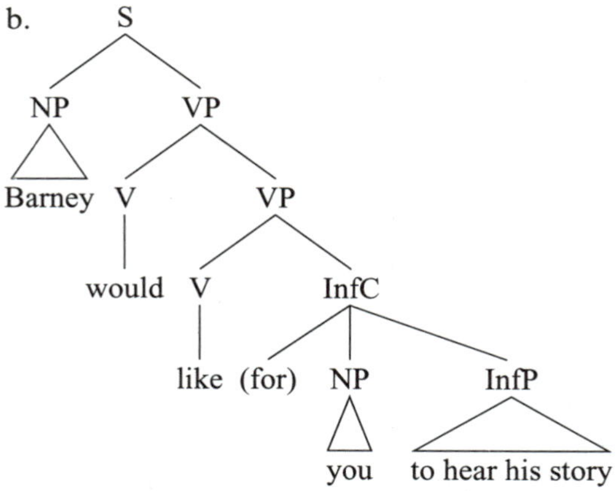

For the purposes of this rule, the pseudocomplements described in the preceding section function just like real complements, as the following pair of sentences shows:

(174) a. It was clear that something needed to be done.
b. It was clear something needed to be done.

The adjective *clear* is thus one of the words that allows the omission, and it is a pseudocomplement clause in which the omission takes place. On the other hand, just as some verbs and adjectives resist the omission in their real complements, so there are some that resist it in their pseudocomplements. The word *regrettable* is one of the latter.

(175) a. It is regrettable that Sharon failed to keep the guinea pig in the cage.
b. ?It is regrettable Sharon failed to keep the guinea pig in the cage.

Chapter 5

Noun Phrases

In chapter 2, we used the standard term *noun phrase* to refer to a large class of sequences that can serve as subjects and also as objects of verbs and prepositions. Since that point, the particular noun phrases that we have used have been of a few very simple kinds. The purpose of this chapter is to give a more detailed picture of how noun phrases are constructed.

In section 5.1, we will look at *elementary* noun phrases, a class that includes such phrases as *she, Joseph, the tadpole, your dog, one sandbag,* and *every carpenter*. In section 5.2, we will examine *partitive* noun phrases, in which an *of* phrase plays a prominent role (*one of the dominoes, several of the cards, a pound of beans,* etc.). Section 5.3 is an interpretive interlude in which the use of the definite article is discussed. Finally, in section 5.4, we will look at the *gerundive* construction, a special sentence-like noun-phrase structure.

5.1 ELEMENTARY NOUN PHRASES

5.1.1 Pronouns and Proper Nouns

In order to begin our inventory of noun-phrase types with the simplest ones, let us start with the pronouns. Pronouns as a group have the property of being able to make up entire noun phrases themselves. In a sentence such as *I see you,* the pronoun *I* is the entire subject noun phrase, and the pronoun *you* is the entire object noun phrase. Thus, we can give the following rule:

(1) A noun phrase can consist of a pronoun (abbreviated *Pro*).

NP

Pro

The major syntactic complication concerning pronouns is that they are the only English forms that retain a distinction between *nominative case* (the case of the subject) and *accusative case* (the case used for objects). Thus, for instance, we have the following contrasts:

(2) a.   I love her and she loves me.
    b.   *Me love she and her loves I.

In addition to the nominative and accusative pronouns, there is a set of corresponding *genitives* (*my, your, his, her,* etc.), which will be analyzed in detail in subsection 5.1.3.

We will refer to these as *ordinary* pronouns, to distinguish them from another set of pronouns, the so-called *reflexive* pronouns. These pronouns, whose form we examined briefly in chapter 1, include *myself, yourself, himself, herself, ourselves,* and so forth. Like the accusative ordinary pronouns, these can occur as objects of verbs and prepositions. Roughly speaking, the reflexive form takes precedence over the ordinary form when the noun phrase in question refers to the same person or thing as the nearest subject or object does (if there is an object).

(3) a.   John believes that [*we* deceived *ourselves*].
    b.   *John believes that [*we* deceived *us*].

(4) a.   John believes that [Nora told *us* about *ourselves*].
    b.   *John believes that [Nora told *us* about *us*].

By contrast, when the nearest subject and the nearest object (if there is one) refer to someone or something else, then an ordinary pronoun must be used.

(5) a.   *We* believe that [John distrusts *ourselves*].
    b.   *We* believe that [John distrusts *us*].

(6) a.   *We* believe that [John told Nora about *ourselves*].
    b.   *We* believe that [John told Nora about *us*].

Section 8.7 will give a fuller treatment of the relation between reflexives and "nearest subjects," making use of the more sophisticated idea of subjecthood developed in that chapter.

One final type of English pronoun, which can occur as either an accusative or a genitive, is the *reciprocal* pronoun *each other,* whose use is illustrated in (7).

(7) a. *Fred and Martha* sent messages to *each other*.
    b. *Fred and Martha* sent messages to *each other's* lawyers.

Proper nouns (sometimes referred to as "proper names") constitute another class of words that typically make up noun phrases all by themselves. Three such noun phrases occur in (8).

(8) *David* introduced *Mr. Jones* to *John Smith*.

For these noun phrases, we need the following simple rule:

(9) A noun phrase can consist of a proper noun (abbreviated *PN*).

NP
|
PN

It was stated above that proper nouns "typically" appear alone. The reason for this qualification will become apparent in subsection 5.1.7.

5.1.2 Common-Noun Phrases: A Brief Review

In order to be ready for the principal work of this section, we need to review some ideas first presented in chapter 2. There we noted that a special class of words called *common nouns* can serve as heads of phrases. We called these phrases *common-noun phrases*. There and in subsequent discussions, several examples of this type of phrase were presented, including the following:

(10) a. book
     b. dogs
     c. beer
     d. leader of the army
     e. king of Spain
     f. heir to the throne
     g. faith in Fred's sister
     h. effort to find a vaccine

The common-noun phrases in (10a)–(10c) consist of common-noun heads alone; those in (10d)–(10h) consist of head nouns followed by complements. The complement rules that we need for these examples are listed in (11).

(11) a. [BOOK]
     b. [DOG]
     c. [BEER]
     d. [LEADER *Of*-P]
     e. [KING *Of*-P]
     f. [HEIR *To*-P]
     g. [FAITH *In*-P]
     h. [EFFORT InfP]

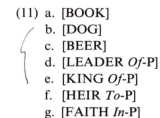

These rules are represented graphically in (12).

(12)

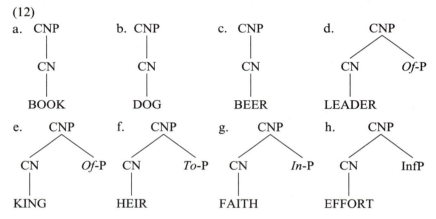

In chapter 10, we will add rules that permit common-noun phrases to contain modifiers as well as complements. These rules, for example, will allow not only *book* as a common-noun phrase, but also *old book, book from England,* and *book that Jill reviewed.* A few simple common-noun phrases will be enough for present purposes, because the remainder of this chapter is concerned with the *external* syntax of common-noun phrases, that is, with the rules that regulate their appearance in larger constructions. The larger constructions in question are just various sorts of what we have called noun phrases. The relation between noun phrases and common-noun phrases can be represented schematically as in (13).

(13)

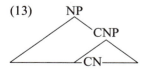

Let us recall here the comments from chapter 2 concerning this terminology. The term *common-noun phrase* is to be understood in the expected way, namely, as a phrase headed by a *common noun*. The term *noun phrase,* on the other hand, is to be understood as a fixed, arbitrary designation for a phrase that can serve as subject, direct object, and so forth. In particular, there are several constructions that are typically included in this class of phrases even though they are not headed by nouns.

Before going on to the main work of this chapter, we need to note two *internal* properties of common-noun phrases that can have an important effect in determining their permitted external environments. As was noted in chapter 1, the general class of English common nouns is divided into *count nouns* and *mass nouns.* The count nouns can be divided further into *singular nouns* and *plural nouns.* In addition to applying the terms *mass, count, singular,* and *plural* to common nouns, we will find good reason to apply them to common-noun phrases as well. This is not the first situation we have seen in which a word passes certain of its properties up to the phrase that it heads. In chapter 2, we saw that verbs of various inflectional types pass their inflectional property up to the phrases that they head. For example, a present-participial marking on a verb has the effect of making the phrase that it heads a present-participial verb *phrase.* In exactly the same fashion, a mass noun will pass its mass property up to the common-noun phrase that it heads, a plural count noun will pass its plural count status up to its common-noun phrase, and so on. These properties of common-noun phrases are represented in (14).

(14)
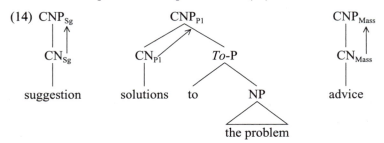

Exercise

1. Draw a tree diagram for each of the common-noun phrases listed below. (For the purposes of this exercise, just represent the noun phrases *London, Fred's dishonesty, Mandalay,* and *the cliff* with triangles.)

   a. coin
   b. maps of London
   c. people

d. porridge
e. evidence of Fred's dishonesty
f. road to Mandalay
g. edge of the cliff
h. decision to intervene

5.1.3 Elementary Noun Phrases Introduced by Determiners and Genitives

We have already seen many noun phrases in which common-noun phrases were preceded by the word *the*, traditionally referred to as the *definite article*. We will refer to the full set of words to which *the* belongs as the class of *determiners*. In addition to *the*, this class includes the four *demonstratives: this, that, these,* and *those*. All of these words combine with common-noun phrases to form noun phrases.

(15) a. the [book]
  b. this [dog]
  c. that [side of the table]
  d. these [students of chemistry]
  e. those [kings of England]

For these noun phrases, we need the rule in (16), which can be expressed either in words or in tree form.

(16) A noun phrase can consist of a determiner plus a common-noun phrase.

Two examples of the structures to which this rule gives rise are shown in (17).

(17)

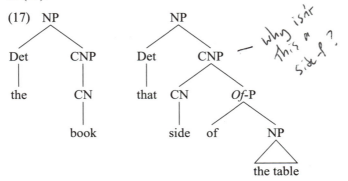

The word *the* is indifferent to the number of the following common-noun phrase; it may be joined to either a singular or a plural phrase. By contrast, the demonstratives have to agree in number with the common-noun phrase: *these* and *those* take plural phrases, whereas *this* and *that* take nonplural phrases.

(18) a.   this [book]   *this [books]
     b.   that [book]   *that [books]

(19) a.   *these [book]   these [books]
     b.   *those [book]   those [books]

The examples in (20) show that mass nouns as well as singular count nouns are to be taken as nonplural.

(20) a.   this [advice]
     b.   *these [advice]
     c.   that [traffic]
     d.   *those [traffic]

A final group of words included in the class of determiners is a surprising one; it consists of the plural pronoun forms *we*, *us*, and *you*, as shown in (21).

(21) a.   we [leaders of the senate]
     b.   us [students of chemistry]
     c.   you [children]

Noun phrases introduced by determiners form part of a special semantic class that we will refer to as *definite noun phrases*. (We will need to refer to this class later in this chapter when we are discussing partitive noun phrases.) Another type of noun phrase that belongs in this class is shown in (22).

(22) a.   Fred's [dog].
     b.   the farmer's [pig]
     c.   your [picture of Fred]

In each of these examples, the bracketed common-noun phrase is preceded by a *genitive construction* (*Fred's, the farmer's, your*). *Genitive* is the traditional name for the construction in English that indicates possession, among other things.

The general rule for forming genitives involves adding a "genitive marker" to a noun phrase. The marker -*'* is added to a noun phrase ending in the plural suffix -*s*.

(23)

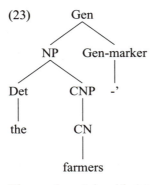

The marker -'s is added to other noun phrases. Some typical structures are given in (24).

(24) a.

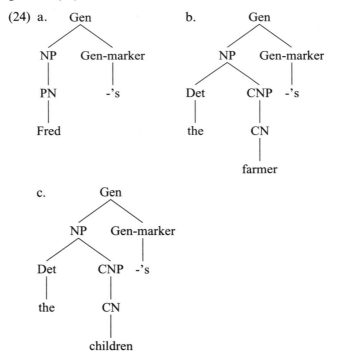

Finally, when we form genitives from pronouns, the forms are more irregular and cannot be predicted from the nongenitive forms (*my* corresponds to *I/me, your* to *you, his* to *he/him,* etc.). What we will do here is represent the pronoun and the genitive marker as fused into a single unit, as indicated in (25).

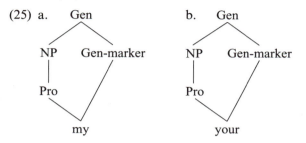

Once we have these structures for genitives, the following rule will give the total noun phrases in (22):

(26) A noun phrase can consist of a genitive construction followed by a common-noun phrase.

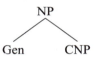

Shown in (27), then, are the complete structures for the noun phrases in (22).

(27) a.   b.

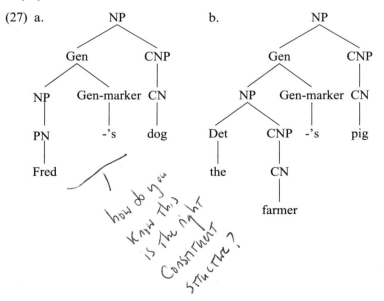

how do you know this is the right Constituent Structure?

c.

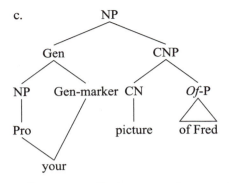

One reason that we can give now for wanting to classify these noun phrases as definite is that they have an interpretation that is close to what we would obtain for a noun phrase introduced by *the*. For example, *Fred's dog* is much closer in meaning to *the dog that Fred owns* than it is to *a dog that Fred owns*. A second reason will become apparent in section 5.2, when we study examples like *several of those dogs* and *several of Fred's dogs*.

One other possibility for forming definite elementary noun phrases is illustrated in (28).

(28) a. the three stooges
   b. these two books
   c. this one concert
   d. the victim's four brothers
   e. Linda's one regret
   f. Gary's many supporters

In these examples, the same elements introduce the noun phrases as in the examples considered earlier (determiners in (28a–c) and genitive noun phrases in (28d–f)). The extra element in each case is either an outright numeral, as in (28a–e), or a word that is close in meaning to a numeral, as in (28f). For noun phrases such as these, we need the following added rule:

(29) A noun phrase can consist of either a determiner or a genitive, followed by a numeral (or a numeral-like word), followed by a common-noun phrase.

Structures for two of the examples in (28) are given in (30).

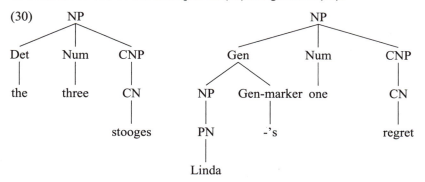

Exercises

1. Draw a detailed tree diagram for each of the following noun phrases.
   a. these distortions of Pat's views
   b. this appraiser's estimates of the damage
   c. Joseph's idea of his rights
   d. my three sons
   e. these two reports to the governor

2. The rules for demonstratives presented here give us a straightforward experimental way of deciding whether a certain noun in English is plural or nonplural. Construct noun phrases (some acceptable, some unacceptable) that show that *cattle* is a plural noun, whereas *traffic* is a nonplural noun.

3. Draw a tree diagram for the noun phrase *Ruth's father's orchard*. Hint: As a preliminary matter, you might want to draw a tree diagram for the noun phrase *Ruth's father*.

5.1.4 Elementary Noun Phrases Introduced by Quantity Words

Another important type of elementary noun phrase consists of a *quantity word* (abbreviated *Quant*) plus a common-noun phrase. The class of quantity words includes *some, many, much, any, no, little, few,* and also the numerals *one, two, three,* and so on. Some examples of noun phrases introduced by these words are given in (31). Each example is accompanied by an indication of the basic properties of the common-noun phrase.

(31) a. some [books]   (plural)
     b. some [vegetation]   (mass)
     c. many [suggestions]   (plural)
     d. several [marbles]   (plural)

e.	much [advice]	(mass)
f.	no [bottles]	(plural)
g.	no [evidence]	(mass)
h.	no [card]	(singular)
i.	any [bottles]	(plural)
j.	any [evidence]	(mass)
k.	any [card]	(singular)
l.	few [opportunities]	(plural)
m.	little [evidence]	(mass)
n.	one [side]	(singular)
o.	three [attempts]	(plural)
p.	all [suggestions]	(plural)
q.	all [advice]	(mass)
r.	each [suggestion]	(singular)
s.	every [suggestion]	(singular)
t.	most [suggestions]	(plural)
u.	most [advice]	(mass)

For these noun phrases, we need the following rule:

(32) A noun phrase can consist of a quantity word followed by a common-noun phrase.

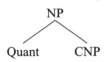

Four sample noun-phrase trees that this rule yields are given in (33).

(33)

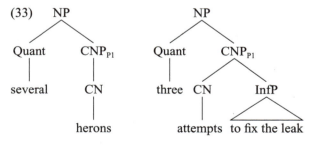

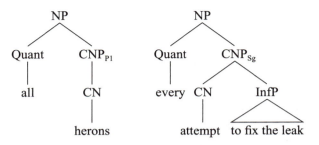

As the examples in (34) show, particular quantity words are limited with respect to the common-noun phrases that they can take.

(34) a. *many [suggestion]   (singular)
     b. *many [advice]   (mass)
     c. *three [advice]   (mass)
     d. *three [suggestion]   (singular)
     e. *much [suggestion]   (singular)
     f. *much [suggestions]   (plural)
     g. *one [suggestions]   (plural)
     h. *one [advice]   (mass)
     i. *all [suggestion]   (singular)
     j. *each [suggestions]   (plural)
     k. *each [advice]   (mass)
     l. *every [suggestions]   (plural)
     m. *every [advice]   (mass)
     n. *most [suggestion]   (singular)

Thus, each quantity word must have associated with it one or more rules saying what kind(s) of common-noun phrases it will accept. The specifications for several of these words are given in (35).

(35) a. [MANY CNP$_{Pl}$]
     b. [THREE CNP$_{Pl}$]
     c. [SOME CNP$_{Pl}$]
     d. [SOME CNP$_{Mass}$]
     e. [ONE CNP$_{Sg}$]
     f. [MUCH CNP$_{Mass}$]
     g. [ANY CNP$_{Pl}$]
     h. [ANY CNP$_{Sg}$]
     i. [ANY CNP$_{Mass}$]
     j. [ALL CNP$_{Pl}$]

     k. [ALL CNP$_{Mass}$]
     l. [EACH CNP$_{Sg}$]
     m. [EVERY CNP$_{Sg}$]
     n. [MOST CNP$_{Pl}$]
     o. [MOST CNP$_{Mass}$]

Four of these words allow more than one type of common-noun phrase. SOME, ALL, and MOST allow either a plural noun or a mass noun, and ANY allows all three of the relevant types.

Exercises

1. For each of the following noun phrases, draw a detailed tree diagram:
     a. many gargoyles
     b. some people
     c. all water
     d. every picture of Fred
     e. several approaches to the problem

2. Below are listed several English nouns. With each one are two specifications. The first indicates whether the noun can be a count noun; the second indicates whether it can be a mass noun. For each of the sixteen specifications, give an example to justify it. Note: The justification for a "no" specification should be an *unacceptable* example.

		Count noun?	*Mass noun?*
a.	pie	yes	yes
b.	thing	yes	no
c.	paper	yes	yes
d.	evidence	no	yes
e.	shoe	yes	no
f.	clothing	no	yes
g.	machine	yes	no
h.	equipment	no	yes

5.1.5   Bare Noun Phrases

In all of the noun phrases that we have examined so far, the common-noun phrase combines with some preceding word or phrase to make up a noun phrase. English also allows noun phrases in which the common-noun phrase occurs without any accompanying element. Each of the following sentences contains one noun phrase of this type:

(36) a. Jock wants to buy *cookies*.
     b. Smith sells *pictures of the White House*.

     c. Horton eats *veal.*

     d. *Advice* is cheap.

The above examples are all either plural nouns or mass nouns. The sentences in (37) show that the same possibility is not available for singular nouns.

(37) a. *Jock wants to buy *cookie.*

     b. *Smith sells *picture of the White House.*

For convenience, we will refer to noun phrases of the type in (36) as *bare noun phrases.* Their structure is given in the following rule:

(38) A noun phrase can consist of a mass or plural common-noun phrase alone.

For the italicized noun phrases in (36), this rule gives the structures in (39).

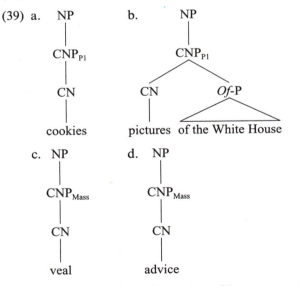

Let us turn now from the syntax of bare noun phrases to a consideration of how they are used in English. We will find that the simplicity of the syntactic rules for their formation is not matched by a corresponding simplicity in the rules for their interpretation. The next few paragraphs will give a brief sketch of the possibilities.

To begin with, bare noun phrases are the most usual choice for predicate noun phrases when plural nouns or mass nouns are involved.

(40) a. Your friends are *Europeans*.
　　b. This substance is *fructose*.

In addition, these noun phrases are used in so-called *generic* sentences, which convey some general truth.

(41) a. *Ostriches* are large flightless birds.
　　b. *Beer* is made from barley and hops.
　　c. *Pepper* makes people sneeze.

Another use is seen in sentences like those in (42), in which habitual activities of the subjects are identified.

(42) a. John sells *shoes*.
　　b. Sally brews *beer*.

A final use is seen in sentences that are neither generic nor habitual, where the use of a quantity word like unstressed *some* is also quite natural.

(43) a. Norma has *mice* in her kitchen.
　　b. Norma has *some mice* in her kitchen.

(44) a. Gerald must have put *rum* in these cookies.
　　b. Gerald must have put *some rum* in these cookies.

The difference in meaning between the (a) and (b) sentences in these pairs is very small, and not easy to describe. It seems to be primarily that the (a) sentences express something about kind, but nothing about quantity. By contrast, the (b) sentences give at least a minimal indication of quantity, even if this indication only comes from *some,* the vaguest of the English quantity words.

In section 5.2, we will discover one other important use for bare noun phrases.

5.1.6　Elementary Noun Phrases Introduced by *A (n)*

A final variety of elementary noun phrase is illustrated in (45).

(45) a. a fossil
　　b. an apple
　　c. a cousin of the king

These noun phrases consist of the word *a* or *an* followed by a common-noun phrase.

As a preliminary matter, let us note that the choice between *a* and *an* depends completely on the first sound of the following word. If the first sound is a consonant, then *a* is used; if the first sound is a vowel, then *an* is chosen. For the operation of this rule, the actual sound is more important than the spelling. Thus, we find contrasts such as the one in (46).

(46) a. Fred is *an only child.*
     b. We are planning *a one-year celebration.*

Even though both *only* and *one* start with the same letter, the first actual sound of *only* is [o], whereas the first actual sound of *one* is [w].

For the purposes of syntax, then, we can think of these two words *a* and *an* as different forms of a single linguistic element. Adopting the traditional term for this element, we will refer to it as the *indefinite article* (*Art* in tree diagrams). The relevant rule for noun phrases is given in (47).

(47) A noun phrase can consist of the indefinite article plus a common-noun phrase.

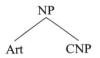

Tree diagrams for the sentences in (45) are given in (48).

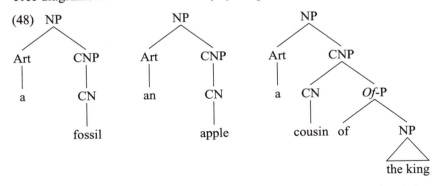

Now let us consider how noun phrases introduced by the indefinite article behave in comparison with noun phrases of types that we have already studied. In some respects, the indefinite article is similar to the numeral *one*, from which it is descended historically. Both elements are limited to common-noun phrases headed by singular count nouns. This shared restriction is illustrated in (49)–(51).

(49) a.   Carol offered *a suggestion*.   (singular count noun)
     b.   Carol offered *one suggestion*.

(50) a.   *Carol offered *a suggestions*.   (plural count noun)
     b.   *Carol offered *one suggestions*.

(51) a.   *Carol offered *an advice*.   (mass noun)
     b.   *Carol offered *one advice*.

Thus, at first glance, the indefinite article gives the appearance of being a special unstressed form of the numeral *one*.

A careful examination, though, reveals several respects in which the article *a(n)* differs from the numeral *one* and from other numerals. In the first place, *a(n)* is natural in predicate noun phrases, whereas numerals are not.

(52) a.   Jerry's niece is *a doctor*.
     b.   ?Jerry's nieces are *seven doctors*.

In the same way, many nonpredicate noun phrases where *a(n)* is natural sound odd when they are introduced by *unstressed* numerals.

(53) a.   Yesterday Ned succeeded in selling a páinting.
     b.   ?Yesterday Ned succeeded in selling nine páintings.
          (with low stress on *nine*)

An observation of the opposite sort concerns certain special situations in which unstressed numerals occur naturally.

(54) a.   MY three uncles are bigger than YOUR three uncles.
          (low stress on *three*)
     b.   THESE four books are more popular than THOSE four books.
          (low stress on *four*)

In such situations, we might expect that we could also use an unstressed version of *one*. But neither *one* itself nor the indefinite article is acceptable here, and the indefinite article is, if anything, worse.

(55) a.   ?*MY one uncle is bigger than YOUR one uncle.
     b.   *MY an uncle is bigger than YOUR an uncle.

Thus, in the one situation where unstressed numerals are natural, the indefinite article is completely impossible.

If the indefinite article does not belong with the numerals, then what linguistic elements does it belong with? In a number of contexts, it appears to give rise to noun phrases that are the singular equivalents of the bare noun phrases discussed in the preceding subsection. This parallel shows up very clearly in the predicate noun phrases in (56).

(56) a. Jerry's niece is *a doctor*.   (singular predicate noun phrase)
     b. Jerry's nieces are *doctors*.   (plural predicate noun phrase)

It also shows up in the generic noun phrases in (57).

(57) a. *A hummingbird* eats constantly.   (singular generic noun phrase)
     b. *Hummingbirds* eat constantly.   (plural generic noun phrase)

These examples might lead us to suppose that a noun phrase introduced by the indefinite article should just be considered a singular count version of a bare noun phrase.

Other contexts exist, though, in which the indefinite article shows a closer kinship to the unstressed quantity word *some*, itself the vaguest of the quantity words discussed earlier in this chapter. In the context of (58), for instance, a bare noun phrase is much less natural than one introduced by *some*.

(58) a. ?Yesterday Ted finally succeeded in selling *paintings*.
     b. Yesterday Ted finally succeeded in selling *some paintings*.

Even though the bare noun phrase is unnatural here, a noun phrase introduced by the indefinite article sounds perfectly normal.

(59) Yesterday Ted finally succeeded in selling *a painting*.

Thus, in this instance, a singular noun phrase introduced by the indefinite article is closer to a plural introduced by *some* than it is to a bare plural.

The import of all of these observations is that the indefinite article has two distinct uses in English. In its first use, it creates singular noun phrases that correspond to the bare noun phrases of the preceding section. In its second use, it is interpreted as a singular quantity word corresponding to the unstressed *some* that occurs with plurals and mass nouns.

5.1.7 A Special Possibility for Proper Nouns

In section 5.1.1, proper nouns were described as "typically" appearing by themselves in noun phrases. In their most common, basic use, this is exactly what they do. However, the rules of English also allow them to be used as if they were common nouns. This use is illustrated in (60).

(60) a. *No John Smiths* attended the meeting.
    b. *This John Smith* lives in Brookline.
    c. Greta knows *thirteen John Smiths*.
    d. I have never met *a John Smith*.
    e. *John Smiths* almost never have unlisted telephone numbers.

These examples might tempt us to believe that there is really no difference between proper nouns and common nouns. But let us see what the consequences would be if we were to drop this distinction. A first consequence is that if *John Smith* were a common noun, it would have to be a count singular noun, as its occurrence with the indefinite article in (60d) shows. But it would then go against the rule that only plural common nouns and mass common nouns can stand by themselves.

(61) a.   *John Smith* issued a plea.
    b.   *Mayor issued a plea.
       (Compare: *The mayor* issued a plea.)

The best thing to say about these examples, then, seems to be the following: although *John Smith* may be used *as if* it were a common noun (meaning specifically "a person named John Smith"), it is in essence a member of the quite distinct class of proper nouns. In chapter 10, when we consider the possibilities for modification in various types of noun phrases, we will see additional reasons for distinguishing between a proper noun like *John Smith* and a common noun like *mayor*.

There is one additional way in which proper nouns can be used as if they were common nouns.

(62) a. Jack works for *an Adolf Hitler*.
    b. The president of the company doubts that he will be able to hire *any Einsteins*.

In this use, the proper names refer not to people who have certain names, but instead to people who are like certain famous people who have those names.

5.1.8 Some Special Combined Forms

Before leaving the topic of elementary noun phrases, we need to note the existence of some special English words that are interpreted as a combination of a quantity word and a noun. These forms are illustrated in (63).

(63) a. Someone did something.
  b. Nobody said anything to anybody.
  c. Everyone looked everywhere.

The four English quantity words that can serve as the first element in these combinations are *some, any, no,* and *every.* The four noun-like stems to which they can be attached are *-one, -body, -thing,* and *-where.* The first two of these (*-one* and *-body*) denote human entities, *-thing* denotes a nonhuman entity, and *-where* denotes a place and is used to form locative and motion phrases.

Such forms will be referred to as *quantifier + noun combinations* and will be analyzed as fusions of a quantity element and a (highly defective) common-noun phrase. This analysis gives rise to the very special tree diagrams in (64).

(64)

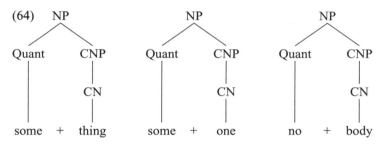

5.2 PARTITIVE NOUN PHRASES

In this section, we examine *partitive noun phrases*—special noun-phrase constructions in which *of* phrases play a role analogous to that played by common-noun phrases in the structures considered up to this point.

5.2.1 Partitive Noun Phrases Introduced by Quantity Words

Let us first consider a situation in which we wish to refer to a part of some plural or mass entity that we can identify by a noun phrase. In the following sets of noun phrases, the (a) phrase is just a noun phrase, and the remaining examples illustrate larger noun phrases denoting parts of these entities.

(65) a. [those suggestions]
  b. *some* of [those suggestions]
  c. *many* of [those suggestions]

    d. *three* of [those suggestions]
    e. *all* of [those suggestions]

(66) a. [George's advice]
      b. *some* of [George's advice]
      c. *much* of [George's advice]
      d. *all* of [George's advice]

For these noun phrases, we need the rule in (67).

(67) **A noun phrase can be formed by combining a quantity word with an *of* phrase.**

The trees in (68) show complete structures for one example each from (65) and (66).

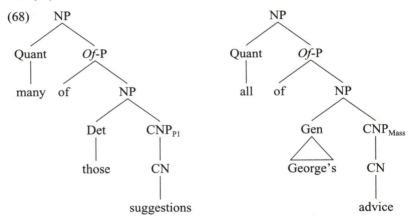

It is necessary to impose restrictions on the use of quantity words when they occur in partitive structures, just as it is when they occur in elementary noun phrases. For instance, we saw earlier that *many* may not combine with a mass common-noun phrase to make an elementary noun phrase (*many advice). Likewise, *many* cannot be used in a partitive structure with a noun phrase built around a mass noun (**many of the advice*).

In one respect, however, the restrictions that hold for nonpartitive noun phrases are different from those that hold for partitive noun phrases. We see the difference when we look at examples involving words like *one* and *each*.

(69) a. one suggestion   *one of the suggestion
     b. *one suggestions   one of the suggestions

(70) a. each suggestion   *each of the suggestion
     b. *each suggestions   each of the suggestions

These examples show that words like *one* and *each*, which require a singular count noun in nonpartitive noun phrases, require a plural count noun when they occur with a partitive *of* phrase. Thus, as far as the partitive construction is concerned, the major division in the class of quantity words is between those that can occur with a plural noun phrase (*many, several, one, three, each*) and those that can occur with a mass noun phrase (*much, less*). Several words, of course, belong to both subclasses (*some, any, none, enough*).

Exercises

1. Draw a detailed tree diagram for each of the following noun phrases:
   a. much of this cheese
   b. many of George's colleagues
   c. few of Martha's portraits of Bill
   d. two of Alice's sister's articles

For the last of these noun phrases, review your answer to exercise 3 at the end of subsection 5.1.3.

2. All of the partitive structures presented in the text have been built up from noun phrases containing either mass nouns or plural count nouns. These are by far the most commonly used nouns in partitive structures. However, it is also possible to find partitive structures built around singular count nouns, as the following sentences show:

(i)   [Most of John's *boat*] has been repainted.
(ii)   [Some of the *record*] contained evidence of wrongdoing.
(iii) [None of the *story*] has appeared in your newspaper.
(iv)   [Much of that *theory*] is unfounded.

(Here we can take *none* to be the equivalent in the partitive construction of the *no* that appears as a quantity word in elementary noun phrases.)
    Not all quantity words are acceptable with singular-count-noun partitives.

(v)   *[Each of John's *boat*] has been repainted.
(vi)   *[Many of the *record*] contained evidence of wrongdoing.
(vii) *[One of the *story*] has appeared in your newspaper.

Try to devise a general rule that dictates which quantity words allow partitives built on singular count nouns. The rule might take the following form: "If a certain quantity word allows ... in elementary noun phrases, then it allows partitive structures based on singular count nouns."

5.2.2 Partitive Noun Phrases Built around Measure Nouns

In the preceding sections, we have seen several examples of English words that indicate quantity (*many, several, three,* etc.). In addition to these words, there are a large number of quantity-indicating words that are much more noun-like in their behavior, in that they themselves can be preceded by quantity words and the indefinite article. These words include common terms for weight, length, and volume (e.g., *pound, ounce, yard, inch, quart,* and *pint*) and also words that have an alternative use as names of containers (*bottle, can, carton,* and *bag*). We can use these words to form partitive constructions based on definite noun phrases, just as we could with *several, much,* and *three.*

(71) a. one *pound* of [those beans]
     b. three *feet* of [that wire]
     c. a *quart* of [Bob's cider]
     d. two *cartons* of [the yogurt]
     e. several *boxes* of [those strawberries]

The structures that we propose for these examples will be different from those proposed for quantity words. Each of these measure nouns will be treated in the same way as other common nouns. In particular, each will head a common-noun phrase and take an *of* phrase as a complement. An illustrative tree diagram is given in (72).

(72)

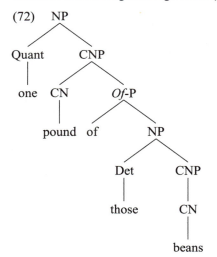

In addition to permitting *of* phrases that contain definite noun phrases, measure nouns permit *of* phrases that contain bare noun phrases.

(73) a. one pound of [beans]
    b. three feet of [wire]
    c. a quart of [cider]
    d. two cartons of [yogurt]
    e. several boxes of [strawberries]

Here measure nouns part company with quantity words, as the unacceptable examples in (74) show.

(74) a. *many of [beans]
    b. *some of [wire]
    c. *much of [cider]
    d. *none of [yogurt]
    e. *one of [strawberries]

One possible explanation for the unacceptability of these examples is that another structure already exists for these words that does the same work, namely, the elementary structure discussed in subsection 5.1.4. In effect, the partitive noun phrases in (74) are "crowded out" by the elementary noun phrases in (75).

(75) a. many beans
    b. some wire
    c. much cider
    d. no yogurt
    e. one strawberry

For measure nouns, the situation is different. As the examples in (76) show, they cannot occur in elementary structures (if we leave aside the special abbreviated syntax of recipes).

(76) a. *one pound beans
    b. *three feet wire
    c. *a quart cider
    d. *two cartons yogurt
    e. *several boxes strawberries

Since these measure nouns do not occur in elementary structures, there is no elementary-noun-phrase competitor for the partitive construction with a bare noun phrase. As a result, such partitive constructions are possible with measure nouns, so that *one pound of beans* and *three feet of wire* are perfectly acceptable.

Exercise

1. Draw a detailed tree diagram for each of the following noun phrases:
    a. several truckloads of furniture
    b. three bushels of those peaches
    c. two boxes of John's letters to Marsha

5.2.3   Some Defective Measure Nouns

In the last two subsections, we have seen reasons for distinguishing between quantity words and measure nouns. We can summarize the differences as follows:

(77) a. Quantity words may occur in elementary noun phrases (*one book, many apples*), whereas measure nouns may not (**one pound beans, *three feet wire*).

   b. Quantity words may not occur with bare-noun-phrase partitive structures (**one of books, *many of apples*), whereas measure nouns may (*one pound of beans, three feet of wire*).

   c. Quantity words may not be preceded by numerals (**one many of the books, *several much of the beer*), whereas measure nouns may (*one pound of the beans, three feet of the wire*).

In this section, we will consider several English words whose behavior places them halfway between these two clear classes.

The first word that deserves special mention is the word *few*. In the use that we have seen already (*few books, few of your friends*), it is just an ordinary quantity word. However, it also occurs in combination with the word *a*, which gives it a somewhat noun-like appearance

(78) a few of your friends

Despite its article + noun appearance, though, *a few* does not really act like an article followed by a measure noun. In the first place, it occurs in elementary structures rather than bare-noun-phrase partitive structures, thus resembling a quantity word like *several* rather than an article + measure-noun sequence like *a pound*.

(79) a.   a few olives, *a few of olives
    b.   several olives, *several of olives
    c.   *a pound olives, a pound of olives

In the second place, we cannot replace the indefinite article preceding *few* by the numeral *one*, as we can the indefinite article before a measure noun.

(80) a. *one few olives
     b. one pound of olives

These contrasts suggest that the two-word sequence *a few* should be treated as a single compound quantity word. The tree diagrams in (81) indicate the structures that arise in this analysis.

(81)

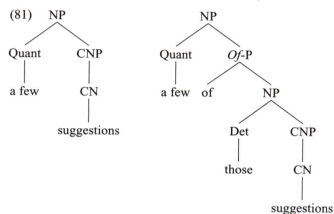

Another intermediate word is *lot*, which occurs either with the indefinite article (*a lot*) or by itself in the plural (*lots*). Unlike *a few*, both *a lot* and *lots* occur in partitive structures rather than in elementary structures.

(82) a. a lot of suggestions, lots of suggestions
     b. *a lot suggestions, *lots suggestions

However, unlike measure nouns, *lot* and *lots* may not be counted, if we ignore the technical meaning that the word has in commercial affairs (*John bought several lots of old books*).

(83) a. *one lot of suggestions
     b. *several lots of suggestions

We see a similar pattern for the word *deal*, as used in the combinations *a good deal* and *a great deal*.

(84) a. a good deal of money, a great deal of money
     b. *a good deal money, *a great deal money
     c. *several good deals of money, *several great deals of money

In view of their similarity to measure nouns in every characteristic except the possibility of being counted, we will treat *lot* and *deal* as "defective" measure nouns. As shown in (85), we will assign them structures just like those of other measure nouns.

(85)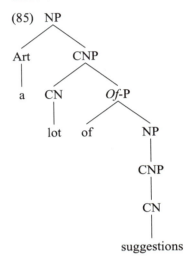

The major difference between *lot* and the ordinary measure nouns is that *lot* has no independent meaning as a noun, but instead must combine either with *a* or with the plural marker to make a fixed idiom. Because of its lack of an independent meaning, any attempt to preface it with other quantity words results in a combination that has no meaning attached to it.

Another class of words whose behavior leaves them somewhere between quantity words and measure nouns consists of number words such as *dozen, hundred,* and *thousand.* These words are like measure nouns in their capacity to be preceded by numerals and quantity words.

(86) a. one dozen of your eggs
      b. one hundred of his books

Yet even here, they are peculiar in requiring a singular form even when the word before them would ordinarily require a plural noun.

(87) a.   three hundred of your friends
      b. *three hundreds of your friends

(88) a.   several thousand of Karen's supporters
      b. *several thousands of Karen's supporters

In addition, they are like quantity words and unlike measure nouns in that they occur in elementary noun phrases rather than in bare-noun-phrase partitives.

(89) a. one dozen roses   *one dozen of roses
     b. three hundred books   *three hundred of books
     c. several thousand supporters   *several thousand of supporters

Even here, though, there is a complication. These words may all be used in plural form when they are not accompanied by a preceding quantity word. When they do occur in this way, they require partitive structures rather than elementary structures.

(90) a. dozens of roses   *dozens roses
     b. hundreds of friends   *hundreds friends
     c. thousands of supporters *thousands supporters

Exercise

1. *Number* and *bunch* are two more English words that allow partitive structures.

(i)   A number of letters were sent.
(ii) Joe earned a bunch of prizes.

Construct some experimental sentences that will provide evidence indicating how *a number* and *a bunch* behave. In particular, do they resemble *a few, a lot,* or *a(n)* plus a measure noun? (Do not consider here the word *bunch* as it is used to refer to a collection of flowers, vegetables, fruits, and so on. On this use, *bunch* is a straightforward measure noun.)

5.2.4 A Special Compound Structure: *All* + Numeral

The quantity word *all* can combine with a following numeral to form a two-word sequence that itself has the force of a quantity word. The partitive noun phrases italicized in (91) provide examples.

(91) a. *All four of your sons* are geniuses.
     b. Gordon ate *all thirteen of the pancakes.*

These special forms can be given by the rule in (92).

(92) A special compound quantity structure can be formed by combining *all* with a numeral.

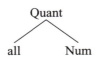

The tree diagram in (93) shows the structure of the noun phrase in (91a) that contains a compound quantity structure.

(93)

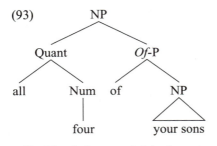

Besides being special in its own right, this combination of *all* plus a numeral enters into a special larger structure, illustrated in (94).

(94) a. *All four lions* eat meat.
    b. George replied to *all three letters*.

An obvious structure for these noun phrases is one in which they are treated as elementary noun phrases.

(95) a.   b.

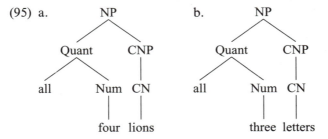

Although these seem to be perfectly ordinary structures, their interpretation is not ordinary at all. Unlike what happens with the partitive examples discussed in the preceding subsection, the omission of the numeral from the sentences in (94) changes their interpretations quite drastically.

(96) a. *All lions* eat meat.
    b. George replied to *all letters*.

In order to get close paraphrases of the sentences in (94), we need to resort to partitive noun phrases.

(97) a. *All four of the lions* eat meat.
    b. George replied to *all three of the letters*.

Thus, noun phrases such as *all four lions* have the odd property of being elementary in form, but partitive in interpretation.

5.2.5   Special Noun Phrases Introduced by *All* and *Both*

As noted in subsection 5.2.1, *all* is like other quantity words in its capacity to occur in partitive noun phrases.

(98) a. Karen met *all of the senators.*
     b. Joseph insulted *all of Fred's cousins.*

As a special extra possibility, *all* can occur with the same following definite noun phrases, but without any intervening *of*:

(99) a. Karen met *all the senators.*
     b. Joseph insulted *all Fred's cousins.*

Here again we clearly have noun phrases with a partitive interpretation. These examples appear to call for the following rule:

(100) A noun phrase can consist of the quantity word *all* followed by a noun phrase.

This rule gives rise to the structures in (101) for the italicized noun phrases in (99).

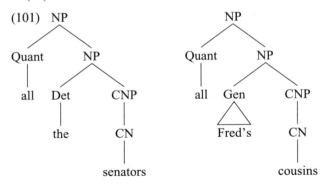

The last special structure to be dealt with involves the word *both.* In addition to appearing in the regular partitive structure illustrated in (102a), *both* appears in the structure illustrated in (102b).

(102) a. Julie fed *both of the alligators.*
      b. Julie fed *both alligators.*

Like *all four lions,* the structure in (102b) is elementary in form, but partitive in interpretation. The structure for *both alligators* is diagrammed in (103).

(103)

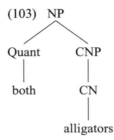

5.3   THE USE OF THE DEFINITE ARTICLE

Now that we have examined the structures of a variety of types of noun phrases, including structures introduced by the determiner *the,* let us look briefly at the conditions under which this particular word must be used. *The* is one of the most common words in the English language. In even a short conversation, a fluent speaker in effect decides many times whether or not to use it. Decades of linguistic research have shown that the unconscious rules responsible for the use of this word require complex calculations on the part of speakers and hearers. Besides being a source of challenging puzzles for linguists, these complexities have been a source of frustration for many adult learners of English. The following subsections will summarize the most essential conditions on its use.

5.3.1   The Use of the Definite Article to Mark "Registration" of Entities

As noted in subsection 5.1.3, noun phrases introduced by definite articles belong to the larger class of *definite noun phrases,* in company with pronouns and noun phrases introduced by genitives. This class stands in contrast to the general class of *indefinite noun phrases,* which includes noun phrases introduced by quantity words, numerals, and the indefinite article, as well as bare noun phrases of the sort described in subsection 5.1.5. Whether a speaker should use a definite noun phrase or an indefinite one depends to a significant degree on whether the entity being referred to has the status of *registered* or *unregistered* in the discourse at that point. The general rule is given in (104).

(104) A definite noun phrase must be used if the entity is already
registered in the discourse; an indefinite noun phrase must be used
if the entity is unregistered.

Two simple examples illustrating the concept of registration are given
in (105).

(105) a. George found *three bananas* on the counter and *two
apples* in the refrigerator. *The bananas* were green, but
the apples were ripe.
   b. On the way to market yesterday, we met *a man* and *a woman*.
The man was playing a fiddle, and *the woman* was playing a
guitar.

In (105a), the noun phrases introduced by *three* and *two* register new
entities in the discourse. Once these entities are registered, the references
to them in the next sentence make use of the definite article. We see
exactly the same distinction in (105b).

In both instances, it would have been odd to start out with definite
articles, assuming that the entities had not been mentioned earlier in the
discourse.

(106) a. ?George found *the three bananas* on the counter and *the two
apples* in the refrigerator. *The bananas* were green, but *the
apples* were ripe.
   b. ?On the way to market yesterday, we met *the man* and *the
woman*. *The man* was playing a fiddle, and *the woman* was
playing a guitar.

Example (106a) would be acceptable only if prior reference had been
made to the three bananas and the two apples, in other words, only if
these entities had been registered earlier in this discourse or in some prior
discourse that formed part of the background for this one. The same
comments hold true for (106b).

At least as unnatural are the examples in (107), which display a repeti-
tion of indefinite noun phrases instead of a switch to definite ones.

(107) a. ?George found *three bananas* on the counter and *two apples* in
the refrigerator. *Three bananas* were green, but *two apples* were
ripe.
   b. ?On the way to market yesterday, we met *a man* and *a woman*.
A man was playing a fiddle, and *a woman* was playing a guitar.

What makes these examples unnatural is the continued use of indefinite noun phrases after the entities being referred to have already been registered.

Let us consider now in more detail how an entity is "registered" in a discourse. We have already seen one extremely basic way, illustrated in (105), where registration is effected by using an indefinite noun phrase to refer to the entity. For convenience in what follows, we will refer to registrations of this type as *standard registrations*.

The following sequence of two sentences shows another way in which an entity may be registered:

(108) We just received *an old Studebaker* today. I told Jonah to check *the carburetor* before he did anything else.

Here, at first glance, it would appear that the only entity that is registered in the first sentence is an old Studebaker, which undergoes a standard registration. With the registration of that entity, however, a number of other entities are registered implicitly, in an operation that is parasitic on the registration of the car. These parasitically registered entities include the following, among many others:

(109) a. a carburetor
       b. a steering wheel
       c. an engine
       d. a brake pedal

Because these additional entities are automatically registered along with the registration of the old Studebaker, they absolutely require the definite article as soon as they are mentioned themselves. Thus, for example, it would be unacceptable to use (110) in a situation where the carburetor referred to in the second sentence is understood as belonging to the car referred to in the first sentence.

(110) ?We just received *an old Studebaker* today. I told Jonah to check *a carburetor* before he did anything else.

Oddly enough, a definite article that marks such a parasitic registration can occur prior to the noun phrase that sets up the standard registration on which it is based. A sequence of this sort is illustrated in (111).

(111) Kevin: What is Henry using to power his home generator?
       Sarah: He took *the engine* out of *a tractor*.

Here the new entity registered in Sarah's answer to Kevin's question is a tractor, and the method of registration is just the standard one of referring to the entity with an indefinite noun phrase (*a tractor*). The use of the definite article in the reference to an engine that has not been previously registered is allowed here on a promissory basis: such a use is permitted if the standard registration on which it is parasitic is provided within the immediately following context.

Another nonstandard use of the definite article is found in certain curious situations in which an indefinite article is also possible. We look first at the version of the dialogue that contains an indefinite article.

(112) Roberta: Where did James meet Clara?
       Gordon: He met her at *a* reception given by the Yale Law dean
       for incoming students in the fall of 1965.

Here now is the same dialogue with a definite article before the noun *reception:*

(113) Roberta: Where did James meet Clara?
       Gordon: He met her at *the* reception given by the Yale Law dean
       for incoming students in the fall of 1965.

The difference between these two versions of Gordon's answer to Roberta's question is rather subtle. In (112), Gordon's choice of the indefinite article signals the registration of a new entity in the standard way. By relying on a standard registration, he in effect acknowledges that this reception may not at this point be part of Roberta's background knowledge. In (113), by contrast, he presents the reception as if it were already registered. In effect, he uses the definite article to reflect the status of the reception as part of his own prior background knowledge, and asks Roberta to make whatever adjustments she needs to make in her prior knowledge in order to catch up. As shown in (114), the latter tactic does not work when the speaker fails to be sufficiently informative about the entity that is to be registered retroactively.

(114) Roberta: Where did James meet Clara?
       Gordon: He met her at the reception.
       Roberta: What reception? What are you talking about?

The conversation in (113) works because the information that Roberta can extract from Gordon's answer is the same as what she could get from the somewhat cumbersome answer given in (115), where use of the definite article in the second part of the sentence is preceded by a standard registration in the first part.

(115) Roberta: Where did James meet Clara?
Gordon: *A* reception was given by the Yale Law dean for incoming students in the fall of 1965, and he met her at *the* reception.

Another nonstandard way in which entities can be registered is simply by being present in the speech situation. Suppose George and Alma are attending a large potluck supper. George can look at the array of dishes spread out on the table, and the following conversation can take place:

(116) George: I wonder who brought *the* carrot cake?
Alma: I don't know. Maybe Kathy will know.

Here the carrot cake counts as being previously registered simply by being present where both conversational participants can see it. In the event that the hearer fails to see it, we typically get the kind of objection shown in (117), where the hearer refuses to acknowledge the registration of any entity bearing this description.

(117) George: I wonder who brought *the* carrot cake.
Alma: What carrot cake? I don't see a carrot cake. What are you talking about?

As a final note, we observe that an entity that has been registered in one conversation can maintain its registration into an entirely new conversation. The sequence in (118) and (119) is illustrative.

(118) (At 10:00 A.M.)
Roger: What are you looking for?
Martha: I had *some* pictures of that accident scene, and I seem to have mislaid them.

(119) (At 11:35 A.M.)
Roger: Why are you looking so cheerful all of a sudden?
Martha: I found *the* pictures of that accident scene.

One extreme case of this continuing registration across conversations is the permanent registration of certain entities, as illustrated in (120).

(120) a. Did anyone remember to feed *the cat*?
b. *The children* need to get booster shots this month.

Here *the cat* might refer to a family pet; likewise, *the children* could be used to refer to the children in the speaker's family. Among the registered entities of this last type are those that have a special, permanent place in the human environment. The noun phrases *the sun, the moon,* and *the stars* are just a few of many examples of this type.

5.3.2   Another Restriction Associated with the Definite Article

In all of the examples considered in subsection 5.3.1, the entity that was referred to with a definite article was the same as the entity that was registered. Slightly more complicated conversational situations provide evidence of another requirement that holds for definite-article use in addition to the requirement that the entity be registered. This requirement shows up most clearly in cases where the registered entity is plural, but the later reference is to some subset of that entity. An example of a sequence of sentences in which this requirement is violated is given in (121).

(121)   ?George found *three bananas* on the counter and *two apples* in the refrigerator. He put *the banana* in his pocket, and ate *the apple* on the spot.

In a case like this, where the references in the second sentence are to only one element of a plural entity, we must make another registration, by means of indefinite partitive structures.

(122)   George found *three bananas* on the counter and *two apples* in the refrigerator. He put *one of the bananas* in his pocket, and ate *one of the apples* on the spot.

We now have two newly registered entities, each a subpart of the original plural entities. The new registration of the single banana in George's pocket can now justify a later definite article.

(123)   George found *three bananas* on the counter and *two apples* in the refrigerator. He put *one of the bananas* in his pocket, and ate *one of the apples* on the spot. He didn't get around to eating *the banana* until late in the evening.

A similar problem with using the definite article arises when multiple entities have been registered that all meet the same description. We see a case of this sort in the conversation in (124), where several different students are mentioned.

(124) Georgia: I've been getting a lot of complaints about your calculus class. One student came in a week ago and said he can't understand your homework assignments. Another one came in a day later and said she can't read your writing on the blackboard. Still another one came in a day after that and said you take a long time to turn their exams back.

Gregory: Actually, the two students came to see me yesterday.

Georgia: Which two of the students are you talking about?

Here Georgia's initial statement has had the effect of registering three separate entities, each of which qualifies as a student. When Gregory uses the definite article to refer to just two of these entities, Georgia quickly registers her confusion. It would have been much more acceptable for Gregory to continue the conversation in the following way:

(125) Gregory: Actually, two of the students came to see me yesterday.

Georgia: Which two were they?

Although Georgia is still asking Gregory for more information, it is clear that in (125) she is not questioning his right to express himself in the manner that he did, as she was in (124). The moral here is that when a definite article is used with a certain description, that description must not apply to registered entities in addition to the one or more to which the speaker intends to refer.

Exceptions to this restriction are possible chiefly in examples like (123). Here one of the originally registered set of three bananas has been given a special registration of its own that sets it apart from the other two. By virtue of the special prominence so conferred, it is entitled to be referred to by itself with a definite article, even though other bananas have been registered.

Exercises

1. In Austin, Texas, a city with several major hospitals, the following discourse would be perfectly natural:

Speaker A: Did you hear the news? John is in the hospital.

Speaker B: That's too bad. Do you know which hospital?

Speaker A: He's at Saint David's.

Explain why the definite article with the noun *hospital* is unexpected, given what was said in the text. What would the text discussion have led you to expect? What special rule could be given for this case? Note: This use of the definite article is characteristic only of American English; the British equivalent would be *John is in hospital.*

2. The following examples illustrate some special situations in which the definite article is required and some special situations in which it is forbidden:

a.	the Mississippi River	*Mississippi River
b.	the Wabash River	*Wabash River
c.	the James River	*James River
d.	*the Clear Lake	Clear Lake
e.	*the Walden Pond	Walden Pond
f.	*the Waller Creek	Waller Creek
g.	the Great Smoky Mountains	*Great Smoky Mountains
h.	the Adirondacks	*Adirondacks
i.	*the Lookout Mountain	Lookout Mountain
j.	*the Nob Hill	Nob Hill

Try to state some informal general rules that give correct results for these cases. (Do not be surprised if the answer you get seems arbitrary. In particular, the distinctions illustrated here do not follow at all from what has been said in this subsection.)

3. The following passage was written by the noted British comic writer P. G. Wodehouse. The first speaker is Stanley Featherstonehaugh Ukridge.

"When I reach that point in my story, you will see that my pawning of Aunt Julia's brooch was perfectly normal, a straightforward matter of business. How else could I have bought half the dog?"

"Half what dog?"

"Didn't I tell you about the dog?"

"No."

"I must have done. It's the nub of the whole affair."

"Well, you didn't."

"I'm getting this story all wrong," said Ukridge. "I'm confusing you. Let me begin at the beginning." ("The Level Business Head," in *Lord Emsworth and Others,* Penguin Books, Harmondsworth, 1966 (reissued 1973, 1975), p. 201 (originally published 1937))

Explain as clearly as you can what the problem is that arises in this conversation and how the problem forces Ukridge to backtrack.

4. Explain why the definite article in the following sentence is unexpected, given the rules set forth in this subsection.

(i) It hit me in the eye.

What would we have expected that the speaker would have to say? Try to state a rule that would relax the standard requirements on the use of the definite article in just the special type of situation that (i) illustrates.

5.4   THE GERUNDIVE CONSTRUCTION

We turn finally to a curious English construction whose internal organization is quite unlike that found in the noun phrases considered in previous sections of this chapter. Structures of this sort, which will be referred to as *gerundives,* are illustrated in (126).

(126) a. We regret *your having called the police.*
      b. *Martha's getting a splinter in her toe* annoyed Sally.
      c. *The mayor's referring to the theft* was inconvenient for Stuart.

In each of these examples, the italicized phrase consists of two parts. The first part is a genitive construction; the second is a present-participial verb phrase. The two parts for the gerundives given in (126) are as follows:

(127)   *Genitive*   *Present-participial verb phrase*
      a. your   having called the police
      b. Martha's   getting a splinter in her toe
      c. the mayor's   referring to the theft

The genitive is actually optional, as the examples in (128) show.

(128) a. We regret *having called the police.*
      b. *Getting a splinter in her toe* annoyed Sally.
      c. *Referring to the theft* was inconvenient for Stuart.

We can thus state the following rule:

(129) A *gerundive* can consist either of a genitive plus a present-participial verb phrase, or of a present-participial verb phrase alone.

Translating the two possibilities in this rule into tree diagrams gives the structures in (130).

(130) a. Gerundive   b. Gerundive

    Gen   VP_PresPart   VP_PresPart

The relation between the genitive and the verb phrase within the gerundive construction is much like the relation between the subject noun phrase and the finite verb phrase of a simple sentence. Thus, in both (131a) and (131b), *the mayor* is understood as the actor in the event of referring.

(131) a. the mayor's referring to the theft
     b. The mayor referred to the theft.

We also saw this relation between the subject and the predicate of a sentence inside a *that* clause, and between the noun phrase after *for* and the infinitival phrase of an infinitival clause.

(132) a. I know [that the mayor referred to the theft].
     b. We would hate [for the mayor to refer to the theft].

From these internal similarities to clauses, we might expect that the gerundive would be clause-like in its external syntax as well. As a matter of fact, though, it is much closer in external behavior to the noun phrases studied earlier in this chapter than it is to the clauses studied in chapter 4. In the first place, gerundives do not appear as pseudocomplements linked to the substitute subject *it*. For instance, of the two examples in (134), each of which corresponds to one of the unpostponed examples in (133), only the first is completely natural.

(133) a. *That John went to town* surprised us.
     b. *John's going to town* surprised us.

(134) a. *It* surprised us *that John went to town.*
     b. ?*It* surprised us *John's going to town.*

To the extent that (134b) is acceptable at all, it is because of a possibility that exists even for ordinary noun phrases, that of using a pronoun as subject, and then, as an afterthought, identifying it by a full noun phrase set off by a special intonation at the end of the sentence.

(135) a. It bit me on the ankle, *the puppy that Howard gave me for my birthday.*
     b. They were very helpful, *the people who operate the sawmill.*

This afterthought interpretation and intonation, which are essential for this construction, are necessary to make (134b) acceptable. Thus, an acceptable version of (134b) should be written with a comma, as in (136), just as commas were used in the sentences in (135).

(136) *It* surprised us, *John's going to town.*

No such special interpretation or intonation is involved with sentences like (134a).

    A second external property that gerundives share with ordinary noun phrases in opposition to clauses concerns their appearance as complements of adjectives. Certain adjectives can directly take clauses as complements.

(137) a. Sandra is uncertain *that Fred is competent.*
       b. Sandra is uncertain *how competent Fred is.*

In contrast, they can take noun phrases only indirectly, with the help of the preposition *of.*

(138) a. *Sandra is uncertain *Fred's competence.*
       b. Sandra is uncertain of *Fred's competence.*

Here the gerundives pattern with ordinary noun phrases rather than with clauses.

(139) a. *Sandra is uncertain *Fred's being competent.*
       b. Sandra is uncertain of *Fred's being competent.*

A final property that gerundives share with ordinary noun phrases is their ability to appear in various sentence-internal positions in which clauses are unacceptable. The unacceptable examples in (140) are taken from subsection 4.2.6; corresponding examples with gerundives are given in (141).

(140) a. *Dorothy considers *that the problem is solvable* unlikely.
       b. *Was *that the money had vanished* obvious?
       c. *Sarah wonders whether *that the money had vanished* was obvious.

(141) a. Dorothy considers *Bill's avoiding the question* quite unimportant.
       b. Was *Bill's avoiding the question* really important?
       c. Sarah wonders whether *Bill's avoiding the question* was really important.

Because of these respects in which the external behavior of gerundives is like that of ordinary noun phrases, we will classify gerundives as noun phrases, thus adopting the following simple rule:

(142) A noun phrase can consist of a gerundive.

NP
|
Gerundive

Thus, the tree diagrams in (143) will be adopted for sentences containing this construction.

(143) a.

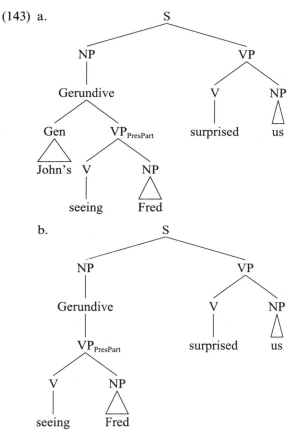

b.

Exercises

1. Draw a tree diagram for each of the following sentences, guiding your efforts at each step by careful attention to the rules developed in this chapter and previous chapters:

  a. Karen's noticing the advertisement prevented the destruction of the neighborhood.
  b. Joe believed that Bernice's congratulating the corporals would make the officers jealous.
  c. Erwin maintains that growing potatoes keeps him young.

2. Some of the present-participial verb phrases that occur without genitive noun phrases clearly deserve to be classified as gerundives. For instance, we would call the italicized phrase in (i) a gerundive, since the longer phrase italicized in (ii) is possible in the same environment.

(i) *Riding in the Derby* disturbed Martha.
(ii) *John's riding in the Derby* disturbed Martha.

However, in other environments, only the verb phrase by itself is acceptable.

(iii)   Janet kept asking for a doctor.
(iv) *Janet kept Bill's asking for a doctor.

These two examples would lead us to say that the verb KEEP takes present-participial verb phrases, rather than saying that it takes gerundives. For each of the following verbs, construct a sentence that shows that the verb can be followed by a present-participial verb phrase. Then construct a sentence that shows whether it should be viewed as taking gerundives or only as taking present-participial verb phrases.

   a. CONTINUE
   b. REPORT
   c. BEGIN
   d. REGRET

Chapter 6

Locative Phrases, Motion Phrases, and Particles

Chapter 3 included some brief remarks about what were referred to as *locative phrases* and *motion phrases*. The purpose at that point was to say just enough to make it possible to talk about complement rules. For instance, we needed to be able to say that *go* combines with a motion phrase to make a verb phrase, whereas *put* makes a verb phrase by combining with a noun phrase and a locative phrase. We noted a few examples of each type of phrase, without looking at the rules for forming them.

6.1 BASIC LOCATIVE-PHRASE AND MOTION-PHRASE STRUCTURES

Perhaps the best way to get an initial idea of the richness of English constructions of these types is to look at some examples. The examples in (1) happen to be locative phrases. With a different verb (*took,* for example), a parallel list could be made for motion phrases.

(1) Joe put the jar

a.	right	back	out	here	in the yard.
b.	——	back	in	there	in the house.
c.	right	——	up	here	on the shelf.
d.	——	——	out	there	in the pasture.
e.	right	——	——	here	in the refrigerator.
f.	——	——	——	here	in the yard.
g.	right	back	——	there	under the cottonwood.
h.	——	back	——	here	in the kitchen.
i.	right	back	up	——	in the attic.
j.	——	back	down	——	in the cellar.
k.	——	back	——	——	in the yard.
l.	right	back	in	here	——.

     m. right back —— here ——.
     n. right —— —— here ——.

All fourteen of the phrases on this list are constructed by combining five elements:

- the word *right*
- the particle *back,* indicating return to a location occupied earlier, or else movement toward, or position in, the rear of some entity
- particles such as *in, out, up,* and *down,* which suggest an implicit contrast relative to some other location
- *here* or *there,* which indicate relative proximity to the speaker
- a prepositional phrase that specifies an absolute location of some kind

All five of these elements are optional, except that at least one of the last four must be present.

With these phrases—in contrast to many of the other phrasal constructions that we have studied—it is difficult to single out one element that is more essential to the phrase than any other and thus can be identified as the head. In the absence of any clear evidence for a more detailed picture of the structure of these phrases, we will assume that they can be divided into two basic parts. The first part is an optional occurrence of the word *right;* the second part is a sequence constructed from the remaining four elements.

(2) A locative phrase or motion phrase can consist of a locative sequence (LocSeq) or a motion sequence (MotSeq), optionally preceded by the word *right*.

(3) A locative or motion sequence can consist of one or more of the following parts, in the order given:

- the particle *back*
- a directional particle
- one of the words *here* or *there*
- a prepositional phrase headed by a preposition of location or motion

These two rules give structures of the sort diagrammed in (4).

(4) a.

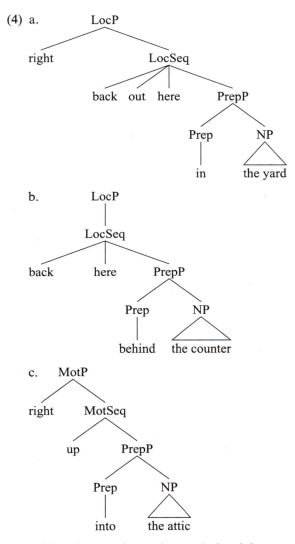

c. At this point, an alternative analysis might appear to be attractive, one in which a sentence like (5) is analyzed as containing four separate motion phrases instead of just one.

(5) John came *back   out   here   into the yard.*

On this alternative analysis, the structure of the verb phrase in this sentence would look like (6).

(6)

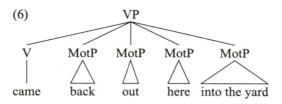

The chief attraction of this view is that each of the parts can appear alone as a motion phrase in its own right.

(7) a. John came *back*.
    b. John came *out*.
    c. John came *here*.
    d. John came *into the yard*.

Despite the initial plausibility of this analysis, there are at least two reasons for viewing *back out here into the yard* as a single phrase in (5). The first is that if each element were really a separate locative phrase in its own right, we would expect a high degree of freedom in the order in which the various elements appear. In fact, we do not find this, as (8) shows.

(8) a. John came   **here   out   back   into the yard*.
    b. John came   **into the yard   out   here   back*.

The second reason for viewing *back out here into the yard* as a single motion phrase is that we can then account for the fact that the whole sequence can move to the front of sentences containing motion verbs such as *come* and *go,* whereas smaller parts cannot move. The sentences in (9) show this.

(9) a.   *Back out here into the yard* came John.
    b. **Here into the yard* came John *back out*.
    c. **Into the yard* came John *back out here*.

6.2 A SPECIAL ORDERING RULE FOR PARTICLES

One syntactic property of certain locative and motion phrases requires special attention. When the locative or motion phrase occurs with the object of a transitive verb, the rules given so far would position it after the object. In some instances, however, we find a different order. In (10) and (11), each (a) example shows the normal order, and each (b) example shows what we will call the *shifted order*.

(10) a. Joe took the garbage *out*.
     b. Joe took *out* the garbage.

(11) a. We carried the money *back*.
     b. We carried *back* the money.

The tree diagrams in (12) show the contrast between the normal order and the shifted order.

(12) a. *Normal order*   b. *Shifted order*

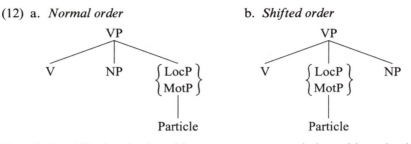

Use of the shifted order is subject to a severe restriction: this order is possible only when the locative or motion phrase consists solely of a particle. The results of violating this restriction are shown in the unacceptable (b) sentences in (13)–(15).

(13) a.   Joe took the garbage *back out*.
     b.   *Joe took *back out* the garbage.

(14) a.   We carried the money *right back*.
     b.   *We carried *right back* the money.

(15) a.   Fred brought some apples *over here*.
     b.   *Fred brought *over here* some apples.

A second condition limiting the shifted word order concerns the object: the particle can be put next to the verb only when the object is not a pronoun. The following sentences show the contrast between full noun phrases and pronouns as direct objects with shifted particles:

(16) a.   Joe brought *Marsha* in.
     b.   Joe brought in *Marsha*.
     c.   Joe brought *her* in.
     d.   *Joe brought in *her*.

(17) a.   We put *the refrigerator* back.
     b.   We put back *the refrigerator*.

    c.   We put *it* back.

    d.   *We put back *it*.

The sentences in (18) show that it is only unstressed pronouns that prevent the shift of the particle.

(18) a. Janice called HIM up.

      b. Janice called up HIM.

This restriction may be a special case of a more general English regularity, to the effect that unstressed pronoun objects cannot be separated from their verbs. Another contrast of this kind is evident in (19).

(19) a.   Jane gave the book to Freddy.

      b.   Jane gave Freddy the book.

      c.   Jane gave it to Freddy.

      d. *Jane gave Freddy it.

Here the noun phrase *the book* can come directly after the verb, as in (19a), or else can be separated from the verb by the indirect object *Freddy,* as in (19b). By contrast, the pronoun *it* has the first option, as in (19c), but does not have the second, as in (19d).

Exercise

1. Draw a tree diagram for each of the following sentences:

    a. Joanna took the packages out.

    b. Jasper brought in the wine.

    c. The sheriff followed us in.

6.3 VERB + PARTICLE IDIOMS

In all of the sentences in which we have seen particles, they have been serving as elements of either locative phrases or motion phrases. Particles used in this way contribute a regular and predictable element of meaning to the sentences in which they occur. In addition, though, we find in English many instances in which particles combine with verbs to give *idiomatic expressions*—expressions whose meanings cannot be deduced from the meanings of their parts. Some intransitive combinations are given in (20), and some transitive ones in (21).

(20) a. Donna *sounded off.* ('Donna stated her opinions forcefully.')

      b. Frank *threw up.*   ('Frank vomited.')

   c. James *flunked out*.   ('James was expelled from school for an excessive number of low grades.')

(21) a. Ruth *sounded* her brother *out*.   ('Ruth elicited her brother's opinions.')
   b. Sidney *called* his boss *up*.   ('Sidney called his boss on the telephone.')
   c. Joe *called* the meeting *off*.   ('Joe canceled the meeting.')
   d. Kevin *knocked* Gregory *out*.   ('Kevin rendered Gregory unconscious.')

The syntax of these particles is almost exactly like the syntax of those that serve as locative or motion phrases. In particular, in a transitive verb phrase they can be shifted to a position immediately after the verb when the object is not a pronoun.

(22) a. Ruth *sounded out* her brother.
   b. Sidney *called up* his boss.
   c. Joe *called off* the meeting.
   d. Kevin *knocked out* Gregory.

For verbs that participate in idioms such as these, complement rules are needed that mention individual particles.

(23) a. [SOUND *off*]
   b. [THROW *up*]
   c. [FLUNK *out*]

(24) a. [SOUND NP *out*]
   b. [CALL NP *up*]
   c. [CALL NP *off*]
   d. [KNOCK NP *out*]

In addition to these special complement rules, these idioms require special semantic statements about the unpredictable meanings associated with them.

Exercise

1. For each of the following sentences, decide whether the particle that it contains is (a) a locative or motion phrase, or (b) part of an idiomatic verb + particle combination. (For some of the examples, the answer may be that it could be either one.) Briefly justify each of your answers.
   a. The airplane took off.
   b. George took his jacket off.

    c. Nancy carried it in.
    d. Sherman carried out Grant's orders.
    e. Jeremy blended in the raisins.
    f. Jerry rubbed out his competitors.
    g. Sandra strolled out.
    h. Terry struck out.
    i. Florence put it down.
    j. Harry knocked it off.

6.4 DISTINGUISHING SHIFTED PARTICLES FROM PREPOSITIONS

Because of the possibility of putting particles between transitive verbs and their objects, two different structures can arise that yield similar sequences of words. The two structures are those shown in (25).

(25) a. *Shifted-particle structure*   b. *Intransitive prepositional structure*

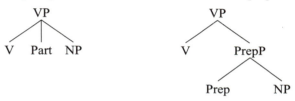

The sentences in (26) illustrate the kind of practical problem that can arise.

(26) a. Nina brought in the armchair.
     b. Nina sat in the armchair.

For each of these sentences, we would like to answer two questions:

• Can it have the shifted-particle structure?
• Can it have the intransitive prepositional structure?

As with many of the practical problems that we have studied, attempting to answer these questions about the particular sentences in (26) forces us to ask the corresponding questions about the verbs BRING and SIT:

• Does this verb allow a shifted-particle structure?
• Does this verb allow an intransitive prepositional structure?

Let us begin by asking the first of these questions. The key experiment depends on something that we already know about particles. If a certain verb truly allows a particle along with a direct object, then putting the particle in the normal position on the right side of the presumptive direct object should yield an acceptable sentence. The simple experimental sentences in (27) give us the answers to our question.

(27) a.   Nina brought the armchair in.
     b.   *Nina sat the armchair in.

Sentence (27a) shows that BRING can take a following direct object and a particle. Thus, we also conclude that BRING can occur in the shifted-particle configuration in (25a). On the other hand, (27b) shows that SIT cannot take a following direct object and a particle. From this we conclude that (26a) is not an instance of the shifted-particle construction. As a side issue, it is worth noting that the affirmative answer in the case of (26a) does not follow from a complement rule that directly associates the verb BRING with the particle *in*. Instead, it follows indirectly from the more general complement rule in (28a), combined with the statement about motion phrases in (28b).

(28) a.   [BRING NP MotP]
     b.   A motion phrase can consist of the particle *in*.

Let us now ask our second question: can the sequence of words *in the armchair* be analyzed as a prepositional phrase in the two sentences in (26)? One of the rules that we discussed above can help to answer this question. As we noted, a particle cannot come between a verb and a pronoun object. Thus, whenever the sequence *in* + pronoun appears and the sentence is acceptable, we know that the sequence can only be a prepositional phrase. To see whether BRING and SIT occur in the prepositional structure shown in (25b), we can simply replace the noun phrase in each original example with a pronoun.

(29) a.   *Nina brought in it.
     b.   Nina sat in it.

From these results we can conclude that SIT can appear in the intransitive prepositional structure, whereas BRING cannot. This conclusion clearly implies that only (26b) can have the intransitive prepositional structure.

For some speakers of English, this last test is difficult to apply, since it rests on a rather subtle judgment. Fortunately, there is another test that can be used to determine whether a certain verb allows a prepositional structure. This test relies on properties of a construction that we will be talking about in chapter 10, the *bound relative clause*. The main fact of interest for us right now is that a prepositional structure allows the formation of a relative clause in which the preposition stands at the beginning of the relative clause, whereas a particle can never stand at the beginning of this construction. We see this in (30) and (31), where each (a) example is a sentence and each (b) example is a noun phrase modified by a relative clause based on that sentence.

(30) a. Nina sat in the chair.
     b. the chair [in which Nina sat]

(31) a. Nina brought in the chair.
     b. *the chair [in which Nina brought]

The acceptability of (30b) shows that the sequence *in the chair* can be a prepositional phrase in (30a). By contrast, the unacceptability of (31b) shows that the same sequence cannot be a prepositional phrase in (31a). The results of this second test yield exactly the same conclusion as the results of the first test: SIT can take an immediately following prepositional phrase, whereas BRING cannot.

Before leaving this topic, let us ask the same two questions about one additional example.

(32) Conrad looked over the newspaper.

To see whether *over* could be a particle in (32), we construct a sentence in which the order of particle and noun phrase is reversed.

(33) Conrad looked the newspaper over.

The acceptability of this second sentence shows that LOOK can take a direct object and a particle and thus that (32) can have the shifted-particle structure. Turning to the question of whether *over* could be a preposition in (32), we try replacing *the newspaper* by a pronoun.

(34) Conrad looked over it.

The acceptability of this sentence shows that LOOK can also occur in the intransitive prepositional structure. If we had any doubt about our judgment of this sentence, we could apply the other preposition test.

(35) the newspaper [over which Conrad looked]

Here again, the acceptability of the result indicates that the intransitive prepositional structure is one in which LOOK can appear. Thus, we are led to conclude that (31) can have either of two structures. This structural ambiguity is associated with a corresponding semantic ambiguity: Conrad can be examining the newspaper (the interpretation that goes with the shifted-particle structure), or he can be looking over the top of the newspaper (the interpretation that goes with the intransitive prepositional structure). The point of this particular example, then, is that some sentences can have both the shifted-particle structure and the intransitive prepositional structure. One practical consequence is that a yes answer to either of our questions does not necessarily imply that the answer to the other one is no. Thus, for instance, we cannot use an affirmative result on the particle test to justify a negative answer to the prepositional question. Likewise, we cannot conclude from an affirmative result on one of the two preposition tests that the sentence cannot have the particle structure. Because this ambiguity is possible, then, we always need to ask the two questions separately.

One final word of caution is in order. We cannot conclude from the ambiguity of (32) that all sentences containing LOOK and *over* and a noun phrase are ambiguous in the same way. Indeed, a careful reexamination of (33)–(35) shows that all three of them are completely unambiguous, in each instance for reasons that are immediately apparent. Since only particles can appear by themselves to the right of a noun phrase, (33) can only be analyzed as a particle structure. On the other hand, since only prepositions can appear with a following pronoun and only prepositions can introduce a relative clause, (34) and (35) are unambiguously prepositional.

Exercises

1. For each of the following sentences, answer two questions:
    A. Can the sentence be analyzed as having the shifted-particle structure?
    B. Can it be analyzed as having the intransitive prepositional structure?
Indicate how you decided on each answer.
    a. Jonah stayed on the platform.
    b. Holmes called in the inspector.
    c. Freddy ate up the cookies.
    d. Horace carried out the orders.
    e. The manager spoke over the intercom.
    f. Pete rolled over the barrel.
    g. Over which barrel did Pete roll?
    h. James pulled on the sweater.
    i. James pulled on it.

2. At first glance, the following two sentences might appear to have identical structures:

(i) Martha turned off the highway.

(ii) Martha turned off the radio.

Construct some experimental examples of your own to see whether the structures of these sentences are really similar. State as clearly as you can what your evidence shows about these two sentences.

Chapter 7

Free Relative Clauses

In this chapter, we turn our attention to two major constructions that help to fill out various phrase types in English. These phrase types include noun phrases very prominently, but they also include adjective phrases, locative and motion phrases, time phrases, and a variety of other types. The two constructions will be grouped under the single term *free relative clause* (*free relative* for short), by which we will understand a relative clause that stands alone rather than attaching to a head noun. The first type of free relative will be referred to as *definite*, the second as *conditional*; the reason for using the latter two terms will be discussed in section 7.4.

7.1 DEFINITE FREE RELATIVES

The definite free relative is illustrated in (1).

(1) a. Karen ate [what Fred offered to her].
    b. [What Harry fixed for Sally] went into the trash.

A close look at these bracketed sequences reveals that each consists of two parts. The first part is just the single word *what*. The second part is a sequence that sounds like an incomplete independent sentence.

(2) a. *Fred offered to her.
    b. *Harry fixed for Sally.

Each of these sentences is incomplete by virtue of needing one more noun phrase than it actually has. When the word *something* is inserted after *offered* and after *fixed*, the sentences become perfectly acceptable.

(3) a. Fred offered *something* to her.
    b. Harry fixed *something* for Sally.

Thus, a better representation for the sequences that come after *what* in (1) would include blanks to indicate the position of missing noun phrases.

(4) a. Fred offered _____ to her.
    b. Harry fixed _____ for Sally.

These representations show clearly that this is a construction based on a sentence with a missing noun phrase. Thus, the structure of these examples might be represented as in (5).

(5)   ??

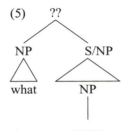

We have seen sequences like this before; they look exactly like the indirect questions discussed in chapter 4.

7.1.1 Definite Free Relatives Contrasted with Indirect Questions

Given this striking resemblance between the bracketed sequences in (1) and the indirect questions studied earlier, we might wonder whether the present sequences really represent a new construction. What reasons are there to believe that they are not indirect questions?

If we look just at the two sequences in isolation, we find no grounds for viewing them as anything other than indirect questions.

(6) a. [what Fred offered to her]
    b. [what Harry fixed for Sally]

The rules that we developed in chapter 4 for indirect questions definitely allow the creation of these sequences. Thus, we will not be able to differentiate the bracketed sequences in (1) from indirect questions on the basis of their internal structure.

When we turn our attention to the external behavior of these sequences, one striking fact becomes immediately apparent: these sequences are found in positions that definitely do not allow a broad range of indirect questions. This fact becomes clear when we try to substitute other indirect questions for the bracketed sequences.

(7) a. *Karen ate $\left\{\begin{array}{l}\text{which dish Norton served to her} \\ \text{whose turnips Bill had bought} \\ \text{how much pasta Fred offered to her}\end{array}\right\}$.

b. * $\left\{\begin{array}{l}\text{Which dish Norton served to her} \\ \text{Whose turnips Bill had bought} \\ \text{How much pasta Fred offered to her}\end{array}\right\}$ went into the trash.

These sets of examples contrast sharply with the corresponding sets in which *knew* is used instead of *ate,* and *was unclear* is used instead of *went into the trash.*

(8) a. Karen knew $\left\{\begin{array}{l}\text{which dish Norton served to her} \\ \text{whose turnips Bill had bought} \\ \text{how much pasta Fred offered to her}\end{array}\right\}$.

b. $\left\{\begin{array}{l}\text{Which dish Norton served to her} \\ \text{Whose turnips Bill had bought} \\ \text{How much pasta Fred offered to her}\end{array}\right\}$ was unclear.

The simplest account of these substantial differences in acceptability can be summarized informally as in (9).

(9) a. KNOW allows indirect questions as complements, whereas EAT does not.

b. UNCLEAR allows indirect questions as subjects, whereas GO does not.

If these statements are correct, then we have an initial argument that the original bracketed sequences, repeated in (10), are not indirect questions.

(10) a. Karen ate [what Fred offered to her].

b. [What Harry fixed for Sally] went into the trash.

Our earlier discussion of indirect questions also provides a second justification for viewing the bracketed sequences as representing a different type of construction. The argument applies specifically to occurrences of this construction in subject position, as in (10b). We observed in chapter 4 that whenever an indirect question can be used as a subject, it can also appear as a pseudocomplement linked to the substitute subject *it.* This dual possibility is illustrated in the sentences in (11), both of which contain the predicate UNCLEAR.

(11) a. [What Fred offered to her] was unclear.

b. *It* was unclear [what Fred offered to her].

The same possibility does not exist for the bracketed sequence when the predicate is changed to *went into the trash*.

(12) a.   [What Fred offered to her] went into the trash.
　　 b.   ?**It* went into the trash [what Fred offered to her].

Sentence (12b) is possible only with an "afterthought" interpretation, which requires a distinctive intonation in spoken English and a special comma punctuation in written English.

(13) *It* went into the trash, [what Fred offered to her].

In sum, *what Fred offered to her* can be used as a pseudocomplement when the predicate is one like UNCLEAR—that is, one that allows the full range of indirect questions. However, the same sequence cannot be so used with a predicate that does not allow indirect questions in general. The argument that results from these considerations is given in (14).

(14) a.   Sentences that have indirect questions as subjects are matched by corresponding sentences in which the indirect questions are pseudocomplements.
　　 b.   Sentence (12a) is not matched by a corresponding acceptable sentence in which *what Fred offered to her* is a pseudocomplement.
　　 c.   Therefore, *what Fred offered to her* is not an indirect question in (12a).

Comparing the interpretation of an indirect question with that of our new type of sequences reveals another respect in which the two constructions are markedly different despite their superficial similarity. As was pointed out in chapter 4, the interpretation of a sentence with KNOW plus an indirect question involves knowing an answer. Sentence (15a), for example, has an interpretation that can be paraphrased as in (15b).

(15) a.   John knows [what Martha ate].
　　 b.   John knows the answer to the question "What did Martha eat?"

With the new construction, by contrast, the interpretation is quite different. We can see this by considering the interpretation of (16).

(16) John cooked what Martha ate.

Here it makes no sense to give an interpretation involving an answer to a question.

(17) ??John cooked the answer to the question "What did Martha eat?"

Instead, (16) is best understood as involving the following two propositions:

(18) a. Martha ate *x*.
    b. John cooked *x*.

7.1.2 The Structure of Definite Free Relatives

We now have three arguments to support the view that sequences such as *what Fred offered to her* can be something other than indirect questions. As noted at the beginning of the chapter, we will refer to constructions of this type as *free relative clauses,* or *free relatives* for short (abbreviated *F-Rel* in tree diagrams). In anticipation of the second variety of free relatives to be introduced in this chapter, we will refer to the ones under study now as *definite free relatives.* Let us now try to develop some rules for this new construction.

As noted already, our initial examples of this construction had two basic ingredients: (a) the word *what;* (b) a sentence with a missing noun phrase. These examples, then, conform to the general pattern given in (19).

(19) F-Rel

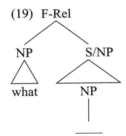

Just as with indirect questions, we can think of the noun phrase *what* as being "donated" to the incomplete sentence, which then uses this donated noun phrase to identify its missing noun phrase, as in (20).

(20)

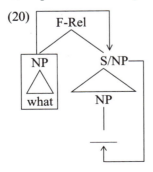

Thus, the particular free relative with which we started this discussion has the structure shown in (21).

(21)

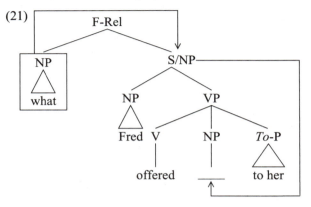

All of the free relatives that we have seen so far have been introduced by the noun phrase *what*. A natural question to ask now is what other kinds of phrases can serve this function. Since *what* can also serve as a questioned phrase, we might look at other questioned phrases. When we do this, we find that the list is extremely small. The following examples show that none of the other kinds of interrogative noun phrases can introduce free relatives:

(22) a. *Fred wants to meet [*who* Sally hired].
     b. *Norton wrote [*how many letters* George wrote].
     c. *George bought [*which car* Sheila wanted to sell to him].

All three of these sentences are easy to interpret, but none of them is acceptable. The conclusion is that *what* is the only noun phrase that can be used to introduce definite free relatives.

When we expand our view to include other types of phrases besides noun phrases, we find two additional words that can introduce definite free relatives.

(23) a. Nathan put the money [*where* Billy told him to put it ____].
     b. The admiral goes [*where* he wants to go ____].
     c. The concert started [*when* the bell rang ____].

The word *where* is joined to a sentence with either a missing locative phrase or a missing motion phrase; *when* is joined to a sentence with a missing time phrase. Other questioned phrases, however, cannot serve in this extra role of introducing free relatives.

(24) a. *You solved the puzzle [*how* Marsha solved it].
(Compare: You solved the puzzle the same way that Marsha solved it.)

    b. *George worked [*how long* Billy worked _____].
(Compare: George worked the same amount of time as Billy worked.)

    c. *Carol walked out of the meeting [*why* Arthur walked out].
(Compare: Carol walked out of the meeting for the same reason that Arthur walked out.)

Thus, our total list of introducing phrases for definite free relatives consists of just the three items *what, where,* and *when,* and the entire set of acceptable structures consists of those given in (25).

(25)

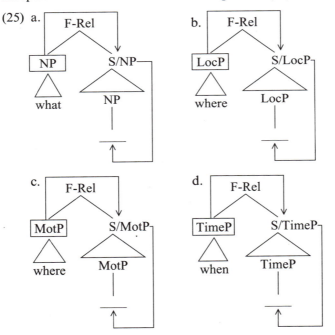

Now let us consider for a moment the other key ingredient of these constructions and ask whether any further sorts of structures can be joined to the introducing phrases. In the case of indirect questions, we found that the structure containing the missing phrase can be either a finite sentence or an infinitival phrase.

(26) a. Jacob always knows [what he should wear ____].
     b. Jacob always knows [what to wear ____].

(27) a. Fido rarely knows [when he should bark ____].
     b. Fido rarely knows [when to bark ____].

The examples in (28) and (29) show that only the former option is available for free relatives.

(28) a. Jacob always wears [what he should wear ____].
     b. *Jacob always wears [what to wear ____].

(29) a. Fido rarely barks [when he should bark ____].
     b. *Fido rarely barks [when to bark ____].

Exercise

1. Draw a tree diagram for each of the following free relatives:
   a. [what Bruce tried to make]
   b. [what Helen asked Christine to bring to the office]
   c. [where Washington wanted to stay]
   d. [where Rex took the dominoes]

7.2 CONDITIONAL FREE RELATIVES

Conditional free relatives are quite distinctive in appearance. These constructions always begin with a phrase that looks like a questioned phrase except for having the suffix *-ever* attached to the interrogative word itself.

(30) a. Fred will say [*whatever* you tell him to say ____].
     b. Keith will read [*whichever book* you leave ____ for him].
     c. Ronnie may keep [*whichever of the toys* he wants to play with ____].
     d. Rhoda dances with [*whoever* ____ asks her to dance].
     e. [*Who(m)ever* you elect ____ to the presidency] will face many problems.
     f. Dorothy can eat [*however many cookies* Clarence bakes ____ for her].

The only questioned noun phrases that fail to have corresponding *-ever* phrases are those introduced by *whose*. Thus, English has a questioned phrase *whose dog*, but no free relative phrases like **whosever dog* or **whoever's dog*. The second of these phrases may not seem drastically unacceptable in isolation, but it creates problems in actual free relatives. In

(31), for example, it is unclear whether it is the dog or the dog's owner that has to make a trip to the pound.

(31) ?[Whoever's dog bit your mailman] will have to make a trip to the pound.

Conditional free relatives can also be introduced by a variety of phrases other than noun phrases and can take on a corresponding variety of roles in the larger sentences in which they appear. This variety is illustrated in the following set of examples:

(32) a. John will sit [*wherever* he wants to sit ____].   (locative phrase)
   b. You should call me [*whenever* you have a question ____]. (time phrase)
   c. George will make the cake [*however big* you want it to be ____].   (adjective phrase)
   d. Candace will call the mayor [*however often* she needs to call him ____].   (frequency adverb)

The only question word in addition to *whose* that fails to have a corresponding *-ever* form is *why*.

(33) *Joanna will file the second petition *whyever* she filed the first one.

Here the problem is not that the intended interpretation is nonsensical. For instance, the rephrasing of the idea given in (34) is perfectly acceptable.

(34) Joanna will file the second petition *for the same reason that* she filed the first one, whatever that reason was.

Just like definite free relatives, conditional free relatives can only be based on finite sentences. The effects of violating this restriction are evident in (35b) and (36b).

(35) a. Jacob always wears [whatever he should wear ____].
   b. *Jacob always wears [whatever to wear ____].

(36) a. Florence always adopts [whichever dog she should adopt ____].
   b. *Florence always adopts [whichever dog to adopt ____].

Exercise

1. Draw a tree diagram for each of the following conditional free relatives. Decide which kind of phrase is introducing each one, but do not bother drawing the internal structure of the introducing phrase.

    a. [whatever Fred ate]
    b. [wherever he put the bananas]
    c. [who(m)ever she found lurking in the pantry]
    d. [whichever book you think that you want to read]
    e. [however much money you asked her to pay]
    f. [however silly his remark might have seemed]

7.3   EXTERNAL BEHAVIOR OF FREE RELATIVES

In the preceding discussion, we have seen many examples of free relatives in the larger context provided by the sentences in which they appear. Although our primary focus has been on free relatives that serve as noun phrases, we have also seen several that serve other functions. Here are two sets of examples, divided between those in which the free relative as a whole serves as a noun phrase and those in which the free relative serves as a phrase of some other type:

(37) a. Karen ate [$_{NP}$ *what* Fred offered ____ to her].
      (Compare: Karen ate [$_{NP}$ something].)
   b. [$_{NP}$ *What* Harry fixed ____ for Sally] went into the trash.
      (Compare: [$_{NP}$ Something] went into the trash.)
   c. Fred will say [$_{NP}$ *whatever* you tell him to say ____].
      (Compare: Fred will say [$_{NP}$ something].)
   d. Ronnie may keep [$_{NP}$ *whichever of the toys* he likes ____].
      (Compare: Ronnie may keep [$_{NP}$ this toy].)
   e. Rhoda dances with [$_{NP}$ *whoever* ____ asks her to dance].
      (Compare: Rhoda dances with [$_{NP}$ someone].)
   f. Dorothy can eat [$_{NP}$ *however many cookies* Clarence bakes ____ for her].
      (Compare: Dorothy can eat [$_{NP}$ ten cookies].)

(38) a. Nathan put the money [$_{LocP}$ *where* Billy told him to put it ____].
      (Compare: Nathan put the money [$_{LocP}$ there].)
   b. The concert started [$_{TimeP}$ *when* the bell rang ____].
      (Compare: The concert started [$_{TimeP}$ then].)
   c. John will sit [$_{LocP}$ *wherever* he wants to sit ____].
      (Compare: John will sit [$_{LocP}$ there].)
   d. Nora will go [$_{MotP}$ *wherever* she wants to go ____].
      (Compare: Nora will go [$_{MotP}$ there].)
   e. George will make the cake [$_{AdjP}$ *however big* you want it to be ____].
      (Compare: George will make the cake [$_{AdjP}$ very big].)

A careful examination of these examples reveals a close connection between the phrase type of the free relative as a whole and the phrase type of the italicized smaller phrase that introduces it. In particular, the free relatives in (37) all occupy noun-phrase positions, and in each sentence the italicized phrase that introduces the free relative is itself a noun phrase. In similar fashion, each of the free relatives in (38) serves a role that is identical to that of the introducing phrase. These individual situations can be pictured as in (39).

(39)

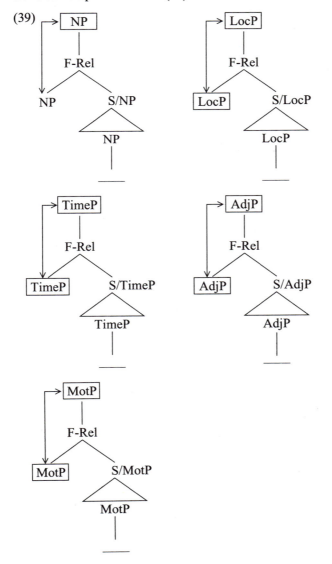

We can summarize this state of affairs in the rule in (40) and represent it in the diagram in (41).

(40) If a free relative is introduced by a certain type of phrase, then the clause as a whole can serve as a phrase of the same type in the sentence of which it is a part.

(41)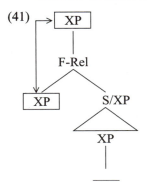

One surprising consequence of this treatment deserves special mention. If we consider whether there are any verbs or adjectives that take free relatives, in the same way that certain verbs and adjectives take indirect questions, we might initially be tempted to think that the answer would have to be yes, given sentences such as those in (1), repeated in (42).

(42) a. Karen ate [what Fred offered to her].
   b. [What Harry fixed for Sally] went into the trash.

These examples might suggest that we need to add special new rules for EAT and GO, those given in (43).

(43) a. NP [EAT F-Rel]
   b. F-Rel [GO MotP]

However, the logic of (40) and (41) suggests that the only rules we need for the sentences in (42) are those in (44), both of which we need independently of free-relative examples, for simple sentences such as those in (45).

(44) a. NP [EAT NP]
     b. NP [GO MotP]

(45) a. Eve ate [$_{NP}$ an apple].
     b. [$_{NP}$ The newspapers] went into the trash.

Since a free relative introduced by a noun phrase is itself a noun phrase, any such free relative automatically qualifies for the object position in (44a) or the subject position in (44b), provided that it is introduced by a noun phrase of a kind that is admitted in that position. For instance, in the case of *what* the noun-phrase position must be one that permits inanimate noun phrases, and in the case of *whoever* the position must be one that permits human noun phrases.

One note of caution is in order here, concerning the rule stated in (40). Although this rule *allows* a free relative to serve as a phrase of the same type as its introducing phrase, it does not *require* it to do so. As we will see in chapter 11, conditional free relatives have another use in English entirely distinct from the one that we have seen in this chapter.

7.4 INTERPRETATION OF FREE RELATIVES

In the preceding sections of this chapter, we have been using the terms *definite* and *conditional* to refer to the two basic types of English free relatives. It is now appropriate to say something about the circumstances in which each can be used, from which it will be clear why these particular terms are appropriate.

A conditional free relative is most natural in a situation in which the entity to which it refers cannot be identified. It has an essentially conditional force, so that (46a) has roughly the import indicated in (46b).

(46) a. George accepted [whichever story Leah submitted to his magazine].
     b. If Leah submitted story$_1$ to his magazine, George accepted story$_1$.
         If Leah submitted story$_2$ to his magazine, George accepted story$_2$.
         If Leah submitted story$_3$ to his magazine, George accepted story$_3$.
         etc.

On the other hand, a conditional free relative is quite bizarre if a specific identification is possible.

(47) ??George accepted [whichever story Leah submitted to his magazine], namely, her story about pioneer life in rural Nebraska.

In part of their range of uses, definite free relatives coincide with conditional free relatives. In particular, the former as well as the latter can be used when no specific identifiable entity is known, in which case they, too, have a conditional force.

(48) a. George accepted [what Leah submitted to his magazine], whatever it was that she submitted.
    b. If Leah submitted x_1 to his magazine, George accepted x_1.
       If Leah submitted x_2 to his magazine, George accepted x_2.
       If Leah submitted x_3 to his magazine, George accepted x_3.
       etc.

However, definite free relatives can also be used when the entity being referred to can be identified quite clearly.

(49) George accepted [what Leah submitted to his magazine], specifically, her story about pioneer life in rural Nebraska.

In this capacity to allow both a nonspecific, conditional interpretation and a specific interpretation, definite free relatives are closely akin to noun phrases introduced by the definite article. In (50a), such a noun phrase is used in a nonspecific, conditional fashion, whereas in (50b), the same noun phrase is used when the entity to which it refers can be more specifically identified.

(50) a. George accepted [the story that Leah submitted to his magazine], whichever one it was that she submitted.
    b. George accepted [the story that Leah submitted to his magazine], specifically, her story about pioneer life in rural Nebraska.

7.5 DISTINGUISHING FREE RELATIVES AND INDIRECT QUESTIONS

In subsection 7.1.1, it was argued that despite their superficial similarities, definite free relatives and indirect questions must be distinguished in the syntactic rules of English. We noted differences both in the rules for forming them and in the rules for their use in larger structures. Our goal in this section will be to look at these differences in a way that will help us to make correct identifications in particular cases.

7.5.1 Internal Requirements

We need to recall at the outset that both a free relative and an indirect question must have a missing phrase of some sort (leaving aside indirect questions introduced by *whether* and *if*). Thus, the presence of a missing phrase will not help us to decide between the two constructions. However, there are other internal characteristics that will help us decide in particular cases.

First, let us consider what structures are allowed as indirect questions. Here there are almost no special restrictions. Indirect questions can be introduced by phrases built up around the full range of *wh* words. In addition, the structure containing the missing phrase can be either a finite sentence or an infinitival phrase.

For definite free relatives, the requirements are much more restrictive. In the first place, the relative-clause structure must be finite; this immediately means that no infinitival construction can possibly be a free relative. In the second place, the only *wh* words that can introduce a definite free relative are *what, where,* and *when.*

Let us see what these conditions imply for several sets of specific examples. The first is given in (51).

(51) a. [whose dog Fred fed]
     b. [how much money Julie earned]
     c. [which picture Smith sold]

Naturally, these sequences qualify as possible indirect questions. However, they fail to satisfy the internal requirements for definite free relatives, since each of them is introduced by some phrase other than *what, where,* or *when.*

Now let us look at a second set of examples.

(52) a. [what to say to Martha]
     b. [where to hide the money]
     c. [when to start the roast]

Here again, all of the sequences clearly qualify as possible indirect questions. In addition, each of the three initial phrases is one that is allowed to introduce free relatives. However, the structures to which these introducing phrases are joined are all infinitival phrases, and that fact disqualifies the sequences as possible free relatives.

Finally, let us consider a third set of examples.

(53) a. [what Carla put in the ice chest]
   b. [where Hans is keeping the chairs]
   c. [when we came to Austin]

Once again, these sequences clearly qualify as possible indirect questions. In addition, they are introduced by *what, where,* and *when,* and the following structures are finite sentences. Thus, at last, we have sequences that satisfy the internal requirements for definite free relatives as well as those for indirect questions.

Exercise

1. For each of the sequences listed below, answer two questions:

A. Does it satisfy the internal requirements for indirect questions?
B. Does it satisfy the internal requirements for free relatives?

Explain each negative answer briefly but clearly. (With some of these sequences, you may want to answer yes to both questions.)

   a. [what to say]
   b. [where Francis wanted to stay]
   c. [how John managed to find the manuscript]
   d. [whose car we should ride in]
   e. [which book to read]
   f. [when the dance began]
   g. [what Karen wants us to do]

7.5.2   External Requirements

Let us begin our comparison of the external requirements for indirect questions and definite free relatives by reviewing what was said in chapter 4 about indirect questions. In that discussion, we saw that every indirect question that occurs as a subject or complement in a sentence must receive an invitation from some particular predicate that specifically permits indirect questions. The sentences in (54) contain examples of such predicates.

(54) a. John *wondered* [how far the travelers would go].
   b. Kate *knows* [how much money we collected].
   c. Jones *told* Smith [why Williams canceled the program].
   d. Robert is not *sure* [how much his opponents know].
   e. [Which candidate will spend the most money] is *clear.*

    f. [Which telephone you use] does not *matter*.

    g. [How much money Bruce made] *depended* on [how many encyclopedias he sold].

Thus, when we want to decide whether a certain sequence satisfies the external requirements for being an indirect question, we need to determine whether it occurs as the subject or complement of one of the permitting words.

In some cases, we may remember that a certain predicate permits indirect questions as complements. Suppose, for instance, that we are given sentence (55).

(55) Brenda knows [what her dog swallowed].

We would be likely to remember, from several earlier examples, that KNOW is a verb that does allow indirect questions. We would then conclude immediately that the sequence in question satisfies the external requirements for being an indirect question.

Suppose, however, that we are given the sentences in (56), neither of which contains a predicate about which we have any previous information.

(56) a. Joe *guessed* [what Marsha gave Bill].

       b. Joe *borrowed* [what Marsha gave Bill].

Here we clearly need to find out whether GUESS allows indirect questions, and then answer the same question for BORROW. At first glance, it might appear that the sentences in (56) would give us an affirmative answer to this question for both verbs. However, the bracketed sequences in these sentences satisfy the internal requirements for free relatives as well as those for indirect questions. Thus, when we look at the bracketed expressions in (56) in the hopes of learning whether these two verbs take indirect questions, we have no way of knowing whether we are really seeing indirect questions.

A natural strategy here is to construct additional sentences containing these two predicates. In particular, we need to provide complements that are unambiguously indirect questions. One possibility is to use a sequence introduced by something other than *what, where,* or *when;* two good choices are *why* and *how much money*. When we take this step, the resulting judgments are clear.

(57) a. Joe *guessed* [why the receipts were unavailable].

       b. Joe *guessed* [how much money Arthur earned].

(58) a. *Joe *borrowed* [why the receipts were unavailable].
   b. *Joe *borrowed* [how much money Arthur earned].

These judgments give us the information that we need: GUESS does allow indirect questions as complements, whereas BORROW does not. It is now easy to answer the question posed about our original examples.

(59) a. Joe *guessed* [what Marsha gave Bill].
   b. Joe *borrowed* [what Marsha gave Bill].

The bracketed sequence in (59a) does satisfy the external requirements for indirect questions, whereas that in (59b) does not.

Let us look now at the external requirements for free relatives. These requirements are quite different from those for indirect questions. Near the end of section 7.3, it was noted that there are no verbs or adjectives that specifically call for free relatives as subjects or complements. Instead, the phrase type of the construction as a whole is determined by the type of the introducing phrase. The particular cases of this rule that apply to definite free relatives can be summarized as follows:

(60) a. Definite free relatives introduced by *what* can be used exactly where nonhuman noun phrases are called for.
   b. Definite free relatives introduced by *where* can be used exactly where locative or motion phrases are permitted.
   c. Definite free relatives introduced by *when* can be used exactly where time phrases are permitted.

Thus, in a situation where a *what* sequence can be a free relative, other inanimate noun phrases (e.g., *something* or *it*) should also be possible. Likewise, in a situation where a *where* sequence can be a free relative, other locative or motion phrases (e.g., *somewhere* or *there*) should also be possible in the same position. Finally, in a situation where a *when* sequence can be a free relative, it should also be possible to substitute other time phrases (e.g., *then, on Tuesday*).

Let us look at some concrete examples. Our first set involves *what* sequences.

(61) a. Fred liked [what he saw].
   b. [What John cooked] made Martha sick.

The positions of both of the bracketed sequences also allow simple nonhuman noun phrases.

(62) a. Fred liked *something*.
  b. *Something* made Martha sick.

Thus, the bracketed sequences in (61) satisfy the external conditions for being free relatives.

Now let us consider the following *where* sequences:

(63) a. Karen stayed [where Cora had wanted to stay].
  b. Karen discovered [where Cora had wanted to stay].

Here substitution of the simple locative phrase *there* gives markedly different results.

(64) a. Karen stayed *there*.
  b. *Karen discovered *there*.

Sentence (64a) shows that locative phrases can occur immediately after STAY, whereas (64b) shows that they are impossible immediately following DISCOVER. Thus, the bracketed sequence in (63a) satisfies the external requirements for being a free relative, whereas that in (63b) does not.

A similar line of reasoning applies to *when* sequences, as the following pair of examples shows:

(65) a. Jacob left [when Elaine stopped playing the piano].
  b. [When Elaine stopped playing the piano] was unclear.

Substituting *then* for the two bracketed sequences yields the following results:

(66) a. Jacob left *then*.
  b. *_Then_ was unclear.

We conclude that only (65a) satisfies the external conditions for being a free relative.

Exercise

1. For each of the bracketed sequences in the sentences below, answer two questions:
  A. Does it satisfy the external requirements for indirect questions?
  B. Does it satisfy the external requirements for free relatives?
For each negative answer, say what requirement is not satisfied.
  a. Bill said [what Norma told him].
  b. [What Shakespeare wrote] is clear.
  c. John put the money [where the children would not find it].

d. [When Shakespeare lived] is clear.

e. George discovered [where Shakespeare lived].

f. George wanted to put up a monument [where Shakespeare lived].

g. [What Shakespeare wrote] is difficult.

7.5.3   A Compatibility Requirement for Free Relatives

Besides satisfying ordinary internal and external requirements, free relatives must satisfy one additional type of condition, a condition that arises naturally as a result of their interpretation. Let us begin by looking again at a free relative introduced by *what* and the interpretation that it has.

(67) a. John cooked [what Martha ate ____].

b. Martha ate x.

John cooked x.

In general, if a free-relative interpretation is to be coherent, then the kinds of entities that could serve in place of x in the first part of the interpretation must include some that could also serve in place of x in the second part. This condition clearly holds for the pair of statements in (67b): we can think of many kinds of entities (spaghetti, boiled potatoes, etc.) that would make sense in place of x in both statements.

In other sentences containing *what* sequences, the compatibility condition fails. The following example provides a clear illustration:

(68) John realized [what Martha ate].

By the rule discussed above, if the bracketed sequence were a free relative, this would have the interpretation given in (69).

(69) Martha ate x.

John realized x.

The problem here is that EAT and REALIZE take different kinds of entities as objects. The objects of EAT must be physical objects (preferably foods), whereas the objects of REALIZE must be true propositions. Thus, the two occurrences of x are incompatible. As a result, it is impossible to view the bracketed sequence in (68) as a free relative. The only coherent interpretation for this sentence is one in which the complement is taken to be an indirect question, in which case compatibility is not relevant.

The compatibility requirement has a special consequence for sentences containing *when* sequences. Such sentences receive the same kind of interpretation as those containing *what* sequences. An example is given in (70).

(70) a. Nora saw the smoke [when the bomb exploded].
    b. Nora saw the smoke at time x.
      The bomb exploded at time x.

Here, there is nothing to prevent the two times from being the same. Thus, the compatibility requirement is satisfied, and the bracketed sequence can be a free relative.

Now let us consider (71a), with the tentative interpretation given in (71b).

(71) a. Nora is telling Peter [when the airplane landed].
    b. Nora is telling Peter at time x.
      The airplane landed at time x.

Here, the times mentioned in the two statements are incompatible. The present-tense form *is* indicates that the telling is going on at the present time, whereas the past-tense form *landed* puts the time of that event earlier than the present. It is thus impossible for the two times to be the same. As a result, the *when* sequence in (71a) cannot be a free relative. Only an indirect-question interpretation is possible.

This restriction to identical times of course holds only for free relatives introduced by *when* and *whenever*. In a *where* free relative, for example, the identity required is not between times but between locations. Thus, the difference of time between the two clauses in (72) does not pose an obstacle to a free-relative interpretation.

(72) The company will put its theme park where the two armies fought.

Exercise

1. Each of the following sentences contains a *wh* sequence. For each one, say whether it satisfies the compatibility requirement for free relatives.
    a. Bill saw [what John constructed].
    b. Kay knows [what her sister knew].
    c. Harley lives [where Washington bought his horses].
    d. [What Anna said] is untrue.
    e. Harley knows [when Washington bought his horses].

7.5.4 Residual Ambiguities

After studying all the differing requirements that indirect questions and free relatives must meet, it might seem likely that every instance of one of these constructions could always be identified unambiguously when it appeared in a sentence. As it happens, however, ambiguous sentences do exist. One example is given in (73).

(73) Martha knows [what John knows].

In isolation, the bracketed sequence would clearly be allowed by the rules for forming indirect questions. In addition, it occurs here as the object of the verb KNOW, one of the verbs that accept indirect questions as objects. Thus, our rules allow this sequence to be analyzed here as an indirect question.

By checking one requirement at a time, we find that a free-relative structure is just as legitimate. The construction is introduced by *what,* one of the permitted phrases. The structure that follows is a finite sentence. Thus, the internal requirements are satisfied. As for the external requirements, the verb KNOW is one that accepts nonhuman noun phrases.

(74) Martha knows *something.*

Finally, the free-relative interpretation would give us the following two statements:

(75) John knows *x.*
Martha knows *x.*

Clearly, the same entities that are objects of John's knowing can also be objects of Martha's knowing. Therefore, this sentence can have a structure in which the bracketed sequence is a free relative.

A very definite ambiguity in meaning goes along with this structural ambiguity. In fact, either of the two interpretations could be true in a situation where the other one was false. On the one hand, Martha might be able to give a correct answer to the question "What does John know?" without having the same knowledge herself. For instance, she might know that he knows the names of the Seven Dwarfs, even though she herself does not know their names. In this situation, the sentence would be true on the indirect-question interpretation, but false on the free-relative interpretation. On the other hand, Martha might not know anything at all about John. In particular, she might have no knowledge of what he knows or doesn't know. But suppose that Martha and John each separately know the names of the Seven Dwarfs. Then the sentence would be true on the free-relative interpretation, but false on the indirect-question interpretation.

Exercise

1. For each of the sentences listed below, answer two questions:

    A. Can it be a free relative?

    B. Can it be an indirect question?

Be sure to check both internal and external requirements in making your determination, and also check the compatibility requirement for free relatives. (Be on the alert for sentences that are ambiguous between the two structures.)

    a. [What Richard said to Sharon] made her laugh.

    b. [What Shakespeare wrote] is unclear.

    c. Jack will tell us [when to leave the room].

    d. John didn't stay [where Bill told him to stay].

    e. John didn't say [where Bill told him to stay].

    f. Harold didn't remember [how Sheila remembered the solution].

    g. Martha told me [what to tell Kevin].

    h. Billy knows [what Einstein knew].

    i. Sarah remembers [why she confessed to Eric].

    j. George believed [what we told him].

Chapter 8

Subjects of Phrases

In chapter 4, it was suggested that verbs and adjectives can impose restrictions on subjects of sentences as well as on complements. In particular, we noted that some words allow only ordinary noun phrases as subjects, whereas others allow clauses of certain types as well. Thus, for instance, we made a distinction between SURPRISE and NOMINATE.

(1) a. NP [SURPRISE NP]
     That-C [SURPRISE NP]
  b. NP [NOMINATE NP]

Although both SURPRISE and NOMINATE take ordinary noun phrases as subjects, only SURPRISE takes *that* clauses as well. These rules were adequate to account for the sentences in (2) and (3).

(2) a. *The explosion* [surprised Bill].
   b. *That the firecracker exploded* [surprised Bill].

(3) a. *The delegates* [nominated Bill].
   b. **That Fred was unpopular* [nominated Bill].

We can see that more needs to be said as soon as we look at some slightly more complicated examples.

(4) a. *The explosion* may have [surprised Bill].
   b. *That the firecracker exploded* may have [surprised Bill].

(5) a. *The delegates* may have [nominated Bill].
   b. **That Fred was unpopular* may have [nominated Bill].

According to the way we are now interpreting the subject/complement rule in (1a), SURPRISE calls for either a noun phrase or a *that* clause as subject. But in neither of the examples in (4) is the verb phrase headed by *surprised* a sentence predicate. As a result, neither verb phrase appears with a "subject" (i.e., a structure that joins with it to make a sentence). In each of the two sentences, the only phrase that does have a subject in this sense of the word is the phrase headed by *may*. In order to solve this problem, we need to expand our idea of what a subject is. After we have taken this step, we will find that subject/complement rules like those in (1) work just as well with complicated sentences as with simple ones.

8.1   AN EXPANDED IDEA OF "SUBJECTS"

What would it mean to speak of "the subject of a phrase"? A convenient way to begin is to think about what we have been calling "the subject of a sentence," and to see what it does for the verb phrase that accompanies it. Consider, for instance, a simple sentence like the one diagrammed in (6), the subject of which is *James*.

(6)

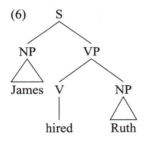

Suppose that we are asked whether the verb phrase *hired Ruth* expresses a complete proposition. Our intuitions would tell us that it does not. What is felt to be lacking is an identification for one of the participants in the event of hiring. In effect, the phrase by itself could be thought of as □ *hired Ruth*. In order to arrive at a complete interpretation for this phrase, we use something that lies outside the verb phrase to identify this absent element. In this case, the noun phrase *James* makes the necessary identification.

The phrase *hired Ruth* is typical of a general pattern: most phrases have some specific part of their interpretation that is not expressed by anything inside the phrase itself, but instead has to be provided by something outside the phrase. In general, when we talk about the *subject of a phrase,* we will be talking about the outside noun phrase or clause that provides this missing part of the interpretation. (When reference is made to "subjects" in connection with infinitival phrases and gerundives serving as complements and subjects, the reference is to be understood as applying to the bare-stem verb phrases and the present-participial verb phrases that serve as their major elements.)

This new idea of subjects can easily be represented in graphic form. Every phrase that serves as a predicate will have with it an empty box, standing for the element in its interpretation that needs to be identified by something outside the phrase. The outside entity that fulfills this role will be linked to this box by an arrow. Thus, the tree for the simple sentence considered above would be redrawn as in (7).

(7)

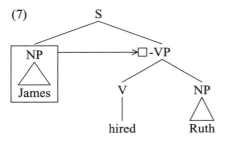

We can express the kind of subject identification found in this very basic situation by the following rule:

(8) If a verb phrase is the predicate of a sentence, then the structure that joins with the verb phrase serves to identify its subject.

In the above sentence, the subject of the verb phrase is identified by (equivalently, "understood as") an ordinary noun phrase; in other examples, of types that we have already seen, a clause of one sort or another serves this role.

In other constructions, the rules for identifying subjects are slightly different. In a full infinitival clause, the subject of the infinitival phrase is identified by the noun phrase that follows *for*. This situation is diagrammed in (9).

(9)

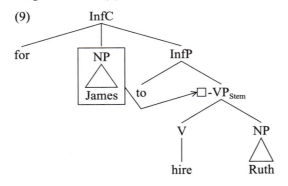

Similarly, in the variety of gerundive construction that contains a genitive, it is the genitive that serves as the subject of the present-participial verb phrase, as indicated in (10).

(10)

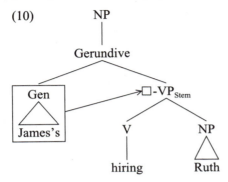

We see yet another situation when we try to identify the subject of the infinitival phrase in sentence (11).

(11) Katy persuaded John to *hire Ruth*.

Just as in (7), (9), and (10), the subject of the verb phrase *hire Ruth* will be the person who did the hiring. By consulting our intuitions as speakers of English, we can tell that *John* is the noun phrase that fulfills this role here. In this instance, then, the object of the larger verb phrase serves also as the subject of the verb phrase in the complement. We can picture this situation as in (12).

(12)

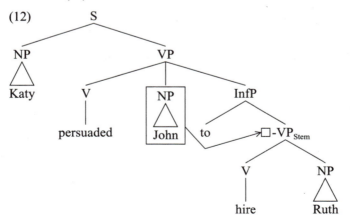

The following simple rule delivers the right results:

(13) If a certain verb phrase occurs as part of a higher verb phrase
     headed by a transitive verb, then the object of the transitive verb
     serves to identify the subject of the lower verb phrase.

In the above situations, the subject of a phrase is identified in an extremely simple and direct way. A situation in which a subject is identified
less directly is given in (14).

(14) John tried to hire Ruth.

What we are concerned with here is identifying the subject of *hire Ruth*.
We have a clear intuition that *John* is to be understood as the agent in the
act of hiring. Thus, the subject of *hire Ruth* is just the subject of the larger
verb phrase that contains it. This two-step identification is pictured
in (15).

(15)

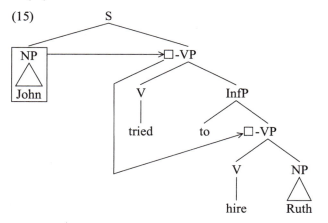

The first identification here is direct: *John* serves as the subject of the verb
phrase headed by *tried,* as dictated by rule (8). Then the second identification is one that we see whenever we look at a verb phrase in an infinitival
complement of TRY. In effect, the subject of this lower verb phrase is
calculated to be the same as whatever turned out to be the subject of the
parent phrase headed by TRY.

The use of the subject of the larger verb phrase in (15) as the subject of
the smaller one is typical of what happens with intransitive verbs in general. We can thus state the following rule:

(16) The subject of a higher phrase headed by an intransitive verb also
     serves to identify the subject of a complement.

This rule provides subjects not only for infinitival constructions but also for gerundives that lack preceding genitive noun phrases.

(17) Cora regrets [living in Toledo].

The way in which the subjects are determined in this sentence is diagrammed in (18).

(18)

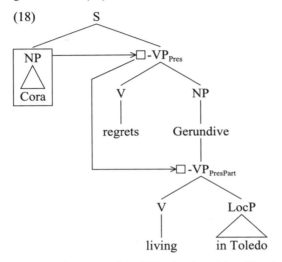

As was the case with (15), the first identification here is direct: the noun phrase *Cora* serves as the subject of the main verb phrase. The second is indirect and falls under rule (16): when we want to find the subject of a complement of REGRET, we first need to determine the subject of the phrase headed by REGRET itself.

In a more complicated sentence, a number of indirect identifications may be required. This successive identification of ever lower subjects is illustrated by the way the rules account for our intuition that *Nelda* is understood as the subject of *finish the book* in (19).

(19) Nelda intends to try to finish the book.

The successive identifications are diagrammed in (20).

(20)

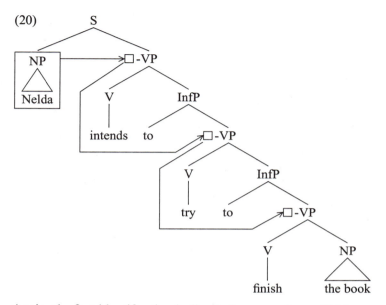

Again, the first identification is direct: the noun phrase *Nelda* serves as the subject of the largest verb phrase. Now, because it is the subject of this top verb phrase and because the top verb phrase does not have an object, *Nelda* is also picked by rule (16) to serve as the subject of the next verb phrase down, the verb phrase headed by *try*. Finally, by virtue of serving as the subject of this intermediate verb phrase, it is picked as the subject of the lowest verb phrase, by yet another application of rule (16).

Exercise

1. In each of the following sentences, a verb phrase is italicized. In each case, say which noun phrase or clause in the sentence identifies the subject of this phrase, and draw a tree diagram in which the successive identifications are indicated by arrows. (In many instances, a chain of two or more identifications will be required.)

    a. Alma asked George to try to remember to *feed the cats.*
    b. Gib may have promised to *let Mae mow the lawn.*
    c. Mark must be refusing to let Debbie *poison the goldfish.*
    d. Kate's wanting to keep *giving parties* bothers Steve.
    e. Pat's taking Lawrence to the veterinarian *relieved Warren.*
    f. The judge would like for Mrs. Bolton to stop *taking his cats to the pound.*
    g. It *surprised Kathy* that Gaylord agreed to plant a magnolia.

8.2 SPECIFICATION OF SUBJECTS

We are now in a position to look again at the question that prompted the discussion in the preceding section—namely, how a subject/complement rule like (21a) could be satisfied by a sentence like (21b), where the *that* clause and the relevant verb phrase are separated by two other verbs.

(21) a. *That*-C [SURPRISE NP]
     b. *That the planters held a meeting* may have [surprised George].

The answer is clear as soon as we look at the tree diagram in (22), where subjects have been identified by the rules stated in section 8.1.

(22)

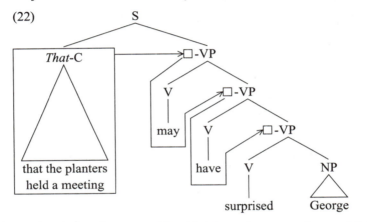

By the chain of separate identifications that our rules establish, the *that* clause that serves as the subject of the largest verb phrase eventually comes to serve also as the subject of the verb phrase *surprised George*. Thus, we really want a subject/complement rule like (21a) to be satisfied whenever the object is an ordinary noun phrase and the subject is identified—either directly or indirectly—as a *that* clause.

8.3 SUBJECTS OF ADJECTIVE PHRASES

So far in this chapter, we have confined our attention to identifying subjects of verb phrases of various sorts. Exactly the same approach works well with adjective phrases. A first example is provided by sentence (23).

(23) That Joe steals hubcaps is [clear].

In chapter 4, one of the subject/complement rules that we assigned to CLEAR was the following:

(24) *That*-C [CLEAR]

In interpreting this specification, we had to ignore temporarily the problem of how the *that* clause could be understood as the subject of CLEAR,
when it was actually joined with a phrase headed by *is*. But if we now treat
CLEAR just as we treated SURPRISE, we find that the *that* clause that
serves as the subject of the sentence as a whole comes to be identified as
the subject of the adjective phrase. The way in which this happens is
shown in (25).

(25)

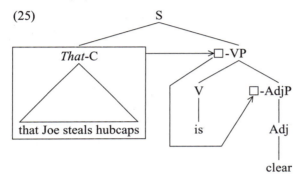

Thus, *clear* in this example satisfies rule (24) so long as we understand the
rule as requiring that the subject of CLEAR be a *that* clause, without
insisting that this *that* clause necessarily be adjacent to the adjective
phrase.

In the same way, an adjective phrase that serves as the complement of
a transitive verb commonly looks to the object of the transitive verb for
its subject. We see this in (26a), which is diagrammed in (26b).

(26) a. Joe made Fido glum.

b.

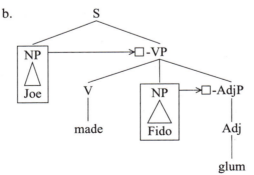

Thus, the requirement that the subject of *glum* be an ordinary noun phrase is satisfied in this example.

A slightly more complex example illustrating the same point is provided by (27).

(27) Joe made it clear that he would resign.

Here the word *it* serves as a clausal substitute, standing in place of a postponed *that* clause. We have said that CLEAR allows a *that* clause as subject. As in chapter 4, we will assume that this subject possibility is just as well satisfied by the word *it* linked to a *that* clause as it is by a *that* clause itself. A complete picture of the various relations between parts of this sentence is given in (28).

(28)

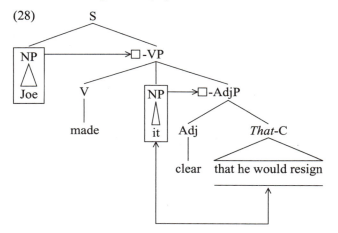

Just as in the simpler example in (26), the object of MAKE serves as the subject of the adjective phrase. In this example, the object is the clausal substitute *it*, which here is linked to a *that* clause. This *that* clause is thus understood as fulfilling any functions of the object. One of these functions is to serve as the subject of the adjective phrase that serves as the complement of MAKE. Thus, by an indirect route, the structure in (28) satisfies the following rule:

(29) *That*-C [CLEAR]

So far in this section, we have seen that adjective phrases deserve to be thought of as having subjects, and deserve to have their subjects identified by much the same rules as do verb phrases. We might also note that adjective phrases are like verb phrases in another respect: they are able to assign their own subject the additional role of serving as the subject of a complement. Example (30) shows this process at work.

(30) Freddy seems eager to *buy the house.*

As shown in (31), the rules that we have developed so far will have the effect of making *Freddy* the subject of the adjective phrase headed by *eager.*

(31)

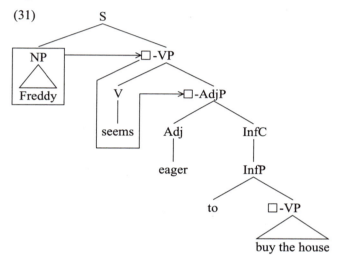

Our intuitions tell us that *Freddy* is also the understood agent of the verb phrase *buy the house.* We can account for this result if we let the adjective EAGER behave just like an intransitive verb, assigning its own subject the added role of identifying the subject of its complement. As shown in (32), this last step finishes creating the indirect link that we want between *Freddy* and the subject of the lowest verb phrase.

(32)

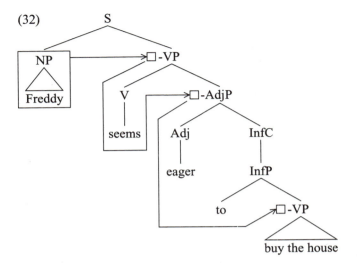

Exercise

1. In each of the following sentences, an adjective phrase is italicized. In each case, say which noun phrase or clause in the sentence serves as the subject of this phrase, and draw a tree diagram in which the successive identifications are indicated by arrows.

    a. George appears to have wanted to be *loyal to the company*.
    b. Fred's receiving a ticket made his sister *angry at the sheriff*.
    c. Carla wants Bill to try to remain *calm*.
    d. Jones would like for it to be *clear to Barry* that the city plans to sue him.

8.4   EXCEPTIONAL VERBS

In the preceding sections, we have assumed a general rule to the effect that in a structure with an object noun phrase it is the object that identifies the subject of a following complement. For most English verbs that take both an object and another complement, this rule holds true. There is a handful of verbs, however, that are exceptional. Even though these verbs take objects followed by predicate complements, it is the subject rather than the object that identifies the subject of the complement.

A first example of a word that is exceptional in this way is PROMISE. In three of the complement configurations that PROMISE allows, nothing out of the ordinary occurs.

(33) a. John promised that he would leave the room.
　　 b. John promised Nancy that he would leave the room.
　　 c. John promised to leave the room.

In (33a) and (33b), the complement subject is just *he,* the subject of the finite sentence within the *that* clause; in (33c), it is the higher subject, as expected. The exceptional case arises with an additional complement configuration allowed by many speakers of English.

(34) John promised Nancy to leave the room.

Here our general rule would lead us to expect that the object noun phrase *Nancy* would serve as the subject of the complement, but instead it is the subject noun phrase *John* that performs this function. This sentence can be contrasted with (35), where the object identifies the complement subject.

(35) John persuaded Nancy to leave the room.

The contrasting patterns of subject determination in these two sentences are shown in (36) and (37), with the normal pattern given first.

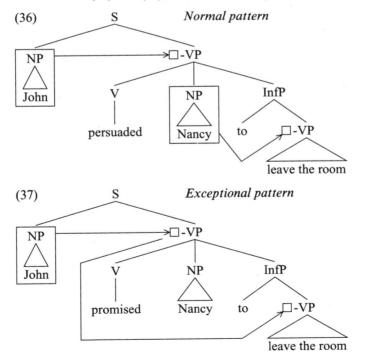

Another pair of verbs shows the same contrast between normal and exceptional behavior with regard to predicate complements. In this instance, the complements are of a type that we have not yet studied. We begin by looking at this new type of complement as it is used with the normal verb REGARD. The complement is italicized in the sentences in (38).

(38) a. Fred [regards John *as capricious*].
    b. Susan [regards Bill *as being eager to succeed*].
    c. Smith [regards Jones *as a threat to the company*].

Each of the italicized complements consists of the word *as* plus another phrase. In (38a), the following phrase is an adjective phrase; in (38b), it is a present-participial verb phrase; and in (38c), it is a noun phrase. Each of these phrases needs to have a subject, and in each case, it is the direct object of REGARD that fills this role. (Similar examples can be constructed that show that the verb VIEW has exactly the same behavior.)

Now let us turn to STRIKE, an exceptional verb taking the same kinds of *as* phrases as REGARD and VIEW.

(39) a. Fred [strikes John *as capricious*].
    b. Susan [strikes Bill *as being eager to succeed*].
    c. Smith [strikes Jones *as a threat to the company*].

Here the choice of the complement subject is entirely different: in each case, it is the subject of STRIKE rather than the object that fills this role. The diagrams in (40) contrast the complement subject choice dictated by REGARD and that dictated by STRIKE.

(40) a.   S   *Normal pattern*

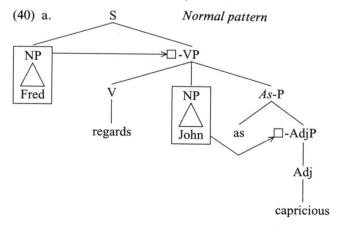

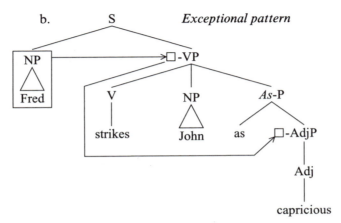

b.   S   *Exceptional pattern*

capricious

As these diagrams indicate, REGARD is normal in much the same way as PERSUADE, whereas STRIKE is exceptional in much the same way as PROMISE.

To summarize, most of the transitive verbs in English that also take predicate complements follow the general rule of having the object serve as the subject of the predicate complement. A few verbs, however, are exceptions to this rule and would need to be so marked in any complete grammar of English.

Exercise

1. Using your intuitions as a guide, say what the understood subject of the infinitival phrase is in each of the following examples:

    a. Karen asked Nellie to wash the car.
    b. Terry told Kevin to feed the dog.
    c. Karen asked Nellie how often to wash the car.
    d. Terry told Kevin how often to feed the dog.

Do the general rules given in the previous sections cover all of these examples, or is it necessary to give one or more exceptional rules? If you think that an exceptional rule is needed, say what it is.

8.5 SUBJECTS OF SUBJECT CONSTRUCTIONS

We have now developed some simple rules that identify subjects of phrases in several different situations. So far, though, our rules say nothing about what happens when infinitives and gerundives occur as subjects themselves.

(41) a. *To move to Vienna now* would be difficult for Jane.

    b. *Reading unfavorable stories* must have bothered Fred.

We will now look briefly at how subjects are identified in this situation.

In (41), the intuitions that we want to account for are that *Jane* is the subject of *move to Vienna* and that *Fred* is the subject of *reading unfavorable stories*. The rules that we developed in the preceding sections dictate that the infinitival clause in (41a) identifies the subject of the phrase *difficult for Jane*. These identifications are shown in (42).

(42)

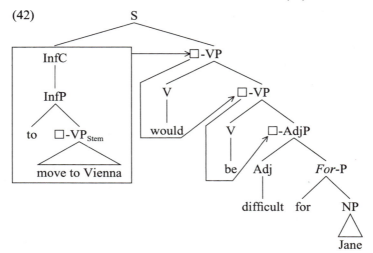

The infinitival construction as a whole serves as the subject of the verb phrase headed by *would* and also indirectly identifies the subject of each of the successive phrases nested below it. What remains to be done can be accomplished by the following rule:

(43) If a gerundive or an infinitival phrase identifies the subject of some other phrase, and this other phrase contains a complement, then this complement can identify the subject of the gerundive or infinitive.

Because *to move to Vienna* identifies the subject of the lowest adjective phrase, and because this adjective phrase has a complement *for* phrase containing the noun phrase *Jane*, rule (43) tells us that *Jane* can identify the subject of the infinitival phrase. This last subject identification is added in (44).

(44)

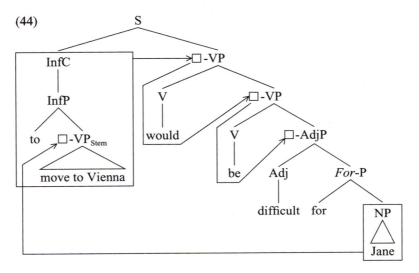

A similar calculation accounts for our intuition that *Fred* is the understood subject of *reading unfavorable stories* in (41b).

Now let us look at a sentence that is similar to (41a) in every respect except one.

(45) To move to Vienna would be difficult.

This sentence is just like the one that we have been discussing, except that the adjective *difficult* has no complement associated with it. Thus, the rule given in (43) does not appear to be applicable to this sentence.

In order to see how the subject of this infinitival clause is identified, it will be helpful to put the sentence as a whole in several different conversational contexts, as in (46)–(48).

(46) I would like to leave Italy and go to Austria, but I haven't saved much money. Thus, *to move to Vienna* would be difficult.

(47) The price of rental housing is very high, and you do not have much money saved. Thus, *to move to Vienna* would be difficult.

(48) The price of rental housing is very high, and George is not being offered much money. Thus, *to move to Vienna* would be difficult.

In (46), it is natural to interpret the subject of the italicized infinitive as being identical to the speaker. In (47), by contrast, the context predisposes us to understand the subject as *you*, the person to whom the speaker is talking. Similarly, in (48), we tend to interpret the missing subject as

George. These conversations help us identify the person for whom something would be difficult. We can say that they help us determine an *understood complement* of the adjective *difficult,* answering the question "Difficult for whom?" This understood complement can do just as well as an expressed complement in identifying the subject of an infinitive or gerundive in subject position.

One more situation deserves attention here. Suppose that we are given the following sentence in isolation:

(49) Riding tigers is difficult.

Even in this situation, speakers of English have a clear idea concerning the subject of the gerundive: the understood subject here is something like "people in general." This identification of the subject is made with the help of two distinct rules. One is the rule that we have already seen, which takes the complement of DIFFICULT and uses it as the subject of the gerundive. The other rule is one that actually provides an understood complement for DIFFICULT in situations like this. It identifies "people in general" as the complement when no other understood complement can be retrieved from the context. As a matter of fact, the same rule operates in a sentence in which no subject gerundive construction is present.

(50) Chemistry problems are difficult.

Just as in the previous example, the understood complement here is taken to be "people in general" (in the absence of a context that picks out someone more specific).

We can indicate the effect of this understood complement in (49) by including a parenthesized complement in the tree diagram, given in (51).

(51)

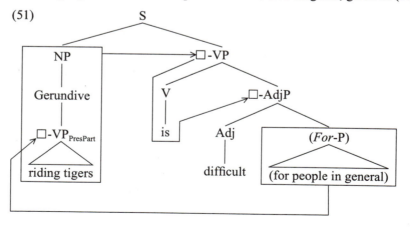

The subject of *riding tigers* is thus identified in the same manner as it would have been if it had occurred in a sentence in which *difficult* had an expressed complement.

Exercise

1. In each of the following sentences, a phrase is italicized. In each case, say which noun phrase or clause in the sentence provides the ultimate identification for the subject of this phrase, and list the steps by which this identification is established. Alternatively, draw a tree diagram in which the successive identifications are indicated by arrows. If you encounter a case where "for people in general" is an understood complement, write it into the tree with parentheses around it to indicate that it is implied but not expressed.

    a. Being able to *understand French* appears to have been important to Jane.
    b. Wanting to be *clever* seems to be natural.
    c. Fred believes that it is easy to avoid *making enemies*.
    d. Carol thinks that being unable to *keep the farm* bothers Henry's mother.

8.6 SUBJECTS AND REFLEXIVE PRONOUNS

So far, our chief reason for giving rules identifying subjects has been to account for the ability of a fluent speaker to look at a sentence and some predicate inside it and pick out the particular noun phrase or clause described by that predicate. The view of subjects that has been developed with this goal in mind receives strong independent support from the behavior of reflexive pronouns.

We looked at reflexive pronouns briefly near the beginning of chapter 5. It was stated there that such pronouns are used just in case the nearest subject or object (if there is an object) refers to the same person or thing. The key examples from the earlier discussion are repeated here.

(52) a.   John believes that [*we* deceived *ourselves*].
    b. *John believes that [*we* deceived *us*].

(53) a.   John believes that [Nora told *us* about *ourselves*].
    b. *John believes that [Nora told *us* about *us*].

(54) a. *We* believe that [John distrusts *ourselves*].
    b.   *We* believe that [John distrusts *us*].

(55) a. *We* believe that [John told Nora about *ourselves*].
    b.   *We* believe that [John told Nora about *us*].

The pairs of examples in (52) and (53) illustrate situations in which a reflexive pronoun is required. In (54) and (55), by contrast, only an ordinary pronoun is allowed.

Although the sentences in (52)–(55) support this treatment, other sentences can be found that appear to pose problems. One such pair of sentences is the following:

(56)   a.   *We made John proud of ourselves.
      b.   We made John proud of us.

According to the idea of subject that we assumed prior to this chapter, the noun phrase *we* would count as the subject nearest to the final pronoun, as shown in (57).

(57)

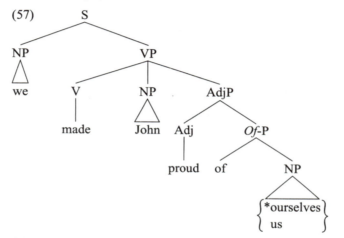

As a consequence, we would expect the reflexive pronoun to be acceptable and the ordinary pronoun to be unacceptable—just the reverse of what is actually the case.

Here the new idea of subjects yields a better result. The treatment that we have developed in this chapter dictates (58) as the structure for these sentences.

(58)

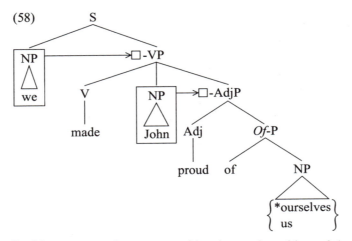

In this structure, the nearest subject is not the subject of the sentence as a whole, but instead is the subject of the adjective phrase, which is identified by the noun phrase *John*. Thus, the noun phrase that serves as the object of the preposition *of* does not refer to the same person or thing as the nearest subject does. As a result, we correctly predict that the reflexive will be unacceptable here.

This new treatment also sheds light on the contrast illustrated in (59) and (60).

(59) a.   Kevin told Anne to be loyal to herself.
      b. *Kevin told Anne to be loyal to her.

(60) a. *Kevin promised Anne to be loyal to herself.
      b.   Kevin promised Anne to be loyal to her.

Prior to this chapter, we would have said that in all four of these sentences the nearest subject was *Kevin* and the nearest object was *Anne*. We would thus have been left without any reason to expect the contrast that we actually find between (59) and (60). However, with the new ideas about subjects, we find that the nearest subject in (59) and the nearest subject in (60) are not the same. The trees in (61) and (62) show the relevant subject identifications.

(61)

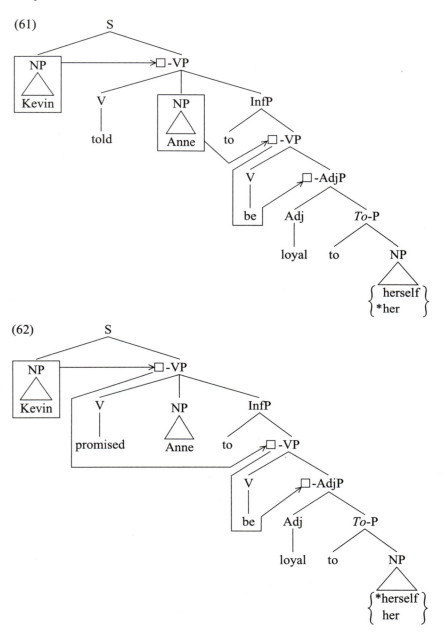

(62)

The verbs TELL and PROMISE identify the subjects of their complements in distinct ways. This difference in the subjects of the two infinitival phrases yields a corresponding difference in the subjects of the adjective phrases. Thus, the nearest subject in (59) is identified by the noun phrase *Anne,* whereas the nearest subject in (60) is identified by *Kevin.*

8.7   A REVISED VIEW OF MISSING SUBJECTS

The rules developed in the preceding sections of this chapter have the effect of picking out one of several noun phrases in a sentence as the "understood subject" of a phrase that does not have an expressed subject of its own. Suppose, for instance, that we are asked to determine the subject of the italicized verb phrase in the following sentence:

(63) Alice told Frank that Jane hopes to *receive a promotion.*

Even though three different noun phrases appear in this sentence, our rules dictate that *Jane* is the only one that can serve as the understood subject of *receive a promotion.* This result agrees with our actual intuition about this sentence: we understand the *that* clause to mean that Jane hopes that she, Jane, will receive a promotion.

However, consideration of some slightly more complex examples suggests that this idea about understood subjects is not quite correct. Although there is no doubt that the person named Jane is the hoped-for promotion recipient, we will see reasons to think that the noun phrase *Jane* is not the understood subject of *receive a promotion*—that instead, the understood subject is more like a pronoun that refers back to Jane.

Let us begin by considering additional examples involving the verb HOPE. The first example is just the sentence contained in the *that* clause of (63).

(64) a. Jane hopes to receive a promotion.

b.

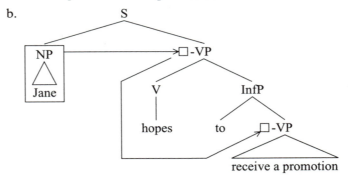

Because HOPE also allows *that* clauses, it is possible to form a sentence with an identical meaning in which the infinitival construction is replaced by a *that* clause. When we do this, the most natural subject for the *that* clause is the pronoun *she*.

(65) *Jane* hopes that *she* will receive a promotion.

In particular, the pronoun is more natural here than a repeated use of the name *Jane*.

(66) ?*Jane* hopes that *Jane* will receive a promotion.

These examples thus give us an initial reason to think that the subject of the infinitival might be very much like a pronoun, rather than a copy of the higher subject.

The case for this view becomes stronger when we look at sentences in which the subject of the sentence as a whole contains a word such as *each* or *every*. The following example illustrates what happens:

(67) *Each woman* hopes to receive a promotion.

Let us once again look for a synonymous sentence in which the complement of HOPE is a *that* clause. Using a pronoun inside the *that* clause gives us a sentence that means exactly the same thing as (67).

(68) *Each woman* hopes that *she* will receive a promotion.

By contrast, if we simply repeat the subject of the sentence as a whole, the resulting example means something entirely different from (67).

(69) *Each woman* hopes that *each woman* will receive a promotion.

We can imagine a situation in which each woman wants a promotion for herself but not for every other woman. In such a situation, (69) would be false, whereas both (67) and (68) would be true. The interpretation of the sentence with an infinitival complement is thus the same as that of the sentence with a *that* clause having a pronoun as subject. Thus, we get the correct interpretation for (67) if we say that the unexpressed subject of the lower verb phrase is understood as if it were a pronoun. On the other hand, we get the wrong interpretation if we maintain that the unexpressed subject of the lower verb phrase is understood as if it were a copy of the subject of the main clause.

There are many other verbs (and also many adjectives) for which the description given above holds true. Consider, for example, the sentence in (70), where the main-clause verb phrase is headed by PERSUADE.

(70) Martha persuaded one of the boys to feed the dog.

Now let us compare the following two revised versions of this sentence, in both of which the infinitival phrase is replaced by a *that* clause:

(71) a. Martha persuaded *one of the boys* that *he* should feed the dog.
　　b. Martha persuaded *one of the boys* that *one of the boys* should feed the dog.

Clearly (71a) is nearer than (71b) to the meaning of (70).

We find evidence for exactly the same view of understood subjects when we look more closely at infinitival and gerundive constructions in subject position. The following sentence provides a clear illustration:

(72) Receiving a ticket annoyed *one of the boys*.

Here again, we have the possibility of expressing the same idea with a *that* clause instead of a gerundive. Moreover, we can compare two possible choices for the subject of the *that* clause. In (73a), we use a pronoun as subject of the sentence; in (73b), we use a repeated occurrence of *one of the boys*.

(73) a. That *he* received a ticket annoyed *one of the boys*.
　　b. That *one of the boys* received a ticket annoyed *one of the boys*.

Sentence (73a) is clearly more accurate than (73b) as a paraphrase for (72). In particular, both (72) and (73a) give the impression that the boy receiving the ticket and the boy who was annoyed are one and the same. In (73b), by contrast, they could very well be different. This finding exactly parallels the result that we obtained with HOPE: the subject of the gerundive is interpreted more like a pronoun than like a full noun phrase. In these two cases, then, the rules as developed in preceding sections should not be thought of as picking out the actual subjects. Instead, the real subjects of these phrases are *understood pronouns,* and the rules pick out their *antecedents* (the noun phrases that we use to determine their reference).

Not all missing subjects are understood in the way just described. For a significant class of verbs in English, it makes sense to say that the understood subject of their complement is *identical* to the subject of the larger phrase, rather than that the understood subject is a pronoun. It is as if the subject that we actually express with these verbs is not understood with them at all, but instead is simply passed down to a complement phrase.

A careful examination of the behavior of the verb SEEM reveals that it has this property. Let us begin by looking at the following sentence:

(74) a. Freddy seems to dislike the principal.

b.

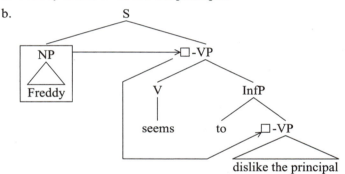

The verb SEEM is like the verb HOPE in allowing *that* clauses as well as infinitivals. In the case of HOPE, the subject of the infinitival phrase was a pronoun that was coreferential with the subject of the main sentence. With SEEM, by contrast, the subject in the infinitival-phrase sentence is referred to only once in the *that*-clause sentence.

(75) a. It seems that Freddy dislikes the principal.
     b. *Freddy seems that he dislikes the principal.

This single role that Freddy plays in (75a) is that of subject of the lower sentence. Thus, we have reason to suspect that (74a), our original SEEM example, is interpreted as if the subject of the lower verb phrase is actually *Freddy,* rather than a pronoun having *Freddy* as its antecedent.

Verbs such as APPEAR and HAPPEN and adjectives such as LIKELY and CERTAIN exhibit the same behavior. Listed in (76)–(79) are several pairs of sentences involving these words. The first sentence in each pair contains an infinitival complement; the second contains a corresponding *that* clause. In each instance, the two sentences are synonymous, and the noun phrase that serves as the subject of the sentence as a whole in the (a) example serves as the lower subject in the (b) example.

(76) a. *Several coins* appear to have vanished.
   b. It appears that *several coins* have vanished.

(77) a. *A policeman* happened to be near the corner.
   b. It happened that *a policeman* was near the corner.

(78) a. *One of the children* is likely to find the egg.
   b. It is likely that *one of the children* will find the egg.

(79) a. *Some of the records* are certain to be faulty.
   b. It is certain that *some of the records* are faulty.

What distinguishes words like HOPE from words like SEEM? The central difference resides in what the two verbs require in order to be interpreted. The verb HOPE has a role associated with it (the role of the "hoper") that needs to be filled in any sentence in which the verb appears, and the job of identifying the occupant of this role falls to the subject of HOPE. By contrast, the verb SEEM does not have any such use of its own for its subject. Instead, the only thing that it does with its subject is to hold it for use as the understood subject of its complement.

From this point on, we will refer to SEEM and other verbs like it as *transparent,* because of the way they let their subjects pass down into their complements. In chapter 13, in the course of studying two special English constructions, we will discover some simple strategies for identifying transparent verbs and adjectives.

Chapter 9

Passives and the *Easy* Construction

In the preceding chapter, we discussed subjects of phrases and stated some rules governing the way in which subjects are identified. We noted that the primary use for subjects is to identify the first role required by the head verb or adjective, and that a secondary use is to serve as the subject of a complement verb phrase or adjective phrase. In this chapter, we will examine two constructions in which the subject of a phrase is used quite differently.

9.1 THE PASSIVE CONSTRUCTION

Traditional grammars of English distinguish between "active voice" and "passive voice," and sometimes also between "active sentences" and "passive sentences." The contrast is often described as a difference in what the subject contributes to the interpretation of the sentence. The following pairs of examples exhibit this contrast:

(1) a. Alice has taken John to the library.   (active)
     b. John has been taken to the library.   (passive)

(2) a. We chose Phil for the position.   (active)
     b. Phil was chosen for the position.   (passive)

The subjects of the active sentences identify the "agents" or "actors," whereas the subjects of the corresponding passive sentences identify the persons toward whom the actions are directed—the persons who "undergo" the action.

9.1.1 Internal Structure of the Passive Construction

In order to understand how passive voice is conveyed in English, it will be useful for us to isolate the following sequences taken from the sentences in (1b) and (2b):

(3) a. taken to the library
    b. chosen for the position

As we will see later in this chapter, the rules of English allow sequences such as these to be used in a variety of circumstances. We will refer to such sequences as *passive phrases*.

The two examples that we have in (3) illustrate two important characteristics of the passive construction. The first is that the head verbs *taken* and *chosen* are past participles. The following examples show that this is the only form that is allowed here:

(4) *John has been $\left\{ \begin{array}{l} \text{take} \\ \text{took} \\ \text{taking} \end{array} \right\}$ to the library.

The second characteristic is that both TAKE and CHOOSE normally require objects, yet none are visible in the sequences in (3). We can see that objects are normally required with these verbs by trying to use these sequences with perfect HAVE.

(5) a. *John has [taken to the library].
    b. *Phil has [chosen for the position].

We can also see that the noun phrase *must* be missing from the passive sequences. If we try to use expressed objects in (1b) and (2b), the results are completely unacceptable.

(6) a. *John has been [taken Bill to the library].
    b. *Phil was [chosen Martha for the position].

We can indicate the missing objects in the phrases in (3) by rewriting them as we did the missing-phrase constructions studied earlier.

(7) a. taken _____ to the library
    b. chosen _____ for the position

By doing this, we express two facts about these phrases: that these verbs normally require objects, and that the objects must be "understood" in this construction, rather than expressed.

We might also note here that only the noun phrase nearest to the verb is eligible to be the missing noun phrase of a passive construction. Thus, we can form passive structures in which an object noun phrase is missing, as in the above examples, or structures in which the object of a preposition is missing, when this preposition comes immediately after the verb.

(8) a. This matter has been [looked into ____].
   b. The baby is being [cared for ____].

On the other hand, it is not possible to form a passive with some other noun phrase missing.

(9) a. *George was [given a book to ____].
      (Someone gave a book to George.)
   b. *Sally was [received a gift from ____].
      (Someone received a gift from Sally.)

To summarize, a passive structure must be headed by a past participle. It must also contain a missing noun phrase, and this noun phrase must be the first one after the verb. If we simply had to express a missing-noun-phrase requirement, we could do it with the symbol $VP_{PastPart}/NP$, meaning a past-participial verb phrase with a missing noun phrase. In order to express the "first noun phrase" requirement as well, we incorporate this additional information into the symbol: $VP_{PastPart}/1stNP$. As formidable as this symbol looks, all it means is a past-participial verb phrase with a missing first noun phrase.

The pairs of tree diagrams in (10) and (11) illustrate the difference between active past-participial verb phrases and the corresponding passive structures.

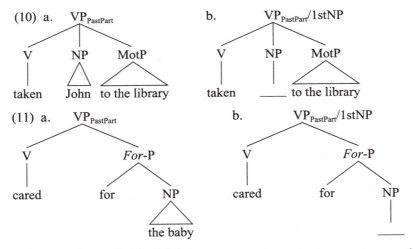

Passive phrases in English have one more important property, one that distinguishes them from passive constructions in many other languages—namely, that they allow an optional *by* phrase to identify the agent of the action expressed by the head verb. For instance, in addition to (12a), which is a structure of the type we have seen already, structures like (12b) with a *by* phrase are possible.

(12) a. John was [taken ____ to the library].
     b. John was [taken ____ to the library *by Alice*].

A tree diagram for the passive phrase in (12b) is given in (13).

(13)

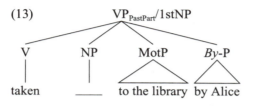

A *by* phrase that identifies the agent of an action is possible only in passive phrases. Trying to use it in active phrases produces unacceptable results.

(14) *Fred has [taken John to the library by Alice].

The only types of *by* phrases that are acceptable in active structures are those that indicate proximity (15a) or those that identify a method of doing something (15b).

(15) a. Fred is standing *by the river*.
     b. Yasir blunted Nigel's attack *by forcing an exchange of queens*.

Exercise

1. For each of the following passive phrases, draw a tree diagram. Be sure to indicate the position of the missing noun phrase.

    a. put on the table
    b. eaten by a tiger
    c. considered intelligent
    d. told that the colonists had revolted
    e. carried into the room by the butler
    f. asked to open the letter

9.1.2   Passive Phrases as Complements

In subsection 9.1.1, we saw how passive phrases are formed; in the present subsection, we will see how they can be used as complements to certain English verbs. In the interests of simplifying the appearance of rules and trees, we will use the symbol *PassP* as an abbreviation for the somewhat cumbersome $VP_{PastPart}/1stNP$.

We have already seen one example of a verb that allows passive phrases as complements, namely, the verb BE.

(16) a. John has [been *taken to the library*].
    b. Phil will [be *chosen for the position*].

Thus, for the verb BE, we want to add the following complement rule:

(17) [BE PassP]

This rule can be expressed in tree form as in (18).

(18) VP

    V   PassP

  BE

There are also several other verbs that allow passive phrases, including the ones illustrated in (19).

(19) a. Fred [got *kicked by the mule*].
      [GET PassP]
    b. Nina [got Bill *elected to the committee*].
      [GET NP PassP]
    c. Sharon [had the carpet *cleaned*].
      [HAVE NP PassP]
    d. Smith [wants the picture *removed from the office*].
      [WANT NP PassP]
    e. George [saw his brother *beaten by the soldiers*].
      [SEE NP PassP]

In later chapters, we will see that passive phrases have several other uses in addition to their use as complements.

Exercises

1. Below are listed several verbs, each accompanied by a complement rule that mentions passive phrases. For each such listing, construct an experimental sentence that indicates whether that verb allows that particular complement configuration. The first is done as an example.

    a. [KEEP PassP]
      Answer: No. *John kept taken to the library by Alice.
    b. [MAKE NP PassP]

   c. [HEAR NP PassP]
   d. [SEEM PassP]
   e. [NEED NP PassP]
   f. [CAUSE NP PassP]

2. Draw a complete tree diagram for each of the following sentences. Feel free to use the symbol *PassP* instead of $VP_{PastPart}/1stNP$. Be sure to indicate the position of the missing noun phrase in any passive phrase that you find.

   a. Peter has been asked to resign.
   b. Frances has had the drapes cleaned.
   c. Shirley seems to have gotten Fred promoted.
   d. Molly must have asked to be taken to the station.

9.1.3 The Interpretation of the Passive Construction

As the preceding subsections make clear, the passive construction differs from ordinary verb phrases in both its internal structure and its external surroundings. As was noted at the beginning of this chapter, it also differs markedly from ordinary verb phrases in the way it uses its subject. It is this difference that accounts for the way the following sentence is interpreted:

(20) John was taken to the library.

In particular, it accounts for the fact that the subject of the sentence as a whole is used to identify the understood object of the verb *taken*.

   Let us look in detail at the interpretation of this sentence. The tree diagram is given in (21), where we revert to the longer symbol $VP_{PastPart}/1stNP$ to stand for the passive phrase.

(21)

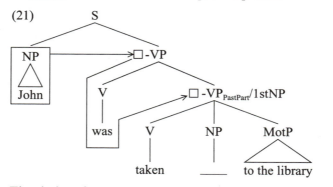

The choice of *John* as the subject of the main verb phrase comes about as a result of the first rule of chapter 8. Since *was* is an intransitive verb, the subject of the phrase that it heads also serves as the subject of its complement, again by one of the rules of chapter 8. Thus, we now have identified *John* as the subject of the passive phrase. If we were to use this subject in the usual way within this lower phrase, we would use it to identify the agent of the verb *taken*. But we know that *John* is not the understood agent of *taken*. What happens instead is that inside the passive phrase, the subject is used to identify the missing noun phrase in object position. Thus, the subject is "deflected" away from making its usual identification and instead identifies a missing noun phrase associated with the construction. We can diagram this entire situation as in (22).

(22)

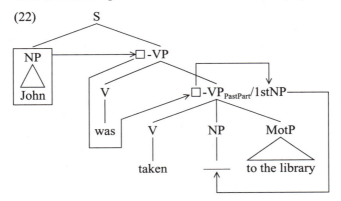

We see the same kind of deflection in a transitive verb phrase in which a passive phrase serves as the second complement. Such a structure is pictured in (23).

(23)

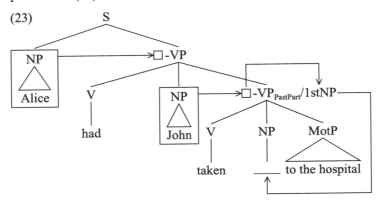

Here the rules of chapter 8 dictate that the direct-object noun phrase should serve as the subject of the complement that follows it. Thus, *John*

is the subject of the passive phrase. But the subject of the passive phrase is now used in the same way as in the previous example. Instead of being used to identify the agent of *taken*, it is used to identify the missing noun phrase associated with the construction.

As noted earlier in this chapter, English makes a special provision for identifying agents within passive phrases. This is the *by* phrase exemplified in (24).

(24) John was taken to the hospital *by the doctor*.

But what about a sentence like (25), where there is no noun phrase that identifies the agent?

(25) John was taken to the hospital.

In such cases, our intuitive interpretation is that some unspecified person is the agent.

Even in situations like this one, in which no agent is expressed, the passive construction requires us to understand one as having played a role. This property of passives stands out quite clearly in the behavior of certain verbs of motion that can occur both in intransitive verb phrases and in passive phrases. *Roll* is one such verb.

(26) a. The barrel [rolled down the hill].   (intransitive verb phrase)
       b. The barrel was [rolled down the hill].   (passive phrase)

In (26a), we have a strong sense that the barrel moved of its own accord, whereas in (26b), we have an equally strong sense that some agent must have been involved in making it roll. The latter interpretation is just as strongly felt here as in the active sentence in (27), in which the agent is identified in the normal way by the subject.

(27) Someone rolled the barrel down the hill.

To summarize, what makes the interpretation of the passive phrase unusual is that its subject is given the role of identifying a missing object of a verb or preposition, rather than the more usual role of identifying an agent. In addition, the agent is either identified by a *by* phrase, or left unidentified.

Exercise

1. Each of the following sentences contains an italicized passive phrase. For each sentence, draw a tree diagram in which you indicate all of the subject identifica-

tions that contribute to the interpretation of the passive phrase. (If the ultimate identifier for the passive object is several phrases away, there will of course be several relevant links.)

    a. Karen was *introduced to Gordon*.
    b. We had John's phone *disconnected*.
    c. Jacob will regret having been *brought to the meeting*.
    d. Trying to be *examined by a specialist* is impossible for Anita.

9.1.4   Passive Phrases with Clausal Subjects

In each of the examples discussed so far in this chapter, the subject of the passive construction has been identified by an ordinary noun phrase, and this noun phrase has then been used to identify the missing noun phrase inside the passive phrase. So far, then, we have no account of sentences such as those in (28).

(28) a. [$_{That-C}$ That Morton is a genius] is believed ____ by my uncle.
     b. [$_{IQ}$ Which attorney will give the closing argument] has been decided ____.

Each of these sentences has a clause as its subject, which identifies the missing direct object within the passive phrase. Corresponding to each of these sentences is a well-formed sentence in which the same clause serves as the direct object of an active structure rather than as the subject of a passive structure.

[29] a. My uncle believes [$_{That-C}$ that Morton is a genius].
     b. Someone has decided [$_{IQ}$ which attorney will give the closing argument].

It thus appears that the passive phrases in (28) should not be characterized as having missing first noun phrases, but instead should be understood as having missing first clauses. In diagram form, the structures of the two passive phrases would be those given in (30).

(30)

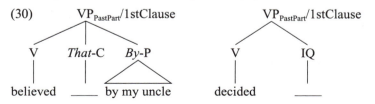

One way of accounting for these examples would be to extend the definition of allowable passive structures in just the way indicated in (30).

Then the clausal subjects of the sentences in (28) would automatically identify the missing clauses in their respective passive phrases. The entire process as it would apply to (28a) is shown in (31).

(31)

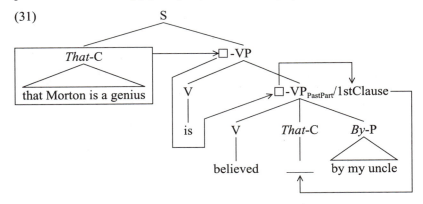

Another possibility, however, is suggested by the relatively high acceptability of examples in which a clausal subject occurs with a passive phrase in which the missing element does not occur in a typical clausal environment. Two such examples are given in (32).

(32) a. [_That-C_ That Joe had a previous arrest] was alluded to _____ by several of the witnesses.

b. [_That-C_ That the convention would end on a happy note] was hinted at _____ by the organizers.

In each of these sentences, the missing element is in the position of a prepositional object, a position in which _that_ clauses are ordinarily unacceptable, as noted in chapter 4. These additional examples, then, suggest the possibility that the missing element in every passive is actually a noun phrase, and that there is some degree of permissiveness with regard to the structures that are allowed to identify this noun phrase. Under this alternative hypothesis, the clausal subject would be allowed to identify the missing noun phrase inside the passive phrase, even though this clausal subject was not itself a noun phrase. Under this hypothesis, the structure for (28a) would be that shown in (33).

(33)

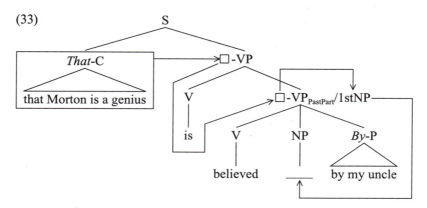

Under either of these accounts, we expect to find alternative versions of all of these sentences in which the place of the clause as subject of the sentence is taken by the substitute subject *it,* and this is indeed what happens.

(34) a. *It* is believed ____ by my uncle [$_{That-C}$ that Morton is a genius].
  b. *It* has been decided [$_{IQ}$ which attorney will give the closing argument].

(35) a. *It* was alluded to ____ by several of the witnesses [$_{That-C}$ that Joe had a previous arrest].
  b. *It* was hinted at ____ by the organizers [$_{That-C}$ that the convention would end on a happy note].

The principle that is relevant here, which was originally stated in chapter 4, is given in (36).

(36) In a situation in which a clause would have some use as a subject, it is possible to employ in its place the clausal substitute *it* linked to a pseudocomplement clause of the same type.

Here the use to which the clausal subject would be put is the indirect identification of the subject of the passive phrase and thus also of the missing element inside the passive phrase. Under these circumstances, (36) allows us to use *it* linked to a pseudocomplement clause instead.

9.1.5   Distinguishing Passive Phrases from Other Verb Phrases

Let us shift our attention now to a more practical matter, that of determining whether specific examples contain a passive phrase or a nonpassive phrase. Even though this discussion will be practical in nature, we will rely heavily on particular rules discussed in this chapter and in earlier chapters. A construction will qualify as a passive phrase only if it satisfies two sets of requirements: *internal requirements* (rules regulating the way the structure itself is built) and *external requirements* (rules stating the larger contexts in which the structure can be used). We will see that both kinds of requirements provide useful clues to correctly identifying phrase types in individual sentences.

9.1.5.1   Internal Requirements of Passive Phrases   Let us begin with the internal requirements of passive phrases. The first rule about passive phrases given in this chapter was that they must be headed by past participles. Thus, the first question to ask about an example phrase is whether or not its head verb in isolation could be analyzed as a past participle. Suppose, for instance, that we were asked about phrases that were headed as follows:

(37) a. [taken...]
   b. [returned...]
   c. [put...]
   d. [forgot...]
   e. [remove...]
   f. [carrying...]

We know that *taken* is a past participle (and nothing else); we also know that *returned* and *put* can be past participles, among other things. By contrast, none of the remaining three verbs can possibly be analyzed as past participles, since the past participles for FORGET, REMOVE, and CARRY are *forgotten, removed,* and *carried.* Our temporary conclusion, then, would be that the first three phrases *might* be passive phrases, whereas the last three could not possibly be.

The other major requirement about the internal structure of passive phrases is that they have a missing first noun phrase, as compared with corresponding active verb phrases. Thus, when we want to know whether a certain phrase could possibly qualify as a passive phrase, our second question should be whether there is an acceptable active verb phrase in which a noun phrase is present after the same verb. In answering this question, we are relying on what we know already, unconsciously or consciously, about complement specifications for individual verbs. Here are some examples:

(38) a. [taken to the office]
　　 b. [killed]
　　 c. [rolled down the hill]
　　 d. [gone to the office]
　　 e. [died]
　　 f. [fallen down the hill]

The verbs in these examples are divided equally between those that allow a direct object in active structures and those that do not. Either we know this already or we can remind ourselves of it by doing experiments as in (39).

(39) a. John [took *Ted* to the office].　　　　[TAKE NP MotP]
　　 b. Shirley [killed *the crabgrass*].　　　　[KILL NP]
　　 c. Sam [rolled *the barrel* down the hill].　[ROLL NP MotP]
　　 d. *John [went *Ted* to the office].　　　　*[GO NP MotP]
　　 e. *Shirley [died *the crabgrass*].　　　　*[DIE NP]
　　 f. *Sam [fell *the barrel* down the hill].　*[FALL NP MotP]

These considerations lead us to conclude that the first three phrases in (38) might ultimately qualify as passive phrases, whereas the last three cannot possibly qualify.

In many situations, looking at internal requirements permits a definite decision about whether a certain phrase is a passive phrase or an active phrase. Yet in one large class of examples, internal requirements by themselves are not sufficient. The problem examples are those whose head verb can occur in active phrases either with an object or without one. EAT, SHAVE, and ROLL all have these dual possibilities.

(40) a. The canary [ate].　　　　　　　[EAT]
　　 b. The canary [ate *its lunch*].　　[EAT NP]

(41) a. Bill [shaved].　　　　　　　　[SHAVE]
　　 b. Bill [shaved *Fred*].　　　　　[SHAVE NP]

(42) a. The barrel [rolled down the hill].　　　　[ROLL MotP]
　　 b. John [rolled *the barrel* down the hill].　[ROLL NP MotP]

Suppose we are given the phrase *eaten* in isolation and asked whether it is a passive phrase or an active phrase. *Eaten* is a past participle, so it could head a passive phrase. Also, the verb EAT allows following objects, so we could analyze this phrase as taking the form [*eaten* ____]. But the past participle *eaten* could also head an active verb phrase, of the sort that we found occurring with the verb HAVE. And EAT can be used in active sentences without an object, as we saw in (40a). Thus, this sequence can be analyzed simply as [*eaten*]. The result of these considerations is that we cannot really identify this phrase one way or another in isolation from a larger context.

We get an even more indeterminate result when we try to identify the phrases *shaved* and *rolled down the hill* in isolation. Both of these sequences can be analyzed as either past-participial active verb phrases or passive phrases. In addition, both qualify as *past-tense* active phrases, since *shaved* and *rolled* serve as past-tense forms as well as past participles.

In view of such examples, it is necessary to study the external requirements of passive phrases, paying particular attention to the ways in which they differ from the external requirements of past-participial and past-tense active phrases. Except for a handful of ambiguous sentences that involve constructions that will be discussed in later chapters, this attention to external requirements will allow us to make clear determinations in situations where internal requirements are not sufficient.

Exercise

1. For each of the following phrases, determine whether it could possibly be a passive phrase. When the answer is yes, construct an example in which the phrase is used as a complement to BE. When the answer is no, say what requirement is not satisfied.

    a. handed to the mayor
    b. roll down the hill
    c. watched Bill open the safe
    d. told to leave the room
    e. traveled to Tehran
    f. moving into the kitchen
    g. closed
    h. flown across the border

9.1.5.2 External Requirements of Passive Phrases Let us review briefly what we have learned about the positions in which passive phrases, past-participial active phrases, and past-tense active phrases can be used. We will be particularly interested in whether the three possibilities overlap at all.

To begin with passive phrases, we have established that they can be used as complements to particular verbs, including BE, GET (both intransitive and transitive), HAVE (transitive), and WANT (transitive). In the following examples, we use the phrase *examined by the specialist,* whose internal structure dictates that it can only be a passive phrase:

(43) a. Fido [was *examined by the specialist*].   [BE PassP]
     b. Fido [got *examined by the specialist*].   [GET PassP]
     c. Alice [got Fido *examined by the specialist*].   [GET NP PassP]
     d. Alice [had Fido *examined by the specialist*].   [HAVE NP PassP]

As for past-participial active phrases, we noted in chapter 3 that they can occur as complements of (intransitive) HAVE. Example (44) contains a phrase that has a direct object and thus can only be active.

(44) Fido [has *examined the specialist*].   [HAVE VP$_{PastPart}$]

Finally, past-tense active phrases have been used in several specific situations so far. They were used in chapter 2 as predicates of simple sentences, in chapter 4 as predicates inside *that* complements and indirect questions, and in chapter 7 as predicates inside free relatives.

(45) a. Fido [*ate* the biscuit].
     b. Fred claims [$_{That-C}$ that Fido [*ate* the biscuit]].
     c. Deborah wants to know [$_{IQ}$ where Thomas [*bought* the car]].
     d. [$_{F-Rel}$ What Joanne [*said* ____]] made sense.

Each of the environments mentioned above is the exclusive domain of just one of the three constructions. We already know from chapter 3 that past-tense active phrases and past-participial active phrases occupy completely different niches. In addition, if we try to use past-tense or past-participial active phrase in one of the situations where passive phrases are allowed, the results are completely unacceptable.

(46) a. *Fido [was *examined the specialist*].   *[BE VP$_{PastPart}$]
     b. *Fido [got *examined the specialist*].   *[GET VP$_{PastPart}$]
     c. *Alice [got Fido *examined the specialist*].   *[GET NP VP$_{PastPart}$]
     d. *Alice [had Fido *examined the specialist*].   *[HAVE NP VP$_{PastPart}$]

We get similar results if we try to use a passive phrase as the complement of intransitive HAVE, or as the predicate of an independent sentence or a sentence within a *that* clause.

(47) *Fido [has *examined by the specialist*].   *[HAVE PassP]

(48) a. *Fido *examined by the specialist*.
     b. *Fred claims that Fido *examined by the specialist*.

This discussion has a pleasant conclusion: in each of the contexts that we have studied so far, only one of the three phrase types under consideration is possible. We can see the full force of this conclusion by putting the phrase *rolled down the hill* in several different contexts. (As we saw in the previous subsection, this phrase in isolation can be either a passive phrase, a past-participial active phrase, or a past-tense active phrase.) Suppose that we are asked to determine how this sequence should be analyzed in each of the following examples:

(49) a. The barrel has *rolled down the hill.*
      b. The barrel was *rolled down the hill.*
      c. Joe had the barrel *rolled down the hill.*
      d. The barrel *rolled down the hill.*
      e. Joe wanted the barrel *rolled down the hill.*
      f. Jane says that the barrel *rolled down the hill.*
      g. Jane says that the barrel has been *rolled down the hill.*

Here are the answers that we can give, along with the reasons:

(50) a. past-participial active phrase—complement of intransitive HAVE
      b. passive phrase—complement of BE
      c. passive phrase—complement of transitive HAVE
      d. past-tense active phrase—finite predicate of independent sentence
      e. passive phrase—complement of transitive WANT
      f. past-tense active phrase—finite predicate of sentence in *that* clause
      g. passive phrase—complement of BE

This demonstration suggests a surprising possibility, namely, that we can distinguish passive phrases from past-tense and past-participial active phrases solely by paying attention to the contexts in which the phrases are used, without having to give any attention to their internal structure beyond making sure that the head verb is a possible past participle. This has significant import for a fluent user of English, whose unconscious syntactic rules we are trying to mirror in our written rules. Suppose that this user is listening to an incoming sentence whose first four words are *The barrel got rolled....* Without hearing the remainder of the sentence, he or she knows already that *rolled* heads a passive phrase. From this the user can deduce that it will be followed by an understood object and that the subject of this passive phrase is to be used to identify this object. On the other hand, suppose that the first four words of the incoming sentence are *The barrel has rolled....* In this sentence, the intransitive *has* tells the hearer to expect a past-participial active phrase, whose subject should be used in the way appropriate in active intransitive sentences.

Our discussion so far has dealt with situations in which we already know whether a certain verb does or does not allow a passive phrase. What can we do, though, in a situation in which we need to determine whether a new verb takes a passive complement or an active complement? For example, suppose that we are asked whether the italicized phrase in (51) is passive, active, or both.

(51) John needs his car *moved to the backyard.*

This particular sequence happens to satisfy the internal requirements of both passive and active constructions, because MOVE can be either intransitive or transitive. The phrase under study appears to be serving as a second complement of the verb *needs,* which we have not discussed in this chapter. Thus, what we want to find out is which of the following two complement specifications is correct for NEED:

(52) a. [NEED NP PassP]
     b. [NEED NP VP$_{PastPart}$]

In order to test the first possibility, we need a phrase that can only be a passive phrase. The simplest possibility here is a phrase that contains an agent *by* phrase, for instance, *repaired by an expert.*

(53) John needs his car *repaired by an expert.*

We can test the second possibility by substituting a phrase whose head verb can only be intransitive. STAY is a good example of such a verb, so that *stayed in the backyard* should tell us what we want to know.

(54) *John needs his car *stayed in the backyard.*

These two experimental sentences show that (52a) is a correct specification for NEED, whereas (52b) is not. In other words, NEED allows passive phrases as second complements, but not past-participial active phrases.

In future chapters, we will discuss several additional contexts in which phrases headed by past participles can appear. Two of these contexts are presented in (55).

(55) a. The barrel *rolled down the hill* belonged to Fred.
     b. When *moved to a new position,* Harrison tries to adapt to his new surroundings.

Without taking up the question of exactly what the rules are that govern these constructions, let us try to determine whether the rules in question call for passive phrases or past-participial phrases. In such a situation, one in which we do not yet know consciously what the rules are, it is once again appropriate to devise experiments that will tell us whether our unconscious rules allow passives, actives, or both. We need to do the same thing that we did with NEED above. That is, we must find phrases that satisfy the internal requirements for only one of the two constructions and substitute these phrases in the sentences in (55). To get phrases that can only be passive, we can include *by* phrases expressing agents.

(56) a. The barrel *rolled down the hill by Alice* belonged to Fred.
　　 b. When *moved to a new position by his superiors,* Harrison tries to adapt to his new surroundings.

From the fact that these two experimental sentences are acceptable, we can conclude that passive phrases are allowed by the rules for the larger constructions.

　　 Now let us see whether past-participial active phrases are also allowed. To test for this possibility, we need to substitute phrases that can only be active. The clearest examples are phrases headed by verbs that are always intransitive and phrases with transitive verbs and expressed objects. Example (57a) is of the former type; example (57b) is of the latter.

(57) a. *The barrel *vanished from the yard* belonged to Alice.
　　 b. *When *received a new job,* Harrison tries to adapt to his new surroundings.

The unacceptability of these sentences shows that the rules for the larger constructions do not allow past-participial active phrases.

Exercises

1. Each of the following sentences contains the sequence *moved into the kitchen.* This sequence satisfies the internal requirements for being either a passive phrase, a past-participial active phrase, or a past-tense active phrase. However, in each of the sentences, there is only one correct analysis for the phrase. Using what was said above about the differing external behavior of these phrase types, identify the correct choice for each sentence, and give your reason.

　　 a. The table has been moved into the kitchen.
　　 b. You should have it moved into the kitchen.
　　 c. The smoke moved into the kitchen.
　　 d. The fact that the table was moved into the kitchen is irrelevant.

e. The dog has been moved into the kitchen.
f. The dog has moved into the kitchen.
g. Sally said that the dog has moved into the kitchen.

2. List all of the passive phrases in the following paragraph. In making your list, try to decide exactly where the passive phrase actually starts and where it ends. It will be helpful to remember that it is identical to a past-participial verb phrase with a missing noun phrase and a possible extra *by* phrase.

If Patricia was told that the books had been returned, then she should have decided to have the bills revised. The customers were persuaded to let their money be refunded. The dealer was informed that strong words were uttered.

9.2   THE *EASY* CONSTRUCTION

We now turn to a second construction in which the subject of a phrase makes an unusual contribution to the interpretation of the phrase. This construction is a certain type of adjective phrase that can be headed by *easy, difficult,* and certain other adjectives. We are already familiar with one of the situations in which these adjectives occur.

(58) a. *It* was easy for Charlie *to solve the problem.*
b. *It* is difficult *to reason with this banker.*

In each of these sentences, the clausal substitute *it* is linked to a postponed infinitival phrase. We find an entirely different situation in the construction to which we now turn.

9.2.1   Syntactic Properties of the *Easy* Construction

Here are two examples of the new construction:

(59) a. The problem was [easy for Charlie *to solve*].
b. This banker is [difficult *to reason with*].

At first glance, this construction does not look too much different from the old one. A close inspection, however, reveals two major differences. The first is that the subject of this construction is an ordinary noun phrase rather than the clausal substitute *it.* The second is that there is something peculiar about the infinitival phrases that follow the adjectives: each sequence lacks a noun phrase in a position where one would normally be required. Both the verb SOLVE and the preposition WITH must have objects, as we can see by trying to do without them in simple sentences.

(60) a. *Charlie solved.
b. *Someone reasoned with.

To see the same point in another way, we observe that infinitival sequences such as the ones in (59) are impossible with our earlier examples of adjectives that allow ordinary infinitival complements, such as EAGER and UNLIKELY.

(61) a. *Charlie is eager to solve.
     b. *Fred is unlikely to reason with.

These adjectives require infinitival phrases that are complete, as in (62).

(62) a. Charlie is eager to solve *the problem*.
     b. Fred is unlikely to reason with *the children*.

As a final observation, we should note that missing noun phrases are absolutely required in the *easy* construction. The same complete infinitival phrases that gave good results in (62) with EAGER and LIKELY give bad results in this new environment.

(63) a. *Charlie is easy to solve *the problem*.
     b. *Fred is difficult to reason with *the children*.

In particular, these sentences are not legitimate as paraphrases for the well-formed sentences in (64).

(64) a. It is easy for Charlie to solve the problem.
     b. It is difficult for Fred to reason with the children.

Because of the missing noun phrases required in this infinitival construction, it might appear tempting at first glance to view it as a variant of the passive construction that we studied in section 9.1. But in fact, the two constructions differ in a significant way. Whereas the missing noun phrase in the passive construction had to be the first noun phrase after the verb, the missing noun phrase in the infinitival after EASY can be farther away from the verb. We see this contrast in (65) and (66).

(65) a. *This drawer was [kept the files in ____].   (passive)
        (Compare: Someone tried to keep the files in *this drawer*.)
     b. This drawer was hard [to keep the files in ____].
        (*easy* construction)

(66) a. *Jane was [tried to persuade ____].   (passive)
        (Compare: Someone tried to persuade *Jane*.)
     b. Jane was hard for us [to try to persuade ____].
        (*easy* construction)

For this construction, then, all that we need to require is that there be a missing noun phrase. We do not have to add the requirement that it be the first one after the verb. What follows the adjective in these examples, then, is just an infinitival phrase with a missing noun phrase, which will be denoted by the symbol *InfP/NP*, just as in the discussion of infinitival indirect questions in chapter 4. With this symbol in hand, we can provide complement rules for the adjectives that take this construction. Here, for example, are the rules for EASY and DIFFICULT:

(67) a. [EASY *For*-P InfP/NP]
     [EASY InfP/NP]
   b. [DIFFICULT *For*-P InfP/NP]
     [DIFFICULT InfP/NP]

Translated into trees, the rules for EASY are as shown in (68).

(68) a.

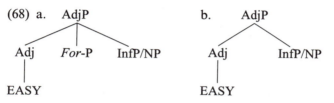

The tree diagrams appropriate for our original sentences (59a–b) are thus as shown in (69).

(69) a.

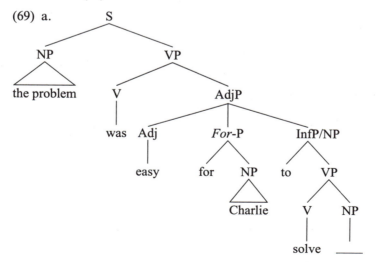

b.

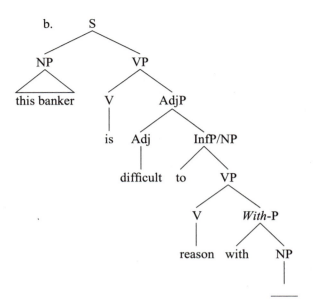

Exercises

1. In the following sentences, insert a blank in the position of the missing noun phrase called for by the *easy* construction:

    a. Amelia was easy to take to Boston.
    b. This fiddle is difficult to play sonatas on.
    c. This horse is hard to keep happy.
    d. John is easy to talk about baseball with, but he is hard to persuade to play.

2. For each of the following sentences, draw the tree that goes with it, being sure to indicate the position of any missing noun phrase:

    a. I consider this sentence hard to diagram.
    b. This question seems easy to answer.
    c. The outline may help to make the material easy for Alice to explain.
    d. That Bill will be easy to talk to is hard for me to believe.

9.2.2   Interpretation of the *Easy* Construction

Let us examine the interpretation of the two central examples from the discussion just concluded.

(70) a. The problem was easy for Charlie to solve.
     b. This banker is difficult to reason with.

If asked to identify the "understood object" of the verb *solve* in (70a), a fluent English speaker would immediately pick out *the problem,* the subject of the sentence as a whole. Similarly, the same speaker would have no trouble in identifying *this banker* as the "understood object" of the preposition *with* in (70b). In this section, we want to consider how this identification takes place—how the link is formed between the subject of the sentence as a whole and the missing noun phrase down inside the infinitival phrase.

Let us begin with (70a), and apply one at a time the subject-identification rules developed in chapter 8. First, the noun phrase *the problem* serves as the subject of the verb phrase headed by *was.* Then, by the rule about complements of intransitive verbs, this subject identifies the subject of the adjective phrase headed by *easy.* Finally, the object of *for* identifies the subject of the infinitival phrase, just as it identifies an infinitival subject when the infinitival phrase itself is the subject of EASY. The three links established so far are shown in (71).

(71)

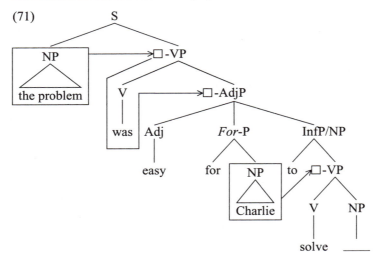

Two other connections need to be made. First, the subject of *easy* needs to be deflected, so that it identifies the missing noun phrase associated with the infinitival construction, rather than identifying the subject of any lower phrase. Second, the empty noun phrase after *solve* needs to be picked out as the missing noun phrase required by the larger constructions. The revised version of the tree in (72) shows these connections.

(72)

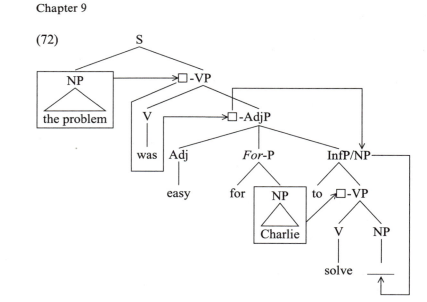

We now have an unbroken chain of links between the subject of the sentence as a whole and the missing noun phrase down inside the infinitival phrase.

The linking of the subject of the sentence with a missing noun phrase proceeds in much the same way when the adjective lacks a *for* phrase. The diagram in (73) shows the links that would be established for (70b).

(73)

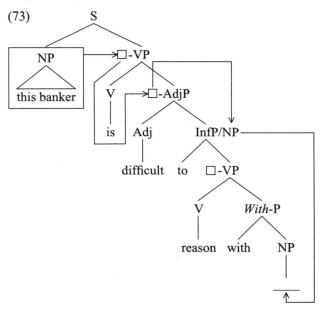

According to the rules that we have used so far, the only subject that is not provided with identification from the outside is the subject of the bare-stem verb phrase inside the infinitival phrase. And this result seems to be consistent with our intuitions as speakers of English: the "understood subject" of this verb phrase is something like the impersonal "people in general," just as it was for some of the subject infinitival constructions examined in chapter 8. Here again, we can describe the results by referring to an understood *for* phrase that goes along with adjectives like EASY and DIFFICULT.

Exercise

1. In exercise 2 at the end of the preceding subsection, you were asked to diagram the following sentences:
    a. I consider this sentence hard to diagram.
    b. This question seems easy to answer.
    c. The outline may help to make the material easy for Alice to explain.
    d. That Bill will be easy to talk to is hard for me to believe.

Add to each tree diagram the links that are relevant for identifying the missing noun phrase in the *easy* construction.

9.3 A MORE SOPHISTICATED VIEW OF MISSING-PHRASE CONSTRUCTIONS

We will begin this section by looking at some examples that are clearly perceived as unacceptable even though they might appear to obey all of the rules and constraints that have been discussed so far. The result will be a more sophisticated and accurate idea concerning the nature of missing-phrase constructions, one that will be useful not only with the constructions taken up in this chapter but also with a variety of other structures in which missing phrases are called for.

The first example to be considered contains an *easy* construction within the type of indirect-question structure studied in chapter 4.

(74) *Ruth wants to know which person Dr. Smith was difficult to operate on.

This sentence clearly contains a missing noun phrase, in the position of the object of *on,* and it has two constructions that require a missing noun phrase: an indirect question and an *easy* construction. From what we have said so far, it might seem that the tree diagram in (75) should represent a

completely legitimate structure for the indirect question contained in this
sentence.

(75)

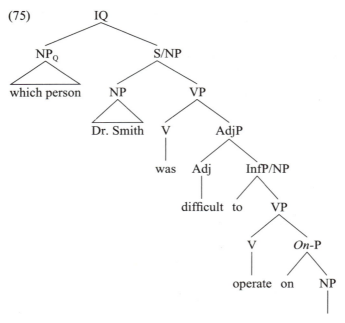

The rule in chapter 4 for phrasal questions says that the second part of an
indirect question of this kind must be a sentence that contains a missing
noun phrase, and indeed, the sentence *Dr. Smith was difficult to operate on
_____* appears to satisfy this requirement. Furthermore, as noted in section
9.2, the formation of the *easy* construction requires that the head adjective
of the adjective phrase be followed by an infinitival phrase with a missing
noun phrase. The infinitival structure *to operate on _____* appears to satisfy
this second requirement.

   We get a first hint of what might be peculiar about this structure when
we think about how this missing noun phrase is to be identified. The
identification process found in indirect questions introduced by noun
phrases was summarized schematically in diagram (36) of subsection 4.1.3
and is repeated in (76).

(76)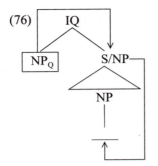

The way in which identification proceeds in the *easy* construction was just illustrated in detail in diagrams (72) and (73), the latter of which is repeated in (77).

(77)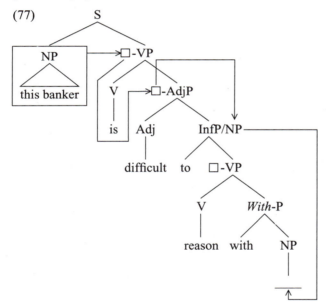

If we try to apply these two types of identification process at the same time to the structure in (75), we get the result shown in (78).

(78)

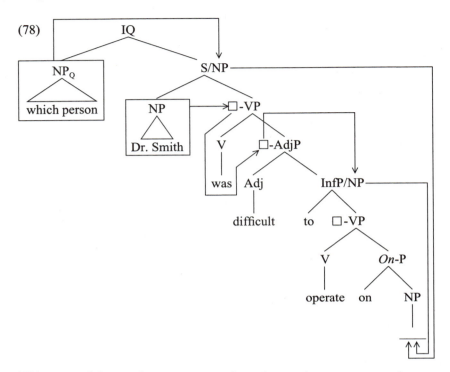

This more elaborated structure reveals an interesting property: only one missing noun phrase is available, and it is being claimed simultaneously by two separate constructions that require such a missing phrase.

Another unacceptable example that looks at first glance as if it satisfies all of the relevant rules and conditions is given in (79).

(79) *Dr. Smith is easy for Bill to be operated on _____.

Here we have a missing noun phrase as the object of the preposition *on*. The phrase *to be operated on* _____ appears to qualify as an infinitival phrase with a missing noun phrase, as required by the adjective **EASY**, and *operated on* _____ likewise appears to qualify as a past-participial verb phrase with a missing first noun phrase. A plausible tree structure for this example would be that given in (80).

(80)

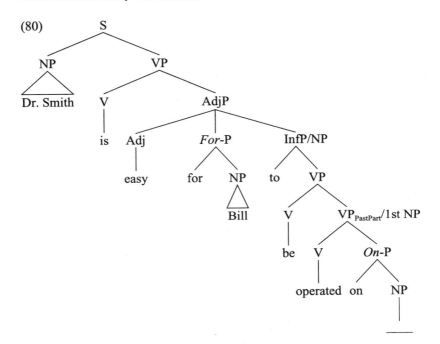

Once again, though, we find that doubling up is necessary when we try to match missing-phrase constructions and missing phrases: here there is only one missing phrase, which has to be shared between two separate constructions, as shown in (81).

(81)

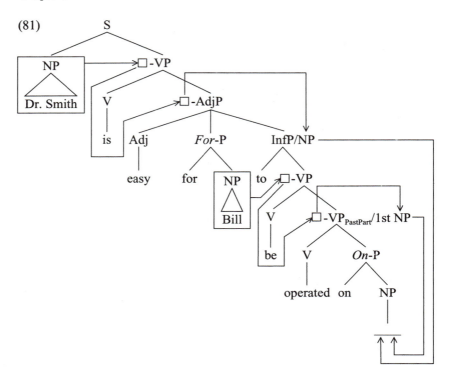

The property that (74) and (79) share—the property that separates them from the large number of acceptable examples that we have seen—is that both associate a single missing noun phrase with two separate constructions. The unacceptability of the sentences that arise under these circumstances warrants the following general principle:

(82) A phrase that satisfies a missing-phrase requirement for one construction cannot simultaneously satisfy a missing-phrase requirement for some other construction.

In effect, this statement implies the following more precise understanding of the symbols *S/NP, InfP/NP,* and *VP$_{PastPart}$/1stNP:*

(83) a. S/NP: a sentence with a missing noun phrase *associated uniquely with it.*

b. InfP/NP: an infinitival phrase with a missing noun phrase *associated uniquely with it.*

c. VP$_{PastPart}$/1stNP: a past-participial verb phrase with a missing first noun phrase *associated uniquely with it.*

One practical moral of this story is that a sequence of words that qualifies as an infinitival phrase with a missing noun phrase in one structure may count as just an ordinary infinitival phrase in another. We see this with the italicized phrases in the two sentences in (84).

(84) a. Jane will tell you that Fred is easy *to work with.*
b. Jane will tell you which colleagues Fred is eager *to work with.*

Although both of these infinitival phrases contain missing noun phrases, only one of the infinitival phrases is a genuine missing-phrase construction. The tree diagrams (85a) (for the *that* clause in (84a)), and (85b) (for the indirect question in (84b)), may help to make it clearer how the two infinitival phrases differ.

(85) a. *That*-C

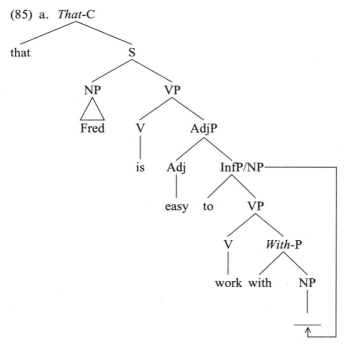

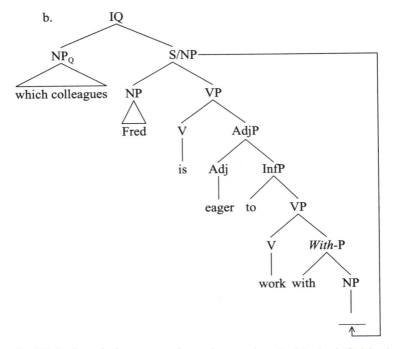

In (85a), the missing noun phrase is associated with the infinitival phrase that serves as a complement of *easy,* making this infinitival a genuine missing-phrase construction. In (85b), by contrast, the missing noun phrase is claimed by a higher constituent, namely, the sentence that combines with *which colleagues* to form an indirect question. Thus, this noun phrase is not available to be associated with the infinitival phrase. As a result, this infinitival phrase is not really a missing-phrase construction, even though it contains a missing phrase.

Exercise

1. The English adjective READY has the unusual property of allowing both the ordinary infinitival phrases that EAGER and RELUCTANT allow, and the infinitival phrases with missing noun phrases that are allowed by EASY and DIFFICULT. These structures are exemplified in (i) and (ii), respectively.

(i)   Smith is ready to operate on Jones.   ([READY InfP])

(ii) Smith is ready to operate on.   ([READY InfP/NP])

For each of the following examples, draw a tree structure in which you indicate the presence of any missing noun phrases and also indicate the missing-phrase construction with which they are associated. In each case, try to be as clear as you can about whether the infinitival phrase after READY is a genuine missing-phrase construction.

a. Margaret wonders which person Smith is ready [to operate on ____].
b. Margaret acknowledged the fact that Smith is ready [to operate on ____].
c. Martha acknowledged the fact that Smith is ready [to be operated on ____].
d. Martha wonders whether Smith is ready [to operate on ____].

PART III
THE SYNTAX OF PHRASES: MODIFICATION

Chapter 10

Modification of Nouns and Noun Phrases

In this chapter, we will discuss the constructions that are employed in English to provide *modification* for nouns and noun phrases. For the purposes of this chapter, we will use the term *modifier* to mean a word or a construction that tells more about the thing modified. We can make a further division between *restrictive modification,* which applies to common-noun phrases, and *nonrestrictive modification,* which applies to noun phrases and other larger syntactic units. In section 10.1, we will look at the semantic effect of restrictive modification. In section 10.2, we will discuss restrictive relative clauses, and in section 10.3, we will examine a variety of nonclausal modifying constructions. In section 10.4, we will look at nonrestrictive relative clauses and note some of the ways in which they differ syntactically and semantically from restrictive clauses.

10.1 RESTRICTIVE MODIFICATION

The general concept of restrictive modification is illustrated by the pairs of related examples in (1)–(3). In each pair, the (a) sentence contains a noun phrase with an unmodified common noun, and the (b) sentence contains a corresponding noun phrase in which the same common noun is restricted.

(1) a. Gregory knows [a pianist].
    b. Gregory knows [a pianist *who lives in Boston*].

(2) a. Janet met [a student].
    b. Janet met [a student *from Sweden*].

(3) a. We spoke with [an artist].
    b. We spoke with [a *young* artist].

We can picture the sets of individuals that belong to the classes of pianists, students, and artists as circles.

(4) pianists   students   artists

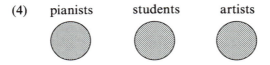

When these nouns stand alone, they denote the entire sets. By contrast, when the same nouns are modified, the sets of individuals denoted by the whole expression are those that belong both to the original set and at the same time to a second set.

(5) pianists   students   artists

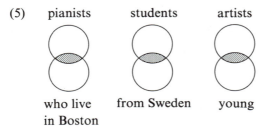

    who live   from Sweden   young
    in Boston

Thus, when these modifiers are combined with their nouns, the set of persons denoted is "more restricted" than the set that the noun by itself denotes. In what follows, we will refer to the construction *who lives in Boston* as a *bound relative clause*, thus distinguishing it from the free relative clauses studied in chapter 7. The phrases *from Sweden* and *young* will be referred to as *nonclausal modifiers*, the former *postnominal* (coming after the noun) and the latter *prenominal* (coming before the noun).

10.2 RESTRICTIVE BOUND RELATIVE CLAUSES

10.2.1 The Structure of Restrictive Bound Relative Clauses

Let us begin our examination of bound relative clauses by looking at some actual examples, grouped according to their internal structure.

(6) a. The senators [who(m) Fred voted for] have resigned.
   b. The report [which Karen submitted] implicated several of her friends.
   c. The guy [whose dog you fed] has left town.
   d. The journalists [who exposed the fraud] are being sued.

(7) a. We read the article [that Smith recommended].
    b. The safe [that Henry keeps his money in] has been stolen.
    c. The people [that voted for Bill] dislike his policies.

(8) a. The accident [Jason caused] will be investigated.
    b. The problem [you told us about] has been resolved.

As with two constructions studied earlier (indirect questions and free relative clauses), it makes sense with the first two of these groups of relative clauses to divide them into an introducing element of some sort, followed by a finite structure.

(9) a. who(m)   Fred voted for
    b. which   Karen submitted
    c. whose dog   you fed
    d. who   exposed the fraud

(10) a. that   Smith recommended
     b. that   Henry keeps his money in
     c. that   voted for Bill

In the third group, the relative clauses consist of finite structures alone, without any introducing element preceding them.

(11) a. ——   Jason caused
     b. ——   you told us about

(For convenience, we will refer to this last type as *bare relative clauses*.) To summarize, the types of relative clauses illustrated above can be introduced

- by a noun phrase that either consists of one of the three "relative pronouns" *who, whom,* or *which,* or else contains the genitive relative pronoun *whose*
- by the word *that*
- by nothing

Let us now look at the right-hand structures in these relative clauses. Besides being finite, they have one other important property: each of them is understood as containing a missing noun phrase.

(12) a. Fred voted for ____   (Compare: Fred voted for *them*.)
     b. Karen submitted ____   (Compare: Karen submitted *it*.)
     c. you fed ____   (Compare: You fed *his dog*.)
     d. ____ exposed the fraud   (Compare: *They* exposed the fraud.)

(13) a. Smith recommended ____   (Compare: Smith recommended *it*.)
     b. Henry keeps his money in   (Compare: Henry keeps his money
        ____   in *it*.)
     c. ____ voted for Bill   (Compare: *They* voted for Bill.)

(14) a. Jason caused ____   (Compare: Jason caused *it*.)
     b. you told us about ____   (Compare: You told us about *it*.)

In all three of these groups, the missing phrase is clearly a noun phrase.

With these observations in hand, we are ready to state rules for forming bound relatives of the kind shown so far. We begin by defining *relative noun phrase* as in (15).

(15) A relative noun phrase consists of one of the following:

   • the word *who*, the word *whom*, or the word *which*
   • the word *whose* plus a common-noun phrase

We can then state the following rule:

(16) A restrictive bound relative clause can consist of one of the following combinations:

   • a relative noun phrase followed by a finite sentence with a missing noun phrase
   • the word *that*, followed by a finite sentence with a missing noun phrase
   • a finite sentence with a missing noun phrase

These possibilities are presented in diagram form as in (17).

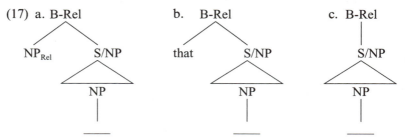

(17) a. B-Rel   b. B-Rel   c. B-Rel

   NP_Rel   S/NP   that   S/NP   S/NP

            NP   NP   NP

   ____   ____   ____

A special restriction needs to be stated for bare relatives, as the following examples indicate:

(18) a. *The journalists [____ exposed the fraud] are being sued.
     b. *The people [____ voted for Bill] dislike his policies.

When the missing noun phrase is the subject of the sentence, the bare relative structure cannot be used. Instead, some introducing phrase must be present—either a relative noun phrase or the word *that*.

(19) a. The journalists [*who* _____ exposed the fraud] are being sued.
     b. The people [*who* _____ voted for Bill] dislike his policies.

(20) a. The journalists [*that* _____ exposed the fraud] are being sued.
     b. The people [*that* _____ voted for Bill] dislike his policies.

Relative clauses are also possible in which the missing phrase is something other than a noun phrase. A first group is exemplified in (21).

(21) a. The official [*to whom* Smith loaned the money] has been indicted.
     b. Martha's sister is the person [*on whom* Fred depends].
     c. The man [*on whose lap* the puppet is sitting] is a ventriloquist.

In these relative clauses, the introducing phrase is clearly a prepositional phrase.

(22) a. to whom   Smith loaned the money
     b. on whom   Fred depends
     c. on whose lap the puppet is sitting

This introductory prepositional phrase consists of a preposition followed by a relative noun phrase. The finite structure that follows this introducing phrase correspondingly contains a missing prepositional phrase of the same kind.

(23) a. Smith loaned the money   (Compare: Smith loaned the money
       _____   *to him*.)
     b. Fred depends _____   (Compare: Fred depends *on her*.)
     c. the puppet is sitting   (Compare: The puppet is sitting
       _____   *on his lap*.)

Two rules give the structure of these relative clauses. The first rule defines *relative prepositional phrases* in terms of the already defined relative noun phrases.

(24) A *relative prepositional phrase* is a prepositional phrase the object of which is a relative noun phrase.

The second rule specifies this kind of relative structure as a whole.

(25) A relative clause can consist of a relative prepositional phrase, followed by a finite sentence with a missing prepositional phrase of the same kind.

Rules (24) and (25) together create structures of the form diagrammed in (26).

(26)

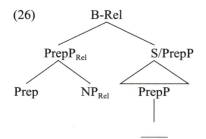

A second group of relative clauses that contain missing phrases other than noun phrases is illustrated in (27).

(27) a. The hotel [where Gloria stays] is being remodeled.
    b. The room [where Joe is taking his tools] is in Byron's basement.
    c. The day [when Jim got fired] was a great day for the board of directors.

These relative clauses can be divided as in (28).

(28) a. where   Gloria stays
    b. where   Joe is taking his tools
    c. when   Jim got fired

The sequences on the right can be understood as containing a locative phrase, a motion phrase, and a time phrase, respectively.

(29) a. Gloria stays ____   (Compare: Gloria stays *there*.)
    b. Joe is taking his tools ____   (Compare: Joe is taking his tools *there*.)
    c. Jim got fired ____   (Compare: Jim got fired *then*.)

These relative clauses, then, can be described by the following rule:

(30) A relative clause can consist of

- the word *where,* followed by a sentence with a missing locative phrase
- the word *where,* followed by a sentence with a missing motion phrase
- the word *when,* followed by a sentence with a missing time phrase

In pictures, these rules take the form shown in (31).

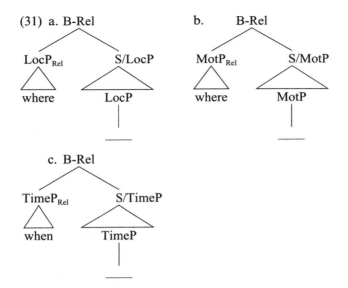

(31) a. B-Rel   b.   B-Rel

LocP_Rel   S/LocP   MotP_Rel   S/MotP

where   LocP   where   MotP

c. B-Rel

TimeP_Rel   S/TimeP

when   TimeP

Exercise

1. Draw a tree diagram for each of the following relative clauses:

   a. [that Harry would object to]
   b. [which Patricia wanted to see]
   c. [that struck Norman]
   d. [Fred ate]
   e. [whose father Joseph cured]
   f. [in which Katy kept the records]
   g. [in which the records were kept]
   h. [where Gloria intends to put the sofa]

10.2.2   An Additional Structure: Infinitival Relative Clauses

Bound relatives of still another sort are based on infinitival structures rather than finite structures. Two of these types are illustrated in (32) and (33).

(32) a. a book [for you to give to Alice]
     b. a bench [for you to sit on]

(33) a. a book [to give to Alice]
     b. a bench [to sit on]

The relatives in (32) are based on full infinitival clauses; those in (33) are built on infinitival clauses that consist of an infinitival phrase alone.

Like all of our previous kinds of relative clauses, these constructions involve missing phrases. We see this when we try to make finite sentences that correspond to the infinitival clauses in (32) and (33).

(34) a. *You gave to Alice.
     b. *You sat on.

Thus, (35) and (36) represent these relative clauses in more revealing fashion.

(35) a. [for you to give ____ to Alice]
     b. [for you to sit on ____]

(36) a. [to give ____ to Alice]
     b. [to sit on ____]

The rule that we can give for them is very simple.

(37) A bound relative clause can consist of an infinitival clause with a missing noun phrase.

This rule gives one of the two structures in (39), depending on whether or not the infinitival clause begins with *for* and a noun phrase.

(38) a. B-Rel   b. B-Rel

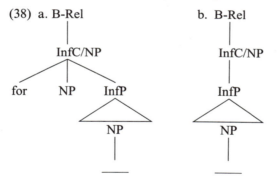

Another infinitival relative structure is also possible.

(39) a. a bench [on which to sit ____]
     b. a refrigerator [in which to put the beer ____]

This construction is introduced by a relative prepositional phrase and has a missing prepositional phrase inside it. In contrast with the previous construction, a full infinitival clause is impossible here.

(40) a. *a bench [on which for Jerry to sit ____]
     b. *a refrigerator [in which for you to put the beer ____]

We might think that we should also be able to introduce an infinitival relative with just a relative noun phrase instead of a relative prepositional phrase. However, this option is not allowed.

(41) a. *a book [which to give ____ to Alice]
     b. *a bench [which to sit on ____]

For the examples in (39), then, we need a rule that limits the introducing phrases to *prepositional* phrases and also requires the following structure to be an infinitival *phrase*.

(42) A bound relative clause can consist of a relative prepositional phrase followed by an infinitival phrase with a missing prepositional phrase of the same kind.

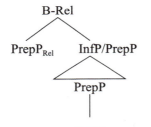

Exercise

1. Draw a tree diagram for each of the following infinitival relatives:
   a. [for Bill to examine]
   b. [to take to Harry's party]
   c. [on whom to rely]
   d. [in which to hide the bottles]

10.2.3   How Bound Relative Clauses Fit into Noun Phrases

In subsections 10.2.1 and 10.2.2, we examined the structure of several different varieties of English relative clauses. It is time now to consider how they fit into noun phrases.

The first fact to be observed is that these relative clauses as a group go particularly well with common-noun phrases—much better than with proper nouns or pronouns. This is particularly clear with relatives introduced by *that*.

(43) a.   the *man* [that grows peaches]
     b.   the *king of England* [that grows peaches]

    c.   *John Smith* [that grows peaches]
    d.   *?him* [that grows peaches]

In view of these differences, we do not want to say that a noun phrase joins with a relative clause to make a bigger noun phrase, as in (44).

(44) NP

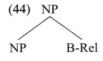

NP   B-Rel

If we adopted such a structure for the noun phrases in (43a) and (43b), our rules would also allow the construction of the unacceptable noun phrases in (43c) and (43d), as shown in (45).

(45)   *NP*   *Rel*
    a.   the man   that grows peaches
    b.   the king of England   that grows peaches
    c.   *John Smith   that grows peaches
    d.   *?him   that grows peaches

This is because *John Smith* and *him* count as noun phrases just as much as *the man* and *the king of England*. Combinations of the type shown in (45d) were possible in English at an earlier time.

(46) a. *He who laughs last* laughs best.
     b. *He who is without sin among you,* let him first cast a stone at her.

However, they are definitely perceived by modern speakers as archaic.

    The analysis that we will adopt instead will rest on a rule that links these relative clauses specifically with common-noun phrases. A partial version of this rule is stated in (47).

(47) A common-noun phrase can be joined with a relative clause. (The phrase so formed is of a type yet to be determined.)

Such a rule would give the structure in (48) for the noun phrase in (43a).

(48)
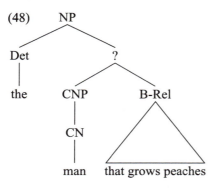

In (48), the undetermined phrase type is indicated by a question mark. Some helpful evidence on what this phrase type might be is provided by the fact that we can join another relative clause to the phrase *man that grows peaches*.

(49) the man [that grows peaches] [that lives near your cousin]

Out of all the men that grow peaches, this second relative clause picks out the one that lives near your cousin. A reasonable structure for this larger noun phrase would be as shown in (50).

(50)
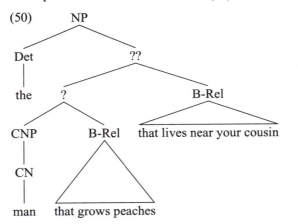

The relative clause *that grows peaches* was brought into the noun phrase by being attached to the common-noun phrase *man*. If we wish to have the second relative clause attached by the same rule, then *man that grows peaches* must itself be analyzed as a common-noun phrase. That is, we want *man that grows peaches* to have the structure shown in (51).

(51)

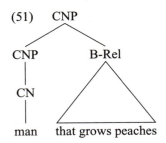

Exactly this structure will allow it to be the "smaller" common-noun phrase to which a second relative clause can be joined.

We can now complete the rule stated in partial form above.

(52) A common-noun phrase joins with a following relative clause to make a (larger) common-noun phrase.

With this finished rule in hand, we are in a position to replace the incomplete diagram in (50) with the more complete one in (53).

(53)

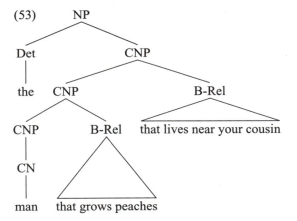

Although relative clauses are most commonly found next to the common-noun phrase that they modify, they may optionally be moved to the end of a sentence. The pairs of sentences in (54) and (55) illustrate this possibility. The first sentence in each pair has the relative clause in its usual place; the second sentence has it at the end.

(54) a. *A man [who likes George's music]* has been found.
       b. *A man* ____ has been found [*who likes George's music*].

(55) a. Harold borrowed *the book [that he had been wanting to read]* from Sally.

b. Harold borrowed *the book* ____ from Sally [*that he had been wanting to read*].

Exercises

1. Draw a tree diagram for each of the noun phrases listed below. Note: Some of the noun phrases contain more than one common-noun phrase, and you will want to decide which one has the relative clause attached to it.

   a. the play that Brenda wrote
   b. several people who knew your brother
   c. a list of the movies that were shown at the festival
   d. a list of the movies that was posted on the bulletin board
   e. a list of the movies that were shown at the festival that was posted on the bulletin board
   f. the pictures of Chicago that John sent to Marsha
   g. the book that Bill wrote that Frank edited

2. The following noun phrase has two possible interpretations:

   the picture of the desk that is kept in Joe's basement

Draw two tree diagrams, one for each of the two structures.

3. The italicized noun phrase in the following sentence from a newspaper story is ambiguous:

   "Others [other TB patients] are like Carol Lewis, *the daughter of a preacher who became a drug abuser*." (Suzanne Gamboa, "Tuberculosis Hits Hardest among Minorities," *Austin American-Statesman,* April 4, 1993, p. A14, italics added)

Draw two tree diagrams for the italicized noun phrase, one for each of its two interpretations.

4. Draw a tree diagram for each of the following sentences. Be sure to give a detailed structure for noun phrases containing relative clauses.

   a. The person who hired Bill has been reprimanded.
   b. Bernice will put the magazines that she has read in Julia's attic.
   c. The keys were kept in the cupboard in which the files were kept.
   d. Velma said that the book that Karen wrote that Mike edited was expensive.

10.2.4   Interpretation of Relative Clauses

We have so far studied the structures that can be employed in bound relative clauses and also the rules governing their use in larger constructions. One additional topic that deserves special attention is the way in which these constructions are interpreted.

Though there are several different ways of describing the interpretation of relative clauses, the one that will be presented here will have the twin advantages of being simple and of being well suited for a practical discussion that will come later in the chapter. The interpretive rules that we will develop will have the effect of associating with a noun phrase like (56a) the somewhat awkward-sounding paraphrase in (56b).

(56) a. the wagon [that Herman wrecked _____]
b. the wagon such that [Herman wrecked *that wagon*]

Essentially, what the rules will do is to bring something into the relative clause from outside. In the change from (56a) to (56b), the relative clause was augmented by the insertion of the noun phrase *that wagon* in the position of the missing noun phrase.

As a first step in building these interpretations, let us assume that every relative clause modifying a common-noun phrase has a special understood noun phrase fabricated for it. This noun phrase consists of either *that* or *those*, together with the smaller common-noun phrase that the relative clause is joined with. The examples of large noun phrases in (57) illustrate how this understood noun phrase is obtained.

(57) a. the woman [that Gordon greeted]
Common-noun phrase to which relative clause is joined: *woman*
Donated noun phrase: *that woman*
b. the king [whose daughter Arnold married]
Common-noun phrase to which relative clause is joined: *king*
Donated noun phrase: *that king*

We can include these donated noun phrases in the relevant tree diagrams in the manner shown in (58).

(58) a.

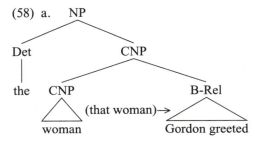

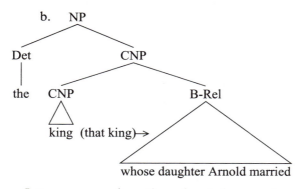

Let us now see how these donated noun phrases are used. When the relative clause is introduced by *that* or by nothing, the donated noun phrase is passed directly to the sentence with the missing noun phrase, which then uses it to identify the missing phrase. Applied to (57a), this procedure gives (59).

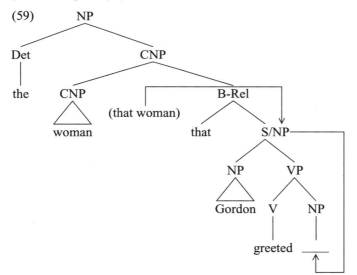

When we carry out the indicated substitution, we get the representation in (60).

(60) the woman such that [Gordon greeted *that woman*]

The situation is more complex in one significant respect when the relative clause starts with a relative noun phrase or prepositional phrase, that is, a phrase containing *who, whom, whose,* or *which.* In this situation, the interpretation has to be accomplished in two steps instead of one. First, the relative clause uses the donated noun phrase to identify the *wh* word. Then the introducing phrase as a whole is handed over to the structure containing the missing phrase, which uses it in the usual way. How this complex process works for the example in (57b) is shown in (61).

(61)

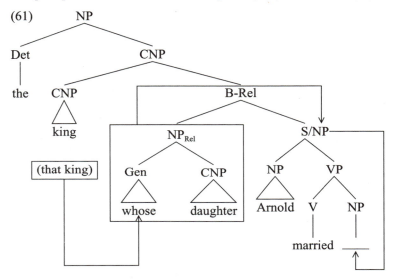

The first step is to substitute the donated noun phrase *that king* for the *who* in *whose.* We then substitute the result as the object of *married.* This gives the representation in (62), which expresses exactly the meaning of the entire noun phrase.

(62) the king such that [Arnold married *that king's daughter*]

Exercises

1. For each of the following noun phrases, give an interpretation of the kind discussed above:

    a. the wagon that Martha painted
    b. the steak we ate
    c. the picture of George that we hung in our attic
    d. the cupboard in which the prints were kept
    e. the person whose dog the postman detests
    f. the woman in whose attic George found a masterpiece
    g. the movie that Shirley enjoyed that bored Alfred

2. As noted in exercise 2 of subsection 10.2.3, the following noun phrase can have two different structures:

the picture of the desk [that is kept in Joe's basement]

Give the two distinct interpretations that result from these different structures.

10.2.5   The Proper Identification of *That* Sequences

The relative-clause structure introduced by *that* is the second kind of subordinate sentence structure we have seen that starts with the word *that*. In chapter 4, we discussed *that* clauses—constructions of the sort illustrated in (63).

(63) a. Martha knows [that John was elected].
     b. [That John was elected] surprised Frank.
     c. It surprised Frank [that John was elected].
     d. The fact [that John was elected] surprised Frank.
     e. Martha told Bill [that John was elected].

Some hints will be given here about how the two constructions can be distinguished when they occur in sentences. As in earlier cases of the same sort, the strategies will rest on ideas about particular syntactic rules. As usual, two groups of rules will be important: those that dictate where these constructions may occur (their external syntax) and those that dictate how they are built (their internal syntax).

10.2.5.1   External Requirements for *That* Clauses   First, let us review the external syntax of *that* clauses. The most important general point here is that this structure always appears with the permission of some particular word. Sometimes this word is a verb or adjective that takes the clause as a complement, as in (64).

(64) a. We *know* [that ...].
     b. We are *certain* [that ...].

Sometimes it is a verb that takes a *that* clause as a second object, after an ordinary noun phrase, as in (65).

(65) a. We *told* Bill [that ...].
     b. We *warned* Bill [that ...].

Sometimes it is one of a limited class of nouns, as in (66).

(66) a. The *fact* [that ...] surprised us.
     b. Emily argued against the *view* [that ...].

Finally, certain verbs and adjectives allow *that* clauses as subjects, either postponed or unpostponed, as in (67).

(67) a. [That . . .] *surprised* us.
    b. It *surprised* us [that . . .].
    c. [That . . .] is *certain.*
    d. It is *certain* [that . . .].

Let us look at a practical problem now. Suppose that we are asked to decide whether the *that* sequences in (68) satisfy the external requirements for *that* clauses.

(68) a. The opinion [that . . .] surprised us.
    b. The number [that . . .] surprised us.

This problem reduces to finding out whether the noun OPINION allows a *that* clause, and then answering the same question for the noun NUMBER. Here we can construct experiments of the kind that we have already seen several times. We proceed by putting something after these nouns that could only be a *that* clause. As we will be reminded when we review the internal syntax of relative clauses, the sequence *that all cows eat grass* cannot be a relative clause under any circumstances. So we now judge the following noun phrases:

(69) a.   the opinion that all cows eat grass
    b. *the number that all cows eat grass

These two experimental examples show us immediately that the noun OPINION does allow *that* clauses, whereas the noun NUMBER does not. These observations about the behavior of the two nouns enable us to answer our original question concerning the examples in (68). The *that* sequence in (68a) could be a *that* clause, at least as far as its external syntax is concerned, whereas the corresponding sequence in (68b) could not possibly be a *that* clause.

We can deal with the examples in (70) in the same way.

(70) a. Joe persuaded the man [that . . .].
    b. Joe kicked the man [that . . .].

Here again, the question of whether the bracketed sequences satisfy the external requirements for *that* clauses reduces to a question about the verbs PERSUADE and KICK: which of these words (if either) allows a *that* clause as a second object? As before, the sequence *that all cows eat grass* cannot be anything but a *that* clause. Thus, we can substitute it for the *that* sequences in (70) and judge how the resulting sentences sound.

(71) a. Joe persuaded the man that all cows eat grass.
  b. *Joe kicked the man that all cows eat grass.

The results are clear: PERSUADE allows a *that* clause as a second object, whereas KICK does not. Thus, the *that* sequence in (70a) satisfies the external conditions for being a *that* clause, whereas the one in (70b) does not.

Exercise

1. For each of the following bracketed sequences, say whether or not it satisfies the external requirements for *that* clauses. (The bracketed sequence used throughout is one that satisfies the internal requirements for both *that* clauses and relative clauses.)

  a. John wants to be sure [that Joe hid in the attic].
  b. We want to remove the papers [that Joe hid in the attic].
  c. We want to tell the reporters [that Joe hid in the attic].
  d. The lamp [that Joe hid in the attic] was useful to the police.
  e. The information [that Joe hid in the attic] was useful to the police.
  f. It surprised the man [that Joe hid in the attic].

10.2.5.2 External Requirements for Relative Clauses For relative clauses introduced by *that,* we find an external requirement of a completely different kind. The basic requirement for these relative clauses is simply that they be associated with common-noun phrases. The simplest kind of common-noun phrase consists of a common noun by itself, as in (72).

(72) a. the *dog* [that ...]
  b. several *people* [that ...]

Other common-noun phrases may consist of a noun plus a complement.

(73) a. the *king of England* [that ...]
  b. the *student of physics* [that ...]

Still others may consist of a common-noun phrase and a relative clause.

(74) a. the *person that Helen interviewed* [that ...]
  b. the *fellow we hired* [that ...]

In most cases, the relative clause will be directly preceded by the common-noun phrase, but in some sentences, it may be shifted to the right, as noted in connection with examples (54) and (55).

As was noted earlier, neither proper nouns used in the usual way nor pronouns give rise to common-noun phrases, and therefore they cannot be modified by relative clauses introduced by *that*. Thus, neither of the *that* sequences in (75) satisfies the external condition for being a relative clause.

(75) a. We told *John* [that ...].
     b. We told *him* [that ...].

Exercise

1. For each of the bracketed sequences in the following sentences, say whether or not it satisfies the external conditions for being a relative clause. (The bracketed sequence used throughout is one that satisfies the internal requirements for both *that* clauses and relative clauses.)

   a. John wants to be sure [that Joe hid in the attic].
   b. We want to remove the papers [that Joe hid in the attic].
   c. We want to tell the reporters [that Joe hid in the attic].
   d. The lamp [that Joe hid in the attic] was useful to the police.
   e. The information [that Joe hid in the attic] was useful to the police.
   f. It surprised the man [that Joe hid in the attic].
   g. It surprised Evelyn [that Joe hid in the attic].
   h. The man was taken into custody [that Joe hid in the attic].

10.2.5.3 The Internal Requirements of the Two Constructions Let us turn now to the internal requirements of these two constructions. The essential internal requirement for a *that* clause is that it consist of *that* plus a sentence, whereas the corresponding requirement for a relative clause is that it consist of *that* plus a sentence with a missing noun phrase. The difference is shown in (76).

(76) a. *That*-C   b. B-Rel

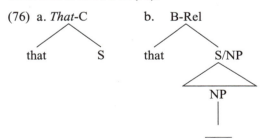

These two tree diagrams look quite different, which might lead to the expectation that the choice between them for particular examples would always be clear. In some instances, the choice actually is easy; in others, it is impossible to tell just by looking at the sequence which of the two structures it represents.

The clear cases are those—such as (77a–d)—in which the sequence after *that* has no room for an extra noun phrase.

(77) a. [that all cows eat grass]
    b. [that Joe disappeared]
    c. [that we will speak with John]
    d. [that I believe Martha will stay at the university]

These particular examples cannot possibly be analyzed as having a missing noun phrase and thus can only be *that* clauses. The same verdict holds for the more interesting examples in (78).

(78) a. [that Beth will be easy for us to work with]
    b. [that Alice was elected to the committee]
    c. [that Sarah ate the pie that George baked]

These examples actually do contain missing noun phrases, as is indicated in (79).

(79) a. [that Beth will be easy for us to work with ____]
    b. [that Alice was elected ____ to the committee]
    c. [that Sarah ate the pie that George baked ____]

However, each of these missing noun phrases is associated with some smaller construction within the sequence: in (79a), with the *easy* construction; in (79b), with the passive phrase; and in (79c), with the small relative clause modifying *pie*. The logic developed in section 9.3 dictates that this association with the smaller construction makes the missing noun phrase unavailable for association with any other structure. As a consequence, each of these missing noun phrases is unavailable for association with the sentence following *that*. Hence, none of the three sentences following *that* in (78) is a genuine missing-phrase construction. Consequently, none of the *that* sequences can be relative clauses.

We have just examined a number of examples in which the sequence after *that* cannot be analyzed as a sentence that has a missing noun phrase associated with it. The tricky cases, to which we now turn, are those in which the sequence after *that* can be interpreted as containing a missing noun phrase that is not associated with any smaller construction.

The following set of examples represents one group where a definite choice is impossible:

(80) a. [that we hid in the attic]
   b. [that Joe reported to the governor]
   c. [that it is easy for us to work with]

Each of the sequences after *that* here can stand as a complete sentence by itself, or else can have another noun phrase added to it.

(81) a. We hid in the attic.   We hid *it* in the attic.
   b. Joe reported to the   Joe reported *the theft* to the
      governor.   governor.
   c. It is easy for us to work   It is easy for us to work with
      with.   *Beth.*

In such cases, we have to look outside the *that* sequence itself to decide whether the structure that follows it is just a sentence or whether it is a sentence with a missing noun phrase.

Another set of sentences for which a definite choice is impossible is shown in (82).

(82) a. [that Joe replaced]
   b. [that they intended to speak with]

At first glance, it might appear that these could not possibly be *that* clauses, since the sequences after *that* cannot stand as independent sentences.

(83) a. *Joe replaced.
   b. *They intended to speak with.

In many instances, they clearly are relative clauses, as in the contexts in (84).

(84) a. The motor [that Joe replaced _____] cost thirty dollars.
   b. The person [that they intended to speak with _____] agreed to reimburse us.

In other situations, however, the same *that* sequences count as *that* clauses. The examples in (85) illustrate these special situations.

(85) a. The motor that Martha thinks [that Joe replaced _____] cost thirty dollars.
   b. The person that you said [that they intended to speak with _____] agreed to reimburse us.

The first thing to be noted is that each of the sentences contains a larger, more inclusive *that* construction. Suppose that we set off both of these larger constructions with brackets, and ask about their status.

(86) a. The motor [that Martha thinks that Joe replaced ____] cost thirty dollars.

   b. The person [that you said that they intended to speak with ____] agreed to reimburse us.

We can tell by looking at the environments of these sequences that they must be relative clauses. Each sequence occurs with a common noun, and neither noun is one of those that allow *that* clauses. From the fact that they are relative clauses, we make a further deduction: each one must consist of *that* plus a sentence that has a missing noun phrase associated with it. Thus, both the object of *replaced* in (86a) and the object of *with* in (86b) must be associated with the S/NPs that form the essential parts of these large relative clauses. We can picture the structures for these large bracketed sequences as in (87).

(87) a. B-Rel

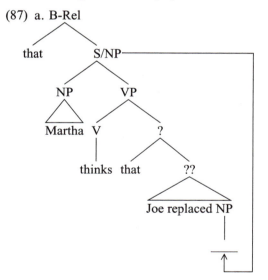

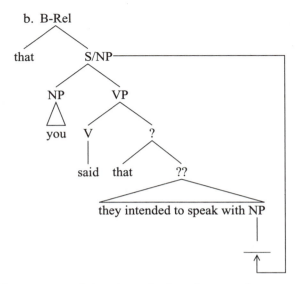

b. B-Rel

Now we can determine whether the constituents marked with double question marks are S/NP or S. They cannot be S/NP, since in each case the only missing noun phrase is already occupied in satisfying the missing-noun-phrase requirement of a larger structure. In other words, in neither tree is there another empty noun phrase with which the double-question-mark structures could be associated. Thus, we are forced to conclude that the smaller structures must be S rather than S/NP. Consequently, the single-question-mark *that* sequences of which they form a part must be *that* clauses rather than relative clauses.

Exercises

1. For each of the following *that* sequences, say whether it can be interpreted as containing a missing noun phrase not associated with any smaller construction. For each positive answer, show where the missing noun phrase is. Do this by showing how a pronoun can be inserted in the sequence after *that* to give an acceptable independent sentence. The first is done as an example.

    a. [that Joseph sent to Cairo]
       Answer: Yes, it can be interpreted as containing a missing noun phrase, as follows:
          that Joseph sent ＿＿ to Cairo
       (Acceptable independent sentence: Joseph sent *it* to Cairo.)
    b. [that Jane would remain]
    c. [that Jane would require]

d. [that it is hard for us to understand]
e. [that the problem is hard for us to understand]
f. [that the person whose brother you talked with has hidden in the attic]
g. [that the person whose brother you talked with has stayed in the attic]
h. [that Bill said that Harry slept in the cellar]
i. [that Bill said that Harry hid in the cellar]
j. [that Bill said that Harry found in the cellar]
k. [that Elena should have spoken to]
l. [that Elena should be spoken to]

2. Each of the following sentences contains a bracketed *that* sequence. Each of the bracketed sequences contains a missing noun phrase that is not associated with any smaller structure. Using clues provided by the larger structures in which the bracketed sequence occurs, determine whether it should be considered a *that* clause or a relative clause.

a. We know the man [that Bill hired ____].
b. Alice knows whose assistant Pete thinks [that Bill hired ____].
c. Alice told Fred that Pete informed the man [that Bill hired ____].
d. We want to determine who told the man [that Bill hired ____].
e. David interviewed the man that Fred claims [that Bill hired ____].

3. The following three sentences are ambiguous. For each sentence, draw two tree structures to indicate what the two interpretations are.

a. The fact that Stanley reported to the governor surprised many reporters.
b. Georgia told the men that we think Sam had hidden in the attic.
c. Joe is aware of the fact that Shirley will discover when Bill visits her sister.

Note: On one interpretation of the third sentence, *when Bill visits her sister* is interpreted as an indirect question, whereas on the other interpretation it is interpreted as a free relative. When interpreted as a free relative, it has an adverbial function. In the next chapter, the basic phrase structure proposed for verb phrases containing phrase-final adverbial modifiers will be as follows:

(i)   VP
           /   \
        VP   Modifier
       / \

For the particular sequence that we are dealing with in this exercise, the diagram corresponding to one of the interpretations will contain a structure of the following form:

(ii)

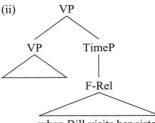

when Bill visits her sister

10.2.5.4 The Compatibility Requirement for Bound Relatives Introduced by *That*   There is one more requirement that a structure needs to satisfy if it is to qualify as a bound relative clause. This is a requirement of compatibility that is similar to the one for free relatives discussed in chapter 7. The effects of this requirement are illustrated by the bracketed sequence in (88).

(88) The fact [that Joe ate at noon] is completely irrelevant.

The bracketed sequence clearly satisfies both external and internal requirements for *that* clauses: it goes with the word *fact,* one of the small group of nouns that allows *that* clauses, and it is completely acceptable as an independent sentence. It also seems that the sequence satisfies both external and internal requirements for relative clauses: it is preceded by a common noun, and there is a place for a missing noun phrase, as (89) shows.

(89) Joe ate *it* at noon.

Yet, in reading sentence (88), we have a strong intuition that the bracketed sequence can only be interpreted as a *that* clause.

The property of sentence (88) that accounts for our intuition that it does not contain a relative clause is that there is a lack of compatibility between being a fact and being eaten by Joe at noon. No imaginable entity of any kind can be both at once. We can see the situation in a particularly dramatic light by applying the interpretive procedure of subsection 10.2.4 to the key noun phrase. This procedure will insert *that fact* in the position where a missing noun phrase is possible, with the following result:

(90) a. the fact that [Joe ate _? ?_ at noon]
      b. the fact such that [Joe ate *that fact* at noon]

This bracketed sequence is clearly nonsensical. As a result, the only natural way to interpret the bracketed sequence in (88) is as a *that* clause. In cases such as this one, our intuitions are based not on grammatical rules as such, but rather on judgments concerning the plausibility or implausibility of the interpretation that the rules yield.

Exercise

1. For each of the following sentences, decide whether the bracketed sequence *in the given context* satisfies the compatibility condition for bound relatives. Specifically, decide whether it could join with the preceding common-noun phrase to give a coherent interpretation. In each case, give the representation that results from the interpretive procedure of section 10.2.4.

a. The book [that Sally wanted Martha to give to the church] cost thirty dollars.

b. The fact [that Sally wanted Martha to give to the church] amazed Bruce.

c. The fact [that Sally wanted Martha to hide from the police] has come to our attention.

d. John told the officer [that Bill reported to the governor].

10.2.6   The Proper Identification of *Wh* Sequences

Bound relative clauses introduced by *who, which, whose, where,* and *when* constitute a third construction on our list of constructions introduced by *wh* words. The indirect-question construction of chapter 4 was the first one, and the definite free relative of chapter 7 was the second. Chapter 7 also included a practical discussion of how to distinguish indirect questions from definite free relatives. In the present section, we will consider how to distinguish bound relatives from the other two constructions.

Let us recall at the outset that all three constructions must be based on a structure that contains a missing phrase of some sort. Thus, the presence of a missing phrase will be of no help in deciding which construction type is present in a particular example. However, other characteristics can be found that serve to distinguish bound relatives from the other two constructions. We will concentrate here on the kinds of considerations that will aid us in answering the question, Can such-and-such a *wh* sequence be a bound relative?

10.2.6.1   Internal Requirements for Bound Relatives   A bound *wh* relative can be either finite or infinitival. If it is finite, it must be introduced by one of the following limited types of phrases:

• a bound-relative noun phrase (*who, whom, which, whose* plus common-noun phrase)

• a bound-relative locative or motion phrase (*where*)

- a bound-relative time phrase (*when*)
- a prepositional phrase having one of the above as its object

If the bound relative is infinitival, there is only one allowable type of introducing phrase, namely, a prepositional phrase with one of the *wh* phrases as its object.

Exercise

1. For each of the following sequences, decide whether it could ever be a bound relative in an appropriate context. Give an explanation for each of your negative answers.

   a. [when Bill returned]
   b. [what Gloria remembered]
   c. [who(m) to send to the office]
   d. [how many books your father wrote]
   e. [where to put the marbles]
   f. [to whom the president was speaking]
   g. [with whom to attend the concert]
   h. [which car he prefers]

10.2.6.2 External Requirements for Bound Relatives   The main external requirement for a bound relative introduced by a *wh* phrase is the same as for a relative introduced by *that:* it must be associated with a common-noun phrase. In the standard case, the relative will be directly adjacent to the common-noun phrase that it modifies. However, it is possible for a bound relative to modify the common-noun phrase at a distance in a case where the relative clause has been postponed to the end of the sentence as a whole.

Exercises

1. Each of the following sentences contains a *wh* sequence whose internal structure would allow it to be either a bound relative or an indirect question. For each such sequence, decide from its external surroundings whether it could possibly be a bound relative. For each positive answer, identify the common-noun phrase that the sequence could modify.

   a. Katy told me [who was present at the lecture].
   b. [Whose dog Fred assaulted] was not clear to the onlookers.
   c. A lady teaches German here [who likes to show slides of Bavaria].
   d. Most of the prisoners [who questioned the authorities] were banished.
   e. Ralph told the officer [who(m) he had hired].
   f. The witness mentioned the time [when everyone heard the bell ring].

2. As a review of the discussions of indirect questions in chapter 4 and chapter 7, decide, for each of the above *wh* sequences, whether it satisfies the external requirements for indirect questions.

10.2.6.3 The Compatibility Condition for *Wh* Bound Relatives Bound relatives introduced by *wh* phrases must satisfy a compatibility condition similar to the one for bound relatives introduced by *that*. As before, a convenient way to check that this condition is satisfied is to try to carry out the interpretive procedure of subsection 10.2.4.

Let us start by looking at a sentence in which this condition is satisfied.

(91) Smith hired the man [whose report you have copied].

The noun phrase that is donated to the relative clause in this example is *that man*. This noun phrase is used to replace the *who* of *whose*, and then the entire introducing phrase is put back in the position of the missing noun phrase.

(92) the man such that [you have copied *that man's* report]

The sentence in brackets here makes perfect sense, and thus the compatibility requirement is satisfied.

Let us look now at another example.

(93) We told the woman [whose widow Jones wants to marry].

We are interested in the possibility that the following subsequence is a noun phrase within the larger sentence:

(94) the woman [whose widow Jones wants to marry]

The noun phrase donated to the relative clause would be *that woman*. Replacing *whose* and inserting the introducing phrase in the position of the missing noun phrase gives (95).

(95) ??the woman such that [Jones wants to marry *that woman's* widow]

Given that only a man can have a widow, the bracketed sequence fails to make sense. For sentence (93), then, a relative-clause interpretation is excluded. The only possible analysis is one in which *the woman* is the first object of the verb *told* and the *wh* sequence is an indirect question serving as the second object.

Exercise

1. Each of the following sentences contains a bracketed *wh* sequence. Each of these sequences satisfies the internal and external requirements for both relative

clauses and indirect questions. For each one, determine whether it satisfies the compatibility requirement for relative clauses.

a. Martha told the man [who wrote the letter].
b. We told the woman [whose wife wrote the letter].
c. We told the woman [whose daughter wrote the letter].
d. John told the woman [who perjured himself].
e. John told the woman [who believed that John perjured himself].

10.3   NONCLAUSAL NOUN MODIFIERS

In the first part of this chapter, we examined the variety of restrictive bound-relative constructions that English allows. In the present section, we will study several important varieties of nonclausal modifiers of nouns —that is, modifying constructions based on phrases and words rather than on sentence-like structures. The discussion will be divided between *postnominal modifiers* (those that come after the noun) and *prenominal modifiers* (those that come before the noun).

10.3.1   Postnominal Modifiers

We begin with several varieties of postnominal modifying phrases that we have encountered in other uses. In particular, all of the postnominal modifiers in these first groups of examples can also be employed as complements of the verb BE.

(96) a. The boy [in the doorway] waved to his father.
         (The boy is [in the doorway].)
     b. The baby [out there in the kitchen] is Jerry's niece.
         (The baby is [out there in the kitchen].)

(97) a. The man [holding the bottle] disappeared.
         (The man is [holding the bottle].)
     b. The boy [waving to his father] lives in Tulsa.
         (The boy is [waving to his father].)

(98) a. The papers [removed from the safe by the robbers] have not
         been found.
         (The papers were [removed from the safe by the robbers].)
     b. The men [brought before the judge] remained silent.
         (The men were [brought before the judge].)

The types of phrases being used as modifiers in these examples are not hard to identify. The modifiers in (96) are locative phrases, those in (97) are present-participial verb phrases, and those in (98) are passive phrases.

As with relative clauses, these modifiers go better with common nouns than with either proper nouns or pronouns.

(99) a.   The boy in the doorway waved to his father.
   b.   *John in the doorway waved to his father.
   c.   *?He in the doorway waved to his father.

Thus, just as with relative clauses, we will assume that these new modifiers join with common-noun phrases and that the resulting phrases are themselves common-noun phrases. The rules we need are shown in graphic form in (100).

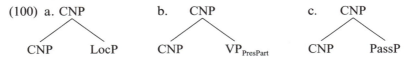

(100) a. CNP   b. CNP   c. CNP

      CNP   LocP   CNP   VP$_{PresPart}$ CNP   PassP

Adjective phrases are one final group of phrases that appear both as complements of BE and as postnominal modifiers. As the examples in (101) show, they are rather marginal as modifiers.

(101) a. ?The woman [eager to start the meeting] is John's sister.
          (Compare: The woman [who is eager to start the meeting] is
          John's sister.)
   b. ?A speaker [hard to understand] should come to the stage.
          (Compare: A speaker [who is hard to understand] should
          come to the stage.)

Even less acceptable as postnominal modifiers are adjective phrases without following complements.

(102) a. *A baby [healthy] was born to Margaret Smith.
   b. *A soldier [very young] just walked into the room.

Anticipating the discussion of the next subsection, we will note that English does provide an alternative means of using adjectives without complements to modify nouns. This alternative is simply to put the adjective before the noun instead of after it.

(103) a. A [healthy] baby was born to Margaret Smith.
   b. A [very young] soldier just walked into the room.

There are two important varieties of nonclausal modifiers that do not serve as complements of BE. The first variety, which is related to simple sentences with HAVE rather than simple sentences with BE, is shown in (104)–(107).

(104) a.   The teams [with good records] will meet in the second round.
b.   *The teams are [with good records].
c.   The teams [have good records].

(105) a.   The fellow [with a fly on his nose] owns this establishment.
b.   *The fellow is [with a fly on his nose].
c.   The fellow [has a fly on his nose].

(106) a.   The student [with a monkey sitting on his lap] deserves a C+.
b.   *The student is [with a monkey sitting on his lap].
c.   The student [has a monkey sitting on his lap].

(107) a.   The woman [with a string tied to her finger] knocked at the door.
b.   *The woman is [with a string tied to her finger].
c.   The woman [has a string tied to her finger].

The modifying phrases in the (a) examples consist of the word *with* followed by a noun phrase and, in (105)–(107), another phrase. This last phrase can be either a locative phrase (*on his nose*), a present-participial verb phrase (*sitting on his lap*), or a passive phrase (*tied to her finger*). Thus, a modifier headed by *with* must have one of the structures in (108).

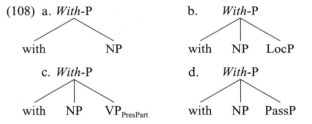

(108) a. *With*-P   b.   *With*-P

      with   NP   with   NP   LocP

c. *With*-P   d.   *With*-P

      with   NP   VP_PresPart   with   NP   PassP

The second kind of postnominal modifier that does not occur as a complement of BE is shown in (109), where brackets mark the noun phrase as a whole and italics indicate the postnominal modifier itself.

(109) We are using [an idea *of Carol's*].

This construction, which we will refer to as *the postnominal genitive,* can be accounted for by the following rule:

(110) A postnominal genitive can be formed by combining the preposition *of* with a genitive.

Postnom-Gen

    of   Gen

This structure can appear with a common-noun phrase in a variety of situations.

(111) a.   I can't get [this car *of Bob's*] to start.
  b.   [The book *of Jane's* that we want you to read] is on the coffee table.
  c.   [Any other possessions *of Carol's*] should be sent to her as soon as possible.
  d.   ?[These portraits of Napoleon *of Jerry's*] will fetch a high price in London.

The one situation in which the construction is unacceptable is shown in (112).

(112) *I can't get [the car *of Bob's*] to start.

In this example, the noun phrase as a whole is of the form *the* + common-noun phrase + postnominal genitive. Perhaps it is not a coincidence that this noun phrase would have exactly the same interpretation as another noun phrase that is made available by rules discussed in chapter 5, namely, the one italicized in (113).

(113) I can't get [*Bob's* car] to start.

Thus, one possible explanation for the unacceptability of (112) is that the alternative structure in (113) in effect crowds it out.

In the above examples, the genitive *Bob's* was used in both the prenominal and the postnominal constructions. This identity of form holds for every class of genitives except one: genitives based on pronouns. As can be seen in the pairs of examples in (114), these genitives differ in every instance except the third-person singular masculine *his*.

(114) a. *my* friend   a friend of *mine*
  b. *our* friend   a friend of *ours*
  c. *your* friend   a friend of *yours*
  d. *his* friend   a friend of *his*
  e. *her* friend   a friend of *hers*
  f. *their* friend   a friend of *theirs*

Let us refer to the genitives in the left column of (114) as *weak genitives* and to the genitives in the right column as *strong genitives*. We can then give the following revised rule for the formation of postnominal genitives:

(115) A postnominal genitive can be formed by combining the preposition *of* with a following genitive. If the genitive is

based on a pronoun, the strong form of the genitive must be used.

We will see an additional use for strong genitives in chapter 16.

As with the other postnominal modifiers that we have seen in this subsection, we will assume that these last two kinds of modifiers combine with the preceding common-noun phrase to make a larger common-noun phrase. These relations are diagrammed in (116).

(116) a. CNP   b.   CNP

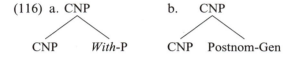

Exercise

1. Draw a tree diagram for each of the following noun phrases:
   a. several people staying at the hotel
   b. the rugs in the attic
   c. the bricks taken from Smith's driveway
   d. the rugs in the attic that were bought from your aunt
   e. the woman with the dog
   f. the necktie with a spot on it
   g. this bicycle of Fred's
   h. the book of yours that Nora wants to read

10.3.2   Modifier or Complement?

In this subsection, we take up a practical question similar to several that we have encountered in earlier discussions. When we are presented with a sentence containing a phrase that occurs sometimes as a postnominal modifier and sometimes as a verb complement, how do we determine whether it can be the first or the second or both? This is a question that might well be raised about the examples in (117), which at first glance look as if they differ only in the choice of verb.

(117) a. Corky put the car in the garage.
      b. Corky owned the car in the garage.
      c. Corky kept the car in the garage.

For each of these sentences, we want to answer two questions: whether the sequence *the car in the garage* can be analyzed as two phrases (a noun phrase followed by a locative phrase), and whether the same sequence can be analyzed as one phrase (a noun phrase). The two relevant verb-phrase configurations are diagrammed in (118).

(118) a.

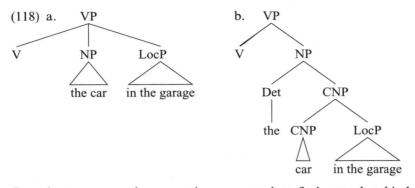

In order to answer these questions, we need to find out what kind of complement configurations these three verbs allow. We can do this by constructing simple experimental sentences in which there is less ambiguity than in the present ones. In order to determine whether a given verb is allowed in the first configuration, we will use a pronoun as the object, since a pronoun cannot be modified by a postnominal locative phrase, as we observed in connection with (99c). We can likewise use a pronoun object without a following locative phrase to test each verb for its comfort in the second configuration. The results are given in (119)–(121).

(119) a. Jack put it in the garage.
      b. *Jack put it.

(121) a. *Jack owns it in the garage.
      b. Jack owns it.

(122) a. Jack kept it in the garage.
      b. Jack kept it.

These examples give us the following information:

- PUT goes only in the [— NP LocP] configuration.
- OWN goes only in the [— NP] configuration.
- KEEP goes in both configurations.

Thus, in (117a), the sequence *the car in the garage* must be two separate phrases; in (117b), it must be a single phrase; and in (117c), it can have either of the two structures. From these conclusions, it follows finally that *in the garage* is a verb complement in (117a), a postnominal modifier in (117b), and either of these in (117c). Exactly the same kind of strategy can be used in examples in which the potential modifiers are something other than locative phrases.

Exercise

1. For each of the following sentences, answer two questions:

   A. Could the italicized phrase be a verb complement in this context?
   B. Could it be a postnominal modifier in this context?

In most cases, some experiments will be useful. In a few examples, however, the answers should be immediate. Explain your answers briefly but clearly.

   a. Joe kept the baby *in his arms.*
   b. We saw the woman *adjusting the telescope.*
   c. We will have three books *removed from the collection.*
   d. The man *in the gray suit* seems to like the play.
   e. The police caught Joe *crawling through a window.*
   f. We talked to the man *holding the weapon.*
   g. John oiled the machine *from the store.*
   h. John removed the machine *from the store.*
   i. Amy locked it *in the garage.*

10.3.3 Prenominal Modifiers

As was mentioned above, English does not generally allow adjectives without complements as postnominal modifiers.

(122) a. *A baby [healthy] was born to Margaret Smith.
      b. *A soldier [very young] just walked into the room.

The alternative construction is one in which the adjectives come before the nouns.

(123) a. A [healthy] baby was born to Margaret Smith.
      b. A [very young] soldier just walked into the room.

Just as adjectives without complements are excluded as postnominal adjective phrases, so adjective phrases that include complements are excluded in prenominal position.

(124) a. *a [fond of chocolates] gentleman
      b. *an [eager to succeed] corporal
      c. *a [reluctant to leave the party] teenager

Despite the unacceptability of these last examples, we will analyze the prenominal modifiers in (123) as adjective phrases, rather than simply viewing them as single-word adjectives. One reason for the phrasal analysis rests in the fact that the adjective can be preceded by a degree modifier like *very,* as seen in (123b). Such an analysis gives rise to structure (125) for (123b).

(125)

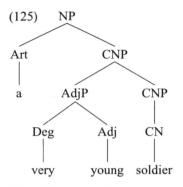

The following rule would give this structure:

(126) A common-noun phrase can be joined with a preceding adjective phrase to form a larger common-noun phrase.

With a rule like this, we would expect to be able to form a sequence of two adjectives before a noun, just by taking the common-noun phrase *young soldier* and joining it with a preceding adjective. Such two-adjective sequences are indeed possible.

(127) a. A tall young soldier entered the room.
      b. A healthy little baby was born to Margaret Smith.

The structure of the subject noun phrase in (127a) is shown in (128).

(128)

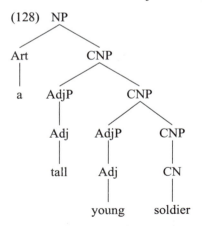

This rule allows the creation of a wide variety of noun phrases with prenominal modifiers. Although it has the advantages of being quite simple and general, we should note several restrictions in the behavior of prenominal modifiers, restrictions that it does not account for.

One problem with the rule stated in (126) is that it imposes no restrictions on the order in which different kinds of adjectives appear in the noun phrase. As examples (129)–(131) show, however, differences in order often carry with them striking differences in acceptability.

(129) a.   a little old wooden house
      b.   *a wooden old little house
      c.   ??an old little wooden house

(130) a.   a nice young soldier
      b.   *a young nice soldier

(131) a.   an old European custom
      b.   *a European old custom

What we find is that adjectives tend to be ordered by general meaning classes. Adjectives having to do with nationality and material have to come as close as possible to the head noun. Adjectives having to do with age and size are next on the left, and adjectives denoting various personality characteristics come next. Before them we also find a small class of adjectives that can only occur prenominally. As shown in (132), this class includes words like *main* and *key* (although in recent years some American speakers have begun to use the latter as a predicate adjective).

(132) a. the main objection
          (*This objection is main.)
      b. the key fact
          (?This fact is key.)

In addition to the restrictions on prenominal adjective order, there are a number of other restrictions that are not well understood. For example, degree modification by *very* is fully acceptable only with the leftmost adjective. Thus, both (133a) and (133b) are acceptable, and so is (133c). By contrast, (133d) and (133e) are both markedly less natural, unless an intonation break is inserted as indicated by the comma in the examples on the right.

(133) a. a very tall soldier
      b. a very young soldier
      c. a very tall young soldier
      d. ?a young very tall soldier   (a young, very tall soldier)
      e. ?a very young very tall soldier   (a very young, very tall soldier)

We will see still more complexities in the behavior of prenominal modifiers in chapter 12 when we look further into the ways in which degree modification can be expressed.

Exercises

1. Draw a tree diagram for each of the following noun phrases:
   a. several young chickens
   b. this very handsome table
   c. the old red rooster
   d. that incompetent king of France

2. As noted in chapter 1 and also at the beginning of chapter 3, the word *one* is often used as a substitute for a repeated common-noun phrase.

(i)   the first *picture* and the second *one*

(ii)   the *picture of King George* that you own and the *one* that I own

(iii) this *funny story* and that *one*

By the rules that we have developed for common-noun phrases, the following sequence can have two possible structures.

(iv)   the old woman from France

First, give the structure that (iv) must have to permit the interpretation of *one* given in (v).

(v)   the *old woman* from France and the *one* from Spain

Then give the structure that it needs to have to allow the interpretation shown in (vi).

(vi)   the old *woman from France* and the young *one*

10.4   MODIFICATION OF SPECIAL COMBINED FORMS

In sections 10.1–10.3, a detailed picture has been developed of the various kinds of restrictive modification that English allows for phrases headed by common nouns. To complete the overall picture, we need to look briefly at the modifying structures allowed with the special combined forms discussed in subsection 5.1.8. This small class of combined forms was made up of words like *someone, nobody, anything,* and *everywhere.*

With regard to modification by relative clauses, these combined forms appear to behave in very much the same way as ordinary sequences consisting of a quantifier or article followed by a common noun. Some illustrative pairs of examples are given in (134)–(139).

(134) a. one student [who speaks Polish]
    b. someone [who speaks Polish]

(135) a. every chair [that Marsha bought from Phillip]
    b. everything [that Marsha bought from Phillip]

(136) a. a safe [in which to keep the jewels]
    b. something [in which to keep the jewels]

(137) a. some official [in France]
    b. someone [in France]

(138) a. no player [with tape on his ankle]
    b. nobody [with tape on his ankle]

(139) a. a possession [of Fred's]
    b. something [of Fred's]

For each of the combined forms in the (b) examples, we can assume a structure parallel to the one already developed for the corresponding (a) example. For example, the tree diagrams for the pairs of noun phrases in (134) and (137) would be as in (140) and (141).

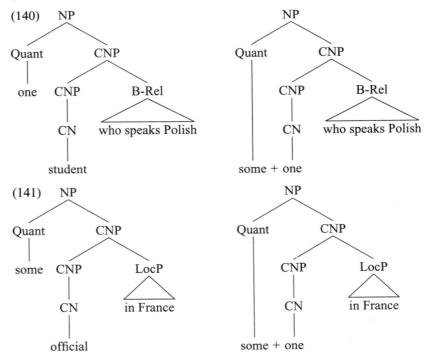

When we look at modification by adjectives, though, we find that ordinary common-noun phrases and special combined forms differ markedly. The pairs of examples in (142) and (143) illustrate the basic differences.

(142) a. *a person intelligent
      b. somebody intelligent

(143) a. an interesting person
      b. *some intelligent body
      c. *intelligent somebody

As (142) and (143) show, the combined forms allow exactly the kind of postnominal modification by adjectives that ordinary common-noun phrases disallow, and vice versa—they disallow the kind of prenominal modification by single adjectives that common-noun phrases do allow. The structure for (142b)—a structure that would have to be restricted specifically to combined forms—is given in (144).

(144)

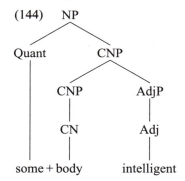

Exercises

1. Draw a tree diagram for each of the following noun phrases:
   a. everything that Marsha bought from Phillip
   b. nobody with tape on his ankle
   c. something of Fred's
   d. nothing edible

2. Review the discussion of example (50) in subsection 10.2.3, a noun phrase with multiple relative-clause modifiers. Then draw a tree diagram for each of the following noun phrases:
   a. anybody from Texas who speaks French
   b. someone easy to work with who knows how to rewire lamps

10.5 NONRESTRICTIVE RELATIVE CLAUSES

So far in this chapter, we have confined our discussion to modifiers that are used to "restrict" a common-noun phrase, that is, to create a narrower set of entities than that denoted by the common-noun phrase alone. In this section, we examine a relative-clause construction that is not used restrictively.

The easiest way to see the difference between restrictive and nonrestrictive relative clauses is to compare two sentences that differ only in the status of the relative clause that they contain.

(145) a. The books which were written by foreign authors were burned.
       b. The books, which were written by foreign authors, were burned.

These two sentences are natural only in situations in which some set of books is understood ahead of time as being relevant to the conversation: all of the books in a certain library or a certain collection. In (145a), a particular subset of these books is picked out (those written by foreign authors), and it is asserted that all of the books in this subset were burned. In (145b), by contrast, we are told that all of the books were burned, and then we are provided with the added assertion that they were all written by foreign authors. The relative clause in (145b) is referred to as nonrestrictive precisely because it does not ask us to form a smaller subset of the set denoted by *books*.

Because these relative clauses do not restrict, we can use them in situations in which restrictive relatives are unacceptable. Neither the noun phrase *Ronald Reagan* nor the noun phrase *the current president of the company* is capable of being modified by a restrictive clause, as we see in (146).

(146) a. *Ronald Reagan who began his career as a radio announcer came to hold the nation's highest office.
       b. *The current president of the company who lives in Buffalo could not attend the ceremony.

In neither of these cases can the relative clause pick out a set that is smaller than the set already picked out by the noun phrases *Ronald Reagan* and *the current president of the company*. In both of these situations, nonrestrictive relative clauses are perfectly acceptable, simply because they are not interpreted as forming smaller sets.

(147) a. Ronald Reagan, who began his career as a radio announcer, came to hold the nation's highest office.

b. The current president of the company, who lives in Buffalo, could not attend the ceremony.

Instead, these relative clauses add independent assertions about the individual or individuals in question.

(148) a. Ronald Reagan began his career as a radio announcer.

b. The current president of the company lives in Buffalo.

Going along with this difference in function are a few small differences in form. In the first place, a nonrestrictive relative inside a larger sentence is set off in speaking by a special "interruption" intonation that occurs before it begins and also when it ends. This intonation, which involves a slight upturn at the end of the final word of the intonational unit, contrasts with the ordinary downturn intonation that we generally find at the end of a sentence. Both types of intonation are seen in (149); the two upturns set off the nonrestrictive relative, and the downturn marks the end of the sentence.

(149) George Washington, who is said to have cut down a cherry tree, became a president.

A nonrestrictive relative that occurs at the end of a sentence is set off differently, in this case by a falling "end" intonation on the material preceding it and the same kind of intonation at the end of the clause.

(150) Cora wrote a letter to Smith's parents, who were pleased to hear from her.

In writing, the spoken intonation breaks are represented by commas, as is other special material that represents an interruption or an independent addition to a sentence.

Another difference between the two types of relative clauses is that nonrestrictive clauses can only be introduced by *wh* phrases. In (151)– (153), restrictives and corresponding nonrestrictives are compared in this regard.

(151) a. The man who(m) the Republicans nominated in 1980 now lives in California.

b. Reagan, who(m) the Republicans nominated in 1980, now lives in California.

(152) a.   The man that the Republicans nominated in 1980 now lives in California.

b.   *Reagan, that the Republicans nominated in 1980, now lives in California.

(153) a.   The man the Republicans nominated in 1980 now lives in California.

b.   *Reagan, the Republicans nominated in 1980, now lives in California.

How to decide on the punctuation appropriate for particular relative clauses is a traditional problem within the prescriptive grammatical tradition. This problem clearly reduces to that of deciding whether a relative clause that one wants to write is being used restrictively or nonrestrictively. With definite noun phrases, it is generally quite easy to decide. If the intention is to pick out a subset of the larger set denoted by the noun alone, then the clause is restrictive and no commas are called for. If the intention is to make an independent assertion about a noun phrase already clearly identified without the help of the relative clause, then the clause is nonrestrictive and commas are required.

With indefinite noun phrases, the choice is typically not so clear. What is the difference between (154a) and (154b)?

(154) a.   Yesterday John saw an animal which resembled his great-uncle Fred.

b.   (?)Yesterday John saw an animal, which resembled his great-uncle Fred.

The situations that these sentences could truthfully describe seem to be indistinguishable. Yet there is a significant difference, and it affords an explanation for the slight oddness of (154b). Simply put, (154a) expresses one single assertion, whereas (154b) expresses two separate ones. The reason that (154b) is slightly odd is that John's seeing an animal would not really be newsworthy in most situations that we can imagine. Thus, what might be called the "news content" of seeing an animal is too slim in its own right to warrant a separate assertion. The same line of reasoning explains why the restrictive clause is the right choice for (155a) and the nonrestrictive clause is more appropriate for (155b).

(155) a.   Last night, John was introduced to a man who had once courted his aunt.

b. Last night, John was introduced to a Martian, who had once courted his aunt.

Being introduced to a man would almost certainly not be news in its own right, whereas being introduced to a Martian might well be news. Thus, the news content of (155a) is enough for only one interesting assertion, whereas the news content of (155b) warrants two.

In all of the examples discussed so far, the nonrestrictive clause is connected to a noun phrase. For these examples, we can analyze the entire sequence of noun phrase + following nonrestrictive as making up a larger noun phrase, as diagrammed in (156).

(156) NP

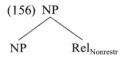

Other types of "antecedent" phrases are also possible. For instance, nonrestrictive clauses can also be linked to adjective phrases, thus forming larger adjective phrases as shown in (157).

(157) AdjP

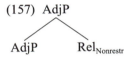

Such a use is evident in (158).

(158) At least Robert is [considerate, *which none of his friends seem to be*].

Here the nearest paraphrase is something like (159).

(159) At least Robert is considerate, and none of his friends seem to be
$$\left\{ \begin{array}{l} \text{considerate} \\ \text{?that} \\ \text{?so} \end{array} \right\} .$$

One more construction to which a nonrestrictive clause can be attached is exemplified in (160).

(160) No one showed up on time, *which Alex didn't like very much.*

Here the nonrestrictive clause is not connected with any phrase within the first clause, but instead adds an independent assertion about the fact reported by the clause as a whole. Thus, the structure that we want for (160) is one in which the nonrestrictive relative attaches to the entire clause that precedes it, as in (161).

(161)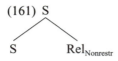

Such sentences can often be paraphrased by using *and* to join the two clauses, and using *that* in the position of the missing noun phrase instead of *which* at the beginning of the sentence. This process yields the following paraphrase for (160):

(162) No one showed up on time, *and* Alex didn't like *that* very much.

Exercise

1. Draw a tree diagram for each of the following sentences:
    a. The woman standing on the porch, who(m) you introduced to Phillip, reads fifteen languages.
    b. Jane gave the car to Martha, who gave it to Florence.
    c. Your friends say that Peter is eloquent, which he seems to want to be.
    d. The waiter found three flies in your soup, which Maxine considered inexcusable.

Chapter 11

Modification of Verb Phrases and Sentences

In the preceding chapter, we examined some of the ways in which English nominal constructions can be modified. Here we will take up the modification of verb phrases and sentences. The modifiers for these structures have an even larger range of semantic effects than is the case for nominal structures. In the present chapter, we will give primary attention to the syntax of these modifiers, sketching their meanings only briefly as a preliminary matter.

In section 11.1, a number of traditional meaning classes of modifiers will be listed. In section 11.2, the basic structural classes of modifiers will be summarized. In section 11.3, the basic positions in which modifiers appear will be discussed. In the rules that will be developed there, reference will be made both to the meaning classes in which modifiers fall and to their structural classes. In section 11.4, some of the syntactic peculiarities of certain clausal modifiers will be considered.

11.1 MEANING CLASSES OF VERBAL MODIFIERS

In the following discussion of the most important meaning classes of verbal modifiers, each class is first described by a general statement and then illustrated with examples.

11.1.1 Locative Modifiers

Locative modifiers show exactly the same internal structure as the locative complements with which we are already familiar. Here are some examples of these phrases used as modifiers:

(1) a. Frank lost three plastic worms *there*.
    b. *Here* you will be safe.

c. *Down there in Brownsville*, Joe worked as a carpenter.
d. Frances read some of Molière's plays *in Paris*.
e. You can grow carrots *wherever you find sandy soil*.
f. Johnny sells souvenirs *where the two armies once clashed*.

11.1.2 Time Modifiers

Time modifiers indicate the time at which some event occurred or some state obtained.

(2) a. We would *then* have called a specialist.
  b. Jones is feeling better *now*.
  c. *Today* our guests will be taken to a bullfight.
  d. *On Thursday*, the Guadalupe River left its banks.
  e. Jane wants to see you *next week*.
  f. *After the match was over*, the teams exchanged shirts.
  g. *When the first bell rings*, everybody will stop working.
  h. Joe locked the door *before he went to lunch*.

11.1.3 Aspectual Modifiers

Aspectual modifiers give information about whether some event or state of affairs is completed, is still going on, and so forth.

(3) a. Carolyn has seen this chapter *already*.
  b. I wonder whether Bruce has seen it *yet*.
  c. Wanda *still* would like to talk about the music festival.
  d. I doubt that Bob thinks about it *any more*.

11.1.4 Duration Modifiers

Duration modifiers indicate how long something lasted. They can perform this function by telling the length of time a certain state or activity lasted (*for three hours*), or by giving its termination point (*until she fell asleep*).

(4) a. *For three hours*, the minister talked about the eye of the needle.
  b. Joanne studied Greek *until she fell asleep*.
  c. The choir sang *(for) a long time*.

11.1.5 Frequency Modifiers

Frequency modifiers indicate the frequency of a certain type of event. Included in this class are modifiers indicating the two opposite extremes (*always* and *never*). Some of these modifiers indicate an absolute frequency (*two times, twice, many times*); others indicate a frequency per time period (*two times a month, twice a week, many times a year*).

(5) a. One *always* hears rumors.
   b. Jimmy *never* has been seen in Washington.
   c. The general would *always* have thought that he could have been a singer.
   d. *Sometimes* an answer is hard to find.
   e. Martha has seen that movie *twice*.
   f. Joe has traveled to Egypt *many times*.
   g. *On several occasions*, the police have found him asleep in his truck.
   h. Gaylord visits his wife and children *several times a year*.

11.1.6 Manner Modifiers

The class of manner modifiers includes a wide variety of expressions that describe the manner or way in which a certain action is performed.

(6) a. John walked onto the stage *slowly*.
   b. *Quickly* Diego chipped the ball into the penalty area.
   c. Doris feeds her guppies *this way*.
   d. Ollie opens jars *like this*.
   e. Johnny introduced his guests *in a relaxed manner*.
   f. Cornelius *sadly* walked out into the pasture.
   g. Velma must have *accidentally* pulled the plug.
   h. Dr. Jekyll has been *carefully* cleaning the wound.

11.1.7 Epistemic Modifiers

Epistemic modifiers let the hearer know something about the "security" of the proposition conveyed in the sentence—whether it is guaranteed to be true, probably true, rumored to be true, and so on down the line.

(7) a. Olivia has *probably* solved the problem.
   b. James has *allegedly* made millions of dollars from illegal enterprises.
   c. Adverbs *undoubtedly* make up a confusing class of words.
   d. *Possibly* some way will be found to save the school.
   e. George would *certainly* be cooperating with Shirley.
   f. *In the teacher's opinion*, use of a form of BE constitutes bad writing.
   g. *According to unidentified sources*, more unconfirmed rumors are expected soon.

11.1.8   Attitudinal Modifiers

Attitudinal modifiers indicate the speaker's emotional attitude toward the state of affairs that he or she is reporting.

(8) a. *Unfortunately*, the state treasury cannot honor your paycheck.
   b. *Regrettably*, people exist who want to put the welfare of the human race ahead of their country's flag.
   c. *Luckily*, such people have very little influence.

11.1.9   Conditional Modifiers

Conditional modifiers put a condition of some sort on the truth of the rest of the sentence.

(9) a. You can succeed *if you try very hard.*
   b. *Unless this colonel is given lots of money*, his lawyer will never become rich.
   c. *Barring a miracle*, the Redskins will have to settle for second place.

A few special types actually have the net effect of asserting that a certain kind of condition is irrelevant.

(10) a. *Whatever kind of work he decides to do*, Edward will find it difficult to make ends meet.
    b. *Whether or not the Celtics win tonight*, the sun will still come up tomorrow.
    c. *No matter how many funny hats she wears*, Julia will never be a star.

11.1.10   Purpose Modifiers

Purpose modifiers indicate the purpose for which some action was performed.

(11) a. Joe sang a lullaby *to quiet the baby.*
    b. *In order to get good seats*, Tim got to the theatre at six in the morning.
    c. Carol writes poems *for money.*
    d. I bought this shredder *for you to put documents into.*

11.1.11   Causal Modifiers

Causal modifiers identify the cause of whatever event or state is conveyed by the rest of the sentence.

(12) a. *Because Mabel has lost her license,* Fred is driving her to work.
b. The program failed *because of a minor typing error.*
c. *On account of a shortage of clean dishes,* Ollie is eating out tonight.

11.1.12 Universal Modifiers

The class of universal modifiers includes the three universal quantity words *each, both,* and *all.* In some varieties of English, it also includes several partitive noun phrases (*each of them, all of them, both of them, neither of them, either of them, none of them*). When used as verbal modifiers, these universal words and noun phrases emphasize the universal applicability or nonapplicability of the predicate to the subject.

(13) a. The students have *each* given a pint of blood.
b. The twins will *both* be running in the first race.
c. Your friends should *all* have received invitations.
d. The players have *all of them* flatly refused to leave the field.
e. Your friends are *neither of them* very diplomatic.

11.1.13 Focusing Modifiers

The class of focusing modifiers consists of the four words *even, only, also,* and *too.* They have the common property of being associated with some special "focused" portion of the sentence in an utterance in which they occur.

(14) a. John *even* speaks ARAMAIC.   (more surprising that speaking Hebrew or Arabic)
b. John *even* SPEAKS Aramaic.   (more surprising than merely reading it)
c. John *only* speaks SPANISH.   (He doesn't speak English or Basque in addition.)
d. John *only* SPEAKS Spanish.   (He doesn't read it or write it.)
e. Kathy *also* wanted to interview BORIS.   (in addition to interviewing Ivan)
f. Kathy *also* wanted to INTERVIEW Boris.   (in addition to photographing him)
g. Dorothy swims in the POND, *too.*   (in addition to swimming in the city pool)
h. Dorothy SWIMS in the pond, *too.*   (in addition to fishing in it)

Also and *too* have the effect of making explicit the parallel between the sentence in which they appear and some earlier sentence in the discourse.

11.2 STRUCTURAL CLASSES OF MODIFIERS

Let us now turn to the classes into which various modifiers fall by virtue of their structure. We can distinguish five basic classes, all of which have already been exemplified:

- adverbs: *usually, often, then, carefully, already, probably, even*
- universal quantity words: *all, both, each*
- noun phrases: *many times, this way, this week, last year, all of them*
- prepositional phrases (also larger locative phrases): *in Austin, out here on the veranda, on Thursday, after the meeting, until ten o'clock, on several occasions, in a relaxed manner, in my opinion*
- clausal modifiers: *where the two armies once clashed, when the first bell rings, before he went to lunch, until she fell asleep, if you try very hard, for you to put documents into*

11.3 RULES GOVERNING MODIFIER POSITIONS

11.3.1 Initial Remarks

Before we try to formulate rules concerning the behavior of particular modifiers, let us make a preliminary list of positions in which modifiers appear. If we were to go through the above sentences one at a time with the aim of making such a list, we might distinguish the five positions listed here.

(15) At the beginning of the sentence:
   a. *Today* our guests will be taken to a bullfight.
   b. *Possibly* some way will be found to save the school.

(16) Before the finite verb:
   a. Wanda *still* would like to talk about the music festival.
   b. Jimmy *never* has been seen in Washington.

(17) After the finite verb:
   a. The general would *always* have thought that he could have been a singer.
   b. George would *certainly* be cooperating with Shirley.

(18) Before the action or state verb:
   a. Velma must have *accidentally* pulled the plug.
   b. Dr. Jekyll has been *carefully* cleaning the wound.

(19) At the end of the verb phrase:
    a. I wonder whether Bruce has seen it *yet*.
    b. Martha has seen that movie *twice*.

Two pairs of the above-named positions are sometimes indistinguishable in a single example. In the first place, "before the finite verb" and "before the action or state verb" determine the same position when it is the action or state verb itself that serves as the finite verb, as in (20).

(20) a. John [before the finite verb] kissed his wife.
    b. John [before the action verb] kissed his wife.

The same kind of overlap arises with the third and fourth positions named above: "after the finite verb" and "before the action or state verb" may also determine one and the same location, as in (21).

(21) a. The queen has [after the finite verb] ordered the servant to leave the room.
    b. The queen has [before the action verb] ordered the servant to leave the room.

This occasional overlap will not create a serious problem for us, though. When we want to construct rules about where various adverbs go, it will always be possible to find examples in which the positions we are interested in are clearly distinguished. In fact, the examples in (15)–(19) all have the useful property of clearly distinguishing the position being illustrated from any of the other positions. In both of the "before the finite verb" examples the finite verbs are different from the action or state verbs, and in both of the "after the finite verb" examples the adverb is followed by a verb different from the action or state verb.

11.3.2 Preliminary Observations on Modifier Position

Let us now try to make some systematic statements concerning the positions that are possible for the various kinds of modifiers we have identified. The first thing we can do is to dispense with the clausal modifiers, the prepositional phrases, and the noun phrases (apart from the universal modifiers). Modifiers of these three syntactic types are most comfortable either at the beginning of the sentence or at the end of the verb phrase. The previous discussion contains many examples of these kinds of modifiers in these two positions. By contrast, they are less acceptable in sentence-internal positions, unless accompanied by a very definite "interruption" intonation or punctuation.

(22) a. *John *before he went to lunch* locked the door.
   b. *You can *wherever you find sandy soil* grow carrots.

(23) a. John, *before he went to lunch,* locked the door.
   b. You can, *wherever you find sandy soil,* grow carrots.

(24) a. *Josephine *in Austin* worked as a carpenter's helper.
   b. *Josephine has *in Austin* been working as a carpenter's helper.

(25) a. ?*You *many times* have asked for loans.
   b. ?*You have *many times* asked for loans.

In view of these observations, the remainder of this discussion will focus on the position of adverbs. Special note will also be made, where appropriate, of the behavior of the other class relevant here, the class of universal modifiers (universal quantity words and noun phrases).

By means of an extensive series of experiments, we can get an idea of where various adverbs are acceptable. In some cases, we can give rules that refer to entire classes; in other cases, it is necessary to single out individual words for special treatment. We will start by looking at the experimental sentences given in (26)–(29). (It needs to be acknowledged here that the (b) sentences in (26), (27), and (29) are perceived as less than fully acceptable by some speakers; this fact will be easily accommodated in the analysis developed in subsection 11.3.4.)

(26) a. *Now* we have been sitting here for three hours.
      (sentence-initial)
   b. We *now* have been sitting here for three hours.
      (before finite verb)
   c. We have *now* been sitting here for three hours.
      (after finite verb)
   d. *We have been *now* sitting here for three hours.
      (before action verb)
   e. We have been sitting here for three hours *now*.
      (end of verb phrase)

(27) a. *Already* George has been making plans.
      (sentence-initial)
   b. George *already* has been making plans.
      (before finite verb)
   c. George has *already* been making plans.
      (after finite verb)

     d. *George has been *already* making plans.
        (before action verb)

     e. George has been making plans *already*.
        (end of verb phrase)

(28) a. *Cheerfully* Vivian ate the tacos.
        (sentence-initial)

     b. *Vivian *cheerfully* has eaten the tacos.
        (before finite verb)

     c. *Vivian must *cheerfully* have eaten the tacos.
        (after finite verb)

     d. Vivian must have *cheerfully* eaten the tacos.
        (before action verb)

     e. Vivian must have eaten the tacos *cheerfully*.
        (end of verb phrase)

(29) a. *Probably* Sally has been listening to Oliver.
        (sentence-initial)

     b. Sally *probably* has been listening to Oliver.
        (before finite verb)

     c. Sally has *probably* been listening to Oliver.
        (after finite verb)

     d. *Sally has been *probably* listening to Oliver.
        (before action verb)

     e. *Sally has been listening to Oliver *probably*.
        (end of verb phrase)

These observations can be summarized in (30).

(30)

	S-initial	Before finite V	After finite V	Before action V	End of VP
a. now	yes	yes	yes	no	yes
b. already	yes	yes	yes	no	yes
c. cheerfully	yes	no	no	yes	yes
d. probably	yes	yes	yes	no	no

The same kinds of experiments with a much wider range of adverbs give the results summarized in (31). Some of the entries in this table refer to individual adverbs; others refer to classes of adverbs.

(31)

	S-initial	Before finite V	After finite V	Before action V	End of VP
a. now	yes	yes	yes	no	yes
b. then	yes	yes	yes	no	yes
c. already	yes	yes	yes	no	yes
d. still	yes	yes	yes	no	yes
e. yet	no	no	no	no	yes
f. any more	no	no	no	no	yes
g. often	yes	yes	yes	no	yes
h. sometimes	yes	yes	yes	no	yes
i. always	no	yes	yes	no	yes?
j. never	yes	yes	yes	no	no
k. Epistemic	yes	yes	yes	no	no
l. Attitudinal	yes	yes	yes	no	no
m. Universal	no	yes	yes	no	no
n. also	no	yes	yes	no	yes
o. too	no	no	no	no	yes
p. even	yes	yes	yes	no	yes?
q. only	yes	yes	yes	no	no

Although individual speakers might disagree with some of the yes and no answers listed here, this chart gives a reasonable overall view of how the five adverbial positions are used.

Before we set out to develop some rules, let us make a note for future reference of one odd coincidence in the way the chart in (31) turned out. For the most part, when we compare two columns, we find that the pattern of answers is different. For instance, although the first and second columns have a broad range of shared answers, there are definite points at which they differ. However, there is one exceptional pair here: the second and third columns contain identical answers for every entry in the chart. We will return to this matter in subsection 11.3.4.

Exercises

1. In (31), three general categories of adverbs are mentioned: epistemic, attitudinal, and universal. Explain why there is no general listing for frequency adverbs.

2. The following sentence is ambiguous, depending on whether the time modifier *today* is understood with the top verb phrase or the bottom one:

(i) John promised to mow the lawn today.

The ambiguity disappears when the modifier occurs at the beginning of the sentence.

(ii) Today John promised to mow the lawn.

Explain in your own words the two meanings of sentence (i), and then say which of these meanings is shared with sentence (ii). Then see if you can think of a principle that would predict the absence of ambiguity in (ii).

3. In some cases, as in (i) and (ii), a manner adverb (which tells something about the way a certain action is carried out) can be put at the beginning of the sentence in which it appears.

(i)   Diego chipped the ball into the penalty area quickly.

(ii) Quickly Diego chipped the ball into the penalty area.

In other cases, however, placing the adverb at the beginning of the sentence gives poor results. Thus, (iv) is unacceptable as a variant of (iii).

(iii)   Diego must have chipped the ball into the penalty area quickly.

(iv) *Quickly Diego must have chipped the ball into the penalty area.

See if you can think of an explanation for the difference in acceptability between (ii) and (iv). Your answer to exercise 2 might prove useful.

11.3.3   Basic Rules for Modifier Positions

With the observations of the preceding subsection in hand, we are ready to try to determine more precisely the nature of the rules that account for the positional behavior of adverbs. Let us begin by reviewing what was said in chapter 10 about the way in which modifiers are joined with common-noun phrases to make larger common-noun phrases. If we use *Mod* as an abbreviation for the various types of modifiers that can attach to common-noun phrases, then the two types of modifying configurations are just those shown in (32).

(32) a. CNP   b.   CNP

     Mod   CNP   CNP   Mod

Diagram (32a) represents prenominal modifying configurations; (32b) represents postnominal modifying configurations.

Let us now consider the possibility of using corresponding structures for the modifiers that we are studying in this chapter. For verb phrases, we would expect the following rule:

(33) A verb phrase can consist of a modifier followed by a (smaller) verb phrase, or a (smaller) verb phrase followed by a modifier.

This rule would yield the two separate configurations shown in (34).

(34) a. VP   b.   VP

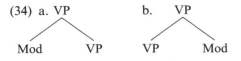

The first of these trees provides immediately for two of the five positions that we have identified. Sentence (35a) has an adverb preceding the finite verb; (35b) has an adverb before the action verb.

(35) a. George *already* has been making plans.
     b. Vivian must have *cheerfully* eaten the tacos.

An adverb like *already* can appear before the finite verb by attaching to the left of the finite verb phrase, as in (36).

(36)

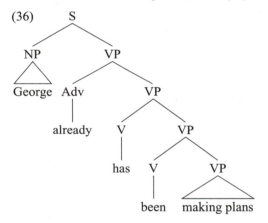

Similarly, an adverb like *cheerfully* can get a position before the action verb by attaching to the left of the phrase that this verb heads, as in (37).

(37)

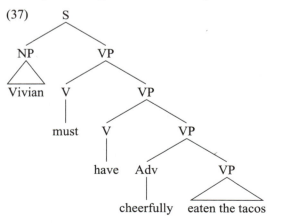

The differing positions of the adverbs in these sentences result from this difference in attachment. Because the verbs come first in the minimal verb phrases that they head, the effect is to put the adverb immediately to the left of the finite verb in the one case, and immediately to the left of the action verb in the other case.

Now let us consider the corresponding examples in which the adverbs come at the end of the verb phrase.

(38) a. George has been making plans already.
      b. Vivian must have eaten the tacos cheerfully.

These examples can be analyzed as having the structure shown in (34b)— the one with the modifier attached on the right side of the verb phrase. On the assumption that the adverbs are attached to the same verb phrases as when they precede the verb phrase, we get the tree diagrams in (39) for these two sentences.

(39) a.

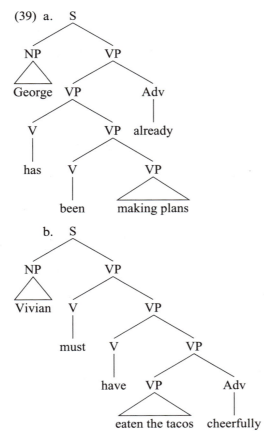

As these diagrams suggest, what appeared to be just one position is really two: to the right of the finite verb phrase and to the right of the action verb phrase. The reason that attachments to the left yield distinct left-to-right positions but attachments to the right do not is that a higher verb phrase and a lower verb phrases typically start at different points in the sentence but end at the same point, as shown in (40).

(40)

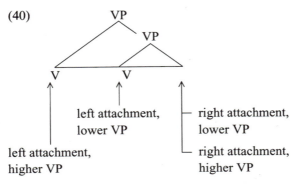

left attachment,
lower VP

right attachment,
lower VP

left attachment,
higher VP

right attachment,
higher VP

To what can we attribute the difference in attachment behavior of an adverb like *already*, which attaches to the phrase headed by the finite verb, and an adverb like *cheerfully*, which attaches to the phrase headed by the action verb? Here we might speculate that the difference in attachment behavior is related to the differing contributions of the head verbs to the meanings of the sentences in which they occur. The finite verb, either by virtue of its tense marking or else in its own right, may indicate something about the time of the reported event, the habituality of the event, or the probable truth of the statement. Thus, with finite verb phrases we find adverbs like *now, already, usually,* and *probably,* which convey information of these kinds. On the other hand, a verb like EAT denotes the central action of the sentence. Since manner adverbs like *cheerfully* describe actions, they occur naturally in combination with phrases headed by verbs of this type.

We are left now with two basic adverbial positions to account for: the sentence-initial position and the position after the finite verb. For the first of these positions, we can adopt the same idea that we adopted for verb phrases, which give the following rule:

(41) A sentence can consist of a modifier combined with a smaller sentence.

For a sentence such as (42a), this rule yields the structure given in (42b).

(42) a. Now we know the answer.

  b.

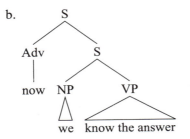

For adverbs that appear after the finite verb, however, the kinds of verb-phrase attachments that we have considered here do not yield a natural account. This is the second respect in which this particular adverbial position poses a special problem.

As a final observation in this section, we note that it is possible to construct sentences in which there is more than a single adverb in a certain position. This possibility is frequently seen with those adverbs that appear before the finite verb, as in (43).

(43) George probably always will be singing that song.

This sentence poses no problem for the rule we have developed. As (44) shows, we just need the same kind of "stacking" that we used with nominal modifiers.

(44)

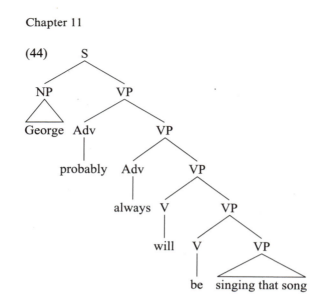

11.3.4   "Before Finite" and "After Finite" as a Single Adverbial Position

In the two preceding subsections, we discussed the various positions in which adverbs can appear, and we tried to develop rules that would account for their appearance in these positions. In the course of our discussions, we noticed two respects in which the position after the finite verb was odd. First, the adverbs that can occur in this position are exactly the same ones that can occur in the position before the finite verb. Second, this position is the only one of the five positions in our list that cannot be readily accounted for by a rule attaching an adverb to one side or the other of a verb phrase or to the beginning of a sentence.

When we look further, we find another mysterious fact about the position after the finite verb: the finite verbs that can be followed by words such as *never, probably,* and *all* are quite limited in number, as the examples in (45) demonstrate.

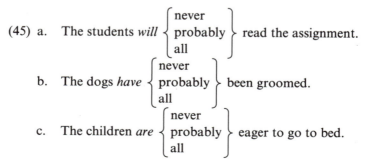

d. *Joe's friends *send* $\left\{\begin{array}{l}\text{never}\\\text{probably}\\\text{all}\end{array}\right\}$ letters to him.

e. *The three friends *became* $\left\{\begin{array}{l}\text{never}\\\text{probably}\\\text{all}\end{array}\right\}$ accountants.

With the verbs *send* and *became,* only the position before the verb is available.

(46) a. Joe's friends $\left\{\begin{array}{l}\text{never}\\\text{probably}\\\text{all}\end{array}\right\}$ *send* letters to him.

b. The three friends $\left\{\begin{array}{l}\text{never}\\\text{probably}\\\text{all}\end{array}\right\}$ *became* accountants.

The only verbs that allow these modifiers to follow them are the modals, the finite forms of BE, and the finite forms of perfect HAVE. Thus, all finite verbs allow these modifiers to precede them, but only a few allow the same modifiers to follow them. This observation might lead us to suspect that the position before the finite verb, which is available with all verbs, is more basic than the position after the verb, which is available with only a few.

An additional surprise is that there are two situations in which the preverbal position is much more natural even with the modals, BE, and HAVE. The first situation is illustrated in (47)–(49).

(47) a. Pete has often visited Grandmother, but Bill *never* has.

b. *Pete has often visited Grandmother, but Bill has *never.*

(48) a. Only a few of the teachers have checked out books, but the students *all* have.

b. *Only a few of the teachers have checked out books, but the students have *all.*

(49) a. John has definitely finished the exercise, and Martha *probably* has, too.

b. *John has definitely finished the exercise, and Martha has *probably,* too.

These examples seem to indicate that when something is "understood" after these verbs, the adverb can only appear before the verb.

The second situation in which the adverb is more natural before the verb than after it is illustrated in (50) and (51).

(50) a.   Bill never WAS much of an electrician.
      b.   *Bill WAS never much of an electrician.

(51) a.   Doris probably COULD play that sonata.
      b.   *Doris COULD probably play that sonata.

These examples seem to indicate that when one of these finite verbs is emphasized, the position after the verb is not available to these adverbs.

Now, do the two above-mentioned special situations have any property in common? We need to look for a property that would distinguish them from the situation in which these adverbs are acceptable after the verb.

(52) a.   Bill has *never* visited Grandmother.
      b.   The students have *all* checked out books.
      c.   Martha has *probably* finished the exercise, too.
      d.   Bill was *never* much of an electrician.
      e.   Doris could *probably* play that sonata.

The distinguishing property is actually rather simple. In the examples in (52), the finite verb is *stressless,* whereas in the examples in (47)–(51), it is stressed. The stressed nature of the verbs in (50) and (51) is obvious, since they receive emphatic stress in these examples. Although the (a) examples of (47)–(49) do not receive this kind of stress, they do receive what we can refer to as *normal stress.* Careful attention to their pronunciation reveals that these verbs are sharply different in pronunciation from those in (52). We can see this most easily by comparing the pronunciations of the verb *has* in the two examples in (53).

(53) a.   Bill never has.   (normal stress on *has*)
      b.   Bill has never visited Grandmother.   (no stress on *has*)

The *has* in (53a) is pronounced [hæz], with a full vowel [æ]. By contrast, the same word in (53b) is pronounced [həz], with the reduced vowel [ə] that appears in English in completely unstressed syllables.

All of our observations to this point are summarized in the following statements:

(54) a.   When the finite verb is stressed, adverbs like *never, probably,* and *all* precede it.
      b.   When the finite verb is unstressed, the same adverbs are allowed to follow it.

The first of these two statements automatically covers ordinary finite verbs like *send* and *became*, since they never lose their stress. It also applies to emphasized verbs and to verbs that have retained their stress because of "understood" material following them.

Even these statements can be simplified. We start by saying that the basic position of adverbs like *never, probably,* and *all* is before the finite verb. In order to account for sentences in which they appear after the finite verb, we simply need to adopt the following rule:

(55) Unstressed finite verbs may be (and for some speakers must be) moved to the left of any preceding adverbs.

This rule has the effect of converting the basic word order in (56a) into the special word order of (56b).

(56) a. Bill   never will read that book.   (no stress on *will*)

    b. Bill will never   read that book.

However, the rule will not apply in either of the situations in (57) and (58).

(57) a. Bill   never WILL read that book.   (emphatic stress on *will*)

    b. *Bill WILL never   read that book.

(58) a. Bill   never will ____.   (normal stress on *will*)

    b. *Bill will never   ____.

In both of these last two cases, the stress on the verb keeps the leftward shift of the verb from taking place.

In the analysis developed here, what makes the modals, BE, and perfect HAVE special is that they are exactly the English verbs that can have their stress reduced. Under ordinary circumstances, this reduction is automatic.

(59) a. Sue can [kən] apply for travel money.
    b. Tony has [həz] papered the walls.
    c. Harvey was [wəz] planning to play tennis.

The reduction fails to take place only if the verb is emphasized, or if the verb is followed by "understood" material.

The structure of a sentence with a shifted finite verb can be represented as in (60).

(60)

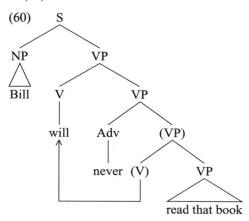

The verb *will* has been shifted to the left, joining with what follows it to make a larger verb phrase. The parenthesized V and VP show the basic position of the verb and the verb phrase that it heads, the position in which the verb would have occurred had the shift not taken place.

What grounds do we have for maintaining that it is the verb that has moved? Could we not just as well say that the adverb moves to the right of the verb? This alternative idea would give us the tree diagram in (61) for sentence (56b), instead of the diagram given in (60).

(61)

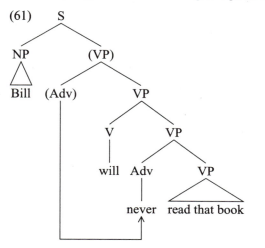

The main reason for preferring the verb-movement idea to the adverb-movement idea is that the former gives a simpler picture for sentences in which additional adverbs are involved. One such sentence is (62).

(62) They are *probably always* playing golf.

The competing structures that the two analyses would yield for this sentence are given in (63).

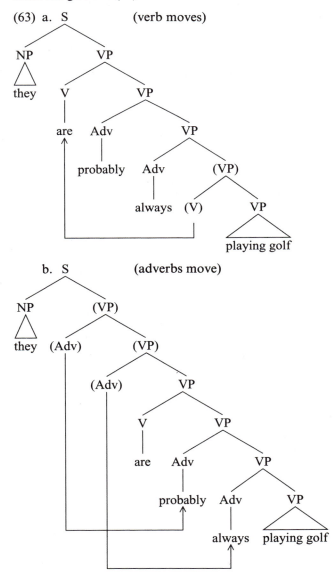

Diagram (63a) is clearly simpler than diagram (63b). Correspondingly, a rule that says "shift the head verb" yields simpler structures than one that says "shift any number of modifiers." This is the justification for claiming that it is the stressless verb that shifts, rather than the modifier.

We have finally succeeded in reducing the basic modifier positions from five to four, by eliminating the position after the finite verb as a separate basic position. We are now left with the following four positions:

- sentence-initial
- before the finite verb
- before the action or state verb
- sentence-final

Exercise

1. For each of the following sentences, draw a tree diagram:
   a. Brenda was usually alert.
   b. Conrad would never have found the answer.
   c. Robert probably always hoped for a miracle.
   d. The clerks were probably all ready to resign.

11.3.5   The Syntax of *Not*

There is one special adverb whose behavior is not accounted for completely by the general word-order system developed above: the negative adverb *not*.

By way of preparation, we need to note that, in many contexts, *not* behaves in very much the same way as *never*. This is particularly clear with certain kinds of nonfinite verbal constructions. The basic position of *never* with gerundives, infinitival phrases, and bare-stem verb phrases is shown in (64).

(64) a. Jane regrets [*never* having seen the movie].
     b. We asked him [*never* to try to call us again].
     c. The rules require that you [*never* miss the monthly meeting].

As the examples in (65) show, the position of *not* is identical.

(65) a. Jane regrets [*not* having seen the movie].
     b. We asked him [*not* to try to call us again].
     c. The rules require that you [*not* miss the monthly meeting].

These examples give us a strong initial reason to believe that *not* is like *never* in the positions that it prefers.

It is with finite verb phrases that *not* and *never* part company. Unlike *never*, *not* requires two special adjustments.

(66) a. Phillip *never* sold Martha's ring.
     b. *Phillip *not* sold Martha's ring.
     c. Phillip did *not* sell Martha's ring.

(67) a. Rhonda *never* reports errors.
     b. *Rhonda *not* reports errors.
     c. Rhonda does *not* report errors.

(68) a. The students *never* ask questions.
     b. *The students *not* ask questions.
     c. The students do *not* ask questions.

In order to see exactly what the first adjustment is, let us leave out *never* and *not* momentarily and display the finite verb phrases in the (a) and (c) sentences above.

(69)   *Ordinary verb phrases*   *Verb phrases headed by DO*
     a. sold Martha's ring   did   sell Martha's ring
        (past-tense verb phrase)   (past DO   + bare-stem verb phrase)
     b. reports errors   does   report errors
        (pres sg verb phrase)   (pres sg DO + bare-stem verb phrase)
     c. ask questions   do   ask questions
        (pres pl verb phrase   (pres pl DO + bare-stem verb phrase)

We see here exactly the same kind of contrast that we saw in chapter 3 between nonemphatic and emphatic sentences. Thus, we conclude that *not*, unlike *never*, requires the use of the special-purpose finite phrase headed by DO.

When we put *not* back in, we note the second adjustment: the head verb must occur to the left of *not* rather than to its right, as seen in (70)–(72).

(70) a. *Phillip *not* did sell Martha's ring.
     b. Phillip did *not* sell Martha's ring.

(71) a. *Rhonda *not* does report errors.
     b. Rhonda does *not* report errors.

(72) a. *The students *not* do ask questions.
     b. The students do *not* ask questions.

In sum, the following special rule is required for verb phrases to which *not* is attached:

(73) When *not* is attached to a finite verb phrase:

- Use a special-purpose finite phrase.
- Shift the head verb to the left of *not*.

Both the similarities between *never* and *not* and their differences are illustrated in (74).

(74) a.

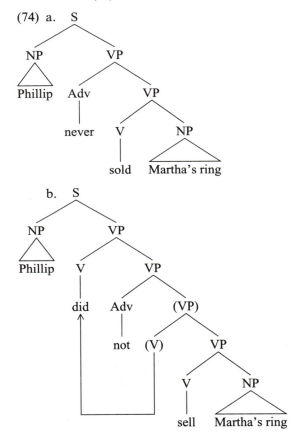

These two diagrams are alike in one respect: the adverbs occupy similar positions in relation to the verb phrase that follows them. However, (74b) differs from (74a) in two significant respects: its verb phrase is the more complicated special-purpose finite, and its head verb has had to be shifted to the left of *not*.

We find that BE, perfect HAVE, and the modals exhibit the same kind of exceptional behavior in negative sentences that they do in emphatic sentences. In each set of sentences in (75)–(77), the (a) sentence is a normal affirmative, the (b) sentence is the incorrect negative that would be expected if these verbs were not exceptional, and the (c) sentence is the correct negative sentence.

(75) a. Max has vanished.
    b. *Max does not have vanished.
    c. Max has not vanished.

(76) a. Smith is a genius.
    b. *Smith does not be a genius.
    c. Smith is not a genius.

(77) a. Sarah will open the package.
    b. *Sarah does not will open the package.
    c. Sarah will not open the package.

The behavior of *not* with these verbs follows immediately from the statement made about them in chapter 3, where we noted that their special-purpose structures are exactly the same as their general-purpose structures. Using this earlier statement in conjunction with rule (73), we automatically account for these new examples. The structures for the acceptable negative sentences in (75)–(77) are given in (78).

(78) a. S   b.   S

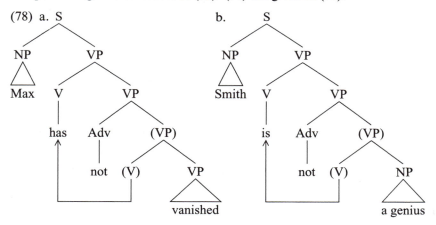

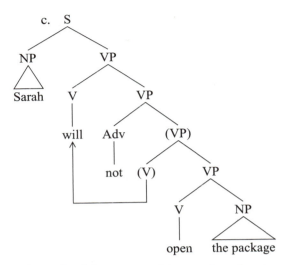

In each of these examples, a verb and *not* occur in a peculiar position relative to one another. Although the analysis just given involves moving the verb, we might ask what grounds there are for believing that the verb has moved to the left of *not*, rather than that *not* has moved to the right of the verb. This alternative analysis would give us the tree diagram in (79b), instead of the one in (74b).

(79)

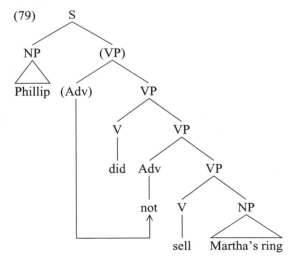

Here the critical kind of evidence is the same as that we saw in the preceding subsection, when we were deciding whether stressless verbs shift across adverbs or vice versa. In particular, it is not difficult to construct sentences in which *not* is accompanied by another adverb. One such sentence is (80).

(80) Fido is not always barking.

The competing structures that these two analyses would yield for this sentence are shown in (81).

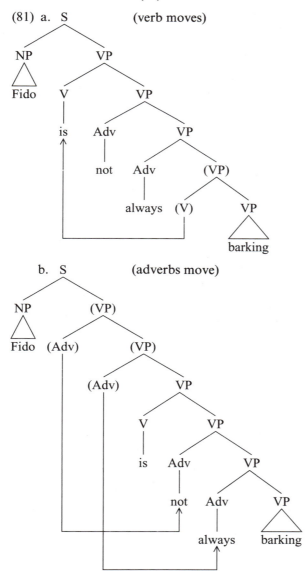

Diagram (81a) is clearly simpler than (81b). Correspondingly, a rule that says "shift the head verb" is simpler than one that says "shift the word *not,* and also any following adverb." This is the justification for claiming that it is the verb that shifts in this construction rather than the adverb *not.*

Exercises

1. For each of the following sentences, draw a tree diagram:
   a. George did not know the answer.
   b. Mabel is not eager to leave the meeting.
   c. Janet does not always type her papers.
   d. The mail will not ever be delivered.

2. In Early Modern English, as represented in the King James Version of the Bible, the formation of sentences with *not* involved movement not just of the auxiliary verbs, as illustrated in (a)–(d), but also of full verbs, as illustrated in (e)–(i).
   a. It *is not* lawful for to put them into the treasury.
   b. Flesh and blood *hath not* revealed it unto thee.
   c. The gates of hell *shall not* prevail against it.
   d. Thou *canst not* make one hair white or black.
   e. To eat with unwashen hands *defileth not* a man.
   f. They *wash not* their hands when they eat bread.
   g. Thou *savourest not* the things that be of God.
   h. Ye *know not* what ye ask.
   i. He saw there a man which *had not* on a wedding garment.

How might the rules developed in the preceding subsection for Modern English be changed in such a way as to account for the sentences in (e)–(i) along with those in (a)–(d)?

3. The following are some additional sentences from the King James Version of the Bible:
   a. I *spake it not* to you concerning bread.
   b. Ye *visited me not.*
   c. Ye *did it not* to me.
   d. I *know you not.*
   e. I was a stranger, and ye *took me not* in.
   f. Ye *believed him not.*

How might the rule developed in the preceding exercise be modified to account for these additional sentences? (Be sure that whatever revision you suggest still leaves you with a viable account for all of the sentences in exercise 2.)

11.3.6 Special-Purpose Head Verbs with Contracted *Not*

Corresponding to the three forms of special-purpose DO and also to most
of the exceptional verbs discussed above, English has combined forms
that end in *-n't,* a contracted form of *not.* Here are some examples:

(82) a. I *did not* go to the post office.
      b. I *didn't* go to the post office.

(83) a. Henry *is not* here.
      b. Henry *isn't* here.

(84) a. The Smiths *could not* see the mountains.
      b. The Smiths *couldn't* see the mountains.

Many of these forms are constructed simply by adding *-n't* to the positive
form (e.g., *isn't* from *is, doesn't* from *does,* and *haven't* from *have*). In a
few cases, though, the relation between the positive and the negative word
is irregular. The most obvious example is *won't,* in place of the expected
**willn't.* In the case of *don't* and *mustn't,* the spellings hide irregularities:
the vowel sound in *don't* is different from the sound in *do,* and the final *t*
in *must* is not pronounced in *mustn't.* In addition, there is at least one
positive form that does not have any contracted negative form at all: *am,*
but **amn't.* Finally, the forms *mayn't, mightn't,* and *shan't,* which still
exist in at least some varieties of British English, are no longer used in
American English.

The easiest way to account for these forms is to hypothesize an optional
process that applies to the uncontracted negative forms after they have
been arranged by the rules set forth in the preceding subsection. Let us
look, for instance, at how the following sentence would be described:

(85) Jones hasn't ever seen the light.

We can think of the sentence as being derived in several steps.

(86) a. Jones not ever has seen the light.
          (*not* and *ever* before special-purpose verb phrase)
      b. Jones has not ever seen the light.
          (head verb shifted to the left of *not*)
      c. Jones hasn't ever seen the light.
          (optional contraction of *not* with *has*)

The structure resulting from this derivation is pictured in (87), where the
plus sign indicates that the two elements are joined into a single word.

(87)

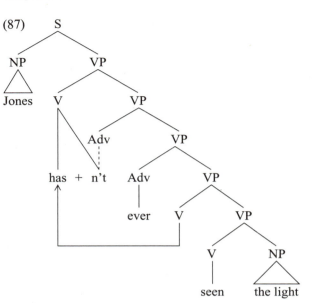

The solid line from the symbol *V* to *n't* indicates that this element has been incorporated into the verb. For the purposes of at least one further rule (which will be discussed in chapter 14), *hasn't* and other contracted forms like it will behave as single units.

Exercises

1. For each of the following sentences, draw a tree diagram.
    a. Holmes doesn't know the answer.
    b. Watson couldn't diagram this sentence.
    c. Wanda hasn't ever really decided to sell the house.
    d. Morton couldn't always waltz.

2. Study the following quotation from one of the novels of the British author P. G. Wodehouse:

(i) "Don't you know that there is no surer way to a woman's heart than [croquet]? At least there usedn't to be when I was ass enough to swing a mallet in my youth." (*Sunset at Blandings,* Penguin Books, London, 1990, p. 51 (originally published 1977))

Describe as precisely as you can the difference between the syntax of *used* shown in this quotation and the syntax of the same verb in the following American English equivalent:

(ii) ... At least there didn't used to be when I was ass enough to swing a mallet in my youth.

11.3.7 A Note on "Verb-Phrase-Final" Position

In subsection 11.3.2, we saw many modifiers that are acceptable in verb-phrase-final position. A representative sample is given in (88).

(88) a. Rhonda loaned some money to her employees *on Thursday*.
 b. We went to a bullfight *today*.
 c. Carol has consulted with her attorney *already*.
 d. Charles walked out the door *quickly*.
 e. George stayed in his hotel room *for three nights*.
 f. Tanya has traveled to Egypt *many times*.
 g. Cornelius walked out the door *slowly*.

In these particular examples, the same modifiers are also acceptable in some position nearer to the verb.

(89) a. Rhonda loaned some money *on Thursday* to her employees.
 b. We went *today* to a bullfight.
 c. Carol has consulted *already* with her attorney.
 d. Charles walked *quickly* out the door.
 e. George stayed *for three nights* in his hotel room.
 f. Tanya has traveled *many times* to Egypt.
 g. Cornelius walked *slowly* out the door.

In this capacity to move nearer to the verb, these relatively short modifiers contrast with clausal modifiers.

(90) a. *Rhonda loaned some money *when she got back to town* to her employees.
 b. *We went *after the reception was over* to a bullfight.
 c. *George stayed *while the legislature was in session* in his hotel room.
 d. *Tanya has traveled *to increase her knowledge of Arabic culture* to Egypt.

Thus, the rule that we will adopt to account for the alternative word order in (89) needs to mention specific structural types of modifiers:.

(91) If a certain verbal modifier can appear at the end of a verb phrase, and is an adverb, a noun phrase, or a prepositional phrase, then it can also optionally be moved closer to the verb.

One firm restriction on this rule is illustrated in the following pairs of sentences:

(92) a.   George saw a play *on Monday.*
     b. *George saw *on Monday* a play.

(93) a.   The baby drank its milk *slowly.*
     b. *The baby drank *slowly* its milk.

The restriction is that these adverbial modifiers are not allowed to come between a verb and its object. This is a special case of what is perhaps the most basic fact in English concerning the order of phrases and words after the verb, namely, that modifiers are not allowed to come between a verb and its direct object. There are only two circumstances in which this restriction is relaxed: when the direct object is a clausal, as in (94), and when it is a "heavy" noun phrase, as in (95).

(94) a.   The governor said *on Monday* [that he would sign the budget bill].
     b.   I would like to ask *at this time* [that all of you find seats].

(95) a.   The jury will reveal *very soon* [the verdict over which they have been laboring for three weeks.]
     b.   I think he mentioned *repeatedly* [a certain man who had come from the northern part of the state in 1958].

In sum, the rule given in (91) can be stated more precisely as follows:

(96) If a certain verbal modifier can appear at the end of a verb phrase, and is an adverb, a noun phrase, or a prepositional phrase, then it can also optionally be moved closer to the verb, provided that it does not separate the verb from a nonclausal nonheavy noun phrase serving as the direct object.

Exercise

1. Two tests for distinguishing between a shifted-particle structure and an intransitive prepositional structure were proposed in chapter 6. The former structure is illustrated in (i), the latter in (ii).

(i) Paul took out the garbage.

(ii) Paul looked out the window.

In (i), *the garbage* is the direct object of the verb *took;* in (ii), *the window* is the object of the preposition *out.* Using the observations just made about the impossibility of an adverb coming between a verb and its object, formulate a third test for determining whether a given verb phrase can have the intransitive prepositional structure. The test should yield a negative result for the structure exemplified in (i) and a positive result for the structure exemplified in (ii).

11.4 SYNTACTICALLY PECULIAR CLAUSAL MODIFIERS

Most of the clausal modifiers that can be attached to verb phrases and sentences are relatively straightforward in structure. The majority of them consist of some "clause-taking preposition" (in traditional terms a "subordinating conjunction") plus a finite sentence. Three examples of this kind of structure are given in (97).

(97) a. Barbara will ask for more money *because we need supplies.*
   b. Kevin left *before the reporters could find him.*
   c. *If it rains tomorrow,* the ceremony will be held next Thursday.

A few other cases exhibit structures that are familiar from previous discussions. Two clear examples are the locative modifier in (98a) and the time modifier in (98b), both of which are definite free relatives.

(98) a. My friends are playing poker *where their grandfathers played before them.*
   b. Marsha called Connie's mother *when the hurricane was over.*

But there are other clausal modifying constructions that either involve familiar structures in an unfamiliar way, or else are structurally different from what we have seen. We will take a quick look at several of these constructions in the remainder of this section.

11.4.1 Conditional Free Relatives as Conditional Modifiers

The first of the familiar structures in an unfamiliar use has already been illustrated in (10a). It is repeated here.

(99) *Whatever kind of work he decides to do,* Edward will find it difficult to make ends meet.

When we studied free relatives in chapter 7, we noted that if a free relative is introduced by a phrase of a certain sort, then it can function as a phrase of that sort in a larger sentence. We also noted, however, that a conditional free relative can serve another function as well. The sentence in (99) illustrates this other function. Even though *whatever kind of work* is clearly a noun phrase, the position in which the clause as a whole occurs in this sentence is definitely not a noun-phrase position. Instead, it is the same kind of adjoined position that a clause introduced by *if* can occupy. Moreover, when we think about the meaning of the sentence as a whole, we can paraphrase it as a conjunction of sentences of the following form:

(100) If he decides to do x kind of work, Edward will find it difficult to make ends meet.
If he decides to do y kind of work, Edward will find it difficult to make ends meet.
If he decides to do z kind of work, Edward will find it difficult to make ends meet.

A rather surprising ambiguity affords an interesting demonstration of this contrast between the use of these structures as ordinary phrases and their use as purely conditional clauses. Such an ambiguity is present in the following sentence:

(101) Bob's sister will be happy *wherever he decides to settle.*

On one interpretation, this clause serves as a locative phrase modifier in the main sentence, indicating where Bob's sister will be happy.

(102) If Bob decides to settle at place x, his sister will be happy at place x.
If Bob decides to settle at place y, his sister will be happy at place y.
If Bob decides to settle at place z, his sister will be happy at place z.

On the other interpretation, the purely conditional one, this clause indicates nothing about where Bob's sister will be happy.

(103) If Bob decides to settle at place x, his sister will be happy.
If Bob decides to settle at place y, his sister will be happy.
If Bob decides to settle at place z, his sister will be happy.

One additional variety of modifier that is closely related to these is illustrated in (104).

(104) a. *Whether or not Martha painted that picture,* it is worth a thousand dollars.
b. *Whether John is suing Karen or Karen is suing John,* they ought to settle out of court.

Each of these sentences can be broken down into the conjunction of exactly two conditionals.

(105) If Martha painted that picture, it is worth a thousand dollars.
If Martha did not paint that picture, it is worth a thousand dollars.

(106) If John is suing Karen, they ought to settle out of court.
       If Karen is suing John, they ought to settle out of court.

In older stages of English, there was actually a word *whetherever*, which corresponded more directly to the other *-ever* words and would have been used instead of *whether* in sentences like those in (104).

11.4.2   No Matter

A construction that has almost the same effect as the one just examined is shown in (107).

(107) a. *No matter whether John is suing Karen or Karen is suing John,* they ought to settle out of court.
       b. *No matter whose car is taken to the rodeo,* someone needs to pay the parking fee.
       c. *No matter what he decides to do,* Billy will need to inform his parole officer.
       d. *No matter how many people come to the reception,* we will have enough forks.

Each of these modifiers consists of the fixed expression *no matter* followed by an indirect question. The interpretation of each sentence is once again the conjunction of a set of conditionals. In (107a), exactly two conditionals are implied, whereas for (107b–d), the set of conditionals is indefinitely large.

(108) If John is suing Karen, they ought to settle out of court.
       If Karen is suing John, they ought to settle out of court.

(109) If x's car is taken to the rodeo, someone needs to pay the parking fee.
       If y's car is taken to the rodeo, someone needs to pay the parking fee.
       If z's car is taken to the rodeo, someone needs to pay the parking fee.

11.4.3   Two Varieties of Purpose Clauses

As noted in subsection 11.1.10, English provides several ways to indicate the purpose of some action. One important way of doing this is to adjoin an infinitival structure to the verb phrase. In some cases, this infinitival structure is just a simple infinitival phrase.

(110) a. Bob went home early *to take a swim.*
     b. Lisa dipped her dog *to reduce the number of fleas in the house.*

In the two examples in (111), a more interesting structure is involved. (Pronoun objects are used in order to make it clear that we are not dealing with infinitival relative clauses.)

(111) a. Bob bought it *to clean his engine with.*
     b. Marie put it up *for Bill to keep his trophies on.*

Here, once again, we are evidently looking at a missing-noun-phrase construction, as we can see when we try to make these verb phrases finite and put them in simple sentences.

(112) a. *Bob cleaned his engine with.
     b. *Bill kept his trophies on.

These examples provide evidence for the following rule:

(113) A purpose clause can consist of an infinitival clause with a missing noun phrase.

As we can tell by the way in which we understand these sentences, the identification of the missing noun phrase is provided by the direct object of the verb phrase. Indeed, when no direct object exists, the constructions are uninterpretable.

(114) a. *Bob went home early *to clean his engine with.*
     b. *Martha worked upstairs *for Bill to put his trophies on.*

The only nontransitive situation in which the construction is acceptable is that shown in (115).

(115) a. This gadget is *to clean the engine with.*
     b. This shelf is *for Bill to put his trophies on.*

Here it is the subject that provides the identification for the missing noun phrase.

11.4.4   Reduced Clausal Modifiers

Many of the words that introduce finite clauses can also be followed by subjectless phrases of various sorts. *When,* for instance, takes several types of phrases.

(116) a. *When waiting for a bus,* one should always try to find the correct change.

    b. *When questioned by the prosecutor,* you should try to keep a straight face.

    c. *When angry,* a polar bear is a dangerous creature.

    d. *When in Rome,* do as the Romans do.

These examples contain a present-participial verb phrase (116a), a passive phrase (116b), an adjective phrase (116c), and a locative phrase (116d). We also find passive phrases with *if* and present-participial verb phrases with *while.*

(117) a. *If opened carelessly,* this package will disintegrate.

     b. *While reading this magazine,* Brenda saw an advertisement for your book.

All of the predicate phrases that we see in these constructions are of kinds that can come after BE. Furthermore, their interpretation is very much the same as it is in corresponding finite constructions in which BE actually appears.

(118) a. *When one is waiting for a bus,* one should always try to find the correct change.

     b. *When you are questioned by the prosecutor,* you should try to keep a straight face.

     c. *When it is angry,* a polar bear is a dangerous creature.

     d. *When you are in Rome,* do as the Romans do.

     e. *If it is opened carelessly,* this package will disintegrate.

     f. *While she was reading this magazine,* Brenda saw an advertisement for your book.

A construction that looks the same at first glance is illustrated in (119).

(119) a. *After reading your letter,* John lost his temper.

     b. *Before buying the house,* Julia had it checked for termites.

In these surroundings, though, the present-participial verb phrases are not interpreted as they would be if they were complements of BE. Instead of understanding these sentences as synonymous with those in (120), we are more likely to equate them with those in (121).

(120) a. ?*After he was reading your letter,* John lost his temper.

     b. ?*Before she was buying the house,* Julia had it checked for termites.

(121) a. *After he read your letter,* John lost his temper.

     b. *Before she bought the house,* Julia had it checked for termites.

Thus, their interpretation is more like that of the verb phrases in the gerundive construction. The gerundive in (122a), for instance, is closer in meaning to the full clause in (122c) than to that in (122b).

(122) a.   John regretted reading your letter.
　　　 b.   ?John regretted that he was reading your letter.
　　　 c.   John regretted that he read your letter.

These constructions provide excellent opportunities for the kind of stylistic pratfall known as the "dangling participle." Some examples are given in (123).

(123) a.   While buying a newspaper, a runaway police horse knocked John over.
　　　 b.   When in the right mood, Sheila's poems really amuse John.

What this sin actually amounts to is trying to use a noun phrase other than the subject of the sentence as a whole to identify the understood subject of one of these subjectless constructions.

Exercise

1. Each of the following passages contains a reduced clausal modifier that strikes many if not most English readers as having a decidedly odd interpretation:

　　　 a.   "Any attempt to remove [sticker] *after being affixed to windshield* will cause sticker to void." (Texas Department of Transportation, notice on the back of 1994 registration renewal stickers)
　　　 b.   "Even the final safeguard—taking the temperature of patients *soon after receiving blood*—had been ignored in some cases." (Walt Bogdanich, *The Great White Lie; Dishonesty, Waste, and Incompetence in the Medical Community,* Simon and Schuster, New York, 1991, p. 227)

　　　 The writer of the first example clearly meant that it is the sticker that is to be affixed to the windshield, and the writer of the second example clearly meant that it is the patients who received blood. Explain how the rules of English conspire to suggest an unwanted interpretation in each case.

Chapter 12
Degree Modification

In this chapter, we will look at degree modification, an area of English syntax that is singularly rich and complex. This kind of modification applies to concepts that have *scales* associated with them. These include, for example, adjectival concepts such as *tall* and *intelligent*, adverbial concepts such as *often* and *quickly*, quantity concepts such as *much* and *many*, and even some noun concepts (*genius, idiot, jerk*, etc.) that can be thought of as being graded along a scale. English makes available a variety of syntactic devices for indicating position on these scales. In section 12.1, we will look at the methods for indicating positions on scales defined by adjectives and adverbs. In section 12.2, we will extend the analysis to include degree modification of the quantity words *much* and *many*. In section 12.3, we will focus on some special methods for indicating the amount of separation between two degrees on a scale. In sections 12.4 and 12.5, we will look at nonquantitative degree modification in noun phrases and at degree modification of verbs. Section 12.6 will be devoted to the various types of clauses that can be associated with degree words. Finally, in section 12.7, we will take a brief look at superlatives.

12.1   SIMPLE DEGREE EXPRESSIONS WITH ADJECTIVES AND ADVERBS

12.1.1   Some Individual Degree Words and Their Interpretations

Let us begin by looking at several separate groups of individual degree words in English. Each group will be shown in the context *Martha is* [_____ *intelligent*]. What we will want to see is the exact way in which degree words from each group place the degree of Martha's intelligence on the general scale of intelligence. The reason for discussing the interpretive properties of these words so early in the chapter is that they will play an important role a few pages later in determining whether various degree-modified expressions can themselves be modified.

The first group, illustrated in (1), consists of words that define a vague general region of the scale and place Martha's intelligence somewhere in that region.

(1) Martha is $\left\{\begin{array}{l} \text{a. } [\textit{very} \text{ intelligent}] \\ \text{b. } [\textit{extremely} \text{ intelligent}] \\ \text{c. } [\textit{unusually} \text{ intelligent}] \end{array}\right\}$.

We can picture this kind of degree meaning in diagram (2), which displays the meaning of sentence (1a).

(2) very intelligent

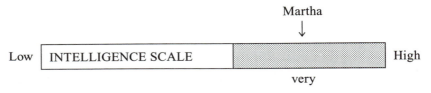

Here the shaded area indicates the vague range covered by the degree word *very*, and the pointer above the scale indicates where Martha's intelligence falls.

A second group of degree words consists of the two words *this* and *that*.

(3) Martha is $\left\{\begin{array}{l} \text{a. } [\textit{this} \text{ intelligent}] \\ \text{b. } [\textit{that} \text{ intelligent}] \end{array}\right\}$.

These two words locate Martha's intelligence on the scale by equating it with some contextually determined degree of intelligence, as in (4).

(4) this intelligent

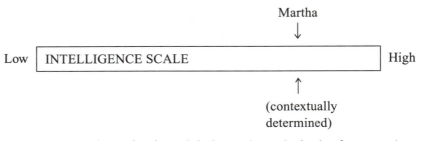

The contextual determination might be made on the basis of, say, an A on an exam, and a person who knows of this performance might make the following comment:

(5) If Martha really is [*this* intelligent], we need to offer her a fellowship immediately.

Degree words in the third group are comparative: they indicate Martha's degree of intelligence in relation to some other degree of intelligence used as a relative standard. (This relative standard, of course, is often defined in an *as* construction or a *than* construction.)

(6) Martha is
$\left\{ \begin{array}{l} \text{a. } [\textit{as} \text{ intelligent}] \\ \text{b. } [\textit{more} \text{ intelligent}] \\ \text{c. } [\textit{less} \text{ intelligent}] \end{array} \right\}$.

Diagrams for the sentences with *as* and *more* are shown in (7).

(7) a. as intelligent

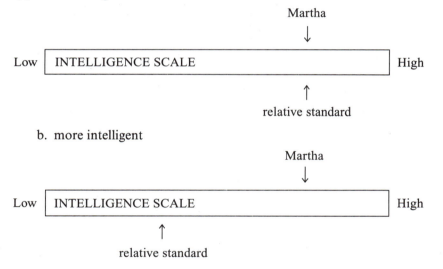

b. more intelligent

Next come three words—*too, so,* and *enough*—that place a certain degree in relation to some region on a scale. Often (but not always), this region is defined as one where a certain result would follow from degrees that fall within the region. Since using a result to define the regions makes for clearer illustrations, some associated result clauses are included in the following examples:

(8) a. Martha is [*too* intelligent] to miss this problem.
　　 b. Martha is [*so* intelligent] that she got an A +.
　　 c. Martha is [intelligent *enough*] to get at least a B.

Diagrams for these sentences are given in (9).

(9) a. too intelligent to miss this problem

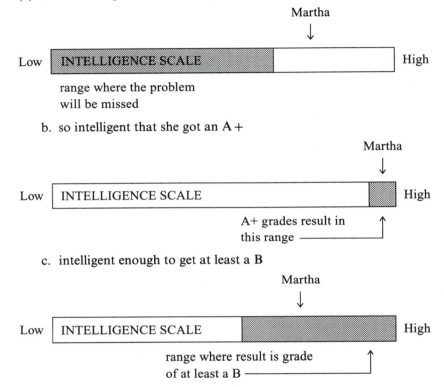

range where the problem
will be missed

b. so intelligent that she got an A +

A+ grades result in
this range ⸻

c. intelligent enough to get at least a B

range where result is grade
of at least a B ⸻

The word *too* puts Martha's intelligence above the range that produces a certain result, whereas *so* and *enough* put her intelligence inside ranges that produce specified results.

One final degree word is *how*.

(10) [*How* intelligent] is Martha?

How is just like other question words in asking for some particular piece of information. Here the information requested is some indication of Martha's intelligence. If we had to give a diagram of this meaning, it might be something like (11).

(11) how intelligent

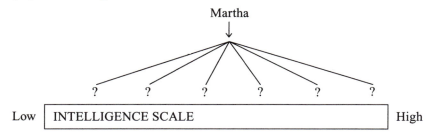

As noted earlier, a major motivation for going into this much detail with regard to the interpretation of the degree words is that these meaning differences will provide an explanation for why certain degree-modified expressions can themselves be modified.

12.1.2   Rules for Creating Degree-Modified Structures

For all but one of these degree + adjective sequences, we will assume that the degree word and the adjective are brought together by the following rule:

(12) A degree expression and an adjective phrase can combine to create a larger adjective phrase.

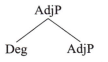

The one exception, of course, is the sequence *intelligent enough*. We might at first think that *enough* comes at the end of adjective phrases. However, with adjective phrases of more than a single word, *enough* follows immediately after the head adjective.

(13) a.   Joe is [_AdjP fond *enough* of algebra].
      b.   *Joe is [_AdjP fond of algebra *enough*].

To account for this odd behavior, let us assume that *enough* is like other degree words in fitting in structures of the type shown in (12). We will then account for the peculiar word order that it induces by adopting a rule that is closely parallel to the special rule adopted in chapter 11 in connection with *not*.

(14) When a phrase is modified by the degree word *enough,* the head of the phrase must be shifted to the left of *enough*.

The two tree diagrams in (15) illustrate the contrast between the ordinary type of degree structure and the special type of degree structure induced by *enough*.

(15) a. AdjP   b.   AdjP

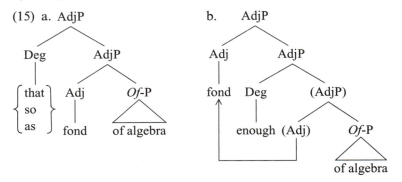

Exactly the same kinds of combinations are possible between degree expressions and adverbs.

(16) Florence finished the work
$\begin{Bmatrix} \text{a.} & [\textit{very} \text{ quickly}] \\ \text{b.} & [\textit{extremely} \text{ quickly}] \\ \text{c.} & [\textit{unusually} \text{ quickly}] \end{Bmatrix}$.

(17) Florence finished the work
$\begin{Bmatrix} \text{a.} & [\textit{this} \text{ quickly}] \\ \text{b.} & [\textit{that} \text{ quickly}] \end{Bmatrix}$.

(18) Florence finished the work
$\begin{Bmatrix} \text{a.} & [\textit{as} \text{ quickly}] \\ \text{b.} & [\textit{more} \text{ quickly}] \\ \text{c.} & [\textit{less} \text{ quickly}] \end{Bmatrix}$.

(19) Florence finished the work
$\begin{Bmatrix} \text{a.} & [\textit{too} \text{ quickly}] \text{ to do a careful job} \\ \text{b.} & [\textit{so} \text{ quickly}] \text{ that she was given a raise} \\ \text{c.} & [\text{quickly } \textit{enough}] \text{ to leave at six o'clock} \end{Bmatrix}$.

(20) [*How* quickly] did Florence finish the work?

These examples demonstrate that the rules given in (12) and (14) for the modification of adjectives really apply to both adjectival and adverbial constructions rather than just to adjectival constructions alone.

12.1.3 Adjectives and Adverbs That Compare without *More*

In every example discussed so far that has involved a compared adjective, the adjective has been preceded by the degree word *more*. Although this is the most common way of forming a compared adjective phrase, another method is used with some adjectives, namely, adding the suffix *-er* to the adjective itself. In (21), we test how various adjectives behave with respect to these two different methods of comparison.

(21) a. smarter than . . .   *more smart than . . .
      b. shorter than . . .   *more short than . . .
      c. higher than . . .   *more high than . . .
      d. lovelier than . . .   more lovely than . . .
      e. narrower than . . .   more narrow than . . .
      f. subtler than . . .   more subtle than . . .
      g. *obeser than . . .   more obese than . . .
      h. *decenter than . . .   more decent than . . .
      i. *deviouser than . . .   more devious than . . .
      j. *intelligenter than . . .   more intelligent than . . .

These adjectives conform to the following traditional rules:

(22) a. The suffix *-er* is allowed by one-syllable adjectives, and also by two-syllable adjectives ending in a vowel or an *-l* sound.
      b. The word *more* is allowed by adjectives of two or more syllables.

For adverbs, the allowed *-er* forms are more limited.

(23) a. faster than . . .   *more fast than . . .
      b. sooner than . . .   *more soon than . . .
      c. *quicklier than . . .   more quickly than . . .
      d. *franklier than . . .   more frankly than . . .

As these examples show, *-er* is allowed only with adverbs having no more than one syllable.

What structure should we propose for adjective phrases compared with the *-er* suffix? Again, as with *enough,* we need to note that the suffix comes after the head of the phrase, and not after the phrase as a whole.

(24) a. George is [fond-*er* of Susan] now.
      b. *George is [fond of Susan]-*er* now.

We can treat the *-er* suffix in the same way we treated *enough.* In particular, we can view *-er* as another degree element that induces the head of the following phrase to shift to the left. The suffix has the additional property of attaching to the adjective to make a single word, much as the contracted negative suffix *n't* attaches to a following verb. This analysis gives the structure in (25) for the adjective phrase in (24a).

(25)

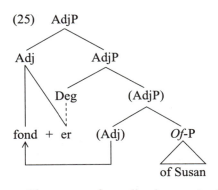

There are a few adjectives and adverbs that have completely irregular comparative forms. The uncompared adjective or adverb, the incorrect regular form, and the correct irregular form are listed in (26).

(26) a. good   *gooder   better
     b. well (adverb)   *weller   better
     c. bad   *badder   worse
     d. far   *farer   farther
     e. little (quantity word)   *littler   less

12.2   DEGREE MODIFICATION OF *MUCH* AND *MANY*

In addition to modifying adjectives or adverbs, degree words can modify the quantity words *much* and *many*. In this way, they can be used as part of a highly elaborate system of indicating quantity in noun phrases. Some simple examples are given in (27) and (28).

(27) Martha would not have eaten
     a. [*very* much] pie or [*very* many] apples.
     b. [*this* much] pie or [*this* many] apples.
     c. [*that* much] pie or [*that* many] apples.
     d. [*as* much] pie or [*as* many] apples.
     e. [*too* much] pie or [*too* many] apples.
     f. [*so* much] pie or [*so* many] apples.

(28) I don't know [*how* much] pie or [*how* many] apples Martha would have eaten.

In order to account for the examples in (27) and (28), we will speak of quantity *phrases* instead of just quantity words. The structure of these phrases is given by the following rules:

(29) A quantity phrase can consist of

- a degree expression plus one of the two quantity words *much* or *many*
- a quantity word alone

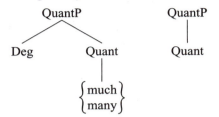

In addition, we will revise the basic rules of chapter 5 so as to allow noun-phrase structures that are introduced by these quantity phrases.

(30) a. A noun phrase can consist of a quantity phrase followed by a common-noun phrase. (This rule yields an elementary noun phrase.)

b. A noun phrase can consist of a quantity phrase followed by an *of* phrase. (This rule yields a partitive noun phrase.)

These rules give the two varieties of noun-phrase structures shown in (31).

(31) a.   VP   b.   NP

QuantP   CNP   QuantP   *Of*-P

Two specific structures that these rules yield are shown in (32).

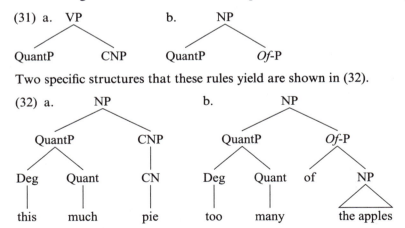

Although these general rules give good results for most degree words, there are three (*more, less,* and *enough*) that cannot modify *much* and *many* in the same way that they modify adjectives and adverbs.

(33) Martha ate
$\left\{\begin{array}{l} \text{*[\textit{more} much] pie and [\textit{more} many] apples} \\ \text{*[\textit{less} much] pie and [\textit{less} many] apples} \\ \text{*[much \textit{enough}] pie and [much \textit{enough}] apples} \end{array}\right\}$.

How can we account for the impossibility of using *more, less,* and *enough* with *much* and *many*? One fact to observe is that for each of the starred sentences, there is a corresponding acceptable sentence in which the expected illegitimate combination is replaced by something else.

(34) a. *Martha ate [*more* much] pie and [*more* many] apples.
     b. Martha ate [*more*] pie and [*more*] apples.

(35) a. *Martha ate [*less* much] pie and [*less* many] apples.
     b. Martha ate [*less*] pie and [*less*] apples.   (many English speakers)
        Martha ate [*less*] pie and [*fewer*] apples   (prescriptive standard English)

(36) a. *Martha ate [much *enough*] pie and [many *enough*] apples.
     b. Martha ate [*enough*] pie and [*enough*] apples.

On the basis of these examples, we can say that *much* is suppressed when it is joined to *more, less,* and *enough,* and that *many* is suppressed when it is joined to *more* and *enough.* Many speakers continue this pattern with regard to **less many,* replacing it simply with *less.* However, the prescribed replacement here is *fewer,* a comparative form built on the quantity word *few.* This suppression can be indicated with parentheses in a tree diagram. Then the structures in (37) and (38) would be assigned to the acceptable noun phrases in (34b) and (36b), respectively.

(37)

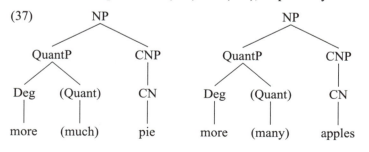

(38)

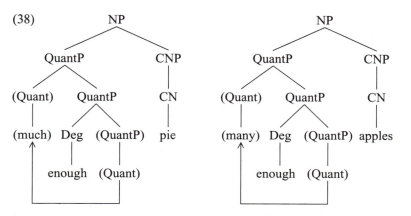

An advantage of this treatment is that it offers an explanation for why *enough* should come after adjectives and adverbs but before nouns. The explanation is that *enough* is not really modifying the noun directly, but instead is part of a quantity phrase. This quantity phrase is just in its normal position in front of the common-noun phrase.

Exercise

1. Draw a tree diagram for each of the following sequences:
    a. so fond of Erin
    b. certain enough of her abilities
    c. this many pictures of Alexandria
    d. how much traffic
    e. too eager to win
    f. as much of your money
    g. too many of the books
    h. more of the dominoes
    i. enough of the soup

12.3 SEPARATION EXPRESSIONS

From most of the degree-modified phrases that we have examined, no larger phrases can be built. But phrases introduced by three degree words (*more, less,* and *too*) allow preceding quantity expressions.

(39) a. Martha is [*much* more intelligent] (than Bill is).
     b. Martha is [*much* less intelligent] (than Bill is).
     c. Martha is [*much* too intelligent] (to miss the problem).

In having this property, these degree words contrast with the others.

(40) a. *Martha is [*much* very intelligent].
   b. *Martha is [*much* so intelligent].
   c. *Martha is [*much* this intelligent].

To see why there should be such a difference between the degree words in (39) and those in (40), we need to review what was said earlier about their meaning. As a look at our earlier diagrams will indicate, the words that do not allow a preceding *much* all have the property of either determining a point that is equal to some other point or else setting a point within a certain region of the scale. In particular, *very* and *so* both set the degree within a certain region, and *this* sets the degree equal to some contextually determined degree. By contrast, the words *more, less,* and *too* all define the degree of Martha's intelligence as being *separated* from some point or region. With both *more* and *less,* the separation is from whatever is serving as the relative standard. With *too,* the separation is from an entire region somewhere below Martha's intelligence. Now it is simple to see what *much* does when it comes before *more, less,* or *too:* it simply indicates the size of this separation. We can see exactly what is involved here by augmenting the diagrams given earlier for *more* and *too* as in (41) to show what the word *much* conveys in sentence (39a).

(41)

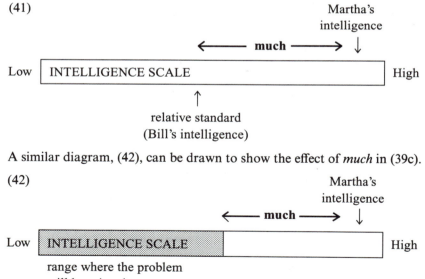

A similar diagram, (42), can be drawn to show the effect of *much* in (39c).

(42)

We will call a word or phrase used in this way a *separation expression,* abbreviated *Sep* in tree diagrams.

Other expressions besides *much* can serve as separation expressions.

(43) a. Joe is *far* more honest (than Fred).
  b. Karen is *far* too sophisticated (to believe your story).

(44) a. Susan is *way* more independent (than Tanya).
  b. Gretchen is *way* too studious (to make a C).

(45) a. Harry caught *many* more fish (than David did).
  b. They caught *three* too many snappers.

(46) a. May is *a lot* more careful (than Avery).
  b. Tony is *a little bit* too talkative (to be able to keep that secret).

(47) a. George is *three inches* taller (than James).
  b. Steve is *ten pounds* too heavy (to be allowed in the welterweight division).

The rule in (48) describes separation expressions, and the rule in (49) spells out the way in which they can combine with certain degree-modified expressions.

(48) A separation expression can consist of

  • the single word *way* or *far*
  • a quantity phrase (*much, several, many*)
  • a measure noun phrase (*a lot, a little bit, three inches, several pounds, five feet*)

(49) A separation expression can be combined with a degree-modified phrase that expresses a separation of degree, to form a larger phrase of the same type.

These rules together give structures of the kinds shown in (50).

(50) a. AdjP   b. AdjP

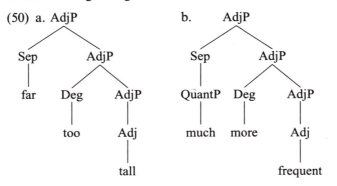

The rules in (48) and (49) allow an even more complex structure. We noted above that *much* and *many* can both be modified by degree expressions themselves; this was in fact the main reason for wanting to talk about quantity *phrases* instead of just quantity *words*. Thus, in addition to using the single word *much* as a separation expression, we can use *much* preceded by a degree word, as in (51).

(51) a. Jonah is [*so much* more polite].
     b. I didn't know that Fred had baked [*that much* more bread].

The tree diagrams in (52) give the structures of the bracketed phrases.

(52) a.

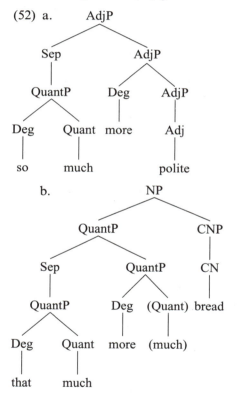

Exercises

1. Draw a tree diagram for each of the following phrases:
   a. this much more frequent
   b. so many more mistakes

c. as much less of his prestige

d. far too much more of your attention

e. enough more intelligent

2. One odd possibility that is allowed by some of the individual words that we have been discussing in this chapter is the kind of "emphatic reduplication" seen in the following examples:

(i)   Enid is *very, very* happy.

(ii) Joe is working *far, far* too slowly.

(iii) Cora and James are *much, much* more confident than they used to be.

Devise some experimental sentences that will help to answer the following questions:

    a. For which specific words is this kind of reduplication possible? For which words is it impossible?

    b. What are the particular conditions under which this reduplication is the most natural for the words that allow it at all? Are there any circumstances where it is not natural even with words such as the three illustrated above?

3. The italicized indirect question in the following quotation is ambiguous:

"When Mrs. Ramo talks about *how much good lawyers can do,* it seems more like the voice of conviction and experience than the Law Day platitudes of some of her 116 male predecessors." (David Margolick, writing about a conversation with Roberta Cooper Ramo, the incoming president of the American Bar Association, in "The A.B.A's Party of the First Part Can Play as Many Parts as Anyone," *New York Times,* February 6, 1994, sec. 4, p. 7)

    A. Say what the two corresponding direct questions are.

    B. Draw tree diagrams for the two distinct structures that the rules of English allow for this indirect question.

    C. Would there have been a corresponding ambiguity if the author had claimed that Mrs. Ramo talked about *how much harm lawyers can do*? Explain your answer.

12.4   DEGREE MODIFICATION IN NOUN-PHRASE STRUCTURES

In the previous section, we saw several examples in which quantities inside noun phrases were modified by degree expressions. Except for the absence of forms in which *more, less,* and *enough* combine with *much* and *many,* the degree expressions that modify quantity words follow the same rules as do the degree expressions that modify adjectives and adverbs. There also exists another kind of degree modification involving noun phrases, which constitutes one of the more bizarre and complicated areas of English syntax. This kind of degree modification arises when we want to indicate a position on a scale defined by some adjective-noun concept (e.g., *tall man* or *good pancake*) or a scale defined by a noun alone (e.g., *genius* or *jerk*).

Let us look first at the cases involving an adjective in addition to a noun. Here there are at least a few degree words that behave as we might expect them to, coming directly before the adjective (or in the case of *enough*, coming directly after it).

(53) a. Thomas is [a *very tall* man].
   b. Jill is [a *more intelligent* woman].
   c. Karen is [a *good enough* painter].

The basic rule given in chapter 10 for prenominal modifiers, together with the rules developed in the present chapter, assigns the structures in (54) to these examples.

(54)

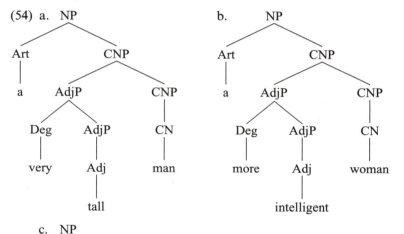

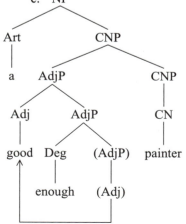

Other degree words such as *extremely, unusually,* and so on, behave like *very* in this regard, and *less* behaves just like *more.*

The complications begin with the degree words *as, so, that,* and *too.*

(55) a. *John is [an *as good* driver].
   b. *Gretchen is [a *so creative* thinker].
   c. *I didn't know we would be able to find [a *that good* singer].
   d. *Joe is [a *too small*] linebacker.

What we find instead are structures in which the degree word and its adjective actually precede the indefinite article.

(56) a. John is [*as good* a driver].
   b. Gretchen is [*so creative* a thinker].
   c. I didn't know we would be able to find [*that good* a singer].
   d. Joe is [*too small* a linebacker].

One additional complication with regard to these structures is that they are only possible with the indefinite article *a(n)*. When any other kind of determiner or quantity structure is involved, neither the normal order shown in (53) nor the special order shown in (56) is possible.

(57) a. *Your friends are [some *as good* drivers].
   b. *Fred is [the *too small* linebacker].

(58) a. *Your friends are [*as good* some drivers].
   b. *Fred is [*too small* the linebacker].

Even examples with bare noun phrases are impossible.

(59) *Your friends are [*as good* drivers].

The very limited circumstances under which these degree words can be used with prenominal adjectives forces us to state two unusually complicated rules. The first of these is a more restrictive version of the rule presented in chapter 10 for prenominal modifiers.

(60) A common-noun phrase can consist of an adjective phrase followed by a smaller common-noun phrase, with the restriction that (a) the adjective phrase must not include a complement; (b) the degree words *as, so, that,* and *too* are not allowed to introduce the adjective phrase.

The second special rule states the idiosyncratic way in which these four degree words can be used.

(61) A noun phrase introduced by *a(n)* can be combined with a preceding adjective phrase introduced by one of the degree words *as, so, that,* and *too,* to form a larger noun phrase.

Rule (61) gives the structure in (62) for (56a).

(62)

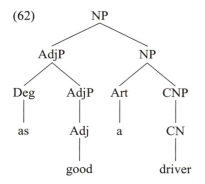

As with the prenominal structures given in chapter 10, this diagram does not itself give any idea of the extremely restricted circumstances under which an adjective phrase and a noun phrase can be combined in this fashion.

   Another word can be used as a special degree modifier in noun phrases. This is the word *such,* which plays much the same role for common-noun phrases that *so* plays for adjectives, adverbs, and quantity expressions. Its behavior is exhibited in (63) and (64).

(63) a. His relatives are [*such* idiots].
      b. This article is [*such* rubbish].
      c. Helen makes [*such* delicious pancakes].
      d. Joe makes [*such* vile chowder].

(64) a. I've never before met [two *such* honest people].
      b. If Bert makes [two more *such* stupid mistakes], Jones will fire him.
      c. [One more *such* disastrous result] could ruin the company.

The examples in (63) and (64) suggest that *such* joins with common-noun phrases. The examples in (64) further suggest that the result is itself a common-noun phrase, a sequence that can combine with a preceding numeral to form a noun phrase. We thus are led to the rule in (65).

(65) A common-noun phrase can be combined with a preceding *such* to form a larger common-noun phrase.

This rule gives the structures in (66).

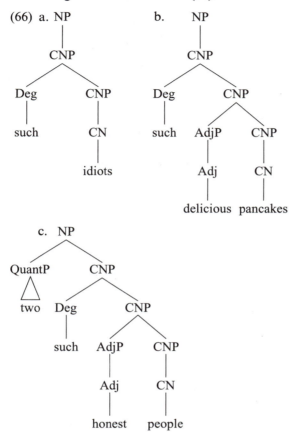

So far, the syntax of *such* has been straightforward. However, with this word—as with several of the other words examined above—a special complication is induced by the indefinite article. Rule (65) would lead us to expect examples like the following:

(67) a. *Alfred is [a *such* genius].
    b. *Frank drives [a *such* old car].

What are actually acceptable are examples in which *such* precedes the indefinite article.

(68) a. Alfred is [*such* a genius].
    b. Frank drives [*such* an old car].

Because of the acceptable examples in (64), we are led to say that the ordinary place for *such* is right before a common-noun phrase. Then, in order to account for the new examples in (68), we need to say that the indefinite article *a(n)* induces a leftward shift of *such,* of the sort shown in (69).

(69) a. NP   b.   NP

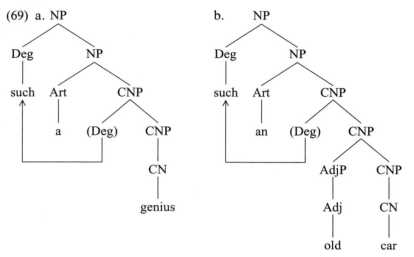

Finally, suppose that we want to use degree words such as *so, that,* or *too* with a noun like *genius* or *idiot.* Doing this depends on attaching these degree words to *much* and following with an *of* phrase.

(70) a. Fred isn't [*so* much of a genius].
    b. Nigel isn't [*that* much of a hothead].
    c. Joe is [*too* much of a prima donna].
    d. Jane isn't [*as* much of a composer].

As we might expect, we also find *more* in place of **more much, less* in place of **less much,* and *enough* in place of **much enough.*

(71) a. *Harry is [*more* much of a hothead].
    b.   Harry is [*more* of a hothead].

(72) a. *Harry is [*less* much of a hothead].
    b.   Harry is [*less* of a hothead].

(73) a. *Harry is [much *enough* of an idiot].
    b.   Harry is [*enough* of an idiot].

Also possible are a small number of quantity expressions other than *much* such as that in (74).

(74) Horatio is [*a little bit* of a liar].

Again, this construction gives good results only in the singular, as we see when we try to construct corresponding examples with plurals.

(75) a. *Fred and Greta aren't [*so* much of geniuses].
    b. *Nigel and Henry aren't [*that* much of hotheads].
    c. *Joe and Betty are [*too* much of prima donnas].
    d. *Jane and Robert aren't [*as* much of composers].
    e. *Harry and Joseph are [*more* of idiots].
    f. *Horatio and Jenny are [*a little bit* of liars].

These observations are summarized in the following rule:

(76) A noun phrase can consist of a quantity phrase followed by an *of* phrase, where the object of *of* is a noun phrase introduced by *a(n)*.

Two of the structures that this rule yields are given in (77).

(77)

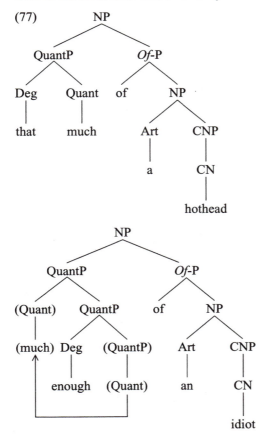

Exercises

1. Draw a tree diagram for each of the following noun phrases:
   a. two extremely fast runners
   b. as big a deficit
   c. this solemn a vow
   d. this devout an old man
   e. such long books
   f. such an ancient legend
   g. three such obnoxious children
   h. so much more of a bureaucrat

2. The bracketed noun phrase in the following sentence is ambiguous:

(i) Flora wants to read [more contemporary novels].

The two distinct readings of the bracketed noun phrase can be paraphrased as follows:

(ii) a. novels that are more contemporary
     b. a greater number of contemporary novels

Corresponding to the two separate interpretations of this noun phrase, our rules give two different structures. Draw tree diagrams for these two noun-phrase structures.

12.5 DEGREE MODIFICATION WITH VERBS

Some verbs have scales associated with them, especially those denoting mental dispositions (e.g., *love* and *admire*). Degrees on such scales are expressed indirectly through the use of quantity expressions, most of them involving *much*.

(78) William loves Brenda
   a. [*very* much]
   b. [*this* much]
   c. [*too* much]
   d. [*as* much] (as James does)
   e. [*so* much] (that he wants to move to Dayton)

As we would expect by this time, *more* and *enough* occur by themselves, without any accompanying *much*.

(79) Jeff admires Lucy
   a. *[*more* much]
   b. [*more*]
   c. *[much *enough*]
   d. [*enough*]

Once again, other quantity expressions are also possible.

(80) Doris admires Arthur $\left\{ \begin{array}{l} \text{a. [a good deal]} \\ \text{b. [a little bit]} \\ \text{c. [quite a lot]} \end{array} \right\}$.

A particularly simple rule will account for these examples.

(81) A verb phrase can be joined with a following quantity phrase to make a larger verb phrase.

This rule gives a type of verb phrase structure, illustrated in (82), that we have seen already in chapter 11 with adverbial modifiers.

(82) a.

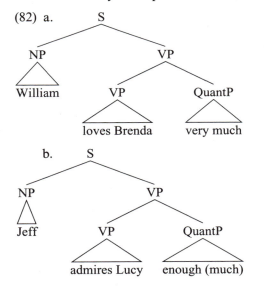

Exercise

1. The following two sentences might appear at first glance to have similar structures:

   a. William snores too much.
   b. William says too much.

Do some experiments to determine what kinds of complement arrangements are preferred by SNORE and SAY, and use your conclusions to arrive at reasonable structures for these two sentences. It might be helpful to consider what the following sentence shows about a possibility for noun phrases that we have not considered previously:

   c. Too much happened during the flight from the city.

12.6   CLAUSES ASSOCIATED WITH DEGREE WORDS

It is time now to discuss in detail the kinds of clauses that are often associated with particular degree words. For this purpose, we can divide the relevant degree words into two groups. Words in the first group (*so, such, too,* and *enough*) take following *result clauses;* those in the second group (*as, more,* and *less*) take following *comparative clauses.* The syntactic properties of the clauses associated with these two groups are quite different, as are their interpretations. We will take up the result clauses first, since their syntax is more straightforward.

12.6.1   Result Clauses

The simplest form of result clause is that found with *so* and *such.*

(83) a. This book is *so* big [that it doesn't fit on the shelf].
      b. *So* many people stayed for lunch [that all of the food was eaten immediately].
      c. Doris ate *such* a big lunch [that she fell asleep in class].
      d. Jerry writes *such* long articles [that his newspaper refuses to print them].

These clauses are clearly just finite *that* clauses, with no missing phrase or other complication. The *that* clause in each sentence simply describes the result that comes about when a certain degree is near the high end of some relevant scale.

With *too* and *enough,* clauses of a different type are used.

(84) The cake is $\begin{Bmatrix} too \text{ hot} \\ \text{cool } enough \end{Bmatrix}$ [for you to remove from the pan].

In both of these sentences an infinitival clause is associated with the degree word, and a careful inspection reveals a missing noun phrase.

(85) a. *You removed from the pan.
      b. You removed *it* from the pan.

Thus, one of the clause types with which *too* and *enough* can occur is an infinitival clause with a missing noun phrase.

(86) The cake is $\begin{Bmatrix} too \text{ hot} \\ \text{cool } enough \end{Bmatrix}$ [$_{\text{InfC/NP}}$ for you to remove ____ from the pan].

The identification of this missing noun phrase is like that for the *easy* construction studied in chapter 9: whatever noun phrase is determined to be the subject of the adjective phrase also provides an identification for the missing noun phrase. In each of the sentences in (84), *the cake* is interpreted as the subject of the adjective phrase and thus also identifies the missing noun phrase inside the infinitival clause.

Another possibility also exists for *too* and *enough,* as (87) shows.

(87) Joel is $\begin{Bmatrix} too \text{ immature} \\ \text{old } enough \end{Bmatrix}$ [to take care of himself].

Here, the infinitival phrase contains no missing noun phrase, and the subject of the adjective phrases (*Joel*) is used to identify the subject of the infinitival phrase rather than some missing noun phrase inside it. Thus, the structure is that shown in (88).

(88) Joel is $\begin{Bmatrix} too \text{ immature} \\ \text{old } enough \end{Bmatrix}$ [$_{InfP}$ to take care of himself].

Exercise

1. The sentences in (84) show that *too* and *enough* may be associated with infinitival clauses with missing noun phrases, that is, with structures of the kind indicated in (86). The clause used in these sentences happens to be one based on an infinitival clause that is introduced by *for*. Construct a sentence in which you show that the same kind of missing-noun-phrase result clause can be based on an infinitival clause that consists of an infinitival phrase alone.

12.6.2 Comparative Clauses

The kinds of clauses that go with comparative degree words are illustrated in (89)–(91).

(89) Joseph became *as* famous [*as* Thelma became].
(Compare: *Joseph became *as* famous [*than* Thelma became].)

(90) Brenda spent *more* money [*than* Bernie spent].
(Compare: *Brenda spent *more* money [*as* Bernie spent].)

(91) Molly encountered *less* trouble [*than* Walter encountered].
(Compare: *Molly encountered *less* trouble [*as* Walter encountered].)

In these examples, we see that the only possible pairings are those between *as* and *as,* between *more* and *than,* and between *less* and *than*. These observations suggest the following rule:

(92) The degree words *more* and *less* permit associated comparative clauses introduced by *than;* the word *as* permits associated comparative clauses introduced by *as.*

Now let us examine the internal structure of these comparative clauses. If we isolate the material after *than* and *as* in the bracketed sequences in (89)–(91), we find immediate evidence of missing phrases.

(93) a. *Thelma became.
     b. *Bernie spent.
     c. *Walter encountered.

In each case, we can make these unacceptable sentences complete by adding a phrase of the same type as the phrase outside the clause introduced by *as, more,* or *less.*

(94) a. Thelma became *very famous.*   (adjective phrase—corresponds to *as famous*)
     b. Bernie spent *too much money.*   (noun phrase—corresponds to *more money*)
     c. Walter encountered *little trouble.*   (noun phrase—corresponds to *less trouble*)

Let us refer to the phrases *as famous, more money,* and *less trouble* in (89)–(91) as *degree-marked phrases.* More generally, we will apply this term to any phrase that is introduced by *as, more,* or *less* (exclusive of the comparative clause). With this concept in hand, we can give the following rule for the formation of comparative clauses:

(95) Comparative clauses consist of either *as* or *than,* followed by a finite sentence with a missing phrase of the same type as an associated degree-marked phrase outside the clause.

For the particular examples in (89)–(91), we have the paired structures in (96).

(96)   *Degree-marked phrases*   *Comparative clauses*

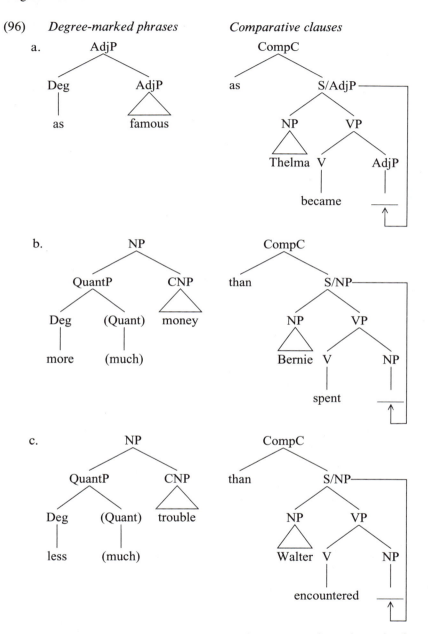

As required by (95), each missing phrase that appears in a clause in the right column is of the same type as the degree-marked phrase on the left.

In cases where the compared phrase happens to be of a type that is optional, we do not get an immediate sensation of a missing phrase inside the comparative clause.

(97) a. Jane writes stories *more often* [than she writes articles].
      b. Joe proofreads footnotes *more carefully* [than he proofreads text].

In each of these examples, the sequence of words after *than* sounds like a complete sentence in its own right.

(98) a. She writes articles.
      b. He proofreads text.

Nevertheless, we will assume that there are missing phrases in the comparative clauses in these examples. In (97a), the missing phrase must be a frequency adverb, to match *more often;* in (97b), it must be a manner adverb, to match *more carefully.* We obtain evidence that there really is a missing-phrase requirement in effect in these examples when we try to add degree-modified adverbial constructions of the relevant type to the comparative clauses in (97). The results are completely unacceptable.

(99) a. *Jane writes stories *more often* [than she writes articles *less frequently*].
      b. *Joe proofreads footnotes *more carefully* [than he proofreads text *very carelessly*].

Thus, the structures of the degree-marked phrases and the comparative clauses in (97) are those shown in (100).

(100)   *Degree-marked phrases*   *Comparative clauses*

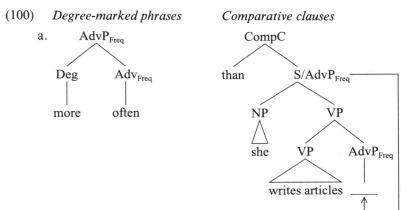

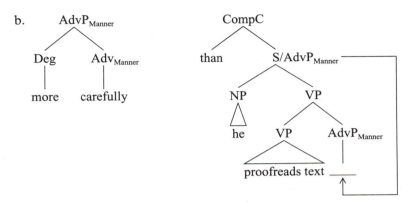

Exercises

1. For each of the following sentences, draw a tree diagram for the degree-marked phrase and also for the comparative clause. Make sure that the missing phrase inside the comparative clause is of the same type as the degree-marked phrase.

   a. Janet reads stories more often than Bill reads articles.
   b. Janet reads more stories than Bill reads.
   c. More people from Connecticut live in frame houses than live in stone houses.
   d. Norma is more of a clown than Robert is.
   e. Barbara put more books in the study than Joe put in the attic.
   f. Barbara read more of the letters from Franklin than Joe read.
   g. Ted was not as much heavier as he had hoped to become.

2. For each of the bracketed comparative clauses in the following examples, draw a tree diagram.

   a. George eats more vegetables [than Brian eats].
   b. George eats more often [than Brian eats].
   c. George eats more enthusiastically [than Brian eats].

Note: Even though the comparative clauses in these examples have an identical appearance, rule (95) implies that their structures are different.

3. What kind of phrase is missing inside the comparative clause in the following sentence, and what is the degree-marked phrase that corresponds to it?

(i) Jones constructed as persuasive an argument as we expected him to construct.

4. Explain why the following sentence does not quite conform to rule (95), with the concept "degree-marked phrase" defined as a phrase introduced by *as*, *more*, or *less:*

(i) Jones constructed a more persuasive argument than we expected him to construct.

In order to bring this sentence within the range of rule (95), Joan Bresnan proposed, in a 1973 article in *Linguistic Inquiry* entitled "Syntax of the Comparative Clause Construction in English," that this sort of degree construction is actually interpreted as if its basic form were as follows:

(ii) ?Jones constructed more persuasive an argument than we expected him to construct.

Say why sentence (ii) is more consistent with rule (95) than sentence (i) is.

12.6.3   Nonmaximal Comparatives

In each of the sentences discussed in the previous subsection, we found a way to match a missing phrase inside the comparative clause with a degree-marked phrase outside the clause. At this point, it might seem that none of these sentences contained more than a single degree-marked phrase, since each one contained only a single degree word. However, a careful look at the italicized sequence in (101) reveals that the number of degree-marked phrases in a sentence is not limited to one, even when we see only one degree word.

(101) Joe bought *as many of the records* [as I bought].

It is obvious that *as many of the records* qualifies as a degree-marked phrase. Indeed, this is the phrase that is matched with the missing noun phrase after *bought* in the comparative clause. However, this is not the only phrase introduced by *as*. In addition, this sentence contains the degree-marked quantifier phrase *as many*. The structure for the sequence *as many of the records* is that shown in (102), with boxes indicating these two degree-marked phrases.

(102)

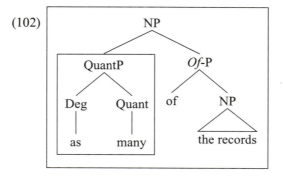

The reason for wanting to identify *as many* as a degree-marked phrase in its own right becomes evident when we look at sentence (103).

(103) Joe bought as many of the records as he bought of the tapes.

Here, as in the examples in (89)–(91), we have clear evidence that the comparative clause contains a missing phrase.

(104) *He bought of the tapes.

What is missing, however, is not a noun phrase corresponding to *as many of the tapes,* but a quantity phrase corresponding to *as many.* Tree diagrams are given in (105) for the relevant degree-marked phrase and the comparative clause.

(105) *Degree-marked phrase   Comparative clause*

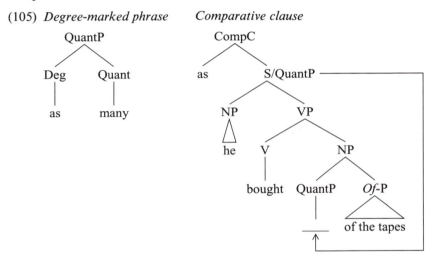

In what follows, the term *nonmaximal comparative* will be used to refer to comparative sentences like (103), that is, to sentences in which the missing phrase inside the comparative clause is matched up with a phrase that is a subphrase of a larger degree-marked phrase. On the other hand, comparative sentences in which the missing phrase is matched by a maximally inclusive degree-marked phrase will be referred to as *maximal comparatives.*

Another example of a nonmaximal comparative is given in (106).

(106) Professor Carson writes as many stories [as she writes articles].

At first glance, the comparative clause in (106) appears not to contain a missing phrase, since the sequence after the second *as* sounds complete in its own right.

(107) She writes articles.

However, rule (95) would lead us to expect a missing phrase of some sort in the comparative clause, one that would match up with a degree-marked phrase outside the clause. There is clearly no place in the comparative clause suitable for a missing noun phrase corresponding to the most inclusive degree-marked phrase *as many stories*. However, there is a place for a missing quantity phrase corresponding to the less inclusive degree-marked phrase *as many*. The structures for the relevant degree-marked phrase and the comparative clause are thus just those given in (108).

(108) *Degree-marked phrase*   *Comparative clause*

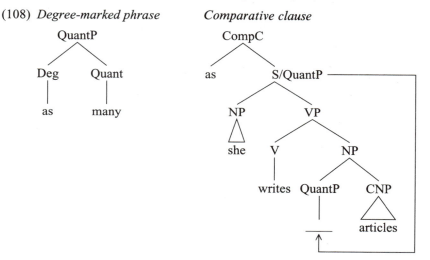

We get evidence of a more direct kind that a missing quantity phrase is involved here if we try to insert a nonempty degree-marked quantity phrase in the position before *articles*.

(109) *Professor Carson writes as many stories as she writes *too many* articles.

A final group of nonmaximal comparatives provides evidence that degree words by themselves should be considered degree-marked phrases. This group is illustrated by the sentence in (110).

(110) David is as erudite as he is creative.

As was the case with (106), it is hard to believe at first that the comparative clause is really a missing-phrase construction, since the sequence after the second *as* sounds like a complete sentence.

(111) He is creative.

But if we try to analyze this sentence in conformity with rule (95), and if we admit *as* as a degree-marked phrase, then the structures in (112) emerge as legitimate possibilities.

(112) *Degree-marked phrase*   *Comparative clause*

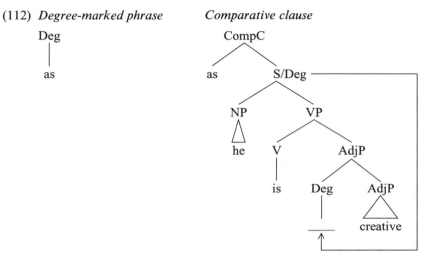

That this analysis is correct is confirmed by the unacceptability of inserting an actual degree word into (110) before *creative*.

(113) *David is as erudite [as he is *very* creative].

This last type of nonmaximal comparative is interpreted as making a comparison that involves two different scales, one associated with erudition and the other with creativity. This type of interpretation can be pictured as in (114).

(114)

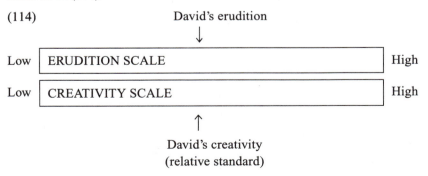

A semantically related construction in which the difference between maximal and nonmaximal comparatives is reflected with particular clarity is the phrasal question. One way to think about the interpretation of comparatives is to view them as requiring us to determine the answer to two separate degree questions and then compare the results. Several of the maximal comparatives that we have examined are listed in (115)–(118), each accompanied by the two degree questions relevant to its interpretation.

(115) Joseph became as famous as Thelma became.
How famous did Joseph become?
How famous did Thelma become?

(116) Brenda spent more money than Bernie spent.
How much money did Brenda spend?
How much money did Bernie spend?

(117) Jane writes stories *more often* than she writes articles.
How often does Jane write stories?
How often does she write articles?

(118) Joe bought as many of the records as I bought.
How many of the records did Joe buy?
How many of the records did I buy?

In each of these pairs of questions, we observe that the initial questioned phrases are exactly the same. Now let us look at some of the nonmaximal comparatives and their associated questions.

(119) Joe bought as many of the records as he bought of the tapes.
How many of the records did Joe buy?
How many of the tapes did he buy?

(120) Professor Carson writes as many stories as she writes articles.
How many stories does Professor Carson write?
How many articles does she write?

(121) David is as erudite as he is creative.
How erudite is David?
How creative is he?

In each of these pairs of questions, the two questioned phrases are distinct, agreeing only in an initial quantity phrase in (119) and (120) and in an initial degree word in (121). In cases where we wish to provide ourselves with an intuitive test after trying to calculate whether a certain comparative is maximal or nonmaximal, looking at question pairs like these is a useful strategy.

Exercises

1. For each of the following sentences, draw a tree diagram for the degree-marked phrase that corresponds to the missing phrase in the comparative clause and also for the comparative clause as a whole:

    a. More pigs eat corn than dogs eat hay.
    b. Students read as many books as professors read articles.
    c. Karen is as fond of you as she is hostile to your boss.

2. For each of the following sentences, decide whether the comparative that it contains is maximal or nonmaximal. In either case, identify the type of the missing phrase inside the comparative clause, and say what the corresponding degree-marked phrase is.

    a. More people drink coffee than drink tea.
    b. More tigers live in zoos than bears live in the wild.
    c. Bob eats pancakes more often than he eats bacon and eggs.
    d. People are more careless than animals are.
    e. Joe sent more letters to senators than he sent telegrams to the president.
    f. The company sent more refrigerators to Siberia than it sent heaters to Kuwait.

12.6.4 Positioning of Clauses Associated with Degree Words

Clauses associated with degree words are generally found in one of two positions, either at the right side of the phrase that contains the associated degree word or at the end of the sentence. These two possibilities are shown schematically in (122).

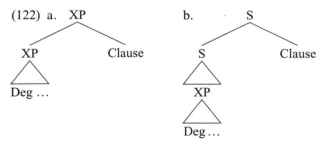

In many of the examples discussed earlier in this section, these two positions are indistinguishable, since the degree-modified phrase is itself at the end of the sentence. Let us therefore look at some examples where a distinction can be made, in order to reach some conclusions about the behavior of different varieties of clauses.

First let us examine some examples containing result clauses.

(123) a. ?**So* many minnows [that Martha lost her temper] were fed to the dog.

   b. *So* many minnows were fed to the dog [that Martha lost her temper].

(124) a. ?**Such* an upsetting meeting [that everyone resigned from the Budget Council] took place yesterday.

   b. *Such* an upsetting meeting took place yesterday [that everyone resigned from the Budget Council].

(125) a. *Too* many relatives [to feed adequately] landed on us on Memorial Day.

   b. *Too* many relatives landed on us on Memorial Day [to feed adequately].

(126) a. *Enough* ice cream [to keep the children happy] had been brought to the picnic.

   b. *Enough* ice cream had been brought to the picnic [to keep the children happy].

We see that although a result clause introduced by *that* is really acceptable only at the end of its sentence, an infinitival clause associated with *too* or *enough* can stay in the phrase in which its degree word appears. Diagrams for two of these sentences—one with the result clause joined onto the sentence as a whole and the other with the result clause joined onto the subject noun phrase—are presented in (127).

(127) a.

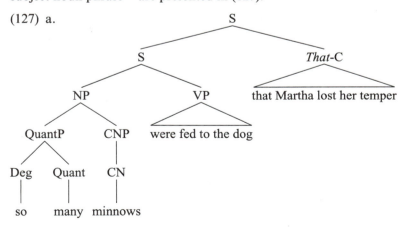

b.

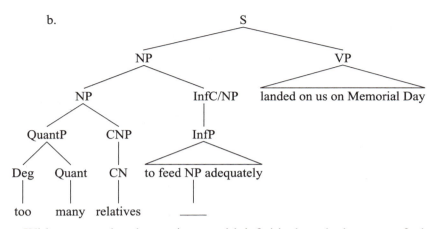

With comparative clauses, just as with infinitival result clauses, we find that both positions are possible.

(128) a. [NP *More* books *than Pete will be able to read*] appeared on the history reading list.

b. [NP *More* books] appeared on the history reading list *than Pete will be able to read*.

(129) a. [NP *As* much money *as John donated in Phil's name*] was donated in Brenda's name.

b. [NP *As* much money] was donated in Brenda's name *as John donated in Phil's name*.

These sentences show that in general the position of the compared clause can be chosen freely. Two qualifications are necessary, however. The first is that nonmaximal comparatives are much better if the comparative clause is at the end of the sentence.

(130) a. *[NP *More* pigs *than dogs eat hay*] eat corn.

b. [NP *More* pigs] eat corn *than dogs eat hay*.

The second is that the choice of location for the comparative clause affects the possibility of applying an optional deletion rule, as we will see in subsection 12.6.5.

Exercise

1. For each of the following sentences, draw a tree diagram:

a. As many shirts as you want to buy will be sent to your house.

b. Joe is less energetic than Francis is.

c. Jonah put so many cans on the table that some of them fell off.
d. Rita put enough money in her account to cover those three checks.
e. Alma gave more cookies to George than she gave doughnuts to Randy.
f. More people visited Arthur than visited David.

12.6.5   Special Ellipsis Rules for Comparative Clauses

All of the comparative clauses that we have examined so far look very much like complete sentences, except for containing missing phrases that correspond to degree-marked phrases in the main clause. English also allows shortened versions of many comparative clauses. These shorter variants are created by two special *ellipsis rules*—rules that allow the omission of certain material that is identical with material elsewhere in a sentence or discourse.

The first of the two rules relies in many cases on the same kind of special-purpose verbs that we saw in our earlier discussion of emphatic sentences and negative sentences with *not*. Some basic effects of this rule are shown in (131)–(134).

(131) a. Clara sends money to Houston more often than Joe sends money to Houston.
       b. Clara sends money to Houston more often than Joe does ＿＿＿.

(132) a. James read the book more carefully than Joel read the book.
       b. James read the book more carefully than Joel did ＿＿＿.

(133) a. Jock served them more wine than Alice will serve them.
       b. Jock served them more wine than Alice will ＿＿＿.

(134) a. Doris has sent postcards to Pam more often than Nora has sent postcards to Pam.
       b. Doris has sent postcards to Pam more often than Nora has

       ＿＿＿.

The optional conversion of each full comparative (a) sentence into the corresponding elliptical (b) sentence can be described by the following tentative rule:

(135) In a comparative sentence in which two phrases are identical (except for the degree-marked phrase in the main clause and the missing phrase in the comparative clause), revise the comparative clause so that there is a special-purpose verb before the second of the identical phrases, and then delete the second phrase.

The steps that this rule dictates for the derivation of (131b) from (131a) are shown in (136).

(136) a. Clara [sends money to Houston] more often than Joe [sends money to Houston].
(full comparative with identical verb phrases)

   b. Clara [sends money to Houston] more often than Joe does [send money to Houston].
(second identical phrase provided with a preceding special-purpose verb)

   c. Clara [sends money to Houston] more often than Joe does [_____].
(second identical phrase deleted)

The derivation of (133b) from (133a) given in (137) shows why it is necessary to allow the degree-marked phrase and the missing phrase to differ.

(137) a. Jock [served them more wine] than Alice will [serve them _____].
(full comparative with verb phrases identical except for degree-marked phrase and missing phrase)

   b. Jock [served them more wine] than Alice will [serve them _____].
(no change—special-purpose verb *will* already in place)

   c. Jock [served them more wine] than Alice will [_____].
(second identical phrase deleted)

The same ellipsis process may also apply when the two phrases are "nearly identical," where this term means that they contain some additional nonidentical phrase. We see effects of this sort in (138)–(141), where italics indicate the smaller nonidentical phrases contained in the larger phrases.

(138) a. Clara [sends money *to Houston*] more often than Joe [sends money *to Little Rock*].

   b. Clara [sends money *to Houston*] more often than Joe does [_____ *to Little Rock*].

(139) a. James [read *the book*] more carefully than he [read *the play*].

   b. James [read *the book*] more carefully than he did [_____ *the play*].

(140) a. Jock will [serve more *wine* to them] than he will [serve *beer* to them].

    b. Jock will [serve more *wine* to them] than he will [____ *beer*
        ____].

(141) a. Doris has [given *postcards* to Pam] more often than she has
        [given *stamps* to Pam].
    b. Doris has [given *postcards* to Pam] more often than she has
        [____ *stamps* ____].

In addition to special-purpose finites, the elliptical process we are examining allows nonfinite forms of HAVE and BE on the left side of the identical phrase, as well as the infinitival marker *to*. These additional possibilities are illustrated in (142), where parentheses indicate the material that is omitted in the elliptical variant.

(142) a. Hans checked his oil less often than he should have (checked
        his oil).
    b. Roger and Heather were driving their car more carelessly than
        they should have been (driving their car).
    c. Dora had to play recitals more frequently than she wanted to
        (play recitals).

This first rule can be summarized, then, as in (143).

(143) Suppose that we have a comparative sentence in which two
     phrases are identical except for the missing phrase in the
     comparative clause and the associated degree-marked phrase in
     the main clause and possibly one other pair of nonidentical
     phrases. Then an elliptical version of this comparative sentence
     can be formed by (a) making sure that there is a modal or some
     form of perfect HAVE, BE, or DO before the second of the
     identical phrases, and (b) deleting all of the material in the second
     phrase except for the nonidentical phrase, if there is one.

As we will see in chapter 16, there is an ellipsis rule that is similar to but somewhat simpler than this one that applies in a wide variety of English sentences and discourse situations in which comparatives are not involved.

The second ellipsis rule that applies in comparative clauses has a much more drastic effect. It applies when the main clause and the sentence inside the comparative clause are identical except for some single contrasted phrase, as in (144)–(147).

(144) a. *John* listens to music more often [than *Bill* listens to music].
    b. *John* listens to music more often [than *Bill*].

(145) a. John listens *to folk music* more often [than he listens *to jazz*].
      b. John listens *to folk music* more often [than *to jazz*].

(146) a. More people play *soccer* [than play *water polo*].
      b. More people play *soccer* [than *water polo*].

(147) a. John gave more books *to Shirley* [than he gave *to Fred*].
      b. John gave more books *to Shirley* [than *to Fred*].

We can derive the (b) sentences above by applying the following rule to the (a) sentences:

(148) If the comparative clause is identical to the main clause except for a contrasted phrase, optionally remove everything from the comparative clause except for this contrasted phrase.

An important qualification on the operation of this rule is that it can be depended on to give good results only when the comparative clause is at the end of the sentence. Leaving the comparative clause inside the phrase that contains the associated degree words generally yields strikingly unacceptable results, as shown in (149) and (150).

(149) a. ?[NP More people than play *water polo*] play *soccer*.
      b. *[NP More people than *water polo*] play *soccer*.

(150) a. John gave [NP more books than he gave *to Fred*] *to Shirley*.
      b. *John gave [NP more books than *to Fred*] *to Shirley*.

The one exception here is that the results are good when the comparative is a nonmaximal one, and the single phrase remaining is the phrase that is parallel to the maximal compared phrase.

(151) a. [NP More people *than ducks*] play soccer.
      b. [NP More pigs *than dogs*] eat corn.

This exception is surprising, given the fact—noted above—that full nonmaximal comparative clauses are generally not acceptable inside the degree-modified phrases.

(152) a. *[NP More pigs *than dogs eat hay*] eat corn.
      b. [NP More pigs] eat corn *than dogs eat hay*.

Exercises

1. Each of the following sentences contains a full comparative clause, one in which neither of the ellipsis rules discussed in this subsection has been applied. In each example, show the results of applying the first of the two ellipsis rules.

    a. Sarah saved more money than Karen saved.
    b. Warren writes to his children as often as he writes to his parents.
    c. More people go to Spain in August than go to Spain in November.
    d. More beavers live in Wisconsin than monkeys live in Wisconsin.

2. For each of the four sentences in exercise 1, show the results of applying the second ellipsis rule instead of the first.

3. For each of the following sentences, begin by saying what the corresponding sentence would be if no ellipsis rules had applied in the comparative clause. Then say which of the two special ellipsis rules (if either) has applied to give the results shown below. For some of the sentences, the answer will be that neither rule has applied.

    a. Laura is reading more mysteries than she is epics.
    b. More Northerners eat hominy than okra.
    c. Joe ate as many cashews as he could.
    d. Jack is buying more grapes from Bolivia than he is from California.
    e. Bill did more laundry than he had planned to do.
    f. Wanda has more buttons on her hat than Walter has on his shirt.
    g. More people drink beer in restaurants than do in bars.

4. The following sentence is ambiguous:

Martin makes Jack do more laundry than Fred does.

Say as clearly as you can what the two interpretations of this sentence are, and then explain how the ambiguity arises.

12.7 THE SUPERLATIVE CONSTRUCTION

A special alternative to the comparative construction exists in English for cases in which we want to say that some degree on a scale is higher than any other corresponding degree. This alternative construction, the *superlative,* comes in two varieties. The first variety shows a very close syntactic and semantic correspondence to full-sentence comparatives, whereas the second shows a semantic correspondence to comparatives inside relative clauses.

The first of these two varieties is illustrated in the (a) sentences of (153)–(157); the (b) sentences are the corresponding comparatives.

(153) a. Jacob is [$_{\text{AdjP}}$ *the most forthright* of all the children in the class].
      b. Jacob is [$_{\text{AdjP}}$ *more forthright* than any of the other children in the class].

(154) a. Your uncle has improved [$_{\text{AdvP}}$ *the most rapidly* of all the players on the team].

b. Your uncle has improved [_{AdvP} *more rapidly* than any of the other players on the team].

(155) a. This problem required [_{NP} *the most work* of all of the problems in the chapter].

b. This problem required [_{NP} *more work* than any of the other problems in the chapter].

(156) a. Gordon felt the shock [_{QuantP} *the most* of all the members of the family].

b. Gordon felt the shock [_{QuantP} *more* than any of the other members of the family].

(157) a. Ned caught [_{NP} the biggest fish of anyone who was on the lake yesterday].

b. Ned caught [_{NP} a bigger fish than anyone else who was on the lake yesterday].

The superlative constructions in the above examples are almost like the corresponding comparative constructions. The main differences are three in number:

• The superlatives have *most* instead of *more*.
• The superlatives have a preceding definite article.
• The superlatives have an *of* phrase instead of a comparative clause.

Tree diagrams for the bracketed portions of some of these examples are given in (158).

(158) a.

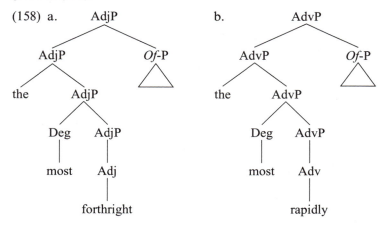

c.

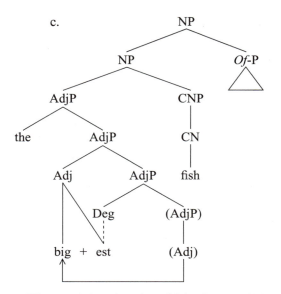

The one situation in which the parallel between comparatives and superlatives of this kind breaks down is with partitive structures, either those that are genuinely quantitative, such as (159), or those peculiar degree constructions discussed in section 12.4, exemplified in (160).

(159) a. *Carol attended [NP *the most of the lectures* of anyone].
      b. Carol attended [NP *more of the lectures* than anyone else].

(160) a. *Oliver is [NP *the most of a liar* of anyone].
      b. Oliver is [NP *more of a liar* than anyone else].

This first variety of superlative receives its interpretation externally, in that we are comparing some set of individuals with one another, with the "first-place" member of the set being some individual referred to outside of the superlative construction itself. We can illustrate by building an interpretation for (153a), which is repeated here.

(161) Jacob is the most forthright of all the children in the class.

The first step is to construct a set of parallel sentences that mention other members of the group to which Jacob belongs and their associated degrees of forthrightness.

(162) Child$_1$ is x_1 forthright.
      Child$_2$ is x_2 forthright.

Child$_3$ is x_3 forthright.

.
.
.

Jacob is x_n forthright.

The second step is to make a claim of superiority for the degree associated with Jacob.

(163) x_n is greater than any of the other x's.

Similar interpretations are possible for the other superlatives given above.

Even when a domain of individuals is identified, however, ambiguities can arise.

(164)   John admires Carol [$_{QuantP}$ *the most* of all the persons in the class].

This sentence can have either of the following interpretations:

(165)   a. Person$_1$ admires Carol x_1 much.
              Person$_2$ admires Carol x_2 much.
.
.
.

        John admires Carol x_n much.
   b. x_n is greater than any of the other x's.

(166)   a. John admires person$_1$ x_1 much.
              John admires person$_2$ x_2 much.
.
.
.

        John admires Carol x_n much.
   b. x_n is greater than any of the other x's.

In spoken English, the ambiguity generally disappears; whichever noun phrase represents the position of the entities that are being considered one at a time generally gets stronger stress than the other. Thus, a pronunciation of this sentence with stress on the word *John* will yield the first interpretation, whereas stress on the word *Carol* will yield the second.

Let us turn now to the second kind of superlatives. With these, there is no *of* phrase to indicate a domain of comparison; the superlative is just an ingredient of an ordinary noun phrase.

(167)   a. Nick just succeeded in catching [the biggest bass in Eagle
              Lake].
   b. Jonathan and Elinor bought [the oldest house in Austin].

In (167a), we are not comparing Nick's bass with a bass that anyone else might have caught. Similarly, in (167b), we are not comparing this house with houses that other people bought; instead, we are simply comparing it with other houses in Austin. Neither Nick in (167a) nor Jonathan and Elinor in (167b) are seen here as belonging to any domains of comparison. To the extent that these sentences can be paraphrased by sentences with comparatives, the comparatives are down inside relative clauses.

(168) a. Nick just succeeded in catching [the bass in Eagle Lake *that was bigger than any other bass in Eagle Lake*].
      b. Jonathan and Elinor bought [the house in Austin *that is older than any other house in Austin*].

Before concluding this section, let us briefly look at the formation of superlatives. We have already seen two examples, (157a) and (167a), in which the superlative is expressed by a suffixed *-est* instead of a preceding *most*. As a general rule, the same adjectives and adverbs that take *-er* as a comparative suffix also take *-est* as a superlative suffix, and those that can only have *more* in the comparative can only have *most* in the superlative.

(169) a.   the smartest   *the most smart
      b.   the shortest   *the most short
      c.   the highest   *the most high
      d.   the loveliest   the most lovely
      e.   the narrowest   the most narrow
      f.   the subtlest   the most subtle
      g. *the obesest   the most obese
      h. *the decentest   the most decent
      i. *the deviousest   the most devious
      j. *the intelligentest   the most intelligent

In addition, the same adjectives and adverbs that have irregular comparative forms also have irregular superlative forms.

(170) a. good   *the goodest   the best
      b. well (adverb)   *the wellest   the best
      c. bad   *the baddest   the worst
      d. far   *the farest   the farthest
      e. little (quantity   *the littlest   the least
         word)

Exercise

1. Draw a tree diagram for each of the following sentences:
   a. Jesse made his statement the most concise.
   b. Jesse made his statement the most concisely.
   c. Harvey wrote the most complicated poem of all the people who entered the contest.
   d. Dorothy regretted the mistake the most of any person in the group.

PART IV
SPECIAL CONSTRUCTIONS

Chapter 13
Special Subject-Predicate Relations

In each of the sentences discussed in earlier chapters, the functions of the subject and predicate can be roughly characterized by saying that the subject identifies some person or entity and the predicate describes it. We see this division of labor in the following sentences:

(1) *Identification*   *Description*
   a. Thomas Jefferson   founded the University of Virginia.
   b. My cat   is on the mat.
   c. You   are fortunate.
   d. What you are saying   makes very little sense.

For ease of reference, we will refer to sentences whose subjects and predicates exhibit this relation as *descriptive sentences.*

In the present chapter, we will consider some sentences that do not have an overall descriptive function of this kind. In section 13.1, we will examine the *existential construction,* which has a special syntax as well as an interpretation that asserts the existence of someone or something rather than asserting that a certain description applies to a subject. In section 13.2, we will investigate a number of sentences that we will describe as *identificational* in function. In such sentences, the verb phrase serves to identify the subject instead of describing it. In section 13.3, we look at the *cleft construction,* an identificational construction that has the same kind of interpretation as the constructions discussed in section 13.2 but has some very marked syntactic peculiarities.

13.1 THE EXISTENTIAL CONSTRUCTION

Two simple examples of the existential construction are given in (2).

(2) a. There is a fly in my soup.
    b. There is a cat on the mat.

Each of these sentences has the word *there* as its subject. This subject is followed by *is,* a noun phrase, and a locative phrase, in that order. The noun phrases serve as the subjects of the locative phrases, in the same way that they would in the following nonexistential sentences:

(3) a. A fly is in my soup.
  b. A cat is on the mat.

We will refer to the noun phrase that comes after BE in the existential construction as the *lower subject,* to distinguish it from the word *there,* which will be referred to as the *upper subject.* Thus, *a fly* and *a cat* are the two lower subjects in (2).

Not every English sentence beginning with *there* is an existential sentence. The sentences in (4) illustrate an entirely different English construction.

(4) a. Thére is Jones.
  b. Thére is the picture of Fred.
  c. Thére goes your brother.

In these sentences, the initial word *there* is a genuine locative phrase or motion phrase. As the accent marks indicate, it always receives a fairly heavy degree of stress when it is spoken. By contrast, the *there* of the existential construction is always spoken without any stress at all. In the present discussion, we will focus our attention on existential constructions, excluding from consideration the sentences that begin with locative *there.*

The form that the existential construction takes varies widely from one language to another, as the examples in (5) indicate.

(5) a. *French*
      Il y a un stylo dans ma poche.
      Literally: it there has a pen in my pocket
      'There is a pen in my pocket.'
  b. *German*
      Es gibt ein Buch auf dem Tisch.
      Literally: it gives a book on the table
      'There is a book on the table.'
  c. *Cairo Arabic*
      Fiih kitaab filbeet.
      Literally: in-it book in-the-house
      'There is a book in the house.'

Even within English we find variation: in certain nonstandard varieties of English, *it* is used as the upper subject in place of the standard English *there*. Thus, for example, speakers of these varieties would use the sentences in (6) in place of those in (2).

(6) a. It's a fly in my soup.
     b. It's a cat on the mat.

The general point illustrated here is that in many if not all languages, the form of the existential is quite arbitrary, especially in the selection of the word used as the upper subject and in the choice of a particular verb, if there is one. Thus, it is not surprising that the appearance of *there* and BE in this construction does not follow from any other properties of the English language, but instead is quite arbitrary. As a result, the construction is best viewed as a kind of sentential idiom, that is, a special combination whose meaning cannot be calculated from the meanings of its individual parts.

13.1.1 The Basic Syntax of the Existential Construction

Let us consider now how the existential construction might be described by a rule. Suppose in particular that we wanted to describe it by giving a special subject/complement rule for the verb BE. The part of the rule that described the complement choice would say that BE could be followed by a noun phrase and a locative phrase, and the part that described its subject would require the word *there*. Thus, the rule as a whole would be as in (7).

(7) *there* [BE NP LocP]

This rule yields (8) as the tree diagram for sentence (2a).

(8)

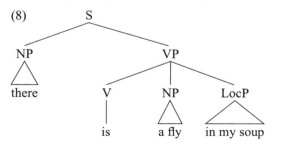

In the sentence just diagrammed, the second complement of the verb BE is a locative phrase. The rules of English also permit two other types of phrases as complements here: present-participial verb phrases and passive phrases. The two sentences in (9) illustrate these possibilities.

(9) a. There is a giraffe *standing on the porch.*   (present-participial verb phrase)
    b. There was a purse *found at the library.*   (passive phrase)

These two configurations call for the additional subject/complement rules given in (10).

(10) a. *there* [BE NP VP$_{PresPart}$]
     b. *there* [BE NP PassP]

In addition, it is possible to build an existential sentence in which there is no complement after the noun phrase.

(11) There is a Santa Claus.

For this sentence, we need the following rule:

(12) *there* [BE NP]

These last three rules give the trees in (13).

(13) a.

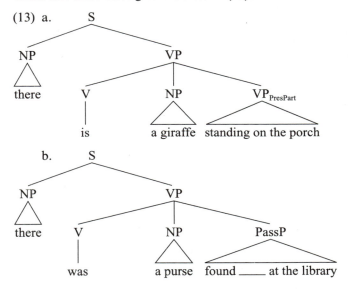

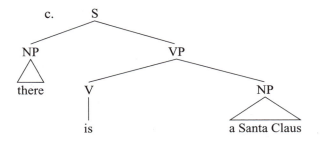

Exercise

1. Draw a tree diagram for each of the following sentences:
   a. There must have been a penny in the cupboard.
   b. There have been some mistakes made.
   c. There were four sailors sitting on the bench.
   d. John wants to know how many chairs there are at the table.
   e. Barbara told us where there were some glasses.

If necessary, review the discussion of indirect questions in chapter 4 to help you determine the structures for the last two sentences.

13.1.2   Number Agreement in Existentials

As illustrated earlier, other languages besides English have an existential construction in which a key element is an arbitrary upper subject. In many if not most of these languages, the verb of the sentence is invariably singular, no matter what the number of the lower subject happens to be. Many nonstandard varieties of English also have this property, so that both examples in (14) are acceptable.

(14) a. There is *a bat* in the belfry.
     b. There is *some bats* in the belfry.

Standard English, however, requires a plural verb when the lower subject of the existential is plural.

(15) a. There is *a bat* in the belfry.
     b. There are *some bats* in the belfry.

We can think of the word *there* as being invisibly marked with the number of the lower subject. *There* then passes its number on to the verb phrase with which it is joined. In some sentences, the word *there* is quite far away from the lower subject. Even in these sentences, a plural lower subject requires that *there*'s verb be plural.

(16) a. *There seems (singular) to have been *three explosions* on the
boat.

    b. There seem (plural) to have been *three explosions* on the boat.

Although *three explosions* is several verb phrases down from SEEM, this noun phrase still manages to transmit its number to the highest verb. It appears to do this by way of its link to the upper subject *there*.

13.1.3 The Noun Phrase in the Existential Construction

The existential construction yields better results with some noun phrases as lower subjects than with others. We have already seen that phrases introduced by *a*, *some*, and *three* give satisfactory results. We also find acceptable existentials with noun phrases introduced by *a lot of*, *several*, and *many*, as well as by noun phrases consisting solely of a plural or mass common-noun phrase.

(17) a. There is *a lot of beer* in the refrigerator.
    b. There are *several manuscripts* in the desk.
    c. There are *many accidents* on Highway 183.
    d. There was *one can* in the cupboard.
    e. There were *ninety-nine bottles of beer* on the wall.
    f. There are *large cracks* in the foundation.
    g. There is *mildew* on the siding.

All of these noun phrases fall in the class of indefinite noun phrases, as described in chapter 5.

The results are much less natural with definite noun phrases.

(18) a. *There are *them* in the room.
    b. *There was *John* on the committee.
    c. *There are *these tomatoes* in the basket.
    d. *There was *my car* stolen by a burglar.

Noun phrases that are introduced by universal quantity words are not acceptable, either.

(19) a. *There is *every apple* on the table.
    b. *There is *each flower* in a pot.
    c. *There are *all guests* in the lounge.

The fact that indefinite noun phrases are much more natural in this construction than members of either of the other two groups may be related to another fact about indefinites: they are often *less* natural than definite and universal noun phrases in the subject position of ordinary sentences, especially when the verb is some form of BE. The sentences in (20) illustrate this point.

(20) a. *The chair* is in the kitchen.   (definite noun phrase)
      b. *Every chair* is in the kitchen.   (universal noun phrase)
      c. ?*A chair* is in the kitchen.   (indefinite noun phrase)
      d. ?*Some chairs* are in the kitchen.   (indefinite noun phrase)

It is as if one of the primary functions of the existential is to enable speakers to avoid using indefinite noun phrases as subjects of sentences such as (20c) and (20d).

Definite noun phrases are acceptable in existentials in one special circumstance: when a question has been asked and the person answering wants to mention one or more alternatives. This type of situation is illustrated in (21) and (22).

(21) Question: Who can we get to watch the children?
      Answer: Well, there's *John*.

(20) Question: What can we read to them?
      Answer: Well, there's *this book,* and there's *the book about Snow White,* and there's *Fred's autobiography*.

Exercise

1. Should *most* be classified as a universal quantity word or as an indefinite quantity word? Base your answer on its behavior in the existential construction, as determined by an experimental sentence that you construct.

13.1.4   The Existential Construction as a Test for Transparency

At the end of chapter 8, SEEM was mentioned as an example of a *transparent* verb, that is, a verb that has the property of not really using its subject itself, instead merely passing it down to its complements. We noted that there are other phrasal heads with this property and that there is a simple strategy for identifying them. We are now in a position to develop this strategy.

As was observed in subsection 13.1.2, it is possible to construct sentences in which the existential word *there* is quite far from the remainder of the existential construction. Our example was the following:

(23) *There* seem to have *been three explosions on the boat*.

In this example, SEEM and the perfect HAVE intervene. The verb BE (represented here by *is*) and the adjective LIKELY show the same capacity.

(24) *There* is likely to *be an explosion on the boat.*

By contrast, many other verbs and adjectives give unacceptable results when they intervene between *there* and the remainder of the construction. Some typical examples are given in (25) and (26).

(25) a. **There* intends to *be an admiral on the committee.*
      b. **There* hope to *be several hurdlers on the team.*

(26) a. **There* is reluctant to *be an admiral on the committee.*
      b. **There* are eager to *be several hurdlers on the team.*

From the above examples, it should be clear that the difference between verbs and adjectives that can intervene and those that cannot is simply that the former are transparent and the latter are nontransparent. Because transparent heads have no use of their own for a subject, they do not impose any restrictions on their subjects. Thus, transparent heads such as SEEM and LIKELY can accept a subject like *there,* which has no interpretation of its own apart from the interpretation it receives in its eventual role as the subject of the existential verb phrase headed by BE. By contrast, each of the nontransparent words INTEND, HOPE, RELUCTANT, and EAGER has a definite use for its subject: it depends on its subject to identify the animate being that is in a particular mental state. These heads have something more pressing to do with a subject than merely to pass it down to some lower predicate. Thus, a meaningless subject such as *there* fails to provide what they require for a complete interpretation of the phrase that they head, and the result is the kind of unacceptability seen in (25) and (26).

These observations indicate that the *there* of existential sentences is significantly different from the *it* that occurs as a substitute for clauses. In the case of *it,* any verb or adjective that calls for a certain kind of clause as subject will be satisfied instead by an *it* linked to a clause of the appropriate sort. Thus, both of the sentences in (27) are perfectly acceptable.

(27) a. [That George will hire Sarah] is clear.
      b. *It* is clear [that George will hire Sarah].

On the other hand, a verb or adjective that calls for a certain kind of noun phrase is not satisfied by an occurrence of *there* that is linked to a noun phrase of the correct type. Thus, only the first of the sentences in (28) is acceptable.

(28) a.   Three doctors hope to be in the auditorium.
     b.   *There hope to be three doctors in the auditorium.

The difference between the pairs of sentences in (27) and (28) indicates that the *it* associated with a pseudocomplement and the *there* used in existential constructions serve fundamentally different roles in sentences in which they appear.

These considerations have an important practical consequence. In chapter 8, it was suggested that there are two possibilities for the understood subject of a phrase with no expressed subject. The first possibility was seen with verbs like HOPE. With these verbs, the subject of the infinitival complement is an understood pronoun, which is coreferential with the subject of HOPE. The second possibility appeared with verbs like SEEM. With these verbs, the subject of SEEM itself serves as the subject of the infinitival complement. Verbs and adjectives like SEEM were referred to as *transparent,* in recognition of the fact that they do not really use their subjects themselves, but simply pass them down to their complement phrases.

Now let us turn to the practical test that is made possible by these differences in behavior between transparent and nontransparent heads. When we want to know which of these two group a certain verb or adjective belongs to, we can construct an experimental sentence in which we let that verb or adjective take *there* as a subject, with the remainder of the existential construction appearing in the complement. If the sentence is acceptable, then the word is transparent; if the sentence is unacceptable, then the word is nontransparent.

Let us apply this test to the adjectives CERTAIN and WILLING, as they are used in the following examples:

(29) a.   The doctor is *certain* to be in the stadium.
     b.   The doctor is *willing* to be in the stadium.

We now construct sentences in which we split an existential such as the one in (30).

(30) There is a doctor in the stadium.

Here are the results:

(31) a.   There is certain to be a doctor in the stadium.
     b.   *There is willing to be a doctor in the stadium.

From this evidence we can conclude that CERTAIN is transparent, whereas WILLING is not.

This test can be used to show that a variety of other verbs and adjectives are transparent in the same way as SEEM, LIKELY, and CERTAIN. Here are some additional examples:

(32) a. There *appears* to be a spot on the rug.
     b. There *happens* to be a fingerprint on the mirror.
     c. There *must* be an apple in the refrigerator.
     d. There *has* been an explosion in the factory.

(29) a. There is *apt* to be a shortage.
     b. There is *sure* to be a revolver in the drawer.

Exercise

1. For each of the following verbs, construct an experimental sentence to determine whether it is or is not transparent. The relevant sentences will contain verb phrases in which the verb is followed immediately by an infinitival phrase.
     a. TRY
     b. REFUSE
     c. TEND
     d. APPEAR
     e. BEGIN
     f. FORGET

13.1.5 Verbs That Do Not Use Their Objects

We have just seen a handful of verbs and adjectives that are transparent, in the sense that they do not use their subjects themselves but merely pass them down to their complement phrases. There is also a small group of verbs in English that treat their direct objects in the same way. A clear example is provided by the verb BELIEVE, as it is used in (34).

(34) Katy believes Fido to be in the garage.

The rule that allows this sentence is that given in (35).

(35) NP [BELIEVE NP InfP]

We can see right away that this sentence can be paraphrased by one in which BELIEVE takes a *that* clause without a preceding object.

(36) Katy believes that Fido is in the garage.

This fact suggests that the object of BELIEVE in (34) is not really being used by BELIEVE but instead is merely being used to identify the subject of the infinitival phrase. This idea can be tested by using *there* as the object of BELIEVE, followed by an infinitival phrase. Here is a relevant pair of examples, the first a simple existential, the second a sentence in which this existential is used with BELIEVE:

(37) a. There is a dog in the garage.
  b. Katy believes there to be a dog in the garage.

The acceptability of (37b) provides confirmation that BELIEVE in this configuration does not really use its object itself. Another verb with the same property is CONSIDER.

(38) a. There is a bug in this program.
  b. George considers there to be a bug in this program.

In contrast to BELIEVE and CONSIDER, many verbs that take direct objects followed by infinitives do use their objects themselves. PERSUADE is one such verb; its object identifies the person whose mind was made up to carry out a certain action. The following pair of sentences shows the result of trying to use the existential *there* as a direct object of this verb.

(39) a. There is a doctor in the stadium.
  b. *Bill persuaded there to be a doctor in the stadium.

Another verb of this type is ASK.

(40) a. There is a bailiff in the hall.
  b. *The judge asked there to be a bailiff in the hall.

Exercise

1. For each of the following verbs, construct an experimental sentence to determine whether it does or does not use its object. Be sure to use verb phrases of the form V + NP + InfP.
  a. ALLOW
  b. PERMIT
  c. EXPECT
  d. INSTRUCT

13.1.6 Other Verbs Occurring in Existentials

In each of the examples we have considered so far, the verb of the sentence has been some form of BE. We also find existential *there* in the company of a small number of other verbs, chiefly those denoting existence or motion of some sort.

(41) a. There exists a smallest positive whole number.
    b. There came a man from Tennessee.
    c. There went out a decree from Caesar Augustus.
    d. There arrived three packages in the mail.

This kind of existential is substantially more marginal than the existential with BE. However, it shares with it the same subject *there,* and the same preference for indefinite noun phrases as lower subjects. Like the existential with BE, its effect seems to be that of avoiding an indefinite noun phrase as the first noun phrase in a sentence.

13.2   IDENTIFICATIONAL SENTENCES

13.2.1   Subjects and Predicates of Identificational Sentences

Among the descriptive sentences discussed in earlier chapters are some in which the verb phrase consists of BE followed by a noun phrase.

(42)

Subject	Description
a. I	am [$_{NP}$ a dentist].
b. You	are [$_{NP}$ the person for whom the job was created].
c. Your mother	is [$_{NP}$ one of Martha's friends].
d. What Fred writes	is [$_{NP}$ unadulterated rubbish].

Many identificational sentences have a similar outward form. They consist of a subject noun phrase—typically a name or a description or even a pronoun—and a verb phrase consisting of BE following by another noun phrase. A first example of this type of sentence is given in (43).

(43) [$_{NP}$ The inventor of the light bulb] was [$_{NP}$ Thomas Alva Edison].

Here the phrase that follows the verb does not describe the inventor of the light bulb; instead, it identifies him. This sentence could in fact constitute an answer to a test question such as "Identify the inventor of the light bulb." Additional examples of identificational sentences are given in (44).

(44) a. [$_{NP}$ The country that won the 1986 World Cup] was [$_{NP}$ Argentina].
    b. [$_{NP}$ The guy who disrupted the meeting last night] was [$_{NP}$ the guy who rents your basement apartment].
    c. [$_{NP}$ I] am [$_{NP}$ Ronald Reagan].

    d. [NP The substance that you are putting on your vegetables right now] is [NP sodium chloride].

    e. [NP Sodium chloride] is [NP the substance that you are putting on your vegetables right now].

    f. [NP Sir William Jones] was [NP the person who first postulated a common parent language for Sanskrit, Latin, and Greek].

    g. [NP The person who first postulated a common parent language for Sanskrit, Latin, and Greek] was [NP Sir William Jones].

These sentences might serve as responses to the following utterances:

(45) a. Identify the country that won the 1986 World Cup.

    b. Who was the guy who disrupted the meeting last night?

    c. Who are you?

    d. What is the substance that I'm putting on my vegetables right now?

    e. Tell me what sodium chloride is.

    f. Who was Sir William Jones?

    g. Name the person who first postulated a common parent language for Sanskrit, Latin, and Greek.

As examples (44d–g) show, the same phrase that serves as the identified phrase in one situation can serve equally well as the identifying phrase in a different situation.

    In addition to identificational sentences in which BE is followed by an ordinary noun phrase, we also find some in which BE is followed by a gerundive, an infinitival clause, or a *that* clause.

(46) a. [NP The thing that bothered Bill] was [NP Molly's forgetting his name].

    b. [NP The project that John is working on now] is [NP fixing the fence].

(47) a. [NP The thing that Beth wants] is [InfC for Grant to sail around the world].

    b. [NP Rhonda's most important goal] is [InfC to finish college in three years].

(48) a. [NP Bill's opinion] is [That–C that we should try to arrange a truce].

    b. [NP The thing that bothers Martha] is [That–C that we haven't made a decision].

One particular variety of identifying sentences is sometimes distinguished from others. This is the so-called *pseudocleft sentence*, illustrated in (49).

(49) a. [NP What Bill put in the safe] was [NP Marcia's necklace].
   b. [NP What Jonah would like for you to bring back] is [NP a pint of yogurt].
   c. [NP What Carol approved of] was [NP Bill's returning the trophy].
   d. [NP What Barbara wants] is [InfC for us to clean the chicken house].
   e. [NP What Tom says] is [That-C that he will call us from Philadelphia].

The subject of each of these sentences is a definite free relative of the sort discussed in chapter 7. The phrases that come after BE are of the same types as those in (44), (46), (47), and (48). Since a free relative is just a special kind of noun phrase, we can regard the pseudocleft sentence as nothing more than the particular version of the identificational sentence that is obtained when the subject happens to be a definite free relative. Thus, we will not treat it as a special construction in its own right.

13.2.2   The Interpretation of Identificational Sentences

As was noted above, the basic import of an identificational sentence is to give a description and then identify the individual or entity or substance that satisfies the description. Although this characterization of these sentences may seem quite simple, it has some unexpected and interesting consequences. In particular, this characterization provides an explanation for some peculiar aspects of subject identification and pronoun interpretation in identificational sentences.

Let us begin by looking more closely at sentence (49a), repeated here.

(50) [NP What Bill put in the safe] was [NP Marcia's necklace].

The interpretation of the free relative in subject position can be roughly approximated as in (51).

(51) the x such that [Bill put x in the safe]

The verb phrase in (50) identifies this x as Marcia's necklace. In so doing, it implies the truth of the statement that we get by substituting *Marcia's necklace* for x in the small sentence in brackets.

(52) Bill put *Marcia's necklace* in the safe.

These initial results may seem obvious, but a more interesting situation arises in (53).

(53) [~NP~ What Bill enjoys] is [~NP~ reading Cicero].

The interesting problem here is to determine how the subject of the gerund *reading Cicero* is identified. Suppose that we just apply the rule given in chapter 8 for sentences in which the verb is followed by a gerundive. For the sentence in (54a), this rule gave us the subject identification shown in (54b).

(54) a. John resents [working in an office].

b.

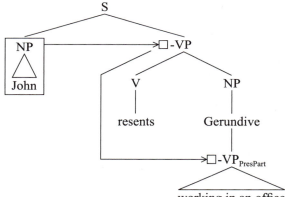

But applying the same rule to (53) picks out *what Bill enjoys* as the understood subject of *reading*. This result is clearly incorrect: the understood subject of *reading* is not *what Bill enjoys* but simply *Bill*.

Here is where our interpretive idea concerning identificational sentences is useful. The interpretation of the free relative comes out as (55).

(55) the *x* such that [~S~ Bill enjoys *x*]

The verb phrase then identifies the *x* in question as *reading Cicero*. If we now substitute *reading Cicero* for *x* in the small sentence in (55), we arrive at the following result:

(56) Bill enjoys *reading Cicero*.

With this structure as a basis for subject interpretation, the rules from chapter 8 do give the correct result, as shown in (57).

(57)

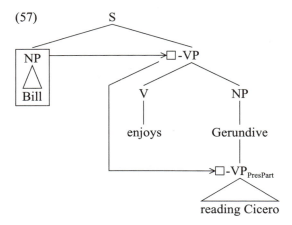

The central point here, then, is this: when we are dealing with an un-expressed subject in the verb phrase of an identificational sentence, the correct identification of that subject requires a computation based on a structure in which the identifying phrase after BE has been substituted somehow in the interpretation of the phrase that tells what is being identified.

The contrast between subject identification in ordinary descriptive sentences and that in identificational sentences is illustrated in a surprising way by the pair of sentences in (58).

(58) a. What *John* enjoys is making *him* sick.
     b. What *John* enjoys is making *himself* sick.

Both of these sentences are acceptable; the challenge is to explain why both the nonreflexive pronoun and the reflexive pronoun can be understood as coreferring with *John*. From our discussion in chapter 8, we know that *him* indicates noncoreference with the subject of *making* and that *himself* indicates coreference with this subject.

In one of the structures that we have seen for verb phrases of the form *is* + present-participial phrase, the lower verb phrase serves as a complement of *is*. This structure, shown in (59), is what we need for (58a).

(59)

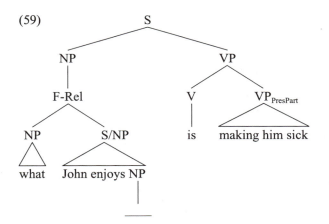

To such a structure, we can apply the subject identification rules of chapter 9 directly, with the result shown in (60).

(60)

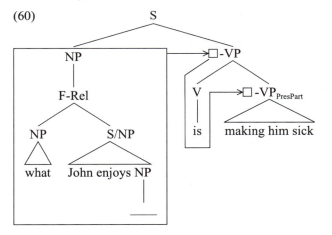

Here the subject of the sentence as a whole has provided the identification for the subject of the present-participial phrase. Since this subject is not coreferential with the object of *making*, the nonreflexive pronoun *him* is called for.

The other structure that we have seen that exhibits a form of BE followed by a present-participial phrase is the kind of identificational structure seen in this chapter, where the present-participial phrase is a gerundive that identifies the subject. Here the interpretation of the initial free relative is as follows:

(61) the x such that [$_s$ John enjoys x]

Substituting the verb phrase *making himself sick* for *x* in the bracketed sentence, we obtain the sequence in (62a), whose structure is given in (62b).

(62) a. John enjoys *making himself sick*.

b.

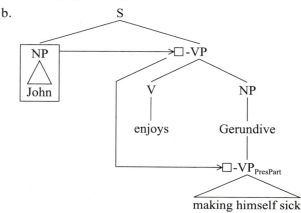

As indicated here, the rules of chapter 8 pick out *John* as the understood subject of *making*. Since *John* and the object pronoun are to be understood as coreferential, the reflexive form is the correct choice here.

Although the substitution idea works well with the last few examples that we have discussed, other examples can be found for which it is hard to see exactly how to apply this technique. One pair of sentences that resists such a treatment is much like the pair of sentences just considered.

(63) a. John's favorite activity is making *him* sick.
b. John's favorite activity is making *himself* sick.

For the first sentence, no problem arises. As with (58a), we treat the verb phrase as consisting of *is* plus a present-participial complement. The noun phrase *John's favorite activity* then becomes the understood subject of *making*. Because this noun phrase is not coreferential with the object of *making*, the nonreflexive *him* is the correct choice.

The problem arises with (63b). This is clearly an identificational sentence. However, the noun phrase *John's favorite activity* does not have a ready-made interpretation of the form shown in (64).

(64) the *x* such that [...]

Without an interpretation like this, we do not have a sentence with a blank into which we can substitute the phrase *making himself sick*. Consequently, we fail to pick out *John* as the understood subject of the gerundive. Here an explanation might possibly depend on some understanding of our unconscious mental definitions of words like *activity*. We might suppose that such definitions themselves have blanks in them. For instance, *x's activity* might mean something like "thing that *x* indulges in ____." Then we might derive the interpretation of (63b) by the same kind of substitution that we used above.

(65) John indulges in [making himself sick].

Once again, the subject-identification rules given in chapter 8 have the effect of picking out *John* to identify the subject of *making*. The result is that the reflexive pronoun is the correct choice for the object of *making*.

One additional kind of identificational sentence that merits special attention is exemplified in (66).

(66) a. [$_{NP}$ The thing that Beth wanted to do] was [$_{VP}$ keep the flame burning].
b. [$_{NP}$ What the teacher does] is [$_{VP}$ grade on the curve].
c. [$_{NP}$ What Roger did] was [$_{VP}$ find the correct analysis].
d. [$_{NP}$ What Bertram seems to have done] is [$_{VP}$ solve the riddle of the Sphinx].
e. [$_{NP}$ What Brenda is doing] is [$_{VP}$ changing the oil].

In each of these sentences, the phrase after BE is a verb phrase. In addition, all of the subjects in these sentences contain an occurrence of the transitive DO found in simple-sentence verb phrases such as *do it* and *do something*. In each of the subjects, this DO is followed by a missing direct object.

(67) a. the thing [$_{B-Rel}$ that [$_{S/NP}$ Beth wanted to do ____]]
b. [$_{F-Rel}$ what [$_{S/NP}$ the teacher does ____]]
c. [$_{F-Rel}$ what [$_{S/NP}$ Roger did ____]]
d. [$_{F-Rel}$ what [$_{S/NP}$ Bertram seems to have done ____]]
e. [$_{F-Rel}$ what [$_{S/NP}$ Brenda is doing ____]]

In (66a–d), the verb phrase after BE is a bare-stem phrase, but in (66e), it is a present-participial phrase. These examples suggest that there is a kind of matching in form between the DO inside the subject and the verb after BE. When the DO is a bare stem, a present tense, a past tense, or a past participle, then the verb after BE should be a bare stem. On the other hand, when the DO is the present-participial form *doing,* then the verb after BE should be a present participle too.

In applying to these examples the kind of substitution that we used with earlier examples, we should note that the verb phrase after BE is substituted not for the blank alone but for DO plus the blank. Thus, from the initial free relative in (68a), we obtain the interpretation given in (68b). Then substitution of the verb phrase after BE for *do* plus the missing noun phrase gives (68c).

(68) a. [$_{NP}$ What Nancy will do ____] is [$_{VP}$ send a note to the teacher].
   b. the *x* such that [Nancy will do *x*]
   c. Nancy will *send a note to the teacher.*

As one incidental point, we observe the same kind of connection between a transitive phrase headed by DO and an ordinary verb phrase in dialogues such as the following:

(69) a. Person A: Do you think that Nancy will [$_{VP}$ do something]?
   b. Person B: Yes; I think that she will [$_{VP}$ send a note to the teacher].

Here again, *send a note to the teacher* constitutes an elaboration not just of the noun phrase *something* but of the full verb phrase *do something.*

Exercises

1. The following sentence is ambiguous:

   What the president wants is to be taken seriously.

   A. Describe this ambiguity, making it as clear as you can what the two different interpretations are.

   B. On one interpretation of this sentence, the understood subject of *taken seriously* is *what the president wants*. On the other interpretation, the understood subject of this passive phrase is *the president*. Say how these quite different subject identifications come about.

   Note: One of the two structures will work exactly like that seen in the following sentence: *The baby is to put his toys away.* Assume here that the relevant complement rule is just [BE InfP] and that the identification of the subject of the infinitival clause proceeds in the same way that it does with other intransitive verb phrases.

2. Answer the same two questions concerning the following ambiguous sentence:

   What the president is doing is leaving scars on the economy.

13.3   THE CLEFT CONSTRUCTION

We turn now to a construction that is specifically designed to serve an identificational function. This construction, which is often referred to by the term *cleft construction,* is illustrated in (70).

(70) a. It was Velma [that you reported to the commissioner].
     b. It must have been Tony [who(m) you sent to the commissary].

13.3.1   Two Plausible but Incorrect Analyses

A quick look at these sentences might give the impression that they represent constructions with which we are already familiar. For this reason, we will begin by comparing the cleft construction with two previously studied constructions to which it is superficially similar.

The first idea to consider is that the examples in (70) involve the *it +* pseudocomplement construction described in chapter 4. To review for a moment, sentences exhibiting this construction have a substitute subject *it* taking the place of a clause that serves as an understood subject. The clause itself then occurs in the position of a complement. Two examples are given in (71).

(71) a. *It* is true [that Gordon discarded the ace].
     b. *It* is obvious [whose car Pete borrowed].

In (71a), the pseudocomplement is a *that* clause; in (71b), it is an indirect question. Turning back to the sentences in (70), we might think that (70a) contains a pseudocomplement *that* clause and that (70b) contains an indirect question.

Two major problems exist for this analysis. The first becomes apparent as soon as we try to put the pseudocomplements back in subject position. When we try to do this with (71), the results are satisfactory.

(72) a. [That Gordon discarded the ace] is true.
     b. [Whose car Pete borrowed] is obvious.

However, when we try to do the same thing with (70), the results are unacceptable.

(73) a. *[That you reported to the commissioner] was Velma.
     b. *[Who(m) you sent to the commissary] is Tony.

The second major problem arises specifically with the idea that the bracketed material in (70a) is a *that* clause. An examination of other examples reveals that what follows *Velma* in this sentence must contain a missing noun phrase. This fact is established by the contrast between (74), where missing-noun-phrase positions can be found, and (75), where there are none.

(74) a.   It was Velma [that you took ____ to the meeting].
     b.   It was Velma [that you talked to ____].

(75) a.   *It was Velma [that you took Beth to the meeting].
     b.   *It was Velma [that you talked to Fred].

This contrast provides solid evidence that the bracketed structure in (70a) cannot be a *that* clause but instead must be a missing-phrase construction of some kind.

The second idea that we might consider is one that would allow us to view the bracketed sequences as missing-phrase constructions. This idea is that the bracketed sequences in (70) are just ordinary relative clauses modifying *Velma* and *Tony,* respectively. The main problem with such an analysis is that it is not consistent with what we have established previously about relative clauses. If the bracketed sequence in (70a) actually were a relative clause, the *that* which introduces it would indicate that it was restrictive rather than nonrestrictive. But having this clause modifying *Velma* would violate the prohibition against having proper nouns modified by restrictive relative clauses. In this example, it would force us to say that the sequence *Velma that you took to the meeting* could be a well-formed noun phrase. Sentence (76) confirms that in fact it cannot be.

(76)   *Velma that you took to the meeting returned your call.

13.3.2   The Structure of the Cleft Construction

Now that we have established that the cleft construction is separate from any we have discussed previously, let us examine its structure, starting with the two sentences we considered at the beginning of the present section.

(77) a.   It was Velma [that you reported to the commissioner].
     b.   It must have been Tony [who(m) you sent to the commissary].

Each of these sentences has as its subject the word *it*. Also, each contains the following elements:

- an occurrence of BE
- a noun phrase

- a sequence that is strikingly similar in internal structure to a restrictive relative clause

In what follows, we will refer to the position of the noun phrase as the *focus* position and to the clause that comes after it as the *cleft clause*. Thus, the diagram in (78) would be appropriate for (77a).

(78)

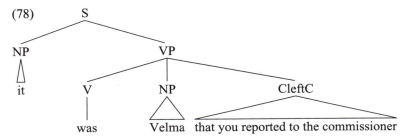

In looking more closely at this construction, we will want to address two general questions:

- What kinds of phrases can occur in the focus position?
- What are the characteristics of the cleft clause?

Let us start with the first of these questions. The two examples that we have seen so far have both had noun phrases in focus position. As the additional examples in (79) show, many other types of phrases are possible.

(79) a. It was *here* that Linda put the molasses.   (locative phrase)
   b. It was *to Boston* that they decided to take the patient ____.
      (motion phrase)
   c. It was *then* that the answer occurred to her ____.   (time phrase)
   d. It was *with a great deal of regret* that I vetoed your legislation
      ____.   (manner phrase)
   e. It was *by starting a fire* that the army avoided defeat ____.
      (means phrase)
   f. It was *three whole days* that the battle lasted ____.   (duration phrase)

There are a few types of phrases that cannot appear in focus position in standard English. These include adjective phrases and verb phrases of various inflectional forms.

(80) a. *It is *fond of Martha* that Harry seems to be ____.   (adjective phrase)

b. *It was *to see his brother* that Harry tried ___.   (infinitival phrase)

c. *It is *stealing apples* that Julia caught Frank ___.   (present-participial verb phrase)

In addition, individual adverbs such as *carefully* and *regretfully* are not acceptable in the focus position, even though prepositional phrases that express the same idea are acceptable.

(81) a. *It was *carefully* that Donna removed the wrapping ___.
(Compare: It was *with care* that Donna removed the wrapping ___.)

b. *It was *regretfully* that Joe fired Pete.
(Compare: It was *with regret* that Joe fired Pete.)

Turning now to the cleft clause, we observe one striking characteristic in the examples in (79). Even though a wide variety of focus phrases occurs in these examples, the word *that* is always acceptable as an introducing element. Thus, the following rule accounts for a broad group of cleft clauses:

(82) A cleft clause can consist of the word *that* plus a sentence with a missing phrase. This missing phrase must be of the same type as the associated focus.

The same rule can be expressed in diagram form as in (83), where the symbol *XP* stands for a phrase of any variety, just as it did in our discussion of indirect questions in chapter 4.

(83)   CleftC

that   S/XP

We do not need to put any special restrictions on the kind of missing phrase allowed, since any type that can appear as the focus can also be the missing phrase in a cleft clause introduced by *that*.

Cleft clauses may also be introduced by a few other elements, primarily *who, whom,* and *whose* plus a common-noun phrase.

(84) a. It was Smiley [*who* ___ spilled beer on this couch].

b. It must have been Dorothy [*who(m)* Fred was referring to ___].

c. It is Martha [*whose work* critics will praise ___].

Also acceptable are prepositional phrases containing these noun phrases.

(85) a. It was Smiley [*on whom* the sheriff placed the blame ____].
     b. It is Margaret [*on whose shoulders* the burden will rest ____].

Surprisingly, though, other *wh* words that serve well in restrictive relatives are not as natural in clefts.

(86) a. ?It is this car [*which* I want you to sell ____].
        (Compare: It is this car [*that* I want you to sell ____].)
     b. ?It was on Thursday [*when* the schedule was announced ____].
        (Compare: It was on Thursday [*that* the schedule was announced ____].)
     c. ?It was in Boston [*where* they held the tea party ____].
        (Compare: It was in Boston [*that* they held the tea party ____].)

Thus, we need the following additional rule for the formation of cleft clauses introduced by certain *wh* phrases:

(87) A cleft clause can have as an introducing phrase either *who, whom,* or *whose* plus a common-noun phrase. In addition, it can be introduced by a prepositional phrase containing one of these noun phrases. In the first case, the adjoined structure is a sentence with a missing noun phrase; in the second case, it is a sentence with a missing prepositional phrase.

The two separate cases of this rule are shown in (88).

(88)

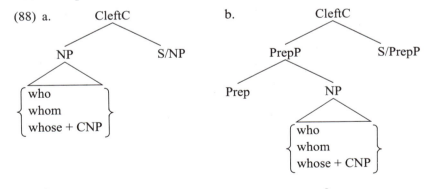

Exercise

1. Draw a tree diagram for each of the following sentences:
   a. It must have been Harold who locked us on the deck.
   b. It was on this desk that Nadine put the keys.

    c. It was Gordon whose car the company repossessed.

    d. Jones knows who it was that Smith wanted to interview.

13.3.3 Interpretating the Cleft Construction

By now we have seen enough to suspect that the identificational function
of cleft constructions is carried out in a way that mimics the process by
which restrictive relative clauses are interpreted. As in the latter process,
we have a structure (here a finite sentence) with a missing phrase. Just as
an understood noun phrase is provided to the restrictive relative clause,
here also an outside phrase is provided, in this case the phrase in focus
position. We can represent this general situation graphically as in (89).

(89)

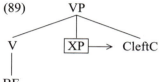

Just as with relative clauses, what happens at this point depends on
whether or not the structure receiving the donated phrase is introduced by
a *wh* phrase. If it is not (if it is introduced either by *that* or by nothing),
then the phrase is donated directly to the sentence with a missing phrase,
which uses it to complete its meaning. This is shown in (90).

(90)

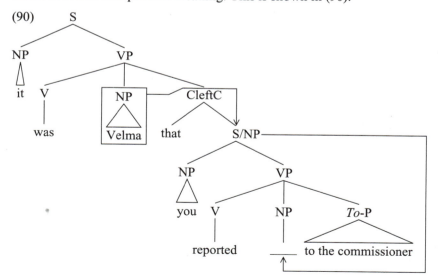

For the sentence diagrammed in (90), this process would yield an interpretation that contained the sentence in (91).

(91) You reported *Velma* to the commissioner.

On the other hand, if the cleft clause is introduced by a *wh* phrase, then the interpretation proceeds in two steps instead of one. First the focused phrase replaces the *wh* word in the introducing phrase. Then this introducing phrase fills in the meaning of the missing phrase. A cleft construction of this kind is shown in (92a); the steps in the interpretation are shown in (92b).

(92) a. It was Meg on whom the burden fell.

b.

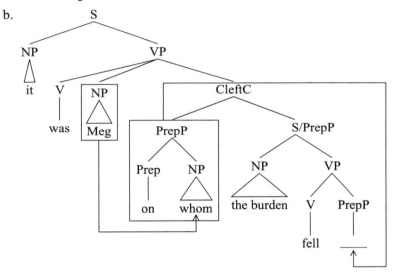

Thus, for (92a), we arrive at an interpretation that implies (93).

(93) The burden fell on *Meg*.

Exercises

1. Take each of the tree diagrams that you drew for the exercise at the end of the preceding subsection and indicate how the interpretation is determined.

2. Draw a tree diagram for the sentence given below. In your diagram, treat *it's* as if it were *it is*. In addition, treat *very things* as a common-noun phrase, without going into its internal structure.

"It's the very things that make it hard for you that make them want to see you do this." (Philip Friedman, *Reasonable Doubt,* Ivy Books, New York, 1990, p. 344)

Assume that the sentence is a cleft sentence, with an interpretation close to the following: [$_{NP}$ The very things that make it hard for you] [$_{VP}$ make them want to see you do it].

13.3.4   The Cleft Construction with Transparent Verbs

Earlier in this chapter, we noted that the existential *there* can be separated from the verb BE only by a transparent head, that is, only by a head that has no use of its own for its subject. Thus, (94a) is possible, since SEEM and HAVE are transparent, whereas (94b) is not.

(94) a.   *There* seem to have *been* three explosions on the boat.
　　 b.   **There* intends to *be* an admiral on the committee.

The cleft construction exhibits exactly the same property. The *it* and the BE can be separated, but only by heads that are transparent. Thus, whereas an ordinary noun phrase like *John* may serve as the subject of either a transparent or a nontransparent head, the *it* of the cleft can only be the subject of a transparent one. We see this contrast in (95) and (96).

(95) a.   John seems to own that house.　　　　(transparent head)
　　 b.   John wants to own that house.　　　　(nontransparent head)

(96) a.   It seems to be John that owns that house.　(transparent head)
　　 b.   *It wants to be John that owns that house.　(nontransparent head)

Thus, just as with existential *there,* the *it* of the cleft construction in no sense serves as a substitute for the noun phrase that occurs in the focus position. In (96b), in particular, the verb WANT needs an animate subject, and the word *it* clearly fails to stand in for *John* as the subject of this verb.

In similar fashion, the *it* of the cleft construction can be an object only for a verb that does not use its object itself. Thus, we find another contrast similar to the one in subsection 13.1.5.

(97) a.   We believed it to be Smith who was leaving the message.
　　 b.   *We persuaded it to be Smith who was leaving the message.

Exercise

1. For each of the following verbs and adjectives, construct an experimental sentence containing a cleft construction to determine whether it is transparent or nontransparent. The relevant sentences will contain verb phrases in which the verb is followed immediately by an infinitival phrase.

    a. ATTEMPT
    b. REFUSE
    c. TEND
    d. APPEAR
    e. APT
    f. EAGER

Chapter 14
Special Sentence Types

Up to this point, we have been concerned solely with declarative sentences, that is, sentences that are used to make statements of various kinds. In this chapter, we will study some types of sentences that are used primarily for other purposes. The first group to be considered consists of direct questions. The second group, similar in form to questions, consists of several kinds of exclamative constructions. The third group consists of imperatives.

14.1 DIRECT QUESTIONS

In chapter 4, we gave a good deal of attention to a special type of clause construction, traditionally referred to as the *indirect question*. These questions are used as subjects and objects of larger sentences. The present section deals with the corresponding constructions that function as independent utterances. Although the outward situation in which direct questions occur is extremely simple, their internal structure is actually more complex in one significant respect than the internal structure of indirect questions.

14.1.1 Yes-No Questions and Alternative Questions

The first group of direct questions that we will examine consists of *yes-no* questions. The contrast between ordinary affirmatives and yes-no questions can be seen in the following pairs:

(1) a. Jack *caught* the measles.
    b. *Did* Jack *catch* the measles?

(2) a. Chris *wants* a drink.
    b. *Does* Chris *want* a drink?

(3) a. The bankers *trust* Smith.
    b. *Do* the bankers *trust* Smith?

We will give a special name to the kind of structure that these questions exhibit, referring to them as *inverted finite structures*. In addition to seeing them serve as direct questions, as in these examples, we will also see them serve as parts of other constructions. This is why we want to have a name for them that is different from *direct yes-no question*. If we can determine how these inverted finite structures are formed, our rule for forming direct yes-no questions can then be stated very simply, as in (4).

(4) A direct question can consist of an inverted finite structure by itself.

Let us look more closely, then, at these structures. Like the emphatic construction discussed in chapter 3 and the *not* construction discussed in chapter 11, this new construction contains a tensed form of DO (either *did, does,* or *do*), together with a bare-stem verb. Clearly, this is another construction that has a special-purpose verb phrase as a basic ingredient. In addition, just as with the negative construction, a change in word order is required: the tensed DO must be shifted to the left of the subject. Thus, a rule for inverted finite structures can be stated as in (5).

(5) To form an inverted finite structure:

  • Use a special-purpose structure.
  • Shift the head verb to the left of the subject noun phrase.

With this rule in mind, we can think of inverted finite structures as being formed in the manner shown in (6).

(6) a. Jack did catch the measles.   (use special-purpose verb phrase)
    b. did Jack catch the measles   (shift head verb to left of subject)

The effects of this derivation are represented in (7), where S_{Inv} is an abbreviation for an inverted finite structure.

(7)

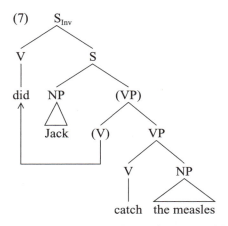

As the rules developed here would lead us to expect, the verbs that were exceptional with regard to the formation of emphatic sentences are exceptional in the same way with regard to the formation of inverted finite structures. The special nature of these verbs is shown in the questions in (8)–(10).

(8)   a.   *_Does_ John _have_ gone to the library?
      b.   _Has_ John gone to the library?

(9)   a.   *_Do_ you _be_ busy?
      b.   _Are_ you busy?

(10) a.   *_Does_ Jack _can_ play the fiddle?
      b.   _Can_ Jack play the fiddle?

Derivations for the inverted structures in the three acceptable (b) examples are given in (11)–(13); they show how the statement about exceptional special-purpose structures and the rule for inverted finite structures work together to give the right results.

(11) a.   John _has_ gone to the library.   (use special-purpose verb phrase)
      b.   _has_ John gone to the library   (shift head verb to left of subject)

(12) a.   you _are_ busy   (use special-purpose verb phrase)
      b.   _are_ you busy   (shift head verb to left of subject)

(13) a.   Jack _can_ play the fiddle.   (use special-purpose verb phrase)
      b.   _can_ Jack play the fiddle   (shift head verb to left of subject)

The structures resulting from these derivations are given in (14).

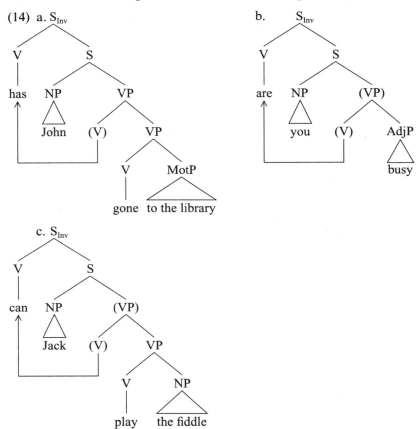

(14) a. S_{Inv}

b. S_{Inv}

c. S_{Inv}

With this examination of the internal properties of inverted finite structures behind us, we have what we need in order to apply rule (4), which states that a direct question can consist of an inverted finite structure by itself. For the example in (13b), considered as a question, the tree diagram would be (15).

(15) DQ

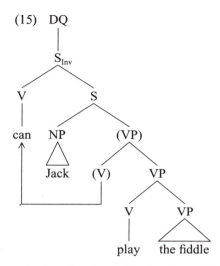

Just as the class of indirect questions includes alternative *whether* questions as well as yes-no *whether* questions, so there are direct alternative questions whose syntax is close to that of direct yes-no questions. The (a) sentences in (16) and (17) both have indirect alternative questions as complements, and the (b) sentences show the corresponding direct questions.

(16) a. We want to know [whether John sued Karen or Karen sued John].
  b. Did John sue Karen or did Karen sue John?

(17) a. Harry didn't tell us [whether Sue played chess or Joe played bridge or Sam played poker].
  b. Did Sue play chess or did Joe play bridge or did Sam play poker?

In (16b), the conjunction *or* joins two inverted finite structures. In (17b), the same conjunction joins three inverted finite structures. Thus, although we will not discuss conjunctions systematically until chapter 16, we can give the following rough rule for this kind of question:

(18) A direct question can consist of two or more inverted finite structures joined by *or*.

The structure that this rule yields for (16b) is shown in (19).

(19)

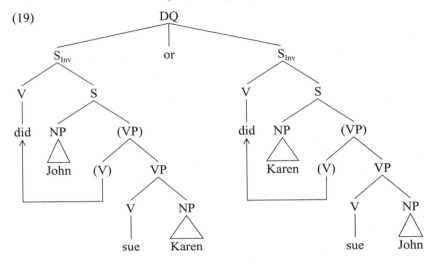

Exercises

1. For each of the following questions, draw a tree diagram:
   a. Does your brother have a job?
   b. Do these people know your cousin?
   c. Could John have been dreaming?
   d. Has your car been washed?
   e. Were the coats made in New York?
   f. Did Sally see the doctor yesterday, or will she see him today?
   g. Is it Beth that you are trying to find?

2. Across various dialects of English, we find two different ways of negating and questioning sentence (i).

(i) John has the necessary money.

The two different questions are given in (ii), and the two different negative sentences are given in (iii).

(ii) a. Does John have the necessary money?
      b. Has John the necessary money?

(iii) a. John doesn't have the necessary money.
      b. John hasn't the necessary money.

On the basis of these examples, give the simplest idea that you can think of concerning how these two varieties of English differ. What should we say about the variety illustrated in the (b) sentences that we do not say about the variety illustrated in the (a) sentences?

14.1.2 Negative Yes-No Questions

The sequences consisting of special-purpose head verbs plus contracted *not* count as special-purpose verbs in their own right. Thus, they can themselves undergo the rule forming inverted finite structures.

(20) a. Didn't Jack return the book?
     b. Isn't Alice with Fred?
     c. Hasn't George written his paper?

A detailed derivation for (20a) is given in (21).

(21) a. Jack *not did* return the book.   (initial sequence with special-purpose verb phrase)
     b. Jack *did not* return the book.   (shift of head verb to left of *not*)
     c. Jack *didn't* return the book.   (optional contraction of *not* with *did*)
     d. *Didn't* Jack return the book?   (shift of head verb to left of subject)

Steps (a)–(c) are those discussed in chapter 11. They result in the structure shown in (22).

(22)

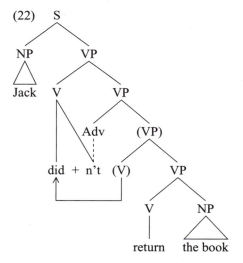

Shifting the finite verb to the left gives the structure in (23).

(23)

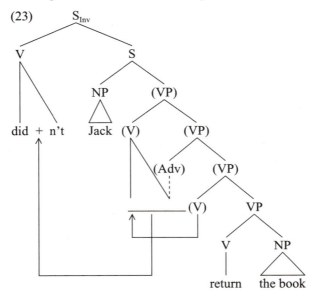

If this diagram seems more than ordinarily complex, it is because of the unusual complexity of the construction whose derivation it represents.

Let us turn now to a different matter: how negative yes-no questions are used. In circumstances in which either a positive or a negative answer is equally likely, such questions are never used. For instance, if we have no idea one way or the other whether Jack returned the book, the appropriate question is not (20a), but (24).

(24) Did Jack return the book?

By contrast, a question like (20a) might be asked in either of two special circumstances. The first is when the person asking the question is sure or virtually sure that the answer is affirmative and wants to force the hearer into giving an affirmative answer. Thus, this type of question crops up frequently in courtroom cross-examination and in news conferences. Examples illustrating this effect are given in (25).

(25) a. Didn't it seem strange to you that your employer sent you home early on the night of the fire?
   b. Didn't you state in your acceptance speech at the convention that you were strongly in favor of a tax cut?

In both cases, the questioner's implication is clearly that only an affirmative answer is appropriate.

The second circumstance in which negative questions are used is when the questioner has just discovered grounds for doubting the truth of something that had previously been taken for granted. For instance, suppose that Carol has been assuming all along that Henry paid the light bill for their apartment, but then they get a letter threatening them with a cutoff of electrical service. It would be natural for Carol to address the following question to Henry:

(26) Didn't you pay the light bill?

Exercise

1. As was shown in this subsection, questions can be formed on negative special-purpose structures as well as on positive special-purpose structures. Give complete derivations for the questions listed below, showing all of the steps that have gone into their formation.

   a. Didn't Janet open the package?
   b. Hasn't Fred made his bed?

14.1.3 Tag Questions

There is one more special type of construction in English that belongs in a discussion of yes-no questions. This *tag question* construction, which has the appearance of an abbreviated yes-no question, is commonly attached to the end of a declarative sentence. Instances of this construction are italicized in (27) and (28).

(27) a. John went to Villanova, *didn't he*?
      b. They know what is going on, *don't they*?
      c. George has spent a lot of money, *hasn't he*?
      d. This cake is quite rich, *isn't it*?
      e. Martha will graduate in May, *won't she*?

(28) a. John didn't go to Villanova, *did he*?
      b. They don't know what's going on, *do they*?
      c. George hasn't spent much money, *has he*?
      d. This cake isn't very sweet, *is it*?
      e. Martha won't graduate in May, *will she*?

Although many other languages have constructions that have the same function in conversation as this particular English construction, in few of these languages is the construction so complicated.

In describing the tag questions in (27) and (28), we can begin by observing three properties of the construction. First, there is a pronoun subject, which in each case agrees with the subject of the preceding declarative. Second, in front of this subject is a special-purpose verb, one that matches the declaratiye verb in tense, number, and person. The tag verb associated with an ordinary verb will be the appropriate positive or negative form of DO, whereas the tag verb associated with a modal, perfect HAVE, or BE will just be a positive or negative form of the same verb. Finally, and most surprisingly, this special-purpose verb is negative if the declarative is positive, and positive if the declarative is negative. The former situation obtains in (27), the latter in (28). Thus, we might give the following rule for forming a tag question to go with a given declarative:

(29) To form the tag question that goes with a given declarative,

- Use as the subject the pronoun that agrees with the subject of the declarative.
- To the left of this subject put a special-purpose verb that fits with the verb of the declarative sentence.
- If the declarative sentence is affirmative, make the special-purpose verb negative, and vice versa.

We can illustrate the operation of this rule by using it to derive a tag to go with the declarative given in (30).

(30) Martin lives in Denver.

The first thing we need to determine is what pronoun is appropriate as a subject noun phrase. For *Martin,* the corresponding pronoun is *he.* The second question is what special-purpose verb corresponds with the verb *lives.* Here the answer is either *does* or *doesn't.* The final question is whether the declarative sentence is affirmative or negative. Since it is affirmative, we use the negative form *doesn't* in the tag. These three choices give us the correct result.

(31) Martin lives in Denver, *doesn't he?*

Tag questions have two different functions in English, and the difference in use goes along with a difference in intonation contour. The first intonation pattern is one that rises on the tag.

(32) Ruth knows about the meeting tomorrow, $\overline{\text{doesn't she}}$?

This question would be asked with this intonation if a speaker suddenly felt insecure about a proposition that had not been questioned previously. Here the previously unquestioned assumption is that Ruth knows about the meeting tomorrow. The utterance serves the function of asking for confirmation of this proposition. Had the questioner not taken this proposition for granted previously, an ordinary yes-no question would have been much more appropriate.

(33) Does Ruth know about the meeting tomorrow?

The other possible intonation on a tag question falls sharply at the end. We might hear this intonation in an utterance of (34).

(34) The weather's nice today, isn't it?

This utterance is clearly not intended to confirm anything about which the utterer is uncertain. Nor is it intended to convey information to the hearer. Instead, it is to be taken as an "invitation to agree" and as such is often used to get a conversation going. In British English, the same construction with the same intonation can also be used as an "invitation to concede a point" and thus can be used to terminate a conversation just as well as to start one. The following is a possible British example:

(35) Your plan would make it awfully difficult to keep our rivals out,
       wouldn't it?

This use is completely foreign to American English.

14.1.4   Direct Phrasal Questions

We now turn our attention to direct questions that are introduced by various sorts of questioned phrases. We saw a good many *indirect* questions of this sort in chapter 4, including the following:

(36) a. whose books Shirley located
      b. which customer George was shouting at
      c. how many employees Karen introduced to the visitors
      d. in which room George stayed
      e. how fond of your aunt the children are
      f. when the concert will begin
      g. where his horse is

For each of these indirect questions, there is a corresponding direct question.

(37) a. Whose books did Shirley locate?
    b. Which customer was George shouting at?
    c. How many employees did Karen introduce to the visitors?
    d. In which room did George stay?
    e. How fond of your aunt are the children?
    f. When will the concert begin?
    g. Where is his horse?

The direct questions are almost exactly like the indirect questions. The only difference is that the sentences on which the direct questions are based are finite inverted structures instead of ordinary finite sentences. That is, their verb phrases are special-purpose phrases, and the head verb has been shifted to the left of the subject. We can thus describe these questions by a relatively simple rule.

(38) To form a direct phrasal question, join a questioned phrase to an inverted finite structure with a missing phrase of the same type as the questioned phrase.

For (37a), this rule yields the tree diagram in (39).

(39)

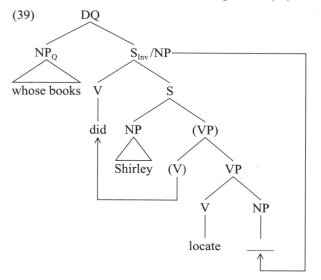

There is one special case where rule (38) gives the wrong result. Among the structures that would surely count as an inverted finite structure with a missing noun phrase would be the structure shown in (40), in which the missing noun phrase is the subject.

(40)

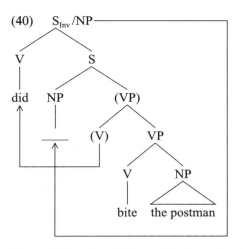

From (40), rule (38) would allow the formation of the question diagrammed in (41).

(41)

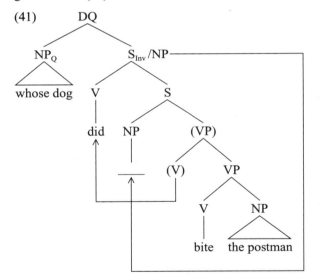

Unless we put emphatic stress on *did,* this is not an acceptable question. The actual question that we get instead is (42).

(42) Whose dog bit the postman?

For this question, we want an uninverted sentence like the one in (43), just as was the case with the corresponding indirect question.

(43)

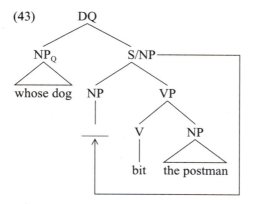

Because of this kind of question, we will amend rule (38) as follows, dividing it into two separate cases:

(44) To form a direct phrasal question, apply whichever of the following rules is appropriate:

- If the questioned phrase is understood as the subject of the question, then join the questioned phrase to an ordinary finite sentence with a missing subject noun phrase.
- Otherwise, join the questioned phrase to an inverted finite structure with a missing phrase of the same type as the questioned phrase.

Exercises

1. For each of the following direct questions, draw a tree diagram:
   a. Which coat did Edgar mend?
   b. What did Fred do with the rug?
   c. Why didn't you keep the change?
   d. How many patients wasn't the doctor able to examine?
   e. What was Erica given?
   f. What could it have been that frightened the herons?

2. The bracketed indirect question in the following sentence is ambiguous:

   I wonder [what Ruth had taken to the market].

Draw tree diagrams for the two structures that this indirect question can have. Then determine what the corresponding direct question is for each of the structures. Explain what it is that makes the ambiguity disappear when we change to the direct questions.

14.2 EXCLAMATIVES

The term *exclamatives* refers to a small class of English constructions whose special function is to express amazement. One of these constructions is illustrated in (45).

(45) a. Didn't John do a great job!
   b. Don't those twins look like their grandmother!
   c. Hasn't this been a terrible summer!
   d. Isn't Horton a jackass!

This construction is identical in every respect except one to negative yes-no questions. The one difference is that these sentences carry a falling intonation contour at the end instead of a rising contour. Although these utterances are not in any way requests for information, they are like questions in calling for some response from the hearer. The kind of response they solicit is an emphatically enthusiastic affirmative answer.

Another exclamative construction has the form of an affirmative yes-no question, except that the intonation falls at the end instead of rising.

(46) a. Did I make a mess of that exam!
   b. Was Smith cross today!
   c. Has that kid grown!
   d. Can Ella sing!

These examples can be made slightly more natural by prefacing them with *boy* or some comparable interjection and by inserting the word *ever* after the subject.

(47) a. Boy, did I ever make a mess of that exam!
   b. Damn, was Smith ever cross today!
   c. Man, has that kid ever grown!
   d. Jesus, can Ella ever sing!

Unlike the exclamatives that look like negative questions, these do not call for a particular type of response from the hearer.

Still other exclamative constructions are used to indicate a high degree. These constructions are exemplified in (48) and (49).

(48) a. *How tall* you have grown ____!
   b. *How soothingly* John reads his poems ____!

(49) a. *What a sullen fellow* Gordon seems to have become ____!
   b. *What a dope* Gordon seems to have become ____!

c. *What beautiful paintings* you bought ____!
d. *What masterpieces* you bought ____!
e. *What tasteless furniture* you have accumulated ____!
f. *What trash* you have accumulated ____!

These examples have three properties in common. First, they have an introductory "exclamative phrase" beginning with *how* or *what*. Second, they contain corresponding missing phrases. These two properties they share with questions, both direct and indirect. Third, all of these exclamatives have a general-purpose verb and normal subject-verb word order, instead of having a special-purpose verb shifted to the left of the subject. This last property has the effect of setting them very clearly apart from direct phrasal questions.

The rules for their introductory phrases are quite simple. The phrase can be an adjective phrase, an adverbial phrase, or a noun phrase starting with the degree word *how*. It can also be a noun phrase that has one of the following three forms:

- *what* + *a(n)* + singular count common-noun phrase
- *what* + plural count common-noun phrase
- *what* + mass common-noun phrase

The exclamative phrases formed with *what* show the same pattern as the noun phrases introduced by *such* that were discussed in chapter 12.

(50) a. *what* a dope   such a dope   (singular count)
     b. *what* masterpieces   such masterpieces (plural count)
     c. *what* trash   such trash   (mass)

One final type of exclamative utterance consists of just one of these introductory exclamative phrases by itself.

(51) a. How stupid!
     b. What a ridiculous price!
     c. What a bargain!
     d. What beautiful dentures!
     e. What idiots!
     f. What beautiful music!
     g. What garbage!

Exercises

1. Construct a pair of examples to show that the phrase *how intelligent* can introduce both a direct question and a nearly identical exclamative. Then construct

another pair of examples to show that *what a genius* is possible only in an exclamative, not in a direct question.

2. Since we know that both direct questions and indirect questions exist, we might ask whether there are any indirect exclamatives that correspond to the "direct" exclamatives that we have been examining in this section. Which of the following examples provides the clearer evidence for the existence of indirect exclamatives?

(i) We told Jack how good the concert was.

(ii) We told Jack what a good concert it was.

Explain your answer briefly but clearly.

14.3 IMPERATIVES

The sentences in our third special class, imperatives, are used primarily to give instructions, orders, commands, invitations, and suggestions for action.

14.3.1 Second-Person Imperatives

The most basic type of imperative consists simply of a verb phrase, with no overt subject preceding it.

(52) a. Eat your spinach.
      b. Sign your name on this line.
      c. Have a cookie.
      d. Be patient.

In these examples, as in all the imperative examples we will see, the verb is in its bare-stem form. Example (52d) shows clearly that it is the bare-stem form and not the present plural form that is required. If we had used the present plural form of BE in this example, we would have obtained the unacceptable sentence in (53).

(53) *Are patient.

Although there is no overt subject in these examples, in each case there is an understood subject *you*. A rule for this type of imperative can thus be stated as follows:

(54) An imperative may consist of a bare-stem verb phrase alone. Such a structure is interpreted as having an understood subject *you*.

A slightly more complex type of imperative exhibits an overt subject.

(55) a. *You* sit down.
      b. *Someone* call a doctor.

c. *Somebody* say something.
d. *Everybody* sit down.

The possible subjects in this construction do not go very far beyond *you, you guys, someone, somebody, everybody,* and so forth. This additional possibility is described in (56).

(56) An imperative can consist of a subject (*you* or some larger noun phrase introduced by *you,* also *somebody, someone*) followed by a bare-stem verb phrase. The subject must be one that can refer to one or more people who are being addressed.

Rules (54) and (56) give the two basic possibilities for affirmative imperatives. For negative imperatives, we start with the same basic structures that are given by rules (54) and (56) and preface them with the word *don't.* This gives the following sets of results, the first lacking subjects and the second showing them:

(57) a. Don't go away.
b. Don't be impatient.

(58) a. Don't you sit down over there.
b. Don't anybody say anything.

(The *anybody* and *anything* that we see in place of *somebody* and *something* are a result of the negative context here; this effect will be discussed in detail in chapter 15.) We can describe negative imperatives, then, as follows:

(59) A negative imperative can consist of *don't* followed by an overt or understood subject followed by a bare-stem verb phrase.

One additional possibility exists for forming a negative imperative. Instead of *don't,* we can use *do not,* as in (60).

(60) a. Do not walk on the grass.
b. Do not post bills.

Unlike the word *don't,* the two-word sequence *do not* cannot be used with imperatives containing an overt subject.

(61) a. *Do not you sit down over there.
b. *Do not anybody say anything.

The rule for these imperatives must therefore be stated as follows:

(62) A negative imperative can consist of *do not* followed by an understood subject *you* followed by a bare-stem verb phrase.

14.3.2   First-Person Imperatives

Besides the imperatives described above, which are generally used to elicit some sort of behavior from the person or persons being addressed, English allows another sort. The primary purpose of this second variety is to suggest a course of action in which the speaker is to be included. The simplest form is exemplified in (63).

(63) a. Let's go to the circus.
     b. Let's be careful.
     c. Let's behave ourselves.

Each of these examples consists of the form *let's* followed by a bare-stem verb phrase. Although there is no overt subject, the understood subject is *we*, as seen most clearly in the reflexive pronoun *ourselves* in (63c). This fact justifies their classification as first-person constructions.

We can also have first-person imperatives in which there is an overt subject, as in (64).

(64) a. Let's everybody take a deep breath.
     b. Let's all five of us go in Fred's car.

In these examples, *let's* is followed by a noun phrase followed by a bare-stem verb phrase.

To make negative first-person imperatives, we merely use *let's not* instead of *let's*.

(65) a. Let's not go to the circus.
     b. Let's not be careless.

(66) a. Let's not everybody talk at the same time.
     b. Let's not all five of us try to crowd into Fred's car.

There is also an alternative negative form that is not standard for American English: instead of *let's not*, the sequence *don't let's* is used.

(67) a. Don't let's go to the circus.
     b. Don't let's be careless.

(68) a. Don't let's everybody talk at the same time.
     b. Don't let's all five of us crowd into Fred's car.

14.3.3   Imperatives with a Conditional Force

All of the imperatives discussed so far have occurred by themselves. In addition to this basic use, they have a rather surprising one in which they are joined to a following declarative by a conjunction. This use is illustrated in (69) and (70).

(69) a. *Eat your spinach,* and you can have some cake.
     b. *Don't spill the beans,* and I'll let your leader live.

(70) a. *Eat your spinach,* or I'll give your cake to the dog.
     b. *Don't spill the beans,* or your leader will get it.

The italicized sequences in these sentences look exactly like the imperatives that we saw above, with a bare-stem verb phrase in the (a) examples and a bare-stem verb phrase preceded by *don't* in the (b) examples. In addition, they have very strongly the import of requesting a certain kind of action. The sentences in (69), with *and,* have the following paraphrases:

(71) a. If you eat your spinach, you can have some cake.
     b. If you don't spill the beans, I'll let your leader live.

By contrast, the sentences in (70), with *or,* have paraphrases that contain *unless* instead of *if.*

(72) a. Unless you eat your spinach, I'll give your cake to the dog.
     b. Unless you don't spill the beans, your leader will get it.

This use of imperatives is also possible when the imperative has a subject.

(73) a. Somebody make a motion for adjournment, and we can all go home.
     b. Don't any of you move, or your leader will get it.

The same use is sometimes found with first-person imperatives as well.

(74) a. Let's leave now, or we'll get stuck in rush-hour traffic.
     b. Let's leave now, and we'll get home in time to watch Nigeria play Bulgaria.

Exercises

1. The imperative constructions examined in this section provide a basic means of ordering, suggesting, or inviting in English. However, a great many English utterances that have these intended effects are similar in their outward form to direct yes-no questions. The following are just a few examples:

(i)   Would/Could you pass the salt?

(ii)   Would you be so good as to lower your voice?

(iii) Would/Could someone help me wrap this package?

(iv)   Will you be quiet?

(v)   Would you mind telling me what you think you're doing in this house?

(vi)   Would you happen to know what time it is?

(vii)   Do you happen to have a pen you could lend me?

Although these sentences would not typically be interpreted as requests for information in the form of a positive or negative answer, they differ in their closeness to outright imperatives. One possible measure of closeness is the naturalness of *please* after the subject. Do experiments with these sentences to determine which ones sound natural with *please* and which ones are less directly imperative in nature.

2. The following set of examples illustrates a curious English construction that bears a superficial resemblance to ordinary *how* questions:

(i) a.   X: How would you like to put your feet up and drink a nice cup of tea?
    Y: I'd love it.
   b.   X: How would you like to help me put away the groceries?
    Y: Just a minute. I'll be right with you.
   c.   X: How would you like to have that tennis racket broken over your skull?
    Y: Gee, you're a tough specimen!

The construction is curious not only because of the variety of different effects it can be used for, but also because we typically find nothing in the answers to such questions that can be related to the *how* in the question.

A.   Describe what it is that makes (ia) an invitation, (ib) a request, and (ic) a threat.

B.   Describe the ambiguity in each of the following two sentences:

a.   How would you like to pay me for the damage that your two-year-old has done?

b.   How would you like to help us bring our fund drive to a successful conclusion?

Give examples of the kinds of answers that you might expect to hear on the two readings.

3. Another construction that brings imperatives and questions together in yet a different way is illustrated in (i) and (ii).

(i)   Why make your own pasta?

(ii)   Why not make your own pasta?

A.   Is this construction related to second-person imperatives or first-person imperatives? Devise some examples with reflexive pronouns to support your answer.

B.   What inflectional type of verb phrase is employed in this construction? Provide acceptable and unacceptable examples that support your answer.

4. The sequence *do X a favor* has a rather odd use in imperatives. Thus, although (ia) and (ib) have the same outward appearance, the speaker clearly is requesting two acts in the first case but only one in the second.

(i) a. X: Sweep the floor and wash the dishes.
     Y: I'll sweep the floor but I won't wash the dishes.

  b. X: Do $\begin{Bmatrix} \text{me} \\ \text{yourself} \end{Bmatrix}$ a favor and sell that blasted fiddle.

     Y: ?I'll do $\begin{Bmatrix} \text{you} \\ \text{myself} \end{Bmatrix}$ a favor, but I won't sell this fiddle.

Sentence (ib) shows this construction in the setting of a straightforward subjectless second-person imperative.

A. Try to construct some other examples with the sequence *do X a favor and,* to see where else it can be used. Among other things, try it out in some of the imperative-like constructions mentioned in the preceding exercises.

B. See if you can think of any other sequences like this in which the action requested is conveyed by the second of two conjoined imperatives, with the first serving mainly to put the request in a certain light.

PART V

SOME TOPICS IN THE SEMANTIC INTERPRETATION OF ENGLISH

Chapter 15
Negation

In dealing with several different syntactic topics, we have observed a number of words that we would intuitively perceive to be negative. In chapter 5, the negative words *no* and *none* were mentioned in their capacity as quantity words, and *nothing, nobody,* and *nowhere* were cited in the discussion of special combined forms. In chapter 11, *never* was listed as one example of a frequency adverb, and two subsections were devoted to the special-purpose verbal constructions involving *not* and its contracted form *-n't*. Sentences containing these words are given in (1).

(1) a. *No* errors were detected.
    b. *None* of the machines have detected intelligent life.
    c. *Nothing* happened during your absence.
    d. Martha *never* mentioned the problem.
    e. Joe did *not* shave before breakfast.
    f. I did*n't* go to the post office.
    g. Greta has *not* returned to her office.

The main project of this chapter is to look at these words in their capacity as negative words, with a view toward developing an overall picture of the manner in which they affect the form and interpretation of sentences in which they occur.

During the initial stages of our discussion, the term *negative sentence* will be used simply as a convenient shorthand for the more cumbersome phrase "sentence containing a negative word." Likewise, the term *affirmative sentence* will be used instead of the expression "sentence that does not contain any negative words." Although these two terms will make the discussion go more quickly, they will not play a role in the rules that are developed and thus will not have any ultimate linguistic significance.

15.1   LOGICAL NEGATIONS OF AFFIRMATIVE SENTENCES

A useful way to approach this topic will be to make some informal comparisons between affirmative sentences and the particular negative sentences that are interpreted as their *logical negations*. Sentence x expresses the logical negation of sentence y if x is true whenever y is false and x is false whenever y is true. Thus, for example, (2b) expresses the logical negation of the proposition expressed by (2a).

(2) a. Smith understands Latin.
    b. Smith does not understand Latin.

If (2a) is true, then (2b) must be false, and if (2a) is false, then (2b) must be true.

This particular pair of sentences makes the relation in form between affirmative sentences and their logical negations look fairly straightforward. To see some examples illustrating a more complex formal relation, let us begin with some affirmative sentences containing the word *some* and its special compound forms.

(3) a. Jack saw *something*.
    b. Connie drank *some* beer.
    c. Shirley *sometimes* gives *some* money to *some* of her friends.

The logical negations of these examples are expressed quite naturally by the following negative sentences:

(4) a. Jack did *not* see *anything*.
    b. Connie did *not* drink *any* beer.
    c. Shirley does*n't ever* give *any* money to *any* of her friends.

There are two chief differences in form between the affirmative sentences in (3) and the corresponding negative sentences in (4). First, the negative sentences contain *not* or *-n't* along with a special-purpose verbal structure. Second, the negative sentences contain *any* and *ever* words in place of the *some* words in the affirmatives. In what follows, we will refer to the *some* words as *assertives,* and to the *any* and *ever* words as *nonassertives*. The two sets of words are listed pairwise in (5).

(5) *Assertive*   *Nonassertive*
    some   any
    someone   anyone

somebody	anybody
something	anything
somewhere	anywhere
sometimes	ever

The negative sentences in (4) constitute one set of logical negations for the affirmative sentences in (3). As it happens, the rules of English allow another set of logical negations as well. These are listed in (6).

(6) a. Jack saw *nothing*.
  b. Connie drank *no* beer.
  c. Shirley *never* gives *any* money to *any* of her friends.

In this alternative group of negative sentences, there is no *not* or *-n't* preceded by a special-purpose verb. Instead, in place of the first assertive word of the affirmative sentence (*something, some, sometimes*), we find a corresponding *negative* word (*nothing, no, never*). The corresponding pairs of nonassertive and negative words involved in these examples are listed in (7).

(7) *Nonassertive*   *Negative*
  a. anything   nothing
  b. any   no
  c. ever   never

As the following unacceptable alternatives to (6c) indicate, a negative word cannot be preceded by a nonassertive:

(8) a. *Shirley *ever* gives *no* money to *any* of her friends.
  b. *Shirley *ever* gives *any* money to *none* of her friends.

For affirmative sentences with assertive words in their subjects, only the second variety of negative sentence is possible as their negation. We can see this by looking at (9)–(11).

(9) a. Someone is sleeping in my bed.
  b. Some zebras can fly.
  c. Something has happened to Bertram's optimism.

(10) a. *Anyone isn't sleeping in my bed.
  b. *Any zebras can't fly.
  c. *Anything hasn't happened to Bertram's optimism.

(11) a.   No one is sleeping in my bed.
     b.   No zebras can fly.
     c.   Nothing has happened to Bertram's optimism.

The sentences in (10) are like those in (8) in having nonassertives to the left of the negatives.

Comparing affirmative sentences with sentences that express their logical negations has provided us with some preliminary observations about the expression of negation in English. It has also given us some useful concepts, specifically, the concepts *assertive, nonassertive,* and *negative,* which refer to important classes of English words.

15.2   SOME ADDITIONAL NEGATIVE SENTENCES

At this point, it might seem that we could state a rule for negative sentences that would derive them by taking affirmative sentences and making some simple changes. In such an approach, we would construct (12b) by starting with (12a), inserting *not,* and changing *something* to *anything.*

(12) a.   The mole will see something.
     b.   The mole will not see anything.

Similarly, we would construct (13b) by taking (13a) and changing the first assertive word to a negative.

(13) a.   Some of the guests signed the register.
     b.   None of the guests signed the register.

The weakness of this approach becomes apparent when we look at additional negative sentences. A first problematic example is given in (14).

(14)   Some of the guests did not sign the register.

From what affirmative sentence would this negative sentence be derived? At first glance, it might appear to represent the logical negation of (15).

(15)   Some of the guests signed the register.

But in fact the negation of (15) is not (14) but (16).

(16)   None of the guests signed the register.

We can prove that (14) is not the logical negation of (15) by imagining a situation in which both sentences would be true at the same time. Let us suppose that ten guests are currently staying in a certain hotel, and that six have signed the register and four have not. In this situation, both (14) and (15) would be true simultaneously; indeed, we would not be speaking paradoxically if we uttered (17).

(17) Some of the guests did not sign the register, and some of the guests did sign the register.

Thus, (14) cannot be the logical negation of (15). This is not to say that (14) is not the logical negation of any affirmative sentence at all. In fact, it is the logical negation of (18).

(18) All of the guests signed the register.

But (14) and (18) do not show the simple correspondence in form that we saw in our earlier pairs of affirmative sentences and their logical negations.

Another negative sentence that would be difficult to describe as the logical negation of an affirmative sentence is (19).

(19) More than three of our neighbors did not vote for Carter.

At first glance, this might appear to express the logical negation of (20).

(20) More than three of our neighbors voted for Carter.

Yet by the same kind of reasoning as in the previous paragraph, we can prove that the meanings of (19) and (20) are not logically opposed to each other. In particular, it is easy to imagine circumstances in which both are true at the same time. If eight of our neighbors did not vote for Carter and seven of our neighbors did, then (19) and (20) are both true. Furthermore, we sense no logical contradiction in (21), where both (19) and (20) are asserted at the same time.

(21) More than three of our neighbors voted for Carter, and more than three of them did not.

If we really want a sentence expressing the logical negation of the affirmative sentence in (20), we need to resort to (22).

(22) Not more than three of our neighbors voted for Carter.

The logical incompatibility of (20) and (22) is shown by the contradiction that we perceive when we join the two sentences, as in (23).

(23) ??More than three of our neighbors voted for Carter, but not more than three of our neighbors voted for Carter.

15.3   THE NOTION OF SCOPE AND THE LEFT-TO-RIGHT RULE

Although we have noted that (14) differs in meaning from (16) and like-wise that (19) differs from (22), we have not yet determined what these differences amount to, or what properties of these sentences bring these differences about. To answer these questions, we will need to consider *scope* relations, relations that hold between the negative words and quantity words in these sentences.

Before we look at the notion of scope as it applies in the interpretation of English sentences, it will be useful to look at the same idea as it can be applied in another domain. Example (24) shows two separate arithmetical expressions, each of which mentions three numbers (60, 3, and 9) and two mathematical operations (division and addition).

(24) a. $(60 \div (3 + 9))$
    b. $((60 \div 3) + 9)$

Because of the differences in the way the numbers and operations are grouped by the two sets of parentheses, we know that the values of the two expressions are not to be computed in the same way. In (24a), we understand that addition has a subordinate role: it is to be performed first, and the result is then to be used in the computation called for by the division operation. We understand exactly the opposite relationship between the two operations in (24b). Here it is the division operation that is subordinate: it is to be performed first, and the result is then to be used as part of the computation called for by the addition operation. The differing procedures by which the values of these two expressions are calculated are shown in (25).

(25) a. $(60 \div (3 + 9))$
       Subordinate operation: Add 3 and 9.
       Result: 12
       Superior operation: Divide 60 by the result of the subordinate operation (i.e., divide 60 by 12).
       Result: 5
    b. $((60 \div 3) + 9)$
       Subordinate operation: Divide 60 by 3.
       Result: 20
       Superior operation: Add the result of the subordinate operation and 9 (i.e., add 20 and 9).
       Result: 29

The basic terms that we will be using are defined in (26).

(26) If A and B are two different operations mentioned in a certain expression, and if the result of the computation called for by B is used in the computation called for by A, then we will say that B is *within the scope of* A. Alternatively, we say that B has *narrower scope* than A, or that A has *wider scope* than B.

Applying this definition to the expressions in (24) gives us the following statements:

(27) a. $(60 \div (3 + 9))$

Addition is *within the scope of* division. Alternatively, we can say that division has *wider scope* than addition in this expression, or that addition has *narrower scope* than division.

b. $((60 \div 3) + 9)$

Division is *within the scope of* addition. Alternatively, we can say that addition has *wider scope* than division in this expression, or that division has *narrower scope* than addition.

With the general idea of scope in mind, let us now see how the truth-values of (19) and (22) are determined in a certain context. The context is provided by the chart in (28), which lists the people living in a certain imaginary neighborhood and indicates the voting behavior of each one in the 1980 U.S. presidential election.

(28)

x	Truth-value of "x voted for Carter"
Kathy	false
Gaylord	false
Warren	true
Pat	true
Mae	false
Gib	false
Steve	true
Kate	true
George	false
Alma	false

The two sentences that we want to evaluate are repeated in (29) and (30); each one is accompanied by a diagram containing a slightly awkward paraphrase in which the meaning is divided among several levels.

(29) More than three of our neighbors did not vote for Carter.

> There are **more than three** of our neighbors x
> for which the following proposition is true:
>
> > It is **not** the case that the following proposition is true:
> >
> > > x voted for Carter.

(30) Not more than three of our neighbors voted for Carter.

> It is **not** the case that the following proposition is true:
>
> > There are **more than three** of our neighbors x
> > for which the following proposition is true:
> >
> > > x voted for Carter.

In both (29) and (30), the sequence *more than three* calls for a counting operation, whereas the word *not* calls for a negating operation (specifically, a reversing of truth-values of the sort described in section 15.1). In what follows, we will see that the relation between the two operations is not the same in the two cases. In particular, we will see that *not* is within the scope of *more than three* in (29), but that *more than three* is within the scope of *not* in (30).

In determining the truth-value of (29), we need to begin by sorting the voters into those that qualify to be counted and those that don't qualify. For each voter x, the requirement for qualification is that the following proposition be true:

(31) It is not the case that the following proposition is true: x voted for Carter.

The truth of this proposition in turn depends on the truth of the following simpler proposition:

(32) x voted for Carter.

If the simpler proposition is true, the negative one is false, and vice versa, as shown in (33).

(33) *x voted for Carter.*   *It is not the case that x voted for Carter.*
     true   false
     false   true

Let us see how this works out for two particular neighbors, Kathy and Warren. As our first step, we extract from (28) the following truth-values:

(34) a. Kathy voted for Carter.   (false)
     b. Warren voted for Carter. (true)

We then apply the reversal of truth-value called for by the word *not,* to determine the truth-values of the propositions in (35).

(35) a. It is not the case that the following proposition is true: Kathy voted for Carter.   (true)
     b. It is not the case that the following proposition is true: Warren voted for Carter.   (false)

The result is that Kathy qualifies for the upcoming counting operation, whereas Warren does not.

Going through the same procedure with each of the neighbors, we obtain the display in (36).

(36) *x*   *Truth-value of "It is not the case that the following proposition is true: x voted for Carter."*

     Kathy   true
     Gaylord   true
     Warren   false
     Pat   false
     Mae   true
     Gib   true
     Steve   false
     Kate   false
     George   true
     Alma   true

We are ready to carry out the *more than three* operation, which we begin by counting the number of occurrences of "true" in (36). Since the number of times we see "true" on this list is six, and since six is greater than three, the sentence as a whole comes out to be true. Here we have clearly used the computation called for by *not* in a subordinate role. In particular, we have used it in arriving at (36), the table that provided the basis for the counting operation. Thus, the operation called for by *not* served to prepare the way for the ultimate operation here, the counting operation called for by *more than three*. The definition in (26) allows us to describe this situation by saying that in (29) *not* has narrower scope than *more than three*, or that *more than three* has wider scope than *not*.

Let us return now to (30), which is repeated here as (37).

(37) Not more than three of our neighbors voted for Carter.

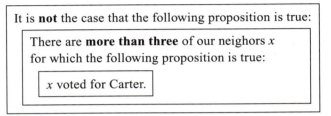

Here we see that the counting takes place on the table given earlier in (26), repeated as (38).

(38) x   *Truth-value of "x voted for Carter"*
       Kathy   false
       Gaylord   false
       Warren   true
       Pat   true
       Mae   false
       Gib   false
       Steve   true
       Kate   true
       George   false
       Alma   false

The number of times we see "true" on this list is four, a number that is greater than three. Thus, the value for the proposition contained in the middle box in (37) is "true." Finally, though, the truth-value determined by this counting operation is reversed by the *not* operation, giving a value of "false" for the entire proposition in (37). This is of course just the opposite of the truth-value that we obtained for (29). In this interpretive process, the scope relation between *not* and *more than three* has been just the reverse of what we saw in (29). The counting operation carried out here did not involve any preparatory use of the negation operation. Instead, the counting operation was an operation that itself had to be performed as a preparation for the negation operation. Thus, in the interpretation of (37), *not* had wider scope than *more than three*.

The following pair of sentences exhibits an exactly parallel difference in meaning:

(39) Calvin often doesn't call us.

> The following proposition is **often** true:
>> It is **not** the case that the following proposition is true:
>>> Calvin calls us.

(40) Calvin doesn't often call us.

> It is **not** the case that the following proposition is true:
>> It is **often** the case that the following proposition is true:
>>> Calvin calls us.

In (39), *often* uses the result of the *not* operation and thus has wider scope than *not*. In (40), by contrast, *not* uses the result of the *often* operation, and thus it is *not* that has wider scope here.

One final pair of examples, a rather surprising one, will prove useful when we try to fashion a coherent set of rules.

(41) Many of the members were not contacted by Carol.

> There are **many** of the members x
> such that the following proposition is true:
>> It is **not** the case that the following proposition is true:
>>> x was contacted by Carol.

(42) Carol did not contact many of the members.

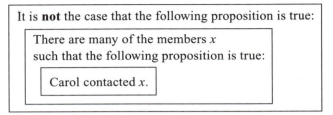

Although active sentences and their corresponding passives usually do not differ in their meanings, we can perceive a clear difference between (41) and (42). Again the critical difference is a difference of relative scope. In (41), wider scope is assigned to *many;* in (42), it is assigned to *not*.

Let us now look for a general rule that will correctly determine relative scope in specific examples. A helpful observation to make here is that in all three sentences in which some element had wider scope than *not,* these words occurred to the left of *not*.

(43) a. *More than three* of our neighbors did *not* vote for Carter.
 b. Calvin *often* does*n't* call us.
 c. *Many* of the members were *not* contacted by Carol.

By contrast, in the three sentences in which *not* had wider scope, it occurred to the left of these elements.

(44) a. *Not more than three* of our neighbors.
 b. Calvin does*n't often* call us.
 c. Carol did *not* contact *many* of the members.

With these examples in mind, then, let us tentatively adopt the following rule:

(45) *Left-to-Right Rule*
 In determining the relative scope of quantity words and negatives, assign scope on the basis of the left-to-right position in the sentence, starting with wider scope for whatever is found on the left.

The effects of this rule can be seen in the explanation that it provides for the active-passive pair mentioned earlier.

(46) a. *Many* of the members were *not* contacted by Carol.
       wide   narrow

b. Carol did *not* contact *many* of the members.
            wide   narrow

In each pair of examples considered in the last few paragraphs, the two negative sentences contained identical quantity words or frequency adverbs. It is now time to turn once again to pairs of sentences in which the quantity words are not the same, one being assertive and the other nonassertive. Two sentences related in this way are given in (47) and (48).

(47) William *sometimes* does*n't* answer his mail.

> It is **sometimes** the case that the following proposition is true:
>> It is **not** the case that the following proposition is true:
>>> William answers his mail.

(48) William does*n't ever* answer his mail.

> It is **not** the case that the following proposition is true:
>> It is **ever** the case that the following proposition is true:
>>> William answers his mail.

The major puzzle posed by this pair of sentences is what makes *sometimes* a good choice in (47) and *ever* a good choice in (48). Here we are really returning to the question of the essential difference between assertives like *sometimes* and nonassertives like *ever*. With this pair of examples in hand, we might hazard the following guess at a rule for nonassertives:

(49) *Nonassertive Rule*
    Nonassertive words are used in situations in which they fall within the scope of a negation, that is, situations in which they have narrower scope than some negative word.

This rule clearly accounts for why (47) and (48) both sound acceptable with their differing frequency adverbs. Beyond that, however, it explains why we cannot replace *sometimes* in (47) by *ever*, as in (50).

(50) *William *ever* does*n't* answer his mail.

The Left-to-Right Rule dictates that *ever* should be assigned wider scope than *n't;* however, this assignment violates the Nonassertive Rule, which requires that *ever* have narrower scope than some negation.

As a matter of fact, we now have an explanation for our earlier observation concerning the impossibility of having *not* as part of the verb phrase along with a nonassertive subject. The relevant sentences are repeated in (51).

(51) a. *Anyone isn't sleeping in my bed.
     b. *Any zebras can't fly.
     c. *Anything hasn't happened to Bertram's optimism.

The left-to-right order of words in these sentences dictates that the non-assertive words should have wider scope than the negatives, but this scope assignment violates the Nonassertive Rule. By contrast, no problems arise with the sentences in which the subject contains the corresponding negative word.

(52) a. No one is sleeping in my bed.
     b. No zebras can fly.
     c. Nothing has happened to Bertram's optimism.

These negative words are interpreted as if they were compounds of *not* plus the corresponding nonassertive.

(53) a. no one = 'not anyone'
     b. no = 'not any'
     c. nothing = 'not anything'

Applying the Left-to-Right Rule to sentence (52a), with *no one* broken up into 'not anyone', we get the following result:

(54) *Not   anyone* is sleeping in my bed.
     wide narrow

This scope assignment satisfies the Nonassertive Rule, which here requires that *anyone* fall within the scope of some negative word. In similar fashion, sentences (52b) and (52c) also satisfy both the Left-to-Right Rule and the Nonassertive Rule.

The combination of the Left-to-Right Rule and the Nonassertive Rule does not strictly forbid the appearance of nonassertives in subject position. We might expect them to appear in this position in any situation in which some negative element precedes the subject of the sentence. As a matter of fact, there are at least three such situations in English.

The first of these occurs when we build a phrasal question out of a negative special-purpose verb. The following question introduced by *why* provides a good example:

(55) Why have*n't any* books been returned?

Because of the inverted order of subject and special-purpose verb in this question, the Left-to-Right Rule assigns *n't* wider scope, which is just what is needed if the occurrence of *any* is to be permitted by the Nonassertive Rule. By contrast, the use of *any* would not be possible in an answer for this question, since here the Left-to-Right Rule would come in conflict with the Nonassertive Rule by assigning wide scope to *any*.

(56) *Any books have*n't* been returned because the library is closed.
        wide   narrow

The second situation in which nonassertives are possible in subject position arises in connection with a special construction that deserves attention in its own right. In this construction, a negative noun phrase or adverb appears at the beginning of a sentence, with a missing phrase left in its place. Associated with this sentence-initial negative phrase, we find the same kind of inversion of subject and special-purpose verb that occurs in direct questions. Here are three examples:

(57) a. *Nothing* have I taken _____ from any members of your family.
        (Compare: I have taken *nothing* from any members of your family.)
     b. *Never* has Ferguson _____ written a book that was as exciting as this new novel.
        (Compare: Ferguson has *never* written a book that was as exciting as this new novel.)
     c. *No more than once a year* does Joe come down from the mountain _____.
        (Compare: Joe comes down from the mountain *no more than once a year*.)

When we substitute nonassertives for the subjects in these sentences, the results are completely acceptable:

(58) a. *Nothing* has *anyone* taken _____ from any members of your family.

b. *Never* has *anyone* _____ written a book that was as exciting as
   this new novel.
c. *No more than once a year* does *anyone* come down from the
   mountain _____.

In each of these three sentences, the nonassertive subject is preceded by
the negative word in the sentence. Consequently, the Left-to-Right Rule
gives wide scope to the negative word and narrow scope to the nonassertive, which is just the scope assignment that the Nonassertive Rule requires. On the other hand, if we put the words into normal word order,
the occurrence of the nonassertives to the left of the negatives gives unacceptable results.

(59) a. *Anyone* has taken *nothing* from any members of your family.
     b. *Anyone* has *never* written a book that was as exciting as this
        new novel.
     c. *Anyone* comes down from the mountain *no more than once a
        year*.

The third situation in which nonassertives occur in subject position
arises in complex sentences such as the following:

(60) a. Karen does*n't* think [that *anyone* will find the ring].
     b. *Nobody* believes [that *anything* can be done].

In each of these sentences, the nonassertive word serving as the subject of
the lower clause falls within the scope of a negative word found in the
main clause.

15.4 NONASSERTIVES WITH OTHER NEGATIVE WORDS

Besides such obviously negative words as *not, no, never,* and *nobody,* there
are a number of words that have a negative-like interpretation, and for
this reason allow nonassertives within their scope. One group of these
words includes *hardly, scarcely, few, little, seldom,* and *rarely.* As the following sentences show, nonassertives behave with them just as they did
with the more obvious negatives:

(61) a. *Hardly any* of the citizens *ever* say *anything*.
     b. *Any* of the citizens *hardly ever* say *anything*.
     c. *Hardly ever* do *any* of the citizens say *anything*.

(62) a. *Few* of the citizens *ever* say *anything*.
     b. *Anything* is *ever* said by *few* of the citizens.

(63) a. *Little* time has he *ever* spent with his family.
    b. *He has *ever* spent *little* time with his family.

As before, the sentences that are acceptable in these examples are those in which every nonassertive falls within the scope of a negative word, with scope being determined strictly by the Left-to-Right Rule.

There is a second group of words whose essentially negative meanings license nonassertives within their scope. These are verbs and adjectives like DOUBT, DENY, INCONCEIVABLE, and UNLIKELY, which allow nonassertives in their object and subject clauses.

(64) a. We *doubt* [that *anyone* will ever say *anything*].
    b. Richard *denied* [that *anyone* had *ever* offered him *any* money].
    c. It is *inconceivable* [that *any* of the papers will *ever* be found].
    d. It is *unlikely* [that the Cubs will *ever* win *any* pennants].

Here it makes good sense to view the scope of these verbs and adjectives as being their clausal subjects and objects. Thus, the appearance of nonassertives in these new sentences falls under the Nonassertive Rule as originally stated.

One final implicitly negative word that licenses nonassertives within its scope is *without*.

(65) I worked in your building for a year [*without ever* hearing *any* complaints].

This sentence can be roughly paraphrased by one in which the negation is easier to see.

(66) I worked in your building for a year, and I did*n't ever* hear *any* complaints.

Exercises

1. Explain briefly why the second sentence is more acceptable than the first.
(i) *I think that anyone ever reads this magazine.
(ii) I doubt that anyone ever reads this magazine.

2. Explain why the second sentence is more acceptable than the first.
(i) *This book is ever given to few readers.
(ii) Few readers are ever given this book.

15.5   OTHER ENVIRONMENTS FOR NONASSERTIVES

There are three other special circumstances that allow nonassertives to be used. First, they are allowed in yes-no questions, both direct and indirect.

(67) a. Did *anyone ever* meet George?
     b. We are trying to determine [whether *anyone ever* met George].

Second, they are found in various conditional clauses, including those introduced by *if, whenever,* and so on.

(68) a. [*If any* of you *ever* see *any* flying saucers], you should report them to Freddy.
     b. [*Whenever anyone* sees *any* flying saucers], Freddy gets very excited.

Third, nonassertives show up regularly in the comparative construction.

(69) a. Jones walked farther [than *any* members of the club had *ever* walked before].
     b. Rachel made more saves [than *any* goalkeeper had *ever* made before].

Thus, the rule given in (49) for nonassertives needs to be extended to that given in (70).

(70) Nonassertive words may be used in yes-no questions, and may also be used within the scope of a negative word, a conditional word, or a comparative.

Exercise

1. For each of the italicized nonassertives below, say what it is that allows it in the sentence.
   a. If *any* of you did not get a questionnaire, Fred will send one to you.
   b. Whether *anyone* will read Joe's book will be decided tomorrow.
   c. John tried to leave the house without disturbing *any* of his neighbors.
   d. Few people believe that Joe's investigation will result in *any* indictments.
   e. Only once did Clara detect *any* sign of life.

15.6   EXCEPTIONS TO THE LEFT-TO-RIGHT RULE

In the past two sections, the Left-to-Right Rule has formed an important part of our explanation for the way nonassertives and negative words behave when they occur together. Despite its importance, this rule does have two major exceptions that need to be noted.

The first exception comes to light when we try to give a rule to regulate the behavior of assertive words like *someone* and *something*. Earlier in this chapter, we examined two sentences that contained assertives in company with negative words.

(71) a. *Some* of the guests did *not* sign the register.
     wide   narrow
   b. William *sometimes* does*n't* answer his mail.
        wide   narrow

We noted that these assertive words have wide scope in these sentences, a fact that would follow from the Left-to-Right Rule. All that we would need to say about the assertive words themselves would be that, unlike nonassertive words, they are capable of occurring outside the scope of a negation.

However, something more needs to be said, as the following examples show:

(72) a. John did*n't* eat *some* of his pie.
   b. Horace did*n't* speak to *some* of his friends.

These examples are at least marginally acceptable, and they call for interpretations in which *some* has wider scope than the negative.

(73) a. For *some* of his pie *x* the following proposition is true:
           it is *not* the case that the following proposition is true:
           John ate *x*.
   b. For *some* of his friends *x* the following proposition is true:
           it is *not* the case that the following proposition is true:
           Horace spoke to *x*.

Even though these interpretations violate the Left-to-Right Rule, they are the correct ones for the sentences in (72). These new examples thus suggest the existence of the following two rules:

(74) *Assertive Rule*
   Assertives are interpreted as having wider scope than negatives.

(75) The Left-to-Right Rule may be relaxed for assertive words.

Two other words that sometimes violate the Left-to-Right Rule are the universal words *all* and *every*. Unlike the assertives, these two words are perfectly capable of appearing within the scope of a negation, as in the following examples:

(76) a. Thelma did*n't* sell *all* of her books.
   b. It is *not* the case that the following proposition is true:
      for *all* of her books *x* the following proposition is true:
      Thelma sold *x*.

(77) a. George did*n't* write to *every* senator.
   b. It is *not* the case that the following proposition is true:
      for *every* senator *x* the following proposition is true:
      George wrote to *x*.

In these two examples, the scope relations are exactly those dictated by the Left-to-Right Rule.

   The problem comes with examples in which the universal precedes the negative. Such examples are quite rare in formal English but are not unusual in spoken English. Two are given in (78).

(78) a. *All* of the packages did*n't* arrive on time.
   b. *Everyone* did*n't* sign Connie's birthday card.

The Left-to-Right Rule would dictate the following interpretations for these sentences:

(79) a. For *all* of the packages *x* the following proposition is true:
      it is *not* the case that the following proposition is true:
      x arrived on time.
   b. For *every* person *x* the following proposition is true:
      it is *not* the case that the following proposition is true:
      x signed Connie's birthday card.

But these interpretations require the same states of affairs as those required by the sentences in (80).

(80) a. *None* of the packages arrived on time.
   b. *No one* signed Connie's birthday card.

These are not generally the interpretations intended when speakers of English use sentences like those in (78). Instead, the intended readings would be those in (81), which clearly violate the Left-to-Right Rule.

(81) a. It is *not* the case that the following proposition is true:
      for *all* of the packages *x* the following proposition is true:
      x arrived on time.

b. It is *not* the case that the following proposition is true:
for *every* person *x* the following proposition is true:
x signed Connie's birthday card.

To accommodate the examples in (78), then, we need to make note of another exception to the Left-to-Right Rule.

(82) The universal words *all* and *every* may fall within the scope of a negative word even when they occur to its left.

This possibility for *all* and *every* may be related to another odd fact about them. Although they are capable of standing by themselves without any negation in their environment, they do not like to be assigned wider scope than a negation in situations where a negation is present. *All* with wide scope plus *not* with narrow scope should mean exactly the same thing as *not* with wide scope plus *any* with narrow scope. But only the *not* + *any* combination is really acceptable in situations in which both should be possible. We see this contrast in acceptability in the following pair of sentences:

(83) a.   ?**All* historians do *not* revere Benedict Arnold.
b.   Benedict Arnold is *not* revered by *any* historians.

Exercise

1. The following two sentences might be used to describe exactly the same situation:

(i) Popeye didn't eat some of his spinach.

(ii) Popeye didn't eat all of his spinach.

At first glance, it might appear that these two sentences should not be equivalent in meaning, since *some* and *all* do not mean the same thing, and there is no other visible difference between the two sentences. Explain how it is possible for them to be equivalent.

Chapter 16

Conjunction and Ellipsis

In this chapter, we will study two special sets of English rules. Rules from the first set take two or more structures, characteristically of some single type, and link them together in a *conjoined structure* that is itself of the same type. Rules from the second set, two of which we have already encountered in our discussion of comparative clauses, spell out the conditions under which it is permissible to perform *ellipsis* operations, that is, to delete material presented earlier in the same sentence or earlier in the discourse. The two sets of rules are grouped together in this chapter primarily because conjoined structures provide excellent contexts in which to study various ellipsis rules. In addition, at least one important ellipsis rule applies only in one particular type of conjoined structure.

16.1 CONJOINED STRUCTURES

16.1.1 Basic Possibilities

Conjoined structures are formed with the help of the so-called *coordinating conjunctions* of traditional grammar. In English, these words are *and, or, nor,* and *but.* For our initial examples of conjoined structures, we will look at some in which the conjunction is *and.* These examples, which are given in (1), illustrate the variety of types of phrases that can be linked by a conjunction.

(1) a. I know that *Trudy is in Atlanta* and *Bob is in Houston.*
   (conjoined sentences)
   b. Smith *hit the ball* and *ran to first base.*
   (conjoined finite verb phrases)
   c. The baby seemed *very tired* and *somewhat cross.*
   (conjoined adjective phrases)

    d. *John* and *the man from Houston* share the same surname.
       (conjoined noun phrases)
    e. Fred seems to have been *tied up* and *left in the garage.*
       (conjoined passive phrases)
    f. We saw many *students of chemistry* and *doctors of medicine.*
       (conjoined common-noun phrases)

In each of these examples, not only are two phrases of the same type joined by *and,* but in addition the larger phrase so formed acts as if it is itself a phrase of the same type. For instance, in (1a), the entire structure made from two conjoined sentences combines with a preceding *that* to make a *that* clause. In (1b), two finite verb phrases are conjoined, and the larger structure so formed is doing something that a finite verb phrase can do, namely, serving as the predicate of an independent sentence. A similar point can be made about each of the remaining examples in (1). These observations are summed up in (2).

(2) If two phrases are of the same type, then they can be joined together by *and,* and the resulting unit is also a phrase of the same type.

Graphically, this preliminary rule gives structures of the form in (3), where *XP* is a symbol for a phrase of any type.

(3)   XP

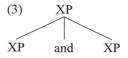

XP   and   XP

For (1a) and (1b), rule (2) gives the structures in (4).

(4) a. S

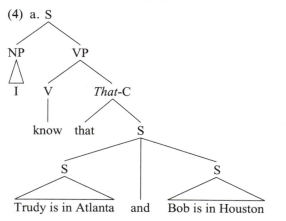

b.

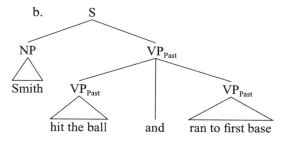

Now that we have a basic idea of how conjoined structures are built, let us look in more detail at the elements that can join their parts. We can see the possibilities by examining the ways in which two adjective phrases can be joined.

(5) a. Joseph is [tired of Houston *and* eager to move back to Topeka].
   b. Joseph is [*both* tired of Houston *and* eager to move back to Topeka].
   c. Joseph is [tired of Houston *or* eager to move back to Topeka].
   d. Joseph is [*either* tired of Houston *or* eager to move back to Topeka].
   e. Joseph is [*neither* tired of Houston *nor* eager to move back to Topeka].

The same kinds of examples can be constructed with other types of phrases. General pictures of the possibilities are given in (6).

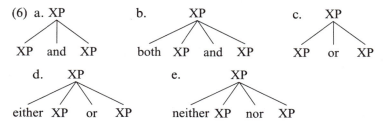

Each of these possibilities except for *both ... and* also works when more than two phrases are being joined.

(7) a.   Martha will [feed the cat *and* lock the door *and* turn off the lights].
   b.   *Martha will [*both* feed the cat *and* lock the door *and* turn off the lights].
   c.   Martha will [feed the cat *or* lock the door *or* turn off the lights].

d. Martha will [*either* feed the cat *or* lock the door *or* turn off the lights].

e. Martha will [*neither* feed the cat *nor* lock the door *nor* turn off the lights].

The failure of the *both* ... *and* combination in (7b) can be attributed to the fact that *both* needs exactly two entities wherever it is used.

The word *but* is another conjunction that resists joining more than two sequences.

(8) a. [Trudy is in Atlanta *but* Bob is in Houston].
   b. Smith [hit the ball *but* failed to get to first base].
   c. The baby seemed [quite energetic *but* somewhat cross].
   d. Richard saw [many shrikes *but* no falcons].

(9) a. *[Trudy is in Atlanta *but* Bob is in Houston *but* Angela is in Dallas].
   b. *Smith [hit the ball *but* failed to get to first base *but* kept on smiling].
   c. *The baby seemed [quite energetic *but* somewhat cross *but* rather cooperative].
   d. *Richard saw [many shrikes *but* no falcons *but* dozens of juncos].

The constraining factor here may be different from that involved with *both*. A semantic condition on the acceptability of *but* structures is that the second conjunct must represent a clear reversal of expectation, given the first. Two successive reversals of expectation may simply be hard for listeners to keep track of. In what follows, then, we will assume that the difference in acceptability between two *and*'s and two *but*'s is attributable to a difference in the semantic properties of the two words, rather than to any difference in their syntax.

16.1.2   Practical Strategies for Dealing with Conjoined Structures

We have just seen that a large variety of English structures can be joined by coordinating conjunctions. Nothing has been said, though, about how to solve the important analytical problem posed by every sentence that contains a conjunction: determining what the structures are that are joined.

Let us begin with a relatively simple example.

(10) Jane opened the door and walked into the library.

This sentence immediately gives us the following two hints:

(11) a. The left-hand structure, whatever it is, ends with *door*.
    b. The right-hand structure, whatever it is, begins with *walked*.

The "candidate structures" that these hints give us as possibilities for this sentence are listed in (12) and (13).

(12) Candidate structures in this sentence that end with *door:*

    door   (common noun)
    the door   (noun phrase)
    opened the door   (verb phrase)
    Jane opened the door   (sentence)

(13) Candidate structures in this sentence that begin with *walked:*

    walked   (verb)
    walked into the library   (verb phrase)

When we compare the two lists, we see that the only type of structure that appears on both lists is verb phrase. In this case, this gives us our answer immediately: the structures joined by *and* in (10) are just those bracketed in (14).

(14) Jane [$_{VP}$ opened the door] and [$_{VP}$ walked into the library].

    A second example where the same strategy suffices is given in (15).

(15) We thought that the car belonged to Peter and that the truck belonged to Beth.

For this example, the list of candidate structures that end with *Peter* appears to be formidably long.

(16) Candidate structures in this sentence that end with *Peter:*

    Peter   (noun phrase)
    to Peter   (*to* phrase)
    belonged to Peter   (verb phrase)
    the car belonged to Peter   (sentence)
    that the car belonged to Peter (*that* clause)
    thought that the car belonged to Peter (verb phrase)
    We thought that the car belonged to Peter (sentence)

Our task is made easy, though, by the fact that the list of candidate structures beginning with *that* has only one item on it.

(17) Candidate structure in this sentence that begins with *that:*

    that the truck belonged to Beth   (*that* clause)

The structures joined by *and* in (15) thus can only be those bracketed in (18).

(18) We thought [$_{That-C}$ that the car belonged to Peter] and [$_{That-C}$ that the truck belonged to Beth].

Sentence (19) requires us to refine our strategy.

(19) Ned hired Marcia and Alice hired Patrick.

Here the lists of candidate structures ending with *Marcia* and beginning with *Alice* are as follows:

(20) Candidate structures in this sentence that end with *Marcia:*

Marcia	(noun phrase)
hired Marcia	(finite verb phrase)
Ned hired Marcia	(sentence)

(21) Candidate structures in this sentence that begin with *Alice:*

Alice	(noun phrase)
Alice hired Patrick	(sentence)

These lists leave us with two distinct possibilities to consider:

(22) a. Ned hired [$_{NP}$ Marcia] and [$_{NP}$ Alice] hired Patrick.
     b. [$_S$ Ned hired Marcia] and [$_S$ Alice hired Patrick].

Let us now make use of a different type of hint that our analysis provides. If *and* is joining the noun phrases *Marcia* and *Alice,* then the result will itself be a larger noun phrase: *Marcia and Alice.* We can now ask whether the environment in which this sequence appears is one in which a noun phrase is really comfortable. In particular, if this is a noun-phrase environment, a simple noun phrase should work just as well. The experimental sentence in (23) shows that the bracketing in (22a) is not legitimate.

(23) *Ned hired [$_{NP}$ the women] hired Patrick.

Thus, we are led to reject (22a), and the structure in (22b) remains as the only viable possibility.

A final lesson is conveyed by the following sentence:

(24) I know John and the girls know Alice.

The two lists of candidate structures are given in (25) and (26).

(25) Candidate structures in this sentence that end with *John:*

John	(noun phrase)
know John	(finite verb phrase)
I know John	(sentence)

(26) Candidate structures in this sentence that begin with *the girls:*

the girls	(noun phrase)
the girls know Alice	(sentence)

Here again, we have two distinct possibilities to consider.

(27) a. [$_S$ I know John] and [$_S$ the girls know Alice].

b. I know [$_{NP}$ John] and [$_{NP}$ the girls] know Alice.

The structure in (27a) is clearly viable: both of the bracketed sequences are legitimate sentences. Can we conclude from this that the structure in (27b) is to be discarded? Let us perform a test similar to that performed in connection with (22a), to determine whether the conjoined noun-phrase structure as a whole is in a position in this sentence where a simple noun phrase would work.

(28) I know [$_{NP}$ those people] know Alice.

The answer is positive: sentence (28) contains a finite clause with omitted *that* serving as a complement to the verb *know.* Consequently, we are led to conclude that (27b) is a legitimate structure for (24). In the present situation, this is a correct conclusion, since we in fact perceive sentence (24) as having such an interpretation. The larger lesson here is simply that there are genuinely ambiguous conjoined structures in which it is actually desirable to have strategies that give indeterminate results.

Exercises

1. In each of the following sentences, two sequences are joined to make a larger sequence of the same type. First decide what types of sequences are conjoined, and then draw a tree diagram for the sentence as a whole.

    a. Gary is scrubbing the floors and repainting the woodwork.

    b. Charles thinks that the king of England and his friends should write a book.

    c. Bob wants Tony to keep the sweaters but return the books.

    d. Martha has put chairs on the lawn and on the patio.

    e. Neither Bruce nor his colleagues know how to restring a racket.

2. At first glance, it would appear that the following two sentences have virtually the same structure, differing only by the presence in the first of the word *that:*

    a. Jones knows that Blake fries hamburgers and that Ali peels potatoes.

    b. Jones knows that Blake fries hamburgers and Ali peels potatoes.

A closer examination shows that the sequences that are joined in (a) are not of the same type as those that are joined in (b). Draw tree diagrams for the two sentences that make the difference clear.

3. Draw a tree diagram for each of the following superficially similar sentences:

    a. I watched Warren and Bill talked to Barbara.

    b. I watched Warren and Bill talk to Barbara.

4. Draw a tree diagram for each of the following two sentences:

    a. I saw Warren and Bill went into the garage.

    b. I saw Warren and Bill taken into the garage.

State which structure(s) you think is/are appropriate for the following additional sentence:

    c. I saw Warren and Bill moved into the garage.

Note: In answering this question, leave out of consideration structures for (a) and (c) in which *saw* takes a finite clause with omitted *that*.

5. The following sentence occurred in a newspaper op-ed column by a well-known American writer:

    "We do not kill young people who oppose their parents or kill adulterers."
    (James Michener, "God Is Not a Homophobe," *New York Times,* March 30,
    1993)

Explain in your own words what the two quite differing interpretations of this sentence are. Then draw the two distinct tree structures that the rules of English dictate for it.

6. Think of one or more sentences that show whether a past-tense verb phrase and a present-tense verb phrase count as "phrases of the same type" for the purposes of being conjoined. Then look for sentences that will answer the same question about bare-stem verb phrases and present-participial verb phrases after the verb SEE.

7. The following quotation appeared in a newspaper story concerning a murder trial in Dallas, Texas:

    "The prosecution and defense attorneys, who called no witnesses, rested their
    cases after Wilson's testimony." (Pauline Arrillaga, "Woman Admits to
    Murder-for-Hire Scheme," *Austin American-Statesman,* August 17, 1994)

At least one reader initially took this sentence to mean that a criminal trial had been held in which neither the prosecution nor the defense called any witnesses, quite an odd occurrence by the usual standards of Texas trial law. When he reread the sentence, it dawned on him that this was not what the reporter had meant to imply. Explain this reader's confusion by giving the two possible structures that the rules of English allow for this sentence. It may be helpful to review the discussion of nonrestrictive relative clauses in section 10.5.

16.1.3   An Alternative Analysis of Conjoined Phrases

At this point, it might seem that a simpler analysis of conjoined structures is possible: one in which we conjoin sentences and then optionally reduce them by keeping just one copy of the material that is the same in both conjuncts. For example, we would derive (29a) from (29b) by keeping just one copy of the two identical subjects and sharing it between the two conjoined verb phrases.

(29) a. Martha [fed the cat *and* locked the door].
    b. [Martha fed the cat *and* Martha locked the door].

In the same way, we would derive (30a) from (30b) by coalescing the two identical verb phrases into one.

(30) a. [Gordon *and* Shirley] missed the meeting.
    b. [Gordon missed the meeting *and* Shirley missed the meeting].

In each of the two cases given above, this analysis has the apparent virtue of deriving one sentence from a longer sentence that has exactly the same interpretation. Unfortunately, however, there are many instances in which deriving conjoined phrases in this way would require a source sentence whose meaning was quite different.

As a first example, sentence (31a) would have to be derived from (31b).

(31) a. Few people belong to the Assembly of God and drink bourbon.
    b. Few people belong to the Assembly of God and few people drink bourbon.

A moment's reflection reveals that these two sentences do not mean the same thing at all. In (31a), the claim is made that there are few people who belong to the Assembly of God and at the same time drink bourbon. By contrast, (31b) claims that there are few people who belong to the Assembly of God and also that there are few people (not necessarily the same few people) who drink bourbon. We might represent these two different meanings as in (32).

(32) a. There are *few* people x such that the following proposition is true:
        (i) is true *and* (ii) is true:
          (i) x belongs to the Assembly of God
          (ii) x drinks bourbon

    b. (i) is true *and* (ii) is true:

       (i) there are *few* people x such that the following proposition is true:

          x belongs to the Assembly of God

       (ii) there are *few* people y such that following proposition is true:

          y drinks bourbon

As these representations suggest, the difference in meaning between (31a) and (31b) is just a difference in scope, of the same general sort as the scope differences that we studied in chapter 15. This scope difference is easier to account for if our rules create conjoined verb phrases as such in their own right, rather than deriving them from conjoined sentences.

A problem of a different sort arises with conjoined subjects. Though it might not seem implausible to derive the conjoined noun phrase in (33a) from the conjoined sentence in (33b), a similar derivation is much less plausible for the conjoined noun phrase in (34a) and (35a).

(33) a. [Gordon *and* Shirley] missed the meeting.
    b. [Gordon missed the meeting *and* Shirley missed the meeting].

(34) a. [Joe *and* Billy] wear the same hat size.
    b. ?[Joe wears the same hat size *and* Billy wears the same hat size].

(35) a. [Charles *and* Marie] embraced.
    b. ?[Charles embraced *and* Marie embraced].

The last two predicates seem to be able to use conjoined subjects (in fact, plural subjects in general) in a way that treats them as a group rather than as separate individuals. Because of the existence of such predicates, we need to be able to create conjoined noun phrases directly, without deriving them from conjoined sentences. This is just what we did in our earlier analysis.

The two bodies of evidence considered above provide arguments for maintaining the analysis with which we began this discussion rather than going to an alternative in which conjoined phrases are derived by way of conjoined sentences. For the remainder of this chapter, we will adhere to the original analysis and view conjoined phrases as just that.

16.1.4 Conjoined Sequences of Phrases

In addition to joining words or phrases with conjunctions, we may also join *sequences* of phrases. Three examples are given in (36).

(36) a. Martha went [to Austin] [on Thursday] *and* [to Dallas] [on Friday].
  b. We gave [doughnuts] [to Angela] *and* [cookies] [to Fred].
  c. Joe sent letters [to Greta] [yesterday] *and* [to Martha] [today].

In (36a), the sequence *to Austin on Thursday* is clearly not a single phrase, but instead is a sequence consisting of two phrases: a motion phrase followed by a time phrase. Likewise, *to Dallas on Friday* must be analyzed as a sequence of two separate phrases rather than as a single phrase. A similar assessment holds for the two sequences *doughnuts to Angela* and *cookies to Fred* in (36b), and also for the two sequences *to Greta yesterday* and *to Martha today* in (36c).

For sentences of this sort, it is very difficult to suggest appropriate tree structures. We can get an idea of the problem involved by looking first at two plausible structures for the first conjunct in (36a), namely, the ones in (37).

(37)

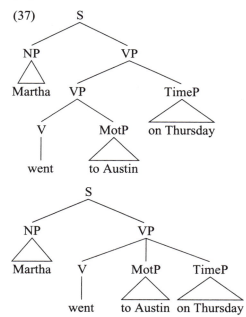

We can then consider the tree in (38) as a representation of the entire conjoined structure.

(38)

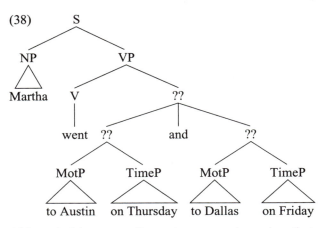

Although this tree conforms to our previous view that a conjunction such as *and* should join two phrases, the phrases in question are themselves suspect. The reason is that in neither of the simple-sentence trees given in (37) do the motion phrase and the time phrase make up a larger phrase. Thus, the conjoined structure in (38) is not consistent with either of the simple-sentence structures in (37).

In sum, although the existence of sentences such as those in (36) needs to be acknowledged, there is currently no completely satisfactory account of these sentences within the general framework adopted in this book.

16.1.5   A Special Possibility for Conjoined Structures

A final kind of conjoined construction can be built from two conjoined sentences or phrases that end in an identical phrase on the right. Two such structures are shown in (39), with the shared phrase in each conjunct italicized.

(39) a. [[John likes *the night watchman*], but [Bill doesn't like *the night watchman*]].

   b. Bob [[is married to *the Secretary of Transportation*], but [rarely eats lunch with *the Secretary of Transportation*]].

To such structures, we can apply *Right Extraction,* a rule that deletes the shared final phrase in its normal position in each conjunct and attaches a copy to the right end of the conjoined structure.

(40) a. [[John likes ____], but [Bill doesn't like ____]], *the night watchman.*

   b. Bob [[is married to ____], but [rarely eats lunch with ____]], *the*
      Secretary of Transportation.

As the above examples show, a special comma punctuation is used after
each of the two conjoined nonidentical parts. These commas correspond
to special intonation breaks in the spoken sentences.

   For sentences like these, we will assume the sorts of structures shown in
(41).

(41) a.

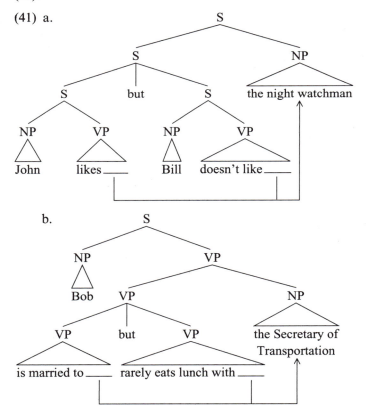

Exercise

1. Draw a tree structure for each of the following sentences:
   a. John taught Bill, and would probably be willing to teach you, how to re-
      build a carburetor.
   b. Marcia looked at, and Marvin thinks that her sister may want to look at,
      the note that Greta left on the refrigerator.

16.1.6   A Closer Look at Alternative Questions

In chapters 4 and 14, we had occasion to study a type of question closely related to yes-no questions. The indirect variety is exemplified by (42a), and the direct variety, by (42b).

(42) a. We want to know [whether John sued Karen or Karen sued John].
     b. Did John sue Karen or did Karen sue John?

We are now in a position to consider these constructions in more detail.

Let us begin with the indirect question in (42a). We know that English has yes-no indirect questions beginning with *whether*. To such questions, exemplified in (43a), we assigned the structure in (43b).

(43) a. [whether Martha is leaving]
     b.

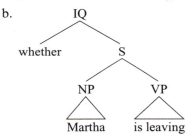

Suppose we also try to treat the indirect question in (42a) by the rule that analyzes it into *whether* and a following sentence. This step is possible now because we have made provisions for conjoined structures. The structure that we would derive is shown in (44).

(44)

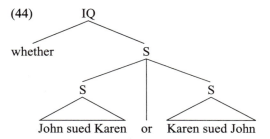

Now we might ask whether alternative questions are possible in which sequences other than full sentences are joined. As (45)–(47) show, they definitely are.

(45) a. We want to know [whether you tried to hire [Martha or Harry]].
   b. Did you try to hire [Martha or Harry]?
   c. Sample answer: I tried to hire *Martha*.

(46) a. Please tell us [whether you consider him [reticent or arrogant]].
   b. Do you consider him [reticent or arrogant]?
   c. Sample answer: I consider him *arrogant*.

(47) a. George didn't say [whether he wanted Bill to [wash the windows first or sweep the floors first]].
   b. Did George want Bill to [wash the windows first or sweep the floors first]?
   c. Sample answer: George wanted Bill to *sweep the floors first*.

The general relation between question and alternatives can be seen with the help of diagram (48a) and the specific instance of it given in (48b).

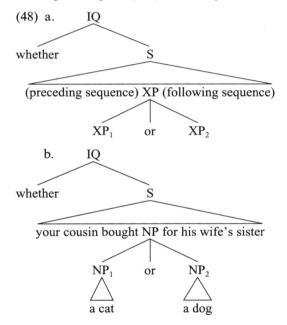

Here *whether* is joined to a sentence that contains two smaller phrases joined by *or*. We can calculate the two alternatives just by leaving everything else in the sentence the same, and replacing the conjoined phrase first by one of the smaller phrases, and then by the other. The resulting alternatives for the general case are shown in (49a), those for the specific example in (49b).

(49) a. (preceding sequence) XP$_1$ (following sequence)
     (preceding sequence) XP$_2$ (following sequence)

   b. your cousin bought [$_{NP}$ a cat] for his wife's sister
      your cousin bought [$_{NP}$ a dog] for his wife's sister

Surprisingly enough, every one of the above *whether* questions has an additional interpretation in written English. Let us look again at the indirect question in (42a), which is repeated here as (50).

(50) [whether John sued Karen or Karen sued John]

The interpretation that we have been assuming all along is one in which the question offers two alternative answers. However, it is also possible to interpret this as an indirect yes-no question. After all, sentence (51) is one that could be either true or false.

(51) John sued Karen or Karen sued John.

On this interpretation, the question would have a positive answer if one or the other of the two sentences that made it up was true, and a negative answer if neither was true.

We get the same type of additional interpretation for (52).

(52) [whether you tried to hire Martha or Harry]

On this second interpretation, this question has a positive answer if the conjoined sentence (53) is true, and a negative answer otherwise.

(53) You tried to hire Martha or Harry.

In spoken English, this ambiguity disappears, by virtue of a sharp difference in intonation patterns. When we intend (52) as an alternative question, we put a sharply rising intonation at the end of the first conjunct.

(54) [whether you tried to hire Martha or Harry]

By contrast, when we intend the same sequence of words as an indirect yes-no question, then the intonation is much flatter prior to the final fall at the end.

(55) [whether you tried to hire Martha or Harry]

One more fact about alternative questions, mentioned briefly in chapter 14, is that it is perfectly possible to give more than two alternatives.

(56) a. We want to know [whether you tried to hire [Martha or Harry or Katy]].
b. Please tell us [whether you consider him [reticent or arrogant or indifferent]].
c. George didn't say [whether he wanted Bill to [wash the windows first or sweep the floors first or put away the chairs first]].

All of these, of course, have corresponding direct questions.

(57) a. Did you try to hire [Martha or Harry or Katy]?
b. Do you consider him [reticent or arrogant or indifferent]?
c. Did he want Bill to [wash the windows first or sweep the floors first or put away the chairs first]?

Exercises

1. Draw a tree diagram for each of the following sentences, on the interpretation where the indirect questions are alternative questions rather than yes-no questions:

a. Horace wants to know whether you expect to leave today or to stay until tomorrow.
b. Whether the voters elect John or Bill, we still will not know whether your party or my party controls the future.

2. Devise an example sentence to show that the treatment of alternative questions in the text needs to be expanded to allow the alternatives to be defined by the conjunction of *sequences* of phrases as well as by the conjunction of single phrases. Review subsection 16.1.4 if necessary.

16.2   ELLIPSIS RULES

We now turn to an important class of syntactic rules that allow us to delete something that is identical to something else in the sentence or discourse. Such rules are generally called *ellipsis rules*. English has several important rules of this type. One of these rules, the first that we will discuss, applies only in conjoined sentences, whereas the other rules apply in a much wider variety of circumstances.

16.2.1   A Special Ellipsis Rule for Conjoined Sentences

The rule that applies specifically to conjoined structures has the effect of removing an identical middle part from sentences after the first in a series of conjoined sentences. Examples are given in (58) and (59).

(58) a. I *work* in a factory and Sam *works* in an office.
     b. I *work* in a factory and Sam, in an office.

(59) a. Pete *must eat* meat, and Fred *must eat* bread.
     b. Pete *must eat* meat, and Fred, bread.

We will refer to this as the *Gapping Rule,* and we can state it as follows:

(60) When two or more sentences are joined by conjunctions, and they are identical except for their subjects and a phrase at the end of the verb phrase, then the identical material can be optionally removed in all of the sentences after the first.

This rule can apply only when we have conjoined *sentences.* As the following pair of examples shows, there is even a contrast here between conjoined sentences and conjoined *that* clauses.

(61) a. Joe knows that [I *work* in a factory] and [Sam, in an office].
     b. *Joe knows [that I *work* in a factory] and [that Sam, in an office].

In addition, the sentences to which this rule applies must be directly joined by *and.* That is, the rule cannot apply if either affected sentence occurs merely as a subordinate part of a conjoined sentence:

(62) a. [Pete likes meat], and I can guarantee that [Fred likes bread].
     b. *[Pete likes meat], and I can guarantee that [Fred, bread].

(63) a. We had originally been told that [Sam nominated Pam], and we were later informed that [Willis nominated Phyllis].
     b. *We had originally been told that [Sam nominated Pam], and we were later informed that [Willis, Phyllis].

As a final note, we observe that the Gapping Rule is impossible with words referred to in traditional grammar as "subordinating conjunctions."

(64) a. Sam called Pam because Willis called Phyllis.
     b. *Sam called Pam because Willis, Phyllis.

This kind of unacceptable sentence provides us with one of many arguments for refusing to group these subordinating words into a single class with the coordinating words *and, but, or,* and *nor.*

16.2.2 Long-Distance Ellipsis Rules

We turn now to a group of ellipsis rules that are much freer in their application. Although they can apply readily between conjoined sentences, they can also apply in a variety of other circumstances. As one special case, they can apply between sentences uttered by two different speakers in a discourse. The formal property that unites them is that each specifies one or more left-hand contexts allowing deletion to take place.

16.2.2.1 Ellipsis after "Small Verbs," *To*, and *Not*   The first such long-distance ellipsis rule, one that is very similar to the first of the two ellipsis rules for comparatives discussed in chapter 12, allows for the deletion of the parenthesized material in the following sentences:

(65) a. John appears to be *fond of ice cream*, but I'm not sure that he really is (*fond of ice cream*).
    b. We thought that Fred would be *working hard on the project*, but it turns out that he hasn't been (*working hard on the project*).
    c. Whenever Martha has *drunk a beer*, Fred has (*drunk a beer*), too.
    d. Carter said that he wouldn't *sign the bill*, but I bet that he will (*sign the bill*).
    e. Barbara once thought that George would soon be *the richest man in Texas*, but now it's doubtful that he ever will be (*the richest man in Texas*).

In each of these examples, forms of BE, perfect HAVE, and the modals (what we might refer to as "small verbs") serve as the left-hand contexts for the deleted material. Another set of small verbs that permit this kind of ellipsis is composed of the finite forms of the special-purpose verb DO.

(66) a. Mabel *speaks French*, and Jerry *speaks French*, too.
    b. Mabel *speaks French*, and Jerry does (*speak French*), too.

(67) a. Hal *perused the article*, and Nat *perused the article*, too.
    b. Hal *perused the article*, and Nat did (*peruse the article*), too.

We can see how important these left-hand contexts are if we try to delete the same types of phrases when the left-hand contexts are not the same. Some illustrative unacceptable results are given in (68)–(71).

(68) a. John seems *fond of ice cream*, and Bill seems *fond of ice cream*, too.

b. *John seems *fond of ice cream*, and Bill seems ____, too. (deleted adjective phrase)

(69) a. Frank wanted Bill to *mow the lawn*, so we had him *mow the lawn*.

b. *Frank wanted Bill to *mow the lawn*, so we had him ____. (deleted bare-stem verb phrase)

(70) a. Beth believes that Fido should *go on a diet*, and we want to insist that the cat *go on a diet*, too.

b. *Beth believes that Fido should *go on a diet*, and we want to insist that the cat ____, too.   (deleted bare-stem verb phrase)

(71) a. Barbara once thought that George would soon become *the richest man in Texas*, but now it's doubtful that he will ever become *the richest man in Texas*.

b. *Barbara once thought that George would soon become *the richest man in Texas*, but now it's doubtful that he will ever become ____.   (deleted predicate noun phrase)

A similar kind of ellipsis is possible after the infinitive marker *to*, and also after an occurrence of *not* that accompanies a special-purpose verb.

(72) a. I'm not positive that John *knows the answer*, but he certainly seems to (*know the answer*).

b. If you ask Martha to *add your name*, I'm sure that she'll be glad to (*add your name*).

(73) a. James is *conscientious*, but Billy is not (*conscientious*).

b. Sandra will *read your reports*, but Harold will not (*read your reports*).

The above observations are summarized in the following rule, which mentions specific neighboring elements:

(74) Optionally delete the second of two identical phrases if the second comes after one of the following elements:

- BE
- perfect HAVE
- modals
- special-purpose DO
- the infinitive marker *to*
- a *not* associated with one of the verbs listed above

As was noted above, this particular rule is a "long-distance" ellipsis rule. The sentences in (75) show that the second occurrence of the phrase can be quite far away from the first.

(75) a. We were originally told that Sam had *nominated Pam,* but we were later informed that Willis had *nominated Pam.*
  b. We were originally told that Sam had *nominated Pam,* but we were later informed that Willis had ____.

As a matter of fact, this pair of sentences is in all other respects very close in form to the pair given in (63), which is repeated here as (76).

(76) a. We had originally been told that [Sam nominated Pam], and we were later informed that [Willis nominated Phyllis].
  b. *We had originally been told that [Sam nominated Pam], and we were later informed that [Willis, Phyllis].

The contrast between sentences (75b) and (76b) provides a striking illustration of the much wider permissibility of ellipsis after a small verb, as compared to the Gapping Rule studied in subsection 16.2.1.

An application of ellipsis after small verbs can actually occur not only within a single sentence but also between two separate sentences uttered by different speakers.

(77) Speaker A: I'm not sure that Sheila has *read the poem.*
  Speaker B: It's clear that Martha has ____, though.

One specific question deserves an answer before this subsection is concluded: what reason is there for thinking that ellipsis after small verbs and the first ellipsis rule studied in the discussion of comparatives are distinct rules? The basic evidence for thinking that they are not quite the same is that leaving behing a contrasted phrase seems fully acceptable only with comparatives. For example, ellipsis seems clearly acceptable in the comparative sentence in (78b), but less acceptable in the noncomparative sentence in (79b).

(78) a. Max has *called* you more often than he has *called* his brother.
  b. Max has *called* you more often than he has ____ his brother.

(79) a. Max has *called* you, and he has *called* his brother, too.
  b. ?Max has *called* you, and he has ____ his brother, too.

16.2.2.2 A Special Construction Involving Ellipsis after Special Purpose Verbs English allows a special elliptical construction that we can treat as an optional variant of the one just considered. Each of the (a) sentences in (80)–(83) shows an ordinary ellipsis after a small verb; the (b) sentences show the special new construction.

(80) a. David knows how much money was taken, and Bill does ____, too.
   b. David knows how much money was taken, and *so does Bill.*

(81) Speaker A: Karen has exceeded the speed limit.

Speaker B: { a. Bill has ____, too. }
              { b. *So has Bill.* }

(82) a. James didn't erase the blackboard, and Bob didn't ____, either.
   b. James didn't erase the blackboard, and *neither did Bob.*

(83) Speaker A: Nora won't remember the password.

Speaker B: { a. George won't ____, either. }
              { b. *Neither will George.* }

This new construction is described in terms of the old one in the following rule:

(84) a. If a sentence has the structure
      NP—special-purpose verb—*too,*
      then optionally substitute for it
      so—special-purpose verb—NP.
   b. If a sentence has the structure
      NP—special-purpose verb + *n't*—*either,*
      then optionally substitute for it
      neither—special-purpose verb—NP.

One extra restriction needs to be put on this rule, as we can see by comparing the acceptable (b) examples in (80)–(83) with the unacceptable ones in (85) and (86).

(85) a. David knows how much money was taken, and I think that Bill does ____, too.
   b. *David knows how much money was taken, and I think that *so does Bill.*

(86) a. George doesn't read Latin, and I am convinced that Joan doesn't ____, either.
   b. *George doesn't read Latin, and I am convinced that *neither does Joan.*

The restriction that we see here is one that limits the special *so* and *either* construction to independent sentences, or to independent sentences joined by conjunctions. What is specifically impossible is the use of this construction in complements and other subordinate clauses.

16.2.2.3 Ellipsis after Questioned Phrases Another important ellipsis rule of English allows for the deletion of repeated material after a questioned phrase. This kind of ellipsis is found in direct questions.

(87) a. Speaker A: Someone is coming.
         Speaker B: *Who* (is coming)?
    b. Speaker A: John moved to Massachusetts.

        Speaker B: $\left\{\begin{array}{l} \textit{When} \\ \textit{Why} \\ \textit{How long ago} \end{array}\right\}$ (did he move to Massachusetts)?

The same kind of ellipsis is also found in indirect questions.

(88) a. Someone is coming, but I don't know *who* (is coming).
    b. We know that John moved to Massachusetts, but we haven't

        been able to determine $\left\{\begin{array}{l} \textit{when} \\ \textit{why} \\ \textit{how long ago} \end{array}\right\}$ (he moved to

        Massachusetts).

A rule for this kind of ellipsis is stated in (89):

(89) Optionally delete the part of the question that follows the questioned phrase, if there is a sentence earlier in the discourse that duplicates the meaning of this second part of the question.

We might wonder here whether this kind of ellipsis occurs only in questions, as rule (89) implies, or whether it applies generally in constructions introduced by *wh* phrases. The contrast shown in (90) and (91) between an indirect question and an identical definite free relative provides clear evidence that the former view is correct.

(90) a. John cooked something, but Betty didn't know [what John cooked]. (indirect question)
    b. John cooked something, but Betty didn't know [what ___].

(91) a. John cooked something, but Betty didn't eat [what John cooked]. (definite free relative clause)
    b. *John cooked something, but Betty didn't eat [what ___].

16.2.2.4   Ellipsis in Noun Phrases   A third kind of long-distance ellipsis in English involves deletions that occur after one of a specified list of elements that are found in noun phrases. This type of deletion is exemplified in (92).

(92) a.   Jack has two pictures of Rockefeller Center, and Agatha has three (pictures of Rockefeller Center).

　　b.   Many animals were saved, but many (animals) were lost.

　　c.   Naturalists have spent many years searching for ivory-billed woodpeckers, but only a few (ivory-billed woodpeckers) have been sighted.

　　d.   John's house is old, but Martha's (house) is new.

As is the case with these examples, the deleted material generally makes up a common-noun phrase. The left-hand elements that permit the deletion include numerals, quantity words like *some, many,* and *few,* and genitive forms like *John's* and *Martha's*.

For genitives that are related to pronouns rather than to full noun phrases, we see the same kind of distinction that we observed in chapter 10. The following examples show the differences:

(93) a.   Karen read Bill's paper, and Bill read *my* paper (*mine* ＿＿＿).

　　b.   Nora fed her dog, and Danny fed *your* dog (*yours* ＿＿＿).

In order to account for the elliptical versions of the above sentences, we need to require that what we earlier called the *strong genitive* be used as the left-hand context for an ellipsis of this kind.

Exercises

1. In each of the following sentences, the first has undergone none of the ellipsis rules studied in this section; the second has undergone one or more of these rules. In each case, identify the rule(s) responsible for the difference between the two sentences.

　　a. i.   Miriam has planted three trees in the front yard and two trees behind the garage.

　　　ii.   Miriam has planted three trees in the front yard and two behind the garage.

　　b. i.   Josie will get to the finish line before Fred gets to the finish line.

　　　ii.   Josie will get to the finish line before Fred does.

　　c. i.   Gary knows that someone is trying to reach him, and he will find out who is trying to reach him, if you ask him to find out who is trying to reach him.

      ii. Gary knows that someone is trying to reach him, and he will find out who, if you ask him to.

  d. i. Ten people would like to attend the reception, but only three people will be able to attend the reception.

      ii. Ten people would like to attend the reception, but only three will be able to.

2. For each of the following sentences, answer three questions:

A. What types of structures are conjoined? Are they single structures or sequences of phrases?

B. Has Right Extraction (described in subsection 16.1.4) applied?

C. Which, if any, ellipsis rules have applied?

For any case where you believe that the sentence shows the effects of Right Extraction or ellipsis, say what the full sentence would have been if no such processes had taken place. The first is done as an example.

a. John should clean the shed, and Peter, mow the lawn.
Answer:
Conjoined sentences.
Right Extraction has not applied.
Gapping has applied.
If Gapping has not applied, the sentence would have been
  John should clean the shed, and Peter should mow the lawn.

b. I wanted to see your parents last week, but didn't get to.

c. George will, and Ruth might, take your course on dolphins.

d. They are able to make a contribution, but probably won't.

e. Adam could have been, but wasn't, watching his favorite program.

f. Brenda was the winner in 1971 and Robert in 1972.

g. Jack was given a railway set, and Jimmy, a baby giraffe.

h. It's cold in January in England but in July in New Zealand.

i. The suggestion made Alice angry and Marcia happy.

j. We discovered that Mike had been playing football and Becky, writing a letter.

k. Alec told us that he had discovered something interesting, but never told us what.

l. Several of Edward's jokes are as long as yours and as stale as Gordon's.

m. The indirect variety is exemplified by (42a), and the direct variety, by (42b).

Chapter 17

Time Relations and Aspect

In this chapter, we turn our attention to two additional sets of semantic rules for English. The first set plays a role in determining *temporal interpretations* of English sentences. The temporal interpretation of the sentence provides information about how the time of each state or events mentioned in the sentence is related to other times. The rules in the second group are concerned with what has traditionally been called *aspect*. Aspectual rules determine the answers to such questions as whether a certain event happened just once or is repeated regularly, or whether a certain activity is to be viewed as completed at a certain time or as still going on. These two sets of rules are intimately related, in that we sometimes need to know the temporal interpretation of a given sentence before we can make a correct aspectual determination.

17.1 TIME RELATIONS

17.1.1 Temporal Interpretations of Simple Sentences

We can begin our study of time relations in English by looking at the relations that are expressed in simple sentences. At the beginning, what will be said will have the air of being so familiar that it hardly needs to be said at all. But in order to be prepared to understand more complex and interesting cases, we will need to examine some familiar examples in a clear light.

17.1.1.1 Temporal Relations Assigned by Individual Elements

Imagine that we hear the following sentences:

(1) a. Joseph was happy.
    b. Joseph is happy.
    c. Joseph will be happy.

Each of these sentences reports a state of being happy. When asked to consider each sentence in turn and say when the reported state was in effect, we might say that it was in effect in the past in (1a), in the present in (1b), and in the future in (1c). If we are pressed to say in more detail what we mean by these three familiar terms, we might begin by saying that all of them are understood with respect to the moment when the sentences are uttered. In what follows, we will refer to this basic point in time as *utterance time*. In (1a), the time of Joseph's being happy is earlier than utterance time; in (1b), it is identical with utterance time; and in (1c), it is later than utterance time. These relations are pictured (2), where *Past* refers to past-tense inflection (in this case, the past-tense inflection in *was*) and *Present* refers to present-tense inflection (in this case, the present-tense inflection in *is*).

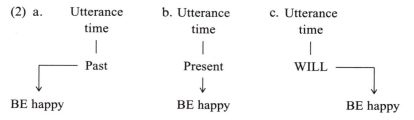

With examples like these in mind, we can give initial versions of general rules for interpreting past-tense inflection, present-tense inflection, and the modal *will*. Each of these rules will be an instruction concerning the way in which the time of an associated verb phrase is determined, and each of them will be accompanied by a diagram that expresses the rule in picture form. For past-tense inflection and present-tense inflection, the "associated verb phrase" is just the verb phrase whose head contains the inflection. For WILL, the "associated verb phrase" is the verb phrase that serves as a complement of WILL. The rules are stated in (3)–(5).

(3) Past-tense inflection can be interpreted as indicating that the time of the associated verb phrase is *earlier*.

```
       ┌──────── Past
       │
       ↓
```

(4) Present-tense inflection can be interpreted as indicating that the time of the associated verb phrase is *identical*.

Present

↓

(5) The modal WILL can be interpreted as indicating that the time of the associated verb phrase is *later*.

WILL ⎯⎯⎯⎯⎤
         ↓

In addition to these three basic linguistic elements, there are a number of other expressions that are interpreted as indicating a temporal relation. To begin with, the special verb USED takes complement infinitival phrases that express states or habitual actions, and assigns to them an earlier time.

(6) a. John *used to* understand the problem.
     b. Carol *used to* hang wallpaper.

(7) USED assigns to the associated infinitival phrase an *earlier* time.

⎡⎯⎯⎯ USED
↓

Another important temporal element is BE GOING, which clearly gives us an extra way of assigning a time later than utterance time.

(8) a. John *is going to* leave for Europe tomorrow.
     b. The weather *is going to* improve tomorrow.

(9) The phrase BE GOING plus infinitive is interpreted as assigning a *later* time to its associated verb phrase.

BE GOING ⎯⎯⎯⎤
              ↓

Finally, English has three special constructions that can be interpreted as assigning a later time to a complement verb phrase.

(10) a. John *is leaving* for Europe tomorrow.
      b. John *is to* leave for Europe tomorrow.
      c. John *leaves* for Europe tomorrow.

In constrast to the WILL and BE GOING constructions, these last three constructions are best when they can be interpreted as "scheduled futures." We can see this most clearly when we try to use them to predict the future occurrence of an event that cannot really be scheduled. Meteorological events (raining, snowing, etc.) fall in this category.

(11) a. It will rain hard tomorrow.
      b. It is going to rain hard tomorrow.

(12) a. ?It is raining hard tomorrow.
   b. ?It is to rain hard tomorrow.
   c. ?It rains hard tomorrow.

In each of the examples discussed so far, the relation of the time of a verb phrase to utterance time is expressed by some linguistic element that contributes very little else to the meaning of the sentence. We now turn to some examples of words whose contributions to the interpretation of a sentence are temporal and nontemporal simultaneously.

A first example is HOPE, a verb whose primary function is to denote a certain mental attitude. When we use this verb with a finite complement (a *that* clause), we find that it does not impose any temporal interpretation on what is hoped for. Instead, we are free to impose any of the three basic temporal relations on the complement by a choice of tense or modal within the complement itself, as in (13).

(13) a. John hopes that he *was* in the correct room.   (earlier)
   b. John hopes that he *is* in the correct room.   (identical)
   c. John hopes that he *will be* in the correct room.   (later)

By contrast, when we use this verb with an infinitival complement, the only possible interpretation is one in which being in the correct room occurs at a later time.

(14) John hopes to be in the correct room.

Of the three sentences in (13), only (13c) is equivalent in meaning to (14). For this reason, we need to provide the following temporal rule for HOPE:

(15) HOPE assigns to its complement infinitival phrase a *later* time.

HOPE ⎯⎯⎯⎯⎯⎯⎐
                    ↓

Other verbs that take infinitival complements have a different temporal effect. SEEM, for instance, imposes an 'identical' interpretation on its complement infinitival phrase.

(16) John seems to be in the correct room.

Of the three sentences in (17), only the second is synonymous with (16).

(17) a. It seems that John *was* in the correct room.
   b. It seems that John *is* in the correct room.
   c. It seems that John *will be* in the correct room.

Thus, we need the following rule for SEEM:

(18) SEEM assigns its complement infinitival phrase an *identical* time.

SEEM
↓

The verbs HOPE and SEEM both insist on just one time assignment for their infinitival complements. With some adjectives, by contrast, both identical and later times can be assigned to infinitival complements. CERTAIN provides a clear example.

(19) John is certain to be at home.

The three basic possibilities for finite clauses with CERTAIN are shown in (20).

(20) a. It is certain that John *was* at home.
         (cannot be paraphrased by (19)).
      b. It is certain that John *is* at home.
         (can be paraphrased by (19)).
      c. It is certain that John *will be* at home.
         (can be paraphrased by (19)).

Thus, for CERTAIN the following rule is justified:

(21) CERTAIN can assign either an *identical* time or a *later* time to an infinitival complement.

Many English modals are similar to these verbs and adjectives in making a temporal as well as a nontemporal contribution to the interpretation of a sentence that contains them. The modal MAY, for instance, has several different nontemporal interpretations, one of which is 'possibility'. This is the interpretation that it has in the following two sentences:

(22) a. It may be raining in Mobile right now.
      b. It may be raining in Mobile tomorrow night.

These sentences show that the MAY of possibility allows the time of its complement verb phrase to be either identical with or later than utterance time. The sentence in (23) shows that it clearly excludes an earlier event time.

(23) *It may be raining in Mobile yesterday afternoon.

For MAY, then, we need the following rule:

(24) MAY (under the interpretation 'logical possibility') assigns either
      an *identical* time or a *later* time to its complement verb phrase.

MAY   MAY _____
(logical possibility)   (logical possibility)
    ↓   ↓

The modal MUST is another example of a word with several different
senses, each one of which imposes a time relation on the complement verb
phrase. One of the primary senses of MUST is something like 'logical
necessity.' The following sentences illustrate the kind of time interpretation that it imposes:

(25) a.   It must be raining in Mobile right now.
      b.   *It must be raining in Mobile tomorrow night.
      c.   *It must be raining in Mobile yesterday afternoon.

These examples show that MUST is like MAY in excluding an 'earlier'
interpretation, but that it differs from MAY in that it also excludes a
'later' interpretation. Thus, we need the following rule for the MUST of
logical necessity:

(26) MUST (under the interpretation of 'logical necessity') assigns an
      identical time to its complement verb phrase.

MUST
(logical necessity)
    ↓

On other interpretations, both MAY and MUST assign a later time.
The interpretations in question are 'permission' (for MAY) and 'obligation' (for MUST).

(27) a. You may come to the meeting tomorrow (if you wish to).
      b. You must come to the meeting tomorrow (whether you want to
          or not).

Other modals besides these two have time interpretations that vary
according to which of their nontime interpretations we pick. To take one
final example, we can observe a subtle distinction between a use of CAN
indicating 'ability' and a use indicating 'possibility'. Along with this contrast goes a contrast in time interpretation. The 'ability' interpretation

assigns an identical time, whereas the 'possibility' interpretation assigns a later time. These facts are illustrated by the sentences in (28).

(28) a. Joe can do eighty push-ups. (ability)
  b. *He can't do eighty push-ups at the end of next summer. (ability)
      (Compare: He won't be able to do eighty push-ups at the end of next summer.)
  c. Joe can return to his diet at the end of next summer. (possibility)

17.1.1.2 Combinations of Temporal Elements: The Time-Assignment Principle We have now examined several English constructions in which a time of some sort is imposed on a verb phrase. In each sentence considered so far, the relations such as 'earlier', 'identical', and 'later' have all been understood with respect to utterance time. When we look at slightly more complex examples, we see that the reference point with respect to which the basic time relations are calculated need not be utterance time. A good first example is (29).

(29) Janet hoped to win the election.

We have two basic intuitions about the temporal relations expressed in this sentence. The first is that the time of hoping to win is earlier than utterance time. The second is that the time of winning the election is later than the time of hoping, but not necessarily later than utterance time. There is a simple way to obtain this result from the rules that we have set up already. The past-tense on HOPE pushes the hoping to an earlier time. When we then use HOPE's own rule and assign a later time to the winning of the election, we measure not from utterance time but from the time of hoping. The relations we want are expressed in diagram form in (30).

(30)

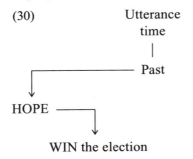

The general principles that have been used here are stated in (31).

(31) a. When a rule assigns a time to a construction that serves as an independent utterance, the point from which the calculation proceeds is just utterance time.

b. When a rule assigns a time to a complement phrase, the point from which the calculation proceeds is the time assigned to the larger phrase of which the complement is a part.

Principle (31a) serves to get a temporal interpretation started. Principle (31b), which we will refer to as the *Time-Assignment Principle,* takes over once we move down past the first temporal assigner in a sentence.

Exercise

1. For each of the following sentences, draw a time diagram indicating its temporal structure:

a. Florence is going to want to keep the notes.   (Assume that WANT is like HOPE.)

b. George must intend to boycott the meeting.   (Assume that INTEND is like HOPE.)

17.1.1.3 Perfect HAVE as 'Earlier' We have seen that a common means of expressing the 'earlier' relation is the past-tense inflection on a verb. As useful as the past-tense inflection is, there are several situations in English in which it cannot be used. As a first example, suppose that we want to use the modal MAY in a sentence in which we are asserting the possibility that it was raining yesterday. As noted above, we cannot simply use *may* followed by *be raining*.

(32) *It may be raining yesterday.

On the other hand, if we were to use *was* instead of *be,* we would violate the requirement that MAY be followed by a bare-stem verb phrase.

(33) *It may *was* raining yesterday.

In situations of this sort, when English rules exclude the use of a past-tense inflection, we have a second means of expressing the 'earlier' relation: use of HAVE plus past-participial verb phrase, as in (34).

(34) It may *have been* raining yesterday.

Perfect HAVE substitutes for a forbidden past-tense inflection with a variety of other modals, and also in infinitival constructions.

(35) a. *John should *took* the shirts to the cleaners yesterday.
     b. John should *have taken* the shirts to the cleaners yesterday.

(36) a. *John must *took* the shirts to the cleaners yesterday.
     b. John must *have taken* the shirts to the cleaners yesterday.

(37) a. *Andrea might *forgot* to leave a message last Thursday.
     b. Andrea might *have forgotten* to leave a message last Thursday.

(38) a. *Harry appears to *took* the wrong bus last night.
     b. Harry appears to *have taken* the wrong bus last night.

(39) a. *We believe Beth to *was* telling the truth this morning.
     b. We believe Beth to *have been* telling the truth this morning.

For this use of HAVE, we need the following rule:

(40) HAVE can assign an *earlier* time to its complement past-participial
     verb phrase.

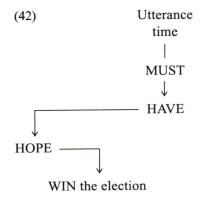

We can see how this rule for HAVE can be used with the other rules
proposed above by looking at a more complex example.

(41) Janet must have hoped to win the election.

By starting with utterance time, and then using the rules for MUST,
HAVE, and HOPE in that order, we arrive at the diagram in (42).

(42)

One important point to note here and to keep in mind during the ensuing discussion concerns the -ed suffix on *hoped.* Even though it looks like a past-tense suffix, it makes no contribution to the temporal interpretation of this sentence. The reason is that it is a past-participial inflection rather than a past-tense inflection, and is present in the sentence only because perfect HAVE demands that its complement be headed by a past participle.

The same use of HAVE occurs in the past-perfect construction found in finite sentences.

(43) a. Joe had changed the oil just the day before.
     b. Sue had paid for the ticket on the 20th.

Such sentences typically function as "flashback" sentences in discourses, providing background information for the main narrative sequence. We see an example of this function in the following simple discourse of three sentences, where a past-perfect sentence is sandwiched between two past-tense sentences:

(44) a. Fred did not know why the oil light was flashing.
        (simple past tense)
     b. The oil had been changed just three days ago.
        (past perfect)
     c. He decided to stop in at the Gulf station on his way home.
        (simple past tense)

In this discourse, two primary events are described (sentences (44a) and (44c)), both of them taking place on the same day. The sentence that occurs between them provides a description of a background event that occurred previously. The time of this background event is earlier than the time of the primary events, which are themselves earlier than the utterance time of the discourse. We can think of the past perfect as consisting of two parts: the past-tense inflection itself and HAVE. The past-tense inflection is interpreted as shifting the time of its verb phrase to an earlier time, typically the time of the primary events being narrated. We do not now have the option of using another past-tense inflection to shift the time even further back, since the rules of English word formation do not allow forms like *changeded* (CHANGE + Past + Past). Here HAVE makes its usefulness felt by imposing another shift in an earlier direction. By the rules suggested so far, then, we would derive the temporal structure given in (45b) for the past-perfect sentence in (45a).

(45) a. Janet had won the election.

      b.

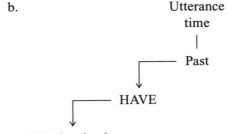

          WIN the election

The same use for perfect HAVE can be observed in certain situations that call for a present-participial verb phrase. One such situation is exemplified in (46).

(46) Existing from week to week on bread and water, Joe is secretly fascinated with gourmet cooking.

The temporal interpretation of this sentence implies that Joe is existing from week to week on bread and water at the same time that he is secretly fascinated with gourmet cooking—in this case, utterance time. Suppose that we want to indicate that the time of Joe's existing on bread and water was earlier than the time of his being fascinated with gourmet cooking. We cannot merely put an -ing suffix onto the past-tense form *existed,* as in (47).

(47) *Existeding* all through 1957 on bread and water, Joe is secretly fascinated with gourmet cooking.

Here once more, perfect HAVE serves the desired purpose.

(48) *Having existed* all through 1957 on bread and water, Joe is secretly fascinated with gourmet cooking.

Exercise

1. Draw a time diagram for each of the following sentences:
   a. Jones may have hoped to win the election.
   b. Jones had hoped to win the election.
   c. Maxwell seems to have promised to make the bed. (Assume that PROMISE imposes the same kind of time interpretation on its infinitival complement as HOPE does.)

17.1.2   The Time-Assignment Principle Applied to Finite Clauses

In the preceding three subsections, we have seen how the relative positions of various times are determined in simple sentences, including those with nonfinite structures of various sorts. When we examine finite complements, we find the same interpretations for past-tense inflection, present-tense inflection, and modals. However, just as with the various time assignments calculated in the last several subsections, the time assignments imposed by tenses and modals in complements are generally understood in relation to the time of the larger phrase of which the finite complement forms a part.

To see how the temporal interpretation for a finite complement is calculated, imagine the following situation. It is now Monday, the day before an exam. We suspect that Joe will not come to the exam the next day, and we are thinking already about the excuse that Joe will make on Thursday for not having come to the exam. Here is a rough picture of the critical times involved in this situation:

(49) Monday   Tuesday   Thursday
      (day we are talking) (day of exam)   (day of Joe's excuse)
      ___|_____|_____|_____

In this situation, we are entitled to utter the following sentence:

(50) Joe *will* tell everyone on Thursday that he *overslept* on Tuesday.

The main point of interest here is the interpretation of the past-tense inflection on *overslept*. We clearly do not interpret it as earlier than utterance time, since the time of the alleged oversleeping is in fact on the day after utterance time. However, we can still view the past-tense inflection as expressing an 'earlier' relation. Instead of understanding this relation with respect to utterance time, we need to understand it with respect to the time of the telling. Thus, (51) is the diagram that we want for the temporal structure of this sentence.

(51)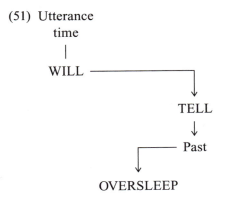

The absence of an arrow on the line below *tell* signifies that the verb does not impose any time assignment of its own on its finite complement but merely lends the complement its own time as a point of reference for interpreting whatever tense and modal forms the complement contains. In the present example, the past-tense inflection on *overslept* starts from the time of the telling and moves from that time to an earlier time.

A similar adjustment is required for interpreting present-tense and *will* in the same context, as the following examples show:

(52) a. John will tell you on Thursday that he feels fine.
     b. John will tell you on Thursday that he will write a letter.

In these examples, we again understand the time of John's telling as the reference point with respect to which the present-tense inflection and the *will* in the complements are interpreted. We interpret the present-tense in the complement of (52a) as indicating a time identical with the time of telling. Likewise, we interpret the second *will* in (52b) as indicating a time later than the time of telling. The relevant diagrams are shown in (53).

(53)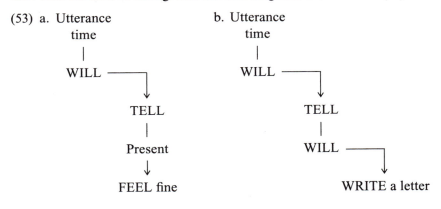

The basic principle governing the imposition of time assignments in complements is the same as that proposed above for nonfinite complements. It is repeated here as (54).

(54) *Time Assignment Principle*

When a rule assigns a time to a complement phrase, the point from which the calculation proceeds is the time assigned to the larger phrase of which the complement is a part.

In the examples given above, this principle dictates that the time of each complement is calculated in relation to the time of the verb phrase headed by *tell* rather than in relation to utterance time.

It may be helpful here to observe an incidental effect of the Time-Assignment Principle as it operates in finite complements. In each of the examples considered above, the tense choice was exactly the same as that which would have been found in the corresponding examples of quoted speech (often referred to as "direct speech"). We can see this parallel in the pairs of sentences in (55)–(57). In each of these pairs, the first sentence contains reported speech and the second contains quoted speech.

(55) a. John will tell everyone on Thursday that he *overslept* on Tuesday.
     b. John will tell everyone on Thursday, "I *overslept* on Tuesday."

(56) a. Maxine will report that Joseph *feels* fine.
     b. Maxine will report, "Joseph *feels* fine."

(57) a. Martha will say tomorrow that she *will* write a letter.
     b. Martha will say tomorrow, "I *will* write a letter."

This parallel between the verb forms in quoted speech and the verb forms dictated by the Time-Assignment Principle for finite complements will give us a quick and efficient tool for recognizing situations where something beyond the Time-Assignment Principle is coming into play. Specifically, when we see pairs of examples where the corresponding verb forms are not the same, we will know that the verb forms of the finite complements are not what would be predicted by the Time-Assignment Principle acting alone. In such cases, we will be led to look for some additional rule or principle.

Exercise

1. For each of the following sentences, draw a time diagram:
   a. Barbara will want to know whether anyone called. (Assume that WANT imposes the same kind of interpretation on an infinitival phrase as HOPE does.)
   b. Fred is certain to say that he doesn't know the answer.

17.1.3   The English Past-Harmony Rule

In each example considered in the previous section, the main clause contained the modal WILL, which had the effect of assigning a later time to the event denoted by the action verb. Here we saw that the Time-Assignment Principle gave exactly the correct results by itself. Correspondingly, tense choice in finite complements turned out to be exactly the same as tense choice in quoted speech.

In many languages, the same degree of simple regularity is found when the main-clause verb is inflected for the past tense. However, English is different in this regard, as we can see by comparing quoted speech and reported speech after the past-tense form *told*. In (58) and (59), each (a) example is a quoted-speech sentence, each (b) example is the corresponding reported-speech sentence, and each (c) example is the unacceptable reported-speech sentence predicted by the Time-Assignment Principle.

(58) a.   When I saw him two years ago, John told me, "I *am* enjoying my first-semester syntax class."
     b.   When I saw him two years ago, John told me that he *was* enjoying his first-semester syntax class.
     c.   *When I saw him two years ago, John told me that he *is* enjoying his first-semester syntax class.

(59) a.   John told me last April, "I *will* graduate in May" (but he didn't graduate after all).
     b.   John told me last April that he *would* graduate in May (but he didn't graduate after all).
     c.   *John told me last April that he *will* graduate in May (but he didn't graduate after all).

As a careful examination of the diagrams in (60) will show, the Time-Assignment Principle yields perfectly reasonable temporal structures for the unacceptable sentences in (58c) and (59c).

(60)

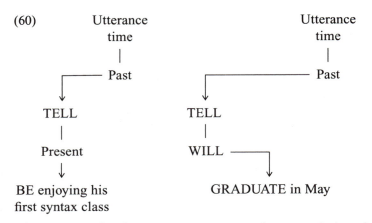

Thus, we see that in past-tense contexts, the tense choices depart from what the Time-Assignment Principle would lead us to expect.

17.1.3.1 Differences between Expected and Occurring Verb Forms We have just seen two pairs of sentences in which there is a difference between the verb form of a direct quotation and the verb form in the corresponding finite complement. Additional contrasting examples are given in (61)–(63).

(61) a. Yesterday afternoon, Dewey said, "Dora *hears* something in the chimney."
   b. Yesterday afternoon, Dewey said that Dora *heard* something in the chimney.

(62) a. Karen said, "William *is* going to attend the meeting," but in the end he didn't.
   b. Karen said that William *was* going to attend the meeting, but in the end he didn't.

(63) a. Last night at the play, Fred said, "Nelda *can't* see the stage."
   b. Last night at the play, Fred said that Nelda *couldn't* see the stage.

The contrasts that we have found are as follows:

(64) *Predicted by the*   *Actually*
     Time Assignment Principle   *occurring*
     hears   heard
     is   was

will	would
is going	was going
can't	couldn't

The difference between the predicted forms and the actually occurring forms is just that the latter look like past forms whereas the former look like nonpast forms. *Hears* vs. *heard, is* vs. *was,* and *is going* vs. *was going* are clear examples of a simple contrast between present-tense inflection and past-tense inflection. The *will-would* contrast and the *can-could* contrast may be treated in the same way. That is, contrary to the analysis of chapter 2, we have grounds here for analyzing *would* and *will* as the past-tense and present-tense forms of WILL, and *could* and *can* as past-tense and present-tense forms of CAN. Thus, where the Time-Assignment Principle would lead us to expect a present-tense form, we simply find the corresponding past-tense form. In what follows, the actually occurring forms will often be called *past-harmonic* versions of the expected forms. So, for instance, we would say that *heard* is the past-harmonic version of *hear(s),* that *would* is the past-harmonic version of *will,* and so on. More generally, we can give the following rule:

(65) The past-harmonic version of a non-past-tense verb form is just the corresponding past-tense form.

There is one more unexpected verb form that can be induced in complements by a past-tense inflection. Considering the following sentence:

(66) Yesterday John told me, "I returned the book on Tuesday."

The temporal situation in this sentence is diagrammed in (67), where the quotation marks indicate quoted speech.

(67)

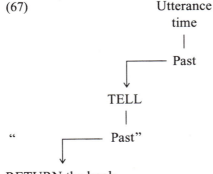

The main clause here has an earlier event time, and this earlier event time itself serves as a reference point for the 'earlier' relation of the event time in the complement. One relatively informal way of expressing this message in reported speech is given in (68).

(68) Yesterday John told me that he returned the book on Tuesday.

Here the verb in the complement is the same as in the corresponding direct quotation in (66). The above statement about a correspondence between expected non-past-tense and actually occurring past-tense would not be relevant here, since the expected complement verb is already past. Leaving the quoted-speech form unchanged gives a result that is correct for this variety of English. However, in a more formal variety of English, the same content would be expressed by a sentence that contained a past-perfect form in the complement.

(69) Yesterday John told me that he *had returned* the book on Tuesday.

This sentence thus requires us to add that where the Time-Assignment Principle would call for a past-tense inflection, we find instead a past perfect. In other words, the past-harmonic version of a past tense is a past perfect.

One particular word of English has no past-harmonic version and thus cannot be used in complements of past-tense sentences. The word is the modal MUST, as we can see when we try to report a past utterance of the sentence in (70).

(70) a.   Yesterday Ann said, "Karen must finish the paper within two hours."
     b.   *Yesterday Ann said that Karen must finish the paper within two hours.

The problem here is that *must* does not have a corresponding past-tense form. That is, there is no word in English that does for *must* what *was* does for *is* or what *would* does for *will*. The strategy that English speakers use when they are faced with situations of this sort is to look for some verbal element that means the same thing and that does have a corresponding past-tense form. In the case of *must,* a natural choice is HAVE TO.

(71) a.   Yesterday Ann said, "Karen *has* to finish the paper within two hours."

b. Yesterday Ann said that Karen *had* to finish the paper within two hours.

17.1.3.2   Formulation of a Past-Harmony Rule   In the preceding subsection, we focused exclusively on determining the past-harmonic versions of various English verb forms. We need to turn back now to the exact circumstances under which these forms are induced.

In each example given in the preceding paragraphs, it is an actual past-tense inflection on a verb such as SAY or TELL that forces the use of past-harmony forms in the complements below it. As it happens, the past-tense inflection does not necessarily have to appear on these verbs of saying.

(72) a. Rachel *intended* to tell us, "I *won't* be able to attend the meeting."

    b. Rachel *intended* to tell us that [she *wouldn't* be able to attend the meeting].

(73) a. John *hoped* to be able to say, "Peter won't swallow any more goldfish."

    b. John *hoped* to be able to say that [Peter *wouldn't* swallow any more goldfish].

(74) a. Karen *used* to tell us, "Cornelius *doesn't* know what he *is* doing."

    b. Karen *used* to tell us that [Cornelius *didn't* know what he *was* doing].

(With regard to the sentences in (74), it might be reasonable to classify the special form *used* as a past-tense form, even though there is no corresponding present-tense form that we can point to.)

Beyond past-tense inflections, though, there is one additional element that induces the same past-harmony effects in complement clauses. This is the perfect HAVE, in its 'earlier' interpretation.

(75) a. Abigail seems to *have* told Fred, "John *will* attend the party."

    b. Abigail seems to *have* told Fred that [John *would* attend the party].

Taken as a group, all of these examples suggest that past-harmony effects in complements are induced whenever there is an 'earlier' time assignment associated with a phrase higher up, whether this 'earlier' shift is expressed by a past-tense inflection or by perfect HAVE.

A single 'earlier' element high up in a structure can make its presence felt all the way down through a chain of finite complements. Some idea of the extensiveness of this effect can be gained by noting the difference between the tenses found in the quoted speech in (76a) and those found in the corresponding reported speech in (76b).

(76) a. Phyllis *wanted* to tell Arthur, "John *doesn't* think that he *will* ever find out whether anyone *knows* when his baggage *will* arrive."

   b. Phyllis wanted to tell Arthur that [John *didn't* think that he *would* ever find out whether anyone *knew* when his baggage *would* arrive].

Here it is the past-tense inflection on *wanted* that induces the past-harmony effects, and it induces them all the way down into the lowest complement, with no help from any other 'earlier' shift along the way.

With all of the preceding discussion in mind, we are now in a position to give a comprehensive formulation of the Past Harmony rule.

(77) *Past Harmony Rule*
   In the portion of a temporal structure that lies below an 'earlier' element, replace every form predicted by the Time-Assignment Principle by its corresponding past-harmonic form.

This rule says in effect that a past-tense inflection or a HAVE makes the entire structure below it a "past-harmony domain" in which changes of the indicated type must take place. This domain can easily be expressed graphically. The diagrams in (78) represent the temporal structures of the two sentences with which we began our discussion.

(78) a. John told me that he *was* enjoying his first-semester syntax course.

   b. John told me last April that he *would* graduate in May.

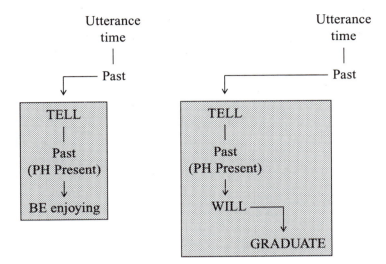

Here the shaded areas indicate the borders of past-harmony domains, and *PH Present* stands for past-harmonic version of present-tense inflection.

Exercises

1. For each of the following sentences, draw a time diagram:
   a. George seems to have thought that Bill would win the competition.
   b. We were sure that Carol would insist that David was competent.
   c. Jerry will assume that Fred forgot that Susan was in Toledo.
   d. Diane must know that Ralph told Frank that Alice would feed the horses.
   e. Jane should have realized that Steve did not understand the problem.

2. The following quotation strike many speakers of English as slightly odd:

   "I really had a feeling there that I am observing unleashed human evils, and that's why I was so shaken." (Natasha Dudinska, a native of Slovakia, quoted by Marc C. Charney in "From Prague, a Student of Lost Ideals and New-Found Evils," *New York Times,* June 13, 1993, sec. 4, p. 7)

Say how the thought would normally be expressed in English, and what rule of English was omitted in the statement as quoted.

17.1.3.3 Usurpation and the Nonapplication of the Past-Harmony Rule

There is one special group of situations in which the Past-Harmony Rule does not apply. Under special circumstances, the earlier time of some lower clause can be "usurped" by a nonearlier time from the clause above it. To see this clearly, we can begin by looking at the example of quoted speech in (79).

(79) John *told* me on Sunday, "Marsha *doesn't* like the plan."

By the rules that we have developed, the corresponding reported-speech sentence would be contained in a past-harmony domain.

(80) John *told* me on Sunday that Marsha *didn't* like the plan.

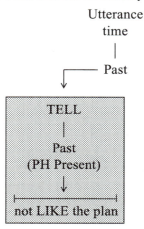

Yet under certain circumstances, we can also report this utterance of John's as in (81).

(81) John *told* me on Sunday that Marsha *doesn't* like the plan.

Our intuition about this sentence is that Marsha's not liking the plan is a state of affairs that exists not only at the time when John is speaking but also at utterance time. The temporal structure of sentence (81) can thus be represented as in (82).

(82)   Utterance
time

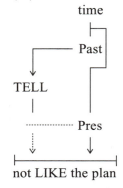

The essential ideas expressed in (82) are as follows. The state of not liking the plan extends far enough through time to include utterance time as well as the earlier time of telling. In this situation, utterance time can usurp the rights of the left-hand branch of the temporal structure. Time relations of complements are then calculated with respect to utterance time rather than with respect to the time of telling. A major consequence is that the verb of the complement does not show any past-harmony marking, since it is no longer connected to an 'earlier' shift in the structure above it.

In the situation described with sentence (81), the state of not liking the plan extended from at least the time of John's speaking through utterance time. Had this state of affairs terminated before utterance time, then usurpation would not have been possible, and the Past-Harmony Rule would have been applied. We can see the impossibility of usurpation here by adding something to sentences (80) and (81) to indicate that Marsha changed her mind at some point between John's speech and our speech.

(83) a. *John *told* me on Sunday that Marsha *does* not like the plan, but she seems to have changed her mind.

b. John *told* me on Sunday that Marsha *did* not like the plan, but she seems to have changed her mind.

The corresponding diagram here is given in (84).

(84)

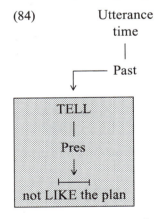

In this situation, the relation to the time of telling ('identical') is different from the relation to utterance time ('earlier'). Thus, the utterance time cannot usurp the 'earlier' branch in this diagram the same way that it did in the case where the time of not liking the plan had a longer span. The 'earlier' branch remains dominant, and thus a past-harmony domain is created. This is why (83b) is more acceptable than (83a).

A similar possibility for usurpation arises in connection with events that are later than utterance time as well as later than the time of telling. Suppose that it is now Wednesday, and that the Monday and Friday in (85) are in the same week.

(85) On Monday John told me, "I will come to the meeting on Friday."

If we express this as reported speech and do not take the option of having utterance time usurp, we get sentence (86).

(86) On Monday John *told* me that he *would* come to the meeting on Friday.

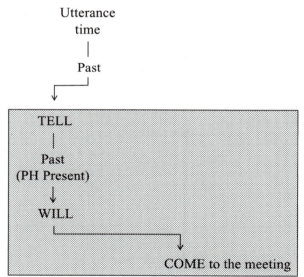

On the other hand, if we do take the usurpation option, we get sentence (87), with the temporal structure shown.

(87) On Monday John told me that he will come to the meeting on Friday.

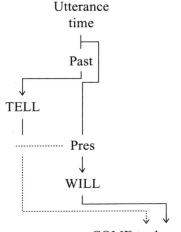

COME to the meeting

Again, as with the structure in (82), we no longer have conditions that create a past-harmony domain. As a consequence, the complement contains *will* instead of *would*.

Exercises

1. Draw a time diagram for each of the following sentences:
   a. John said that George will find a solution.
   b. Barbara told us that Harry will claim that he didn't think that he would see the letter.

2. Study the following pair of sentences:
   (i)   John said that he will come to the picnic, and I'm sure that he will come.
   (ii)   *John said that he will come to the picnic, and I'm sure that he did come.

   Explain as clearly as you can why (i) is acceptable and (ii) is not.

17.1.4 Special Uses of Present-Tense Inflection and Past-Tense Inflection

In the previous subsection, we saw a clear case of a complication in the relationship between syntactic tense marking and semantic temporal relation. In particular, we saw instances of past-tense inflections that were not interpreted as 'earlier' but instead were interpreted as past-harmonic versions of present-tense inflections. There are several other situations in English in which past-tense and present-tense inflections do not have their ordinary interpretations. The purpose of this section is to briefly survey these situations.

17.1.4.1 Present-Tense Inflection with 'Later' Interpretation: Temporal Clauses One important situation of this type is illustrated in the sentences in (88), each of which contains a subordinate clause serving as a temporal modifier.

(88) a. [Before Aaron *leaves* for Akron tomorrow], Joe *will* introduce him to you.
     b. [After the party *is* over], Fred *will* drive Sam to the airport.
     c. [When Sue *arrives* at the airport], someone *will* give her a ticket.
     d. [While Marsha *is* interviewing Tom], you *will* be interviewing Alice.

In each of these sentences, the main clause contains the verb WILL, which indicates that the time of the accompanying verb phrase is later than utterance time. By contrast, none of the adverbial subordinate clauses contain either WILL or any other verb imposing a shift in a later direction. Yet we understand the event reported in each of these clauses as occurring later than utterance time. For these cases, then, we need the following special rule:

(89) If a present-tense sentence occurs in a clause introduced by a temporal word (*before, after, when, while*), and if the main clause has a future interpretation, then the present-tense inflection can be given the interpretation 'later'.

17.1.4.2 Present-Tense Inflection with 'Later' Interpretation: Conditional Clauses We find additional instances of present-tenses inflections with 'later' interpretations when we look at subordinate clauses that have a conditional interpretation. The most obvious examples are clauses introduced by *if*.

(90) a. [If Geraldine *asks* us to help her], we *will* call you.
     b. [If I *am* not here when you call], Dorothy *will* write down your message.

However, there are many other examples of the same sort in which the conditional meaning, though less apparent, is no less real.

(91) a. [Whoever *crosses* the line first] *can* adopt this orphaned rabbit. (*If x* crosses the line first, *x* can adopt this orphaned rabbit, likewise for *y* and so on.)
     b. We *will* award the prize to the person [who *submits* the best essay].

(*If* person *x* submits the best essay, we will award the prize to *x*, likewise for person *y* and so on.)

c. [Whether or not Shirley *agrees* with tomorrow's vote], she *should* abide by the decision of the group.
(*If* Shirley agrees with tomorrow's vote, she should abide by the decision of the group; *if* she does not agree with it, she should still abide by the decision of the group.)

d. Bill *is going* to be difficult to work with during the summer, [no matter how many new employees *are* hired next month to help him].
(Bill is going to be difficult to work with during the summer *if x* employees are hired, likewise *if y* employees are hired, and so on.)

These examples require us to add the following rule:

(92) If a present-tense inflection occurs in the subordinate part of a conditional sentence or in a subordinate clause that is understood in a similar way, and if the main clause has a 'later' interpretation, then the present-tense inflection can also be given the interpretation 'later'.

17.1.4.3   Pasts Tenses Interpreted as Present Tenses: Hypothetical Conditionals   Let us turn now to another situation in which past-tenses inflections are interpreted as if they were present-tenses inflections. This situation involves what are often referred to as "hypothetical" conditionals, which are closely related in meaning to the ordinary conditionals of the sort that we examined above. Sentence (93a) is an ordinary conditional, and sentence (93b) is a hypothetical conditional that has the same temporal interpretation.

(93) a. If you *miss* class tomorrow, you *will* not hear Professor Grant's elucidation of Hugo's metaphors.
b. If you *missed* class tomorrow, you *would* not hear Professor Grant's elucidation of Hugo's metaphors.

Despite the differences in their verb forms, the two sentences in (93) share identical temporal structures, with both subordinate clause and main clause moving toward the future. To the extent that there is any meaning difference, it is in a greater feeling of hypotheticality about (93b). These observations suggest that the past-tense inflection in the subordinate clause is to be interpreted as a 'hypothetical' version of the present-tense inflection. Furthermore, since the present-tense inflection in a conditional can have a 'later' interpretation, we now have an explanation for the fact that the past-tense inflection can come to assign a 'later' relation to the verb phrase to which it is attached. The steps in the interpretation are summarized in (94).

(94) a. The past-tense inflection can be interpreted as the 'hypothetical' version of a present-tense inflection.
   b. A present-tense inflection, in the subordinate clause of a conditional, can be interpreted as 'later.'

It is also necessary to state rules for the verb forms that can occur in the main clause of a hypothetical conditional. In (93b), we saw *would,* itself a past-tense form of WILL. The two other possibilities are *could* and *might.*

(95) a. If Alfred *wanted* to leave after midnight, he *could* catch a ride with Mark.
   b. If Alfred *wants* to leave after midnight, he *can* catch a ride with Mark.

(96) a. If you *went* to the station early, you *might* catch a glimpse of the senator.
   b. If you *go* to the station early, you *may* catch a glimpse of the senator.

Having noted the use of special hypothetical verb forms, we need to say something more about what a hypothetical context actually is. We can get some important clues by examining the longer discourse in (97).

(97) If John *decided* not to return next year, we *would* have several problems. When we *went* to the president to ask permission to replace him, we *would* have to argue in writing that the position *needed* to be filled. After we *received* permission, we *would* need to find an acceptable replacement. The replacement that we *hired* *would* find a great deal of rebuilding work to be done.

This discourse begins with a subordinate clause introduced by *if*. This clause asks us to imagine that a certain future event (John's deciding not to return next year) has materialized. In the remainder of that sentence, and in all of the sentences that follow, consequences of that imaginary future event are spelled out. The past-tense forms that we find throughout the discourse indicate that the original supposition is still being assumed.

In order to calculate the time relations in (97), we use exactly the same rules that we used for individual hypothetical sentences. We take each past-tense inflection to be a hypothetical version of a corresponding present-tense inflection. The effect of these rules is to make the time relations in (97) exactly like those in the nonhypothetical discourse in (98).

(98) If John *decides* not to return next year, we *will* have several problems. When we *go* to the president to ask permission to replace him, we *will* have to argue in writing that the position *needs* to be filled. After we *receive* permission, we *will* need to find an acceptable replacement. The replacement that we *hire will* find a great deal of rebuilding work to be done.

The present-tenses inflections on the various verbs in this nonhypothetical discourse are interpreted as follows:

(99) a. *decides:* present-tense inflection in a conditional, interpreted as 'later'
  b. *go:* present-tense inflection in a temporal clause, interpreted as 'later'
  c. *needs:* present-tense inflection in a complement clause, interpreted as 'identical'
  d. *receive:* present-tense inflection in a temporal clause, interpreted as 'later'
  e. *hire:* present-tense in a clause understood as an implicit conditional, interpreted as 'later'

Thus, the past-tenses inflections in the hypothetical discourse in (97) are assigned exactly the same temporal interpretations, once we apply the simple rule that says to treat them as special versions of present-tense inflections.

17.1.4.4 Past Tenses Interpreted as Present Tenses: Counterfactual Conditionals We turn now to a second type of conditional that induces some special verb forms. Conditionals of this new type are defined by the fact that the speaker presupposes the proposition expressed in the *if* clause to be false. Here are some examples:

(100) a. If you *lived* in Dallas now, you could drive home in half a day.
      (Presupposition: You *do* not live in Dallas now.)
   b. If Joe *knew* how to sing, he would have a job at the Metropolitan Opera.
      (Presupposition: Joe *does* not know how to sing.)

Again, as was the case with hypothetical conditionals, past-tense inflections receive a time interpretation that in simple sentences is expressed with present-tense inflections. Thus, in both of the sentences in (100), the past-tense inflection appears to express counterfactuality rather than the 'earlier' relation, and the rule that we need to state here is that the past-tense inflection can serve as the counterfactual version of the present-tense inflection.

When we want to have a counterfactual clause in which an 'earlier' relation is imposed, we go a step farther and resort to the past-perfect construction.

(101) a. (Presupposition: You *were* not here yesterday.)
     If you *had been* here yesterday, you would have met Marsha.
   b. (Presupposition: You *did* not see the movie last night.)
     If you *had seen* the movie last night, you would be laughing, too.

Thus, in counterfactual *if* clauses, past-perfect forms are interpreted as counterfactual versions of ordinary past-tense inflections.

The verb forms that we find in the main clauses of counterfactual conditionals are just *would* and *could* as special versions of present-tense inflection, and *would have* and *could have* as special versions of past-tense inflection.

(102) a. If Geraldine suspected that the money had been spent, she *would be* upset.
   b. If there weren't so many clouds in the sky, you *could see* the mountains from here.

(103) a. If Geraldine had suspected that the money had been spent, she *would have been* upset.
   b. If there hadn't been so many clouds in the sky, you *could have seen* the mountains from here.

Just as was true of hypothetical conditionals, a counterfactual conditional may create a counterfactual context in a larger discourse. The discourse in (104) provides an example.

(104) If Jacob *lived* in Boston, he *would* go to watch the Boston Celtics several times each week during the winter. When the Celtics *won,* he *would* celebrate, and when they *lost,* he *would* weep. Every

winter, the money that he *paid* for tickets *would* add up to several hundred dollars.

We can get some idea of the way in which these verb forms correspond to noncounterfactual forms by imagining the form that a comparable discourse would take if Jacob *did* live in Boston.

(105) Since Jacob *lives* in Boston, he *goes* to watch the Boston Celtics several times each week during the winter. When the Celtics *win,* he *celebrates,* and when they *lose,* he *weeps.* Every winter, the money that he *pays* for tickets *adds* up to several hundred dollars.

In this discourse, the present-tense inflections are interpreted not as 'later' but as 'identical.' This is likewise the interpretation of the corresponding past-tense forms in the counterfactual discourse in (104).

In every sentence discussed so far in which a counterfactual presupposition came into play in a sentence or a discourse, it arrived as part of a conditional sentence. English provides another major means for initiating counterfactual discourses, which is illustrated in (106).

(106) a. Joe *returned* that book yesterday. We wish that he *hadn't* returned it.
    b. Janice *doesn't* live in Texarkana. Caleb wishes that she *did* live there.

As a matter of fact, noncounterfactual complements are unacceptable with *wish.*

(107) a. *We wish that Joe *didn't* return that book yesterday.
    b. *Caleb wishes that Janice *lives* there.

Just as with counterfactual *if* clauses, a counterfactual complement of *wish* may introduce an entire counterfactual discourse.

(108) Caleb wishes that Janice *lived* in Texarkana. She *would* be able to get messages to his parents, and the replies that they *sent* through her *would* give him an idea of how well they *were* getting along.

Again, we can compare this discourse with one where Janice's living in Texarkana is not contrary to fact.

(109) Caleb is glad that Janice *lives* in Texarkana. She *is* able to get messages to his parents, and the replies that they *send* through her *give* him an idea of how well they *are* getting along.

One small addition needs to be made to our statements about counter-factual forms. In the vast majority of cases, the counterfactual version of a present-tense inflection is just the corresponding past-tense inflection. However, under certain circumstances, the counterfactual version of *am* and *is* is *were* rather than the expected *was*. These circumstances are illustrated in (110).

(110) a. If I *were* (*was) you, I would be happy about the outcome of the election.
   b. If he *were* (?*was*) here now, he would be objecting to everything that we are doing.
   c. If I *were* (*was) to raise an objection, I would be overruled.

These occurrences of *were* are little more than frozen relics of an earlier "subjunctive" form that was at one time used in counterfactuals. They are less natural than *was* when the subject is something other than a pronoun, and they are totally impossible when they appear outside the immediate vicinity of the *if*.

(111) a. If the book that Connie wrote *was* (?*were*) still in print, we would assign it to our students.
   b. If someone lived in the house now, whoever it *was* (*were) would have many unwelcome problems with termites.

Our general rule, then, will be that *was* is the counterfactual version of *am* and *is*. We will then add a very narrow special rule to say when *were* is called for instead.

(112) Use *were* as a replacement for the counterfactual form *was* when it is the main verb of a clause introduced by *if*. This replacement is obligatory in the expression *if I were you* and is preferable in the case where the subject is a pronoun. The degree of acceptability falls when the subject is not a pronoun. In positions other than the main-verb position in the *if* clause, the normal form *was* must be used.

Exercises

1. Below are two sentences with the past-tense form *went*. Say what the single common interpretation is for the past-tense inflection here.

(i) John *went* home early.

(ii) If John goes home early tomorrow, Bill will tell everybody the next day that John *went* home early.

2. Below are two more sentences containing a past-tense verb form.

(i) If Joe *lived* in Boston, he would be skiing instead of playing tennis.

(ii) If Joe *lived* in Boston, he must know about the swan boats.

These two past-tense inflections are not interpreted in the same way. How is each one interpreted, and how do you know which interpretation to assign?

17.1.5   Two Additional Uses for Perfect HAVE

As we have seen, the HAVE + past participle construction is often used to express the 'earlier' relation, particularly in circumstances in which no past-tense inflection is possible or in circumstances in which the past-tense inflection expresses something else. This construction is also used with two other interpretations. These interpretations can be seen most clearly in the present-tense form of the perfect construction.

The first use is illustrated in the following sentences:

(113) a. Joe has lived in Austin for sixteen years.
        b. The Smith brothers have sold groceries since 1968.

Both of these sentences assert that a certain state of affairs has existed for a period of time that begins at some point in the past and goes up to and includes utterance time. This interpretation can be represented graphically in (114).

(114)   Utterance
             time

             |

        Present

             ↓

├───────────┤
 LIVE in Austin

For this situation, neither simple present-tense forms nor simple past-tense forms are appropriate. With present-tense forms, the results are simply unacceptable.

(115) a. *Joe lives in Austin for sixteen years.
        b. *The Smith brothers sell groceries since 1968.

If we use the past-tense inflection instead of the perfect HAVE in (113a), we get an acceptable sentence as a result.

(116) Joe lived in Austin for sixteen years.

However, this sentence is only appropriate if Joe no longer lives in Austin —that is, if the state being referred to was before utterance time. Sentence (116), then, would have to be represented as in (117).

(117)

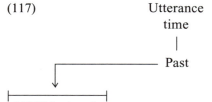

If we try to replace the present perfect in (113b) by a past-tense form, the result is again ill formed.

(118) *The Smith brothers sold groceries since 1968.

The unacceptability of this sentence can be analyzed as arising from a conflict between the past-tense inflection (which puts the state of affairs completely prior to utterance time) and the phrase *since 1968* (which means 'from 1968 to utterance time'). Thus, this use of the present perfect is one that is not duplicated in English by either the present-tense inflection or the past-tense inflection.

The second additional interpretation for the present perfect is illustrated in (119).

(119) a. Joe has written you a letter today.
      b. Kasparov has asked for a postponement.
      c. Marsha has accepted the position.

At first glance, these might appear to have the same 'earlier' interpretation as the occurrences of HAVE that we saw in the examples of subsection 17.1.1.3. In particular, it might seem that these sentences are interpreted in exactly the same way as the corresponding sentences containing past-tense inflections in place of present-perfect forms.

(120) a. Joe wrote you a letter today.
      b. Kasparov asked for a postponement.
      c. Marsha accepted the position.

A careful examination of many examples, however, indicates that the present perfect is much more restricted than either the past-tense inflection or the nonpresent forms of perfect HAVE. The following three-sentence sets illustrate some of the situations in which there is a clear contrast in acceptability:

(121) a. Alice finished her dissertation yesterday.
     b. Alice must have finished her dissertation yesterday.
     c. *Alice has finished her dissertation yesterday.

(122) (Asked at some point after Truman's death)
     a. Did you ever talk with Truman?
     b. Could you ever have talked with Truman?
     c. ?Have you ever talked with Truman?

(123) (Asked of a person who has nearly been run down by a reckless
     driver who has immediately left the scene)
     a. Did you see the guy's license number?
     b. Shouldn't you have seen the guy's license number?
     c. ?Have you seen the guy's license number?

(124) a. Did you hear that explosion?
     b. Shouldn't you have heard that explosion?
     c. ?Have you heard that explosion?

What all of the inappropriate (c) examples have in common becomes
clear if we make use of a new concept, which we can call the *potential
period of occurrence* of a certain kind of event. It will be useful to contrast
(119c), one of the acceptable present perfects, with (124c), one of the
unacceptable ones. In (119c), the type of event with which the statement
is concerned can roughly be referred to as "Marsha's accepting the position." The period during which such an event could occur presumably
includes part of the past, but also extends to the present and beyond. We
can diagram this potential period of occurrence as a rectangle that begins
at some point in the past and includes utterance time (see (125)). Making
the statement in (119c) then involves the claim that an event of this type
actually did occur prior to the moment of speaking.

(125)

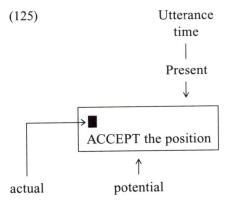

What is important here is that the potential period of occurrence for this event includes utterance time.

The situation with regard to (124c), where the central event is "your hearing that explosion", is quite different. Here the potential period of occurrence is extremely short and actually terminates before utterance time, as shown in (126).

(126)   Utterance
                           time
                            |
                         Present
                            ↓

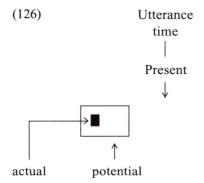

actual   potential

The strangeness of the present perfect here can be explained by noting the failure of the potential period of occurrence to include utterance time. For reasons that vary from one example to the other, the inappropriateness of the present perfects in (120)–(123) can be explained in the same way.

It is worth paying particular attention to the way in which this account of the present perfect excludes adverbs like *yesterday* while allowing *today*. Let us look again at the two examples above in which this difference shows itself.

(127)   Joe has written you a letter today.

(128)   *Alice has finished her dissertation yesterday.

In (127), the event is "Joe's writing you a letter today;" the period during which this event could potentially occur includes utterance time, since this latter point falls within the boundaries of the time period designated by *today*. In (128), by contrast, the event is "Alice's finishing her dissertation yesterday." The potential period of occurrence for this event is the period designated by *yesterday*, a stretch of time that fails to include utterance time.

We see the same contrast in another light when we examine a time adverb like *this morning*, comparing its behavior in a past-tense context and in a present-perfect context.

(129) a. Joe wrote you a letter this morning.
     b. Joe has written you a letter this morning.

In (129a), we can understand the time adverb *this morning* as referring either to a time period that includes utterance time, or to a time period that ended earlier the same day. In (129b), only the first of these interpretations is possible. Thus, (129b) would be an appropriate utterance at 11:30 A.M., but not at 2:00 P.M. This limitation on the present perfect in (129b) follows from our requirement that the potential period of occurrence for the event "Joe's writing you a letter this morning" include utterance time.

These two special interpretations of the present-perfect construction are sometimes available for a single sentence, so that the sentence is ambiguous. Consider (130), for example.

(130) Joe has stood on his head for thirty seconds.

On one interpretation, this sentence can be understood as asserting that a certain action has been going on from some moment in the past up to and including the time of speaking, as shown in (131).

(131)   Utterance
                    time
                     |

             Present
                     ↓

|————————————|
STAND on his head

On the other interpretation, this sentence says something about a certain kind of event, "Joe's standing on his head for thirty seconds." The potential period of occurrence includes utterance time, and the sentence asserts that at least one event of this type took place prior to the moment of speaking.

(132)

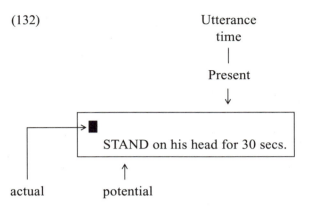

Utterance
time
|
Present
↓

STAND on his head for 30 secs.

↑

actual   potential

The ambiguity of this sentence thus provides evidence that these two interpretations really are distinct and are not merely special cases of a more
general rule of interpretation.

We have now studied in some detail the two interpretations that are
possible for the present-tense form of the perfect HAVE construction. Are
these same two interpretations available for the other forms of the perfect
HAVE construction? In the case of the first special interpretation—that
involving a period of time beginning in the past and continuing up
through utterance time—the answer is clearly yes. Evidence for such an
interpretation is provided by sentences like those in (133).

(133) a. Jane may have lived in Austin since 1968.
       b. Having lived in Austin since 1968, George knows many people
           at City Hall.

With regard to the second interpretation—that requiring a potential period of occurrence that extends through utterance time—it is harder to
give a clear answer. What we need for a clear test is a verb phrase that
sounds more natural in present-perfect form than in simple past form.

Verb phrases containing the adverb *yet* appear to be slightly more acceptable in the present perfect than in the past tense, at least in fairly
formal English.

(134) a. Lisa hasn't opened the letter yet.
       b. ?Lisa didn't open the letter yet.

We can take this as evidence that the word *yet* does not go well with an
'earlier' interpretation. When the perfect HAVE construction appears in
bare-stem form with a modal, *yet* is perfectly acceptable.

(135) Lisa may not have opened the letter yet.

Sentence (135), then, suggests that the bare-stem HAVE construction, just like the present-tense form of HAVE, allows the interpretation involving a potential period of occurrence.

To summarize, the perfect HAVE construction has three separate interpretations. In each form except the present perfect, all three interpretations are possible. In the present perfect, by contrast, the 'earlier' interpretation that is shared with the simple past-tense inflection is not available. This restriction is one of the more troublesome for learners of English as a second language to master. Given the 'earlier' interpretation found in nonfinite perfects like (136) and past perfects like (137), it is natural to believe that (138) should be possible as well.

(136)   a. John must have completed his studies in May.
        b. John appears to have completed his studies in May.
        c. John regrets having completed his studies in May.

(137)   John had completed his studies in May.

(138)   *John has completed his studies in May.

This restriction against using the present form of the perfect HAVE construction to mean 'earlier' is the major restriction to be remembered in connection with this construction.

17.2   ASPECT

So far in this chapter, our concern with time has been restricted to time *relations*—that is, to the manner in which the times of various events in sentences are related to utterance time and to other times. In the present section, we turn to *aspectual* properties of sentences, which involve a completely different way of looking at time. Subsection 17.2.1 provides an initial idea of what is meant by an aspectual property. In subsection 17.2.2, four basic aspectual classes of verb phrases are distinguished. The rules in which these distinctions play a role are sketched in subsection 17.2.3.

17.2.1   The Nature of Aspect

When we examine the aspect of a sentence, we stop looking at the relations between the time of an event or state and some other time, and we focus on the way in which the event or state itself, considered in isolation, spreads out in time. The difference between the temporal relations expressed in a sentence and the aspectual properties of the sentence can be illustrated with the help of two pairs of examples.

Examples (139a) and (139b) exhibit different time relations but the same aspectual structure.

(139) a. Joan wrote a sonnet.
     b. Alfred will eat a peach.

Joan's writing a sonnet and Alfred's eating a peach are placed in different positions relative to utterance time by virtue of the past-tense inflection in the first sentence and the modal WILL in the second. However, the aspectual properties of these two sentences are the same. Both assert the existence of an event that progresses through a series of intermediate stages and has a natural endpoint. In (139a), the natural endpoint occurs when the fourteenth line of the sonnet is written down; in (139b), the natural endpoint occurs when the last bite of the peach disappears. If we justified the truth of these two sentences by showing movies of them, we would see these successive stages quite clearly as both the unwritten portion of the sonnet and the uneaten portion of the peach got smaller. Both the differing relational properties and the identical aspectual properties of these sentences are captured in (140).

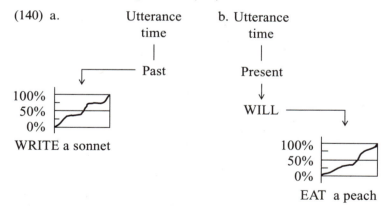

Here the aspectual structure of these two verb phrases is represented by showing a graph of the portion of the task that has been completed at successive times, with 0 percent at the beginning of the interval and 100 percent at the end of the interval.

Our second pair of examples consists of two sentences that exhibit identical time relations (both being earlier than the time of utterance) but quite different aspectual properties.

(141) a. Joan wrote a sonnet.
      b. Roger had a rash.

As noted already, sentence (141a) asserts the existence of an event that progresses through a sequence of stages to a natural endpoint. Sentence (141b), by contrast, asserts the existence of a certain state, one that does not involve an idea of steady progression or successive stages. Although Roger's doctor might notice different stages associated with Roger's rash, there is nothing inherent in the meaning of the sentence that would imply such a succession. These similarities in time relations and differences in aspectual properties are summarized in diagram form in (142).

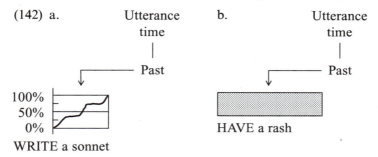

At first glance, aspectual properties of sentences may seem much more subjective than the time relations that were the topic of discussion in section 17.1. Yet there are several important kinds of English rules in which aspectual properties of sentences play a definite role:

- rules governing the appearance of certain aspectual adverbials
- rules governing the interpretation of time adverbs
- rules governing the availability and interpretation of the simple present tense
- rules governing the availability and interpretation of the progressive construction (BE plus present-participial verb phrase)

In subsection 17.2.3, we will discuss these rules in detail. Meanwhile, though, we can get an initial glimpse of the kinds of differences involved, using just the two verb phrases in (141). Here are some contrasting examples that show the effects of these four kinds of rules:

(143) a. ?Joan wrote a sonnet *for fifteen minutes*.   (The *for*-phrase
adverbial is unnatural.)

   b. Roger had a rash *for three days*.   (The *for*-phrase adverbial is
natural.)

(144) a. When Sam arrived for a visit, Joan wrote a sonnet.   (The
time of writing the sonnet *begins with* the time when Sam
arrived.)

   b. When Sam arrived for a visit, Roger had a rash.   (The time
of having the rash *includes* the time when Sam arrived.)

(145) a. *Joan writes a sonnet right now.   (The simple present tense is
unacceptable.)

   b. Roger has a rash right now.   (The simple present tense is
acceptable.)

(146) a. Joan is writing a sonnet right now.   (The progressive is
acceptable.)

   b. *Roger is having a rash right now.   (The progressive is
unacceptable.)

17.2.2   Four Basic Aspectual Classes

This section will introduce four major aspectual classes. Distinguishing
these four classes will greatly simplify the job of stating the rules that
account for the kinds of contrasts that we have just seen. Intuitive descriptions
and a few examples will be given here. Then in the natural course of
studying the rules in which these classes play a role, we will develop some
experimental tests that will help us to determine what class a given verb
phrase belongs to.

17.2.2.1   States   The first aspectual class is the class of *states*. Examples
of sentences that report states are given in (147).

(147) a. Roger had a rash.

   b. Karen felt happy.

   c. Jonah owned a horse.

   d. Fred's grandfather weighed two hundred pounds.

   e. This tree is dead.

   f. Thor has a tumor on his toe.

   g. Nora liked the book.

As noted above, states characteristically are interpreted as being more or less uniform throughout an interval; consequently, they do not have natural endpoints. In addition, they generally do not involve any action on the part of their subject.

17.2.2.2 Activities The aspectual class consisting of *activity* sentences is one whose members, at first glance, look very much like states. Here are some examples:

(148) a. Karen talked to Martha.
      b. Jonah pestered the cat.
      c. Mavis snored.
      d. Martin wandered around.

As their name implies, activities are in general more "active" than states. However, they are similar to states in not having any natural endpoints. For instance, there is no point at which an episode of "talking to Martha" would necessarily come to a conclusion, as "eating a peach" would have to.

17.2.2.3 Accomplishments The next aspectual class of verb phrases is generally referred to by the term *accomplishment*. In contrast with states and activities, accomplishments have natural endpoints. We have already seen two examples of accomplishment verb phrases: *write a sonnet* and *eat a peach*. Other accomplishment verb phrases occur in the following sentences:

(149) a. Ron peeled the carrot.
      b. Jody repaired the toaster.
      c. Dorothy built a house.
      d. Heifetz performed the Third Partita.
      e. Georgia wrote a sonnet.
      f. A man traveled from Jerusalem to Jericho.

The definable endpoints here are the point at which the carrot is completely peeled, the point at which the toaster works again, the point at which the house is finished, and so on.

17.2.2.4 Achievements The final aspectual class of verb phrases consists of *achievements*. Verb phrases of this class are like accomplishment verb phrases in having a clear natural endpoint. Yet, as we will see more clearly below, they differ from accomplishments in attaching much greater importance to the endpoint than to any earlier point. Several examples are given in (150).

(150) a. Linda finished her dissertation.
     b. Joel arrived at the meeting.
     c. Fred's goldfish died.
     d. Carol got to Boston.

17.2.3 Rules in Which the Aspectual Classes Play a Role

In (143)–(146), we got a glimpse of the effects of several rules in which aspectual properties of sentences play a role. Having identified the four major aspectual classes, we are now in a position to undertake a more systematic examination of these rules.

17.2.3.1 Rules concerning Aspectual Adverbial Phrases

Two kinds of adverbial phrases are commonly used to indicate the duration of a state or event. One kind is headed by *in*, the other by *for*.

As a preliminary matter, we need to observe that phrases such as *in four minutes* can be used in two distinct ways, only one of which is relevant in what follows. These phrases can indicate how long a certain event goes on, or they can indicate how long it is before a certain state or event begins. Both readings are possible in the following ambiguous sentence:

(151) Roger Bannister will run a mile in four minutes.

On one reading, the sentence means that the task of running a mile will require four minutes from start to finish. On the other reading, the sentence means that the running of the mile is scheduled to begin four minutes after utterance time. The former interpretation is aspectual in nature, having to do with the time internal to the event itself, whereas the latter interpretation is relational, having to do with the time of the event relative to another time. In what follows, we will be interested exclusively in the aspectual interpretation.

We turn now to the matter of primary concern. *In* phrases are most acceptable in situations in which natural endpoints exist (accomplishments and achievements).

(152) a. Ron peeled the carrot $\left\{ \begin{array}{l} \textit{in three minutes} \\ \textit{?for three minutes} \end{array} \right\}$. (accomplishment)

    b. Linda finished her thesis $\left\{ \begin{array}{l} \textit{in three months} \\ \textit{?for three months} \end{array} \right\}$. (achievement)

By contrast, *for* phrases are most natural in situations in which such endpoints do not exist (states and activities).

(153) a. Roger had a rash $\begin{Bmatrix} \textit{for three days} \\ \textit{?in three days} \end{Bmatrix}$.   (state)

b. Karen talked to Martha $\begin{Bmatrix} \textit{?in thirty minutes} \\ \textit{for thirty minutes} \end{Bmatrix}$.   (activity)

The above discussion affords a practical dividend that merits special attention: the differing hospitality to *for* phrases and *in* phrases provides an effective means for distinguishing between states and activities on one hand, and accomplishments and achievements on the other. For instance, suppose that we want to determine the class membership of the two sentences in (154).

(154) a. Simon treated Roger's rash.

b. Simon healed Roger's rash.

When we add aspectual adverbials of these two kinds to the two sentences, we get a clear result.

(155) a. Simon *treated Roger's rash* for three weeks (*in three weeks).

b. Simon *healed Roger's rash* in three weeks (*for three weeks).

We conclude from this experiment that treating Roger's rash is a state or an activity, whereas healing Roger's rash is an accomplishment or an achievement. (Tests described later will show that the former is an activity rather than a state, and that the latter is an accomplishment rather than an achievement.)

Applied to a variety of verb phrases, this test yields some surprises. In particular, we find many examples in which two nonstate verb phrases are headed by the same verb but nevertheless have to be placed in different classes. One group of examples is given in (156) and (157).

(156) a. Brenda *drove to San Francisco* in an hour (*for an hour).

b. Brenda *drove toward San Francisco* for an hour (*in an hour).

(157) a. Gordon *rowed two miles* in an hour (*for an hour).

b. Gordon *rowed* for an hour (*in an hour).

The contrast between (156a) and (156b) derives from the fact that in the former but not in the latter, a specific goal is attained. Similarly, (157a) asserts that a definite distance was covered, whereas (157b) does not. These examples, then, can be accounted for by the following rule:

(158) Motion verb phrases in which a definite goal is reached or a definite distance is covered count as accomplishments or achievements, whereas motion verb phrases in which neither of these conditions hold count as activities.

The examples in (159)–(162) illustrate another contrast between accomplishments and activities.

(159) a. Freddy *ate a pancake* in two minutes (*for two minutes).
      b. Freddy *ate pancakes* for two hours (*in two hours).

(160) a. Linda *drank a glass of beer* in thirty seconds (*for thirty seconds).
      b. Linda *drank beer* for thirty minutes (*in thirty minutes).

(161) a. Frances *read a story* in thirty minutes (*for thirty minutes).
      b. Frances *read stories* for three hours (*in three hours).

(162) a. Grant *wrote a poem* in three weeks (*for three weeks).
      b. Grant *wrote poetry* for three months (*in three months).

In each of these pairs of examples, the first sentence involves some definite unit or amount of something, whereas the second does not. These examples can be accounted for by the following rule:

(163) If a certain verb phrase has a direct object that denotes a definite number or amount, and the verb phrase is an accomplishment, then a corresponding verb phrase in which the object denotes an indefinite number or amount will count as an activity.

Exercise

1. Apply the *for*-versus-*in* test in each of the following sentences, to decide whether the verb phrase should be classified as an accomplishment or an activity. Some may be classifiable as both.

   a. Harry walked around the block.
   b. Your father built this house.
   c. We ate Joe's biscuits.
   d. Nelda will tell John the story.
   e. The soup cooled.
   f. The squirrels disappeared.
   g. Jody finished your sentence.
   h. Smith managed the company.

17.2.3.2 Interpretation of Time Adverbs The four basic aspectual classes that were described above differ markedly in the way they require ordinary time adverbs to be interpreted. Some of these time adverbs denote individual points of time (*at three o'clock yesterday afternoon, right at that moment*), whereas others denote intervals of time (*yesterday, last year, on Tuesday*). The major differences in interpretation concern where the state or event in question has to lie in relation to the time span denoted by the adverb.

States are the most permissive of the four classes in this regard, as a simple situation illustrates. Suppose that Roger had a rash yesterday from noon until eight o'clock in the evening. Suppose also that Betty came to see him at three o'clock that afternoon. Under these circumstances, both of the sentences in (64) are completely acceptable.

(164) a. Roger had a rash *yesterday*.
　　　b. Roger had a rash *when Betty came to see him at three o'clock*.

The relation between the period of the rash and the time spans denoted by these two adverbs is represented in (165).

(165) a.

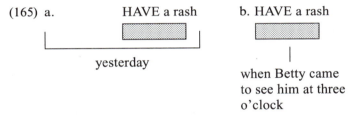

In the first case, the time adverb denotes a period that includes the state, whereas in the second case, the time adverb denotes a point that is itself included in the period in which the state is in effect.

Moving to activities and accomplishments, we find that the possibilities of interpretation are more limited.

(166) a. Karen talked to Martha yesterday.
　　　b. Karen talked to Martha at three o'clock.

(167) a. Joan wrote a sonnet yesterday.
　　　b. Joan wrote a sonnet at three o'clock.

Sentences (166a) and (167a) are interpreted in the same manner as the state sentence (164a). Again, the time span denoted by *yesterday* can include the interval during which the event was going on. But the interpretations of sentences (166b) and (167b) are different from that of the state sentence (164b). Here *at three o'clock* cannot be just some point or other within the interval in which the talking or the writing took place. Instead, it can only be taken as an indication of the moment at which these events started. Thus, the interpretations in (168) are the only ones that we get for activities and accomplishments.

(168) a.   TALK to Martha   b.   TALK to Martha

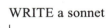

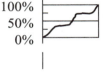

Even this interpretation is impossible for accomplishments that are spread over a longer period, as the following sentence shows:

(169) Marvin read *War and Peace* at three o'clock Friday afternoon.

The only legitimate interpretation for this sentence is that Marvin is an incredibly fast reader. The sentence could not be used to report a situation in which Marvin starts to read *War and Peace* at three o'clock on Friday afternoon, but finishes it only several days later.

Still another interpretation is possible for achievement sentences. In contrast with activities and accomplishments, the only requirement for achievements is that the time span of the adverb cover the final moment of the achievement. The contrast between achievements and accomplishments in this regard is particularly striking.

(170) a.   John spent several years finishing his dissertation. He finally finished it on July 4, 1987 (at three o'clock in the afternoon). (achievement)

      b.   *John spent several years writing his dissertation. He finally wrote it on July 4, 1987 (at three o'clock in the afternoon). (accomplishment)

(171) a.   Carolyn spent several days getting to Boston. She finally got there at three o'clock (at three o'clock this afternoon). (achievement)

b. *Carolyn spent several days driving to Boston. She finally
   drove there at three o'clock (at three o'clock this afternoon).
   (accomplishment)

Even though achievements, like accomplishments, can be described as
taking a long time, we are entitled with achievements to use any time
adverb that covers the final moment, without regard to all of the time that
went before that moment. This requirement is pictured for sentence (170a)
in (172).

(172) FINISH his dissertation

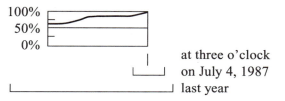

As (170b) and (171b) show, this kind of interpretation, one in which the
time adverb does not include the entire event, is completely impossible for
accomplishments.

Exercise

1. For each of the following sentences, use some time adverbs to test whether the
sentence contains an accomplishment verb phrase or an achievement verb phrase:

   a. Edison invented the phonograph.
   b. Sequoya developed an alphabet.
   c. David noticed the bug.
   d. Frankenstein created a monster.
   e. Harold relinquished his claim.
   f. Katy let go of the rope.
   g. Columbus discovered America.
   h. Nancy won the race.

17.2.3.3 Possibilities for Verb-Phrase Interpretation The third area in
which the basic aspectual classes described above play a role is in determining the possibilities for two contrasting interpretations for verb
phrases. These interpretations, which are themselves aspectual in nature,
can be referred to as *punctual* and *habitual*. A verb phrase with a punctual
interpretation refers to a state or event that occurs either once or some
definite number of times. By contrast, a verb phrase with a habitual
interpretation denotes a state or event that recurs with some degree

of frequency. The following pairs of sentences illustrate these two interpretations:

(173) a. Roger had a rash last week.   (punctual state)
      b. Roger occasionally had a rash.   (habitual state)

(174) a. Jonah pestered the cat last night.   (punctual activity)
      b. Jonah pestered the cat every day.   (habitual activity)

(175) a. Alfred ate a peach yesterday.   (punctual accomplishment)
      b. Alfred ate a peach three times a year.   (habitual accomplishment)

(176) a. Carol discovered a new problem on Thursday.   (punctual achievement)
      b. Carol discovered a new problem several times a month. (habitual achievement)

Now, what are the external circumstances under which these two interpretations are available? For habituals, the answer is simple: so long as the verb phrase itself is one that makes sense with a habitual interpretation, then that interpretation is allowed. The sentences in (177) give some idea of the range of environments that permit a habitual interpretation:

(177) a. Cora *had a headache every day*.   (past tense)
      b. Nora *writes a novel every year*.   (present tense)
      c. Joe's son will *write a letter every week*.   (bare stem as complement of WILL)
      d. *Eating a peach three times a year* is good for you.   (present participial)
      e. Sharon appears to have *finished an essay every month*.   (past participial as complement of perfect HAVE)

With the punctual interpretation, the possibilities are more limited. The most readily apparent restriction concerns the possibility of such an interpretation for simple sentences in the present tense. The sentences in (178) show the possibilities for each of the four basic aspectual classes.

(178) a. John can't talk on the phone now. He *has a headache*.   (state)
      b. Flora is busy right this minute. *She *plays the piano*.   (activity)
      c. Max will see you in a minute. *Right now he *writes a letter*. (accomplishment)
      d. Sarah will be free in just a second. *Right now she *finishes her breakfast*.   (achievement)

The following rule represents an initial attempt at expressing this limitation:

(179) When it occurs in the simple present tense, a nonstate verb phrase cannot receive a punctual interpretation.

Additional examples reveal that this interpretive restriction needs to be stated in a more general form. We find the same effects with nonfinite verb phrases when the event time and the current reference point are the same. A clear example is (180), where the intended interpretation of the modal MUST is 'logical necessity'.

(180) *John must take a bath right now. (I bet that's why he isn't answering the door.)

This sentence with this interpretation is just as unacceptable as (181), in which *take a bath* appears in the present tense.

(181) *It must be the case that John takes a bath right now.

These examples, then, suggest that the statement in (180) should be replaced by one that does not refer specifically to the present tense.

(182) If the event time is the same as the current reference point, a nonstate verb phrase cannot receive a punctual interpretation.

We have here a rule in which a matter concerning aspect (the availability of a punctual interpretation) is determined by a combination of a basic aspectual property (whether the phrase denotes a state) and a property of time relations (whether the event time and the current reference point are the same).

Exercises

1. If we were to examine a great many verb phrases, with a view to determining whether or not they could qualify for a habitual interpretation, we would find that some verb phrases seemed to require a frequency modifier, whereas others did not. Here are examples from both of these groups:

(i)	Jack eats grasshoppers.	Jack eats grasshoppers quite frequently.
(ii)	?Jane makes a mistake.	Jane rarely makes a mistake.
(iii)	?Peter drinks three beers.	Peter drinks three beers every Saturday.
(iv)	?Norbert attends a concert.	Norbert attends a concert every Sunday.
(v)	Hugh eats peas with a knife.	Hugh occasionally eats peas with a knife.
(vi)	Kathleen watches television.	Kathleen often watches television.

(vii) ?Barry sells a truck.   Barry sells a truck about once a week.

(viii) Norma drives a truck.   Norma drives a truck about once a week.

Give a simple statement that distinguishes between the verb phrases that need a frequency modifier in order to have a habitual interpretation and those that do not.

2. As was noted earlier in this chapter, MAY can have two interpretations (logical possibility and permission), and MUST can also have two (logical necessity and obligation). We see both interpretations for MAY in (i), and for MUST in (ii).

(i) John may eat lunch at his office.

(ii) John must eat lunch at his office.

Now look at the following sentences:

(iii) John may destroy this letter.

(iv) John must destroy this letter.

In (iii), MAY has the same two interpretations that it had in (i). However, MUST in (iv) has only the 'obligation' interpretation. Explain why the logical-necessity interpretation is allowed in (ii) but not in (iv). Hint: Look again at the diagrams in (24) and (26).

3. In subsection 17.1.3, which dealt with past harmony, it was noted that in informal speech, a past-tense inflection in quoted speech was matched with a past-tense inflection in the corresponding reported speech.

(i) Carol said, "Janice *collected* the money."

(ii) Carol said that Janice *collected* the money.

In addition, of course, the Past-Harmony Rule sometimes dictates a match-up between a present-tense inflection in quoted speech and a past-tense inflection in reported speech.

(iii) Carol said, "Janice *collects* the money."

(iv) Carol said that Janice *collected* the money.

The following sentence contains a past-tense inflection in the subordinate clause that can be interpreted as 'earlier' but not as a past-harmonic present (meaning 'same time as'):

(v) Carol said that Janice *married* Phil.

Explain why this subordinate past-tense inflection can only be interpreted as 'earlier'.

17.2.3.4 Availability and Interpretation of the Progressive A final area in which the four basic aspectual classes are differentiated involves the progressive construction, which consists of BE plus a present-participial verb phrase. We will begin by considering how it is interpreted with activities and accomplishments, since its interpretation here is the most straightforward.

In our general discussion of activity and accomplishment sentences, we noted that they are interpreted as taking place during an interval. As was observed in subsection 17.2.3.2, a time adverb that refers to a single moment can only be interpreted (if it can be interpreted at all) as indicating the point at which this interval begins. Thus, sentences such as (183a) and (183b) can have only the interpretations in which *at three o'clock* identifies the beginning time of the event.

(183) a. Karen talked to Martha at three o'clock.

TALK to Martha

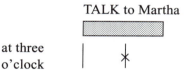

at three
o'clock

b. Joan wrote a sonnet at three o'clock.

WRITE a sonnet

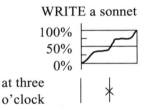

at three
o'clock

It is precisely here that the progressive construction fills a gap. As illustrated in (184), it takes a particular complement verb phrase that by itself would stand for an entire activity or accomplishment stretched over an interval, and creates a larger verb phrase that stands for a slice of an activity or accomplishment—a slice that can be as small as a single moment.

(184) a. Karen was talking to Martha at three o'clock.

BE talking to Martha

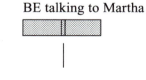

at three
o'clock

b. Joan was writing a sonnet at three o'clock.

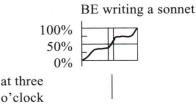

With achievements, the progressive has a similar though not identical effect.

(185) a. On June 18, Linda was finishing her dissertation.
    b. When the clock chimed eight, Joel was arriving at the meeting.
    c. At the time when the phone rang, Fred's goldfish was dying.
    d. At five o'clock, Carol was getting to Boston.

As noted earlier, a single-moment time adverb with an achievement generally denotes the endpoint of the event. However, when we use such an adverb with an achievement verb phrase in a progressive construction, the adverb marks out the time of a prefinal slice of the event. The contrast between a simple achievement and an achievement in a progressive construction is depicted in (186).

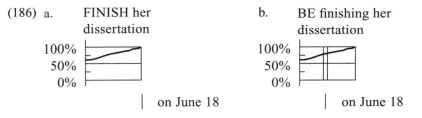

Progressives associated with activities, accomplishments, and achievements serve to fill the gap that we noted in the preceding subsection. Although the examples with the simple present tense in (187) are not acceptable, the corresponding progressive examples in (188) are.

(187) a. *Right now, Georgia plays the piano.   (activity)
    b. *Right this minute, John takes a bath.   (accomplishment)
    c. *At this point, Karen finishes her dissertation.   (achievement)

(188) a. Right now, Georgia is playing the piano.   (activity)
    b. Right this minute, John is taking a bath.   (accomplishment)
    c. At this point, Karen is finishing her dissertation.
       (achievement)

In addition, the 'logical necessity' reading of MUST, which was impossible with *take a bath,* is readily available with the corresponding progressive.

(189) a. *John must take a bath right now. (I bet that's why he isn't answering the door.)

  b. John must be taking a bath right now. (I bet that's why he isn't answering the door.)

Thus, the restriction that nonstates cannot have an event time identical with the current reference point applies only to nonprogressive verb phrases.

Let us turn now to the fourth basic class, the class of states, and see how phrases of this type behave with the progressive construction. As a general rule, state verb phrases are unacceptable with the progressive.

(190) a. *I am knowing the answer to your question.
      (Compare: I know the answer to your question.)

  b. *Joan is owning two cars.
      (Compare: Joan owns two cars.)

  c. *This bar of soap is costing fifty cents.
      (Compare: This bar of soap costs fifty cents.)

  d. *The manager is weighing two hundred pounds.
      (Compare: The manager weighs two hundred pounds.)

This fact might be connected to the fact—noted in subsection 17.2.3.2—that state verb phrases can be asserted for individual "interior points," as well as for intervals. The relevant example is repeated in (191), along with the diagram.

(191) Roger had a rash when Betty came to see him at three o'clock.

HAVE a rash

when Betty came
to see him at three
o'clock

Since the major effect of the progressive construction is to create a predicate with this possibility, and since states already have it, the progressive would be superfluous with them.

In several special cases, however, state verbs can occur in the progressive construction.

(192) a. Karen understands this proof.
     b. Karen is understanding this proof.

(193) a. I really like this performance.
     b. I am really liking this performance.

(194) a. Donald finds your accusations ludicrous.
     b. Donald is finding your accusations ludicrous.

The acceptability of the present tense in the (a) examples shows that all of these really are state verb phrases. Both the (a) and the (b) sentences appear to assert the existence of a judgment of some sort concerning an individual entity or a set of entities. The (a) sentences suggest that the judgment is a final and total judgment. The (b) sentences, by contrast, imply that the judgment is a intermediate one based on only part of the available evidence. Sentence (192b) would typically be used if Karen was only partly done going through the proof, (193b) would be appropriate at an intermediate point in the performance, and (194b) would be used if Donald had only heard some of the accusations.

Another type of situation in which an apparent state verb phrase appears in the progressive construction is illustrated in the (b) sentences of (195)–(197).

(195) a. Jeffrey *resembles his brother.*
     b. Jeffrey is *resembling his brother more and more.*

(196) a. Dana *knows the answer.*
     b. Dana is *knowing more and more of the answers as the course progresses.*

(197) a. The manager *weighs two hundred pounds.*
     b. The manager is *weighing more and more.*

Each of the italicized phrases in the (b) sentences denotes a state that is changing in some way, rather than a state that is staying the same. Thus, the use of the progressive here may be the same as that illustrated in examples that contain change-of-state verbs such as COOL and SOFTEN.

(198) a. The soup is cooling.
     b. The wax is softening.

One final observation about the progressive concerns its interpretation with habitual verb phrases. Some contrasts between the simple present and the present progressive can be seen in (199)–(201).

(199) a. Jonah pesters the cat a lot.
     b. Jonah is pestering the cat a lot this year.

(200) a. Tony goes to Austin every Saturday.
     b. This fall, Tony is going to Austin every Saturday.

(201) a. Lorna proposes a new topic every two weeks or so.
     b. This spring, Lorna is proposing a new topic every two weeks or so.

The difference between the (a) sentences and the corresponding (b) sentences is a subtle one. Each of the (a) sentences seems to assert a permanent habitual state of affairs, whereas the corresponding (b) sentence implies that the habitual state of affairs may be only temporary.

Exercises

1. The English verb HAVE has many different meanings and can be used to head a variety of verb phrases. Several verb phrases headed by HAVE are listed below. For each one, construct an experimental progressive sentence that will indicate whether the verb phrase in question should be classified as a state verb phrase or as a verb phrase of some other kind.

    a. have a good time
    b. have a headache
    c. have a heart attack
    d. have her hat on backwards
    e. have some lunch
    f. have an interview with Fred
    g. have Hal mow the lawn
    h. have two chickens in the pot

2. In this discussion of aspect, we have assumed that there are four basic aspectual classes of verbs and that any habitual verb phrase is related to a nonhabitual verb phrase from one of these four classes. An alternative viewpoint would be that at least some English verbs give rise to phrases that are inherently habitual. One verb for which such an analysis might be adopted is the verb LIVE, as used in the sentence *Quentin lives in Boston.* Think about the way in which you interpret the corresponding progressive, *Quentin is living in Boston,* and use this as evidence to decide whether *live in Boston* should be classified as a stative verb phrase or as an inherently habitual verb phrase.

Appendix A

The Context of English Syntax: Epilogue with References

INTRODUCTORY REMARKS

To the extent that this book has achieved its purpose, most readers who have worked their way through all of it or even a substantial part of it will understand more about the nature of the English language than they did at the outset. In particular, those who are native speakers without prior training in syntax are likely to be much more aware than before of the extent to which speaking and comprehending English depends on the existence of a vast and complex system of rules, a system that is hidden in the unconscious minds of those who use the language. In addition, they will have seen a number of specific hypotheses about what these rules might be and will be able to calculate what sorts of structures these hypothesized rules dictate for a wide variety of specific English sentences. For instance, where an ordinary native speaker can see nothing except the sequence of words in (1), readers of this book (possibly with a bit of time for calculation and reflection) can visualize the structure in (2).

(1) Who will Dr. Smith be ready to operate on?

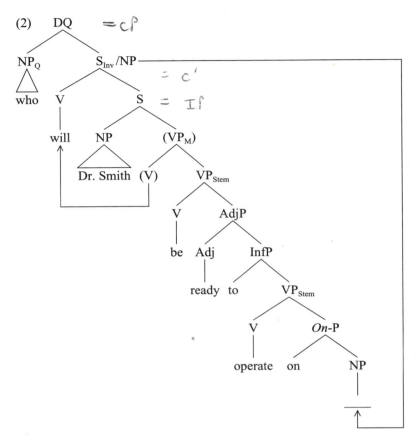

(2)

With the ability to make such structural calculations goes the ability to give concrete explanations for many curious intuitions that virtually all speakers of English have but that very few can explain. For instance, readers who worked their way through section 9.3 can explain why Dr. Smith is taken to be the surgeon in (1) but the patient in the superficially similar (3).

(3) When will Dr. Smith be ready to operate on?

Likewise, the structures that can be calulated for the sentences in (4) and (5) provide a basis for understanding why (4b) is much more acceptable than (5b).

(4) a.   Martha knows what John cooked.
    b.   Martha ate what John cooked.

(5) a.   Martha knows which fish John cooked.
    b.   *Martha ate which fish John cooked.

Some readers may feel that they now know all that they need or want to know about English syntax. Indeed, for many practical purposes and for the satisfaction of general curiosity, what has been conveyed about syntax in this book may be adequate for them, or very close to it. Others, however, may feel that they want to know more. Some in this latter group may want to broaden their knowledge of English syntax to include a more complete inventory of English constructions. For instance, the two-clause comparative structure in (6) and the preposed-adjectival construction with *though* in (7) are just two of many special English constructions that have not been dealt with in this textbook.

(6) [The more of his sonnets Alfred reads ____ to us], [the sleepier we become ____].

(7) Conscientious though you certainly seem to be ____, we are reluctant to leave you alone with the gold.
    (Compare: Though you certainly seem to be conscientious, we are reluctant to leave you alone with the gold.)

These and many other idiosyncratic constructions would be included in a grammar of English that aimed for absolute completeness. All of them can be studied using the same informal methods and experimental techniques that have been illustrated over and over again in the body of this textbook.

Besides aiming for greater breadth of coverage, another possibility is to aim for greater depth. Pursuing this possibility amounts to inquiring into the reasons for certain statements that have been presented in this book, rather than simply accepting them as final answers. An example of a statement that might be explored more deeply is the one in chapter 9 to the effect that the missing noun phrase in the English passive construction must be the first noun phrase after the past-participial verb. This statement is a reasonably accurate description of our observations about what we can and cannot do in forming passive structures, as evidenced by the following examples from chapter 9:

(8) a.   John has been [taken ____ to the library].
    b.   The baby is being [cared for ____].
    c.   *George was [given a book to ____].
    d.   *Sally was [received a gift from ____].

Even though there are many purposes for which this descriptive statement would suffice, we might nevertheless choose not simply to leave matters here, but instead to ask some additional questions.

- Given that the English passive construction exhibits this property, why does it exhibit this property?
- Why isn't the passive construction like the *easy* construction, a construction in which the choice of a missing noun phrase is not limited in this manner?
- Is this limitation on the passive construction an ultimate mental reality in itself, or is it merely a by-product of some more basic reality?

Once we start asking questions like these, we are making our way into a domain of inquiry that does not belong exclusively to English syntax, but instead lies in part in the area generally referred to as *syntactic theory* (or, as in chapter 1, *universal grammar*).

The central purpose of the remainder of this appendix is to indicate briefly what syntactic theory is concerned with and how it is related to the syntax of English. The reason for putting these comments at the end of the book rather than at the beginning is that most readers will be in a much better position to make sense of them now than they would have been earlier, by virtue of their substantially greater sophistication about the basic syntactic properties of English. Because of obvious space limitations, this appendix will not even begin to offer a complete or rigorous view of any particular theory. Nor will it attempt to provide a systematic evaluation of the issues that divide specific syntactic theories from one another. Nevertheless, the partial glimpses given here may prove useful for those who want to take courses or do independent reading in syntactic theory, as well as for those who simply want to satisfy a certain amount of accumulated curiosity about how the view of English syntax developed in this book is related to this more abstract kind of linguistic inquiry.

The discussion will be organized as a brief and unsystematic sketch of a few highlights in the history of generative syntax, beginning with its inception in the middle and late 1950s.[1] In the course of this account, informal descriptions will be provided for a number of concepts that have been important in the development of generative syntactic theory, and mention will also be made of several general ideas, about approaches and methods, that have played a significant role.

GOALS OF GENERATIVE THEORIES

The beginning of the generative syntactic revolution in linguistics can be dated to 1957, the year of publication of a small book by Noam Chomsky entitled *Syntactic Structures* (Chomsky 1957). Chomsky began this book by identifying what he regarded as the two basic goals of research in syntax. The first was to develop grammars (sets of syntactic rules) for various individual languages; the second was to develop a general theory of grammar that would provide an abstract model to be used in constructing grammars of particular languages. He then went on to argue for the inadequacy of two elementary models for human grammars, in each case showing that the model failed to allow an illuminating grammar for English. As an alternative, he proposed a "transformational" model of syntax, which he illustrated with a small, tentative set of rules to account for a few basic constructions and sentence types of English. (This model of syntax will be described in more detail several paragraphs further on.)

A second work by Chomsky that was of major importance in initiating the generative revolution was his review of *Verbal Behavior* by B. F. Skinner (Chomsky 1959). This review, a critical examination of the theory of language advocated by the leading American behavioral psychologist of that time, had an electrifying effect in awakening psychologists and philosophers as well as linguists to the truly remarkable nature of the human capacity for language, and the utter impossibility of accounting for it in terms of the kinds of simple notions that had proved useful for describing artificial learning experiments done with laboratory animals such as pigeons and rats.

The psychological import of a theory of generative syntax was elaborated by Chomsky in *Aspects of the Theory of Syntax* (Chomsky 1965). Here he made more explicit than in *Syntactic Structures* that a generative theory of syntax was to be seen as having a central role to play in an account of language acquisition. Specifically, the theory was viewed as making claims about the innate (i.e., genetically determined) principles humans bring to the task of mastering their native languages. Chapter 1 of *Aspects* included a lengthy discussion of the way in which a body of such innate principles might contribute to an explanation of the capacity that human children have for learning the rules of their native languages. Chomsky's view of the function of these innate principles in the acquisi-

tion of an arbitrary human language L is shown schematically in diagram
(9), a slightly modified version of diagram (26) in chapter 1.

(9)

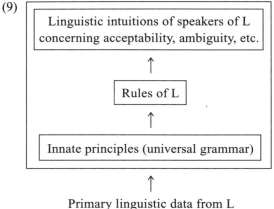

Primary linguistic data from L
(Previously heard sentences, etc.)

Chomsky's belief that innate principles are crucially involved in language acquisition was based on two fundamental considerations. The first
was that he and other generative linguists had provided overwhelming
evidence by 1965 that the systems of unconscious rules learned by human
children are remarkable for their intricacy and complexity. The second
was that the early linguistic experience of young children appears to be
nowhere close to being sufficient to determine the grammars that children
give evidence of having developed. Put another way, there seemed to be
no possibility that one could look at the linguistic experience of children
and predict what unconscious rules they would end up with, if one relied
solely on general rules of logic or vague principles of "analogy" or "similarity." Unless children were assumed to be guided by innate linguistic
principles of some kind, it would remain a complete mystery how they
could develop a coherent set of rules at all, and how this task could be
accomplished "in an astonishingly short time, to a large extent independently of intelligence, and in a comparable way by all children," to use
Chomsky's own formulation (1959, 577). The predicament of a hypothetical language-learner who is not assumed to have the help of any innate
linguistic principles is shown schematically in (10).

(10)

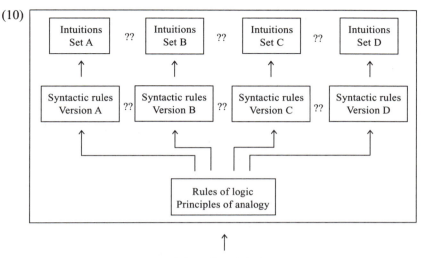

Primary linguistic data
(Previously heard sentences, etc.)

The problem for this hypothetical learner is that there are far too many possible sets of rules that would be consistent with the evidence provided by the linguistic environment, if the learner had guidance only from ordinary logic and analogy. The reason for supposing that human learners are equipped with innate syntactic principles is that these can exclude a great many tempting possibilities in advance. This narrowing of the possibilities would be beneficial if it led to a situation where (a) only one set of rules was consistent with the primary data and also compatible with the innate principles, and (b) the intuitions predicted by this one set of rules were actually correct. Suppose, for instance, that we tested the four versions of the rules in (10) and found that version B did the best job of predicting the intuitions of adult speakers. Then we would have reason to believe that innate principles had excluded versions A, C, and D in advance, but had allowed version B. The kind of guidance that such principles are assumed to provide to the language-learner is shown in (11).

(11)

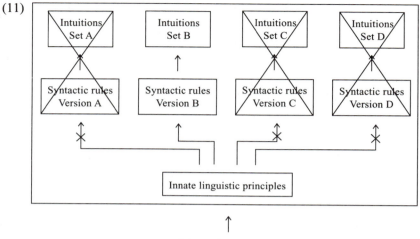

Primary linguistic data
(Previously heard sentences, etc.)

The innate linguistic principles have had the effect of narrowing the learner's options in a beneficial way, excluding in advance the tempting but inadequate sets of rules in versions A, C, and D. The task of a generative syntactic theory is to discover what these innate principles are.[2]

TYPES OF RULES IN A TRANSFORMATIONAL MODEL

At the outset of scholarly work on generative syntax, it was assumed that the guidance provided by these innate principles took the form of definitions of general *types* of rules that children could use in creating a mental grammar of the language that they heard around them. One prominent class of rules defined in the early theories consisted of *phrase-structure rules*—rules that state that a certain kind of structural unit may consist of one or more other structural units. Rules that are implicitly of this type have been seen at many points in the present textbook. Two very basic phrase-structure rules for English are given in (12), in the notation used in many early generative grammars.

(12) a. S → NP VP
     b. VP → V NP

These rules, of course, say just that a sentence may consist of a noun phrase and a verb phrase and that a verb phrase may consist of a verb and a noun phrase. Taken together, they allow the formation of the structure in (13), which provides the basic architecture for simple transitive sentences.

(13)

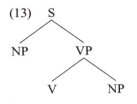

By applying additional phrase-structure rules that build noun phrases and then by inserting individual words, we get the detailed tree diagrams that are associated with particular individual sentences.

Rules of another type, known as *transformational rules,* alter the structures developed by the phrase-structure rules, by moving, adding, or deleting various elements. The present textbook contains several rules that are implicitly of this kind. One such rule is the one in chapter 11 that alters the regular pattern of English verb phrases in a limited set of specific situations by moving special-purpose finite verbs to the left of *not.* Another such rule is used in the formation of the inverted finite structures discussed in chapter 14, which serve as an essential component of direct questions and several other constructions. In many works by Chomsky and others, transformational rules have also been used in the description of what have been characterized in this textbook as "missing-phrase constructions," including in particular the passive construction, the *easy* construction, phrasal questions, and relative clauses. Since transformational rules were the most novel type of rule used in these early generative grammars, they were the type that received special recognition in the term *Transformational Grammar,* a common name for the early generative grammars of particular languages like English, and also for the general syntactic theory that lay behind them.[3]

In a grammar of English that conformed to the model assumed in early transformational theories, a question like *Where was John taken by the police?* might be derived in several stages. First, the phrase structure rules (and, starting with Chomsky 1965, some "subcategorization features"— lexical rules that resembled the complement rules introduced in chapter 3 of this textbook) would give a tree diagram like (14), a structure corresponding to that of a simple active declarative sentence.[4]

(14)

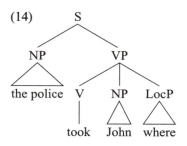

Then several transformational rules would apply to alter this structure in a number of ways. First, a transformational rule (frequently referred to as "Passive") would move *the police* into a *by* phrase, move *John* into the noun-phrase position vacated by *the police,* and insert an extra occurrence of *be.* The way this rule would apply to (14) is shown in simplified form in (15).

(15)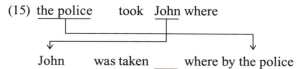

To this transformed structure, two additional transformational rules would apply in sequence. The first (often referred to as "*Wh* Movement") would move the questioned phrase *where* to the beginning of the structure, yielding the new structure in (16).

(16)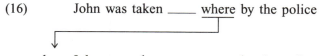

The second (often referred to as "Subject-Auxiliary Inversion") would now move the finite verb *was* to the left of the subject, yielding the desired direct question.

(17) where   John was taken ____ ____ by the police

where was John ___ taken ____ ____ by the police

The term *deep structure* was often used to refer to a structure like (14), that is, to a structure created by phrase-structure rules and lexical rules. The term *surface structure* was used to refer to a structure that resulted from the subsequent application of relevant transformational rules.[5] A general schematic picture of the way in which phrase-structure rules and transformational rules combined to generate sentences in this theory is shown in (18).

(18)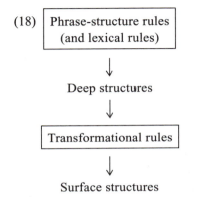

EARLY GENERATIVE RESEARCH ON ENGLISH

From the late 1950s into roughly the middle 1970s, English occupied a dominant position in generative syntactic scholarship, and a large fraction of the research done during this period was devoted specifically to trying to work out adequate transformational accounts of English. A great deal of effort was expended on just trying to get a firm descriptive grasp of the subject matter. This effort involved examining speaker judgments on a more extensive basis than had ever been done before (including especially judgments about what were *not* acceptable English sentences), and then trying to formulate explicit systems of rules that would account for these judgments. In work that was presented at a 1958 conference, Chomsky illustrated his new theory of syntax with a more comprehensive grammar of English (Chomsky 1962b). In the ensuing years, a large number of works were published by other scholars on various more specialized topics in English syntax. Among these were Edward Klima's article on English negation (Klima 1964), Peter Rosenbaum's dissertation on clausal complements (Rosenbaum 1967), and Joan Bresnan's article on degree modification and comparison (Bresnan 1973), to name just a few of many works from this period that were quite influential. Also published during this period was *The Major Syntactic Structures of English* (Stockwell, Schachter, and Partee 1973), a volume that attempted to synthesize a complete and coherent transformational grammar of English out of the growing body of research that had been done on individual topics. All of these works had a dual mission: to arrive at a more complete and detailed understanding of the unconscious rules of English, and to evaluate the validity of the abstract transformational model by looking closely at how illuminating a grammar it allowed for English.

CONDITIONS ON THE APPLICATION OF TRANSFORMATIONAL RULES

Much attention during these years was also given to a problem that had completely escaped notice prior to the inception of generative grammar. This problem was that otherwise valid syntactic rules gave surprisingly poor results when they applied in certain special situations. The first observations about the existence of such special situations were made in Chomsky 1962a, 1964. Chomsky noted, for instance, that (19) was unacceptable, even though it conformed to generally applicable English rules for forming questions and relative clauses and had a reasonable answer.

(19) *What did he see the man read the book that was on ____?
       (Answer: He saw the man read the book that was on *molecular biology*.)

We can get a clearer view of what is going on here by looking at a somewhat simpler structure, the indirect question bracketed in (20).

(20) *Please tell me [which cat he caught the dog that chased ____].
       (Answer: He caught the dog that chased *Rascal*.)

The indirect question in (20a) could have been derived in the following steps:

(21) a. he caught the dog [the dog chased which cat]
           (deep structure)
       b. he caught the dog [that chased which cat]
           (by a special transformational rule for forming relative clauses)
       c. which cat he caught the dog [that chased ____]
           (by *Wh* Movement, the rule illustrated in (16))

Even though all of the rule applications look legitimate, the indirect question is unacceptable. In Chomsky 1964, it was hypothesized that a hidden application of *Wh* Movement was involved in the formation of the relative clause *that chased which cat,* and that the subsequent attempt to move another *wh* phrase out of the same structure was barred by a general condition that was not restricted to English, but instead was common to all languages. This condition prohibited the extraction of some element from a structure if a similar element had already been extracted from the same structure by an earlier transformational operation.

A comprehensive examination of a great many unacceptable examples of this kind was conducted by John R. Ross, who proposed a number of different constraints (Ross 1967). All of them had the effect of defining certain "syntactic islands," structures from which phrases could not be moved by otherwise applicable movement transformations. One such contraint was the Complex-NP Constraint, by virtue of which the relative clause in (21b) would be a syntactic island. The effect of this island in blocking the movement of the *wh* phrase *which cat* is shown in (22), where the x on the arrow indicates that the movement is disallowed.

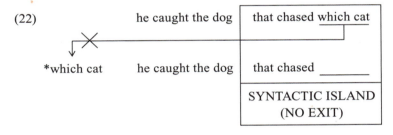

The unacceptable (21c) could only be derived by illegally extracting *which cat* from the island defined by the Complex-NP Constraint. Following the suggestion made in Chomsky 1964, Ross proposed that this constraint and several of his other island constraints were not specific to English, but instead constituted part of the innately given and thus universal component of the human language capacity.

In 1973, Chomsky returned to the discussion of these phenomena himself, proposing an alternative theory for several of the observations made by Ross, a theory based on a new condition that was dubbed the Subjacency Condition. This condition prohibits any element from being moved across more than one "bounding node" in a single movement operation. In the original version of the condition, it was assumed that the class of bounding nodes consisted of just clauses and noun phrases. Given the Subjacency Condition, the indirect question in (21c) is unacceptable because *which cat* has to cross a clause boundary and a noun-phrase boundary to get to its eventual position at the beginning of the indirect question. These two bounding nodes are the two interior boxed structures in (23).[6]

(23)
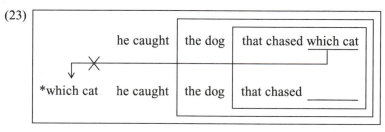

One defensive measure had to be taken in order to make the Subjacency Condition viable. It was necessary to assume that *wh* movements that appeared to cross several clauses were actually accomplished in a series of separate jumps. The problem requiring this "successive-cyclic" assumption was created by the acceptability of the embedded indirect question in (24).

(24) I want to know [what Jane thought that Bill said that Ann bought].

As the diagram in (25) shows, this indirect question would be incorrectly ruled out by the Subjacency Condition if the movement of *what* had to take place in one long jump.

(25)

	Jane thought	that Bill said	that Ann bought what
what	Jane thought	that Bill said	that Ann bought ___

However, if *Wh* Movement could use the initial position in a clause as an intermediate "parking place" and if it could apply successive-cyclically, then the alternative transformational derivation in (26) would be possible.

(26)

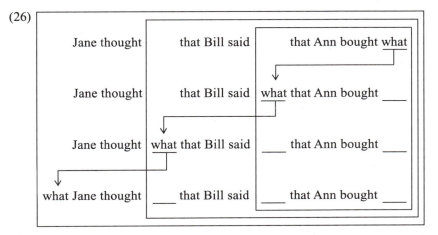

Thus, the hypothesis of successive-cyclic *Wh* Movement removes what would otherwise be a serious obstacle to adopting the Subjacency Condition. As it happened, later research turned up arguments of a less theoretical and more direct sort for successive cyclicity: French and Irish proved to exhibit special syntactic effects exactly in those clause-initial locations that successive-cyclic *Wh* Movement would have used as intermediate parking places.[7]

In the years since these early efforts to understand island phenomena, an enormous amount of additional research has been devoted to this topic, and to other types of situations in which the application of various kinds of syntactic rules appears to be limited by constraints of a general kind. Several different constraints were proposed in the 1970s and 1980s to prevent certain unacceptable extractions not covered by the Subjacency Condition, including extractions of the subjects of indirect questions, as illustrated in (27).[8]

(27)

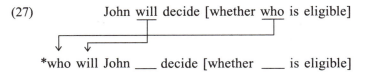

John will decide [whether who is eligible]

*who will John ___ decide [whether ___ is eligible]

Also receiving attention in the form of several proposed constraints were ungrammatical reflexive and reciprocal examples of the kind illustrated in (28).[9]

(28) a. *Marsha* would like for John to hire *herself.*

   b. *Marsha and Tom* would like for John to hire *each other.*

The result of all of this work was the accumulation of a broad collection of data and a number of competing theoretical proposals concerning the precise conditions under which syntactic rules of various types could apply.

EXTENSIONS OF THE *ASPECTS* THEORY

The 1970s witnessed a number of new proposals concerning the sorts of rules that a generative model of syntax should allow. The major goal of these proposals, several of which have remained influential in one form or another to the present time, was to try to put very severe limits on what could be stated in the rule systems of individual languages. This narrowing of possible rule systems has been viewed as a way of achieving a beneficial narrowing of the possibilities that a hypothetical language-learner would have to consider in acquiring a grammar, along the lines of the diagram in (11). One such effort has been seen in the development of *X-bar theory,* which aims to define a more restricted set of possibilities for phrase structure.[10] Although many different versions of X-bar theory have been proposed, all of them are alike in requiring the properties of phrases to be determined by the properties of their heads, rather than allowing phrase-structure rules complete freedom to say almost anything at all about what smaller syntactic units can combine to form a phrase. (In the present textbook, the structures proposed for verb phrases, adjective phrases, and common-noun phrases fall very much within the spirit of X-bar theory, whereas the structures proposed in chapter 6 for locative and motion phrases fall just as clearly outside it.)

In addition to this attempt to limit possible phrase-structure rules, several different efforts have been made to construct a much more restrictive theory of transformational rules. One notable effort of this sort is embodied in the theory of movement rules first proposed in Chomsky 1976. Something of the character of this effort can be seen by comparing what could be said in the original transformational theory and what can be said in the newer theory about the way in which the subject of a passive is determined. In the original theory, it was possible to build certain restrictions directly into the transformational rule. In particular, one could specify (a) that the noun phrase that is moved to the left has to be the first noun phrase after the verb, and (b) that this noun phrase has to be put in the position from which the original subject has been moved. In the revised theory, by contrast, the only rule allowed for this situation is one that just say "Move NP." The theory allows no statement that specifically identifies this rule with the passive construction as such; in fact, the same rule is also assumed to be operative in derivations such as that shown in (29), where a subject that is understood with the nontransparent verb KNOW is moved up to be the subject of the transparent verb SEEM.

(29)   seems [Martha to know the answer]

Martha seems [_____ to know the answer]

An additional restriction is that there cannot be any indication in the rule itself of what noun phrases qualify for movement or where they can be moved. The idea is that any limitations observed in the passive construction or in any other constructions that show the effects of Move NP are to be attributed to the operation of constraints that apply to movement rules in general, among which are those in (30).

(30) a. Under ordinary conditions, if a phrase of any kind is moved by a transformational rule, it must move to a vacant position in which that type of phrase would normally be allowed by phrase-structure rules. (This is the Structure-Preservation Constraint of Emonds 1970, 1976.)
   b. The position to which a phrase is moved must be in a certain structural relation to the position from which the phrase is moved. To use a technical term, the eventual position must "c-command" the original position (roughly speaking, the eventual position must be farther up the tree than the original position).

The one special property of the passive construction that makes Move NP relevant for passive structures and is responsible for the particular choice of missing noun phrase is that identified in (31).

(31) The passive verb in English (like that in some but not all other languages) loses the capacity that the corresponding active verb has to "license" the presence of a following noun phrase. Thus, if a noun phrase starts out in such a position in deep structure, it must be moved somewhere by Move NP.[11]

Taken together, these conditions, along with several others that have an independent justification in regulating the relation of reflexives and reciprocals with their antecedents, achieve much the same effects as were formerly achieved by specific restrictions in the passive transformational rule. The overall strategy seen here is to formulate maximally simple rules that are restricted in their ultimate effects by independent general conditions. This strategy is also much in evidence in Chomsky's theory of the early 1980s (widely known under the label *Government-Binding Theory* or *Principles-and-Parameters Theory*) and has been a prominent feature of his work and the work of many other syntacticians to the present time.[12]

The term *modular* is often applied to theories that have this property of getting their results from the interaction of several simple rules or principles rather than from some single rule or principle of a fairly complicated sort.[13] A brilliant early example of modular thinking in the physical sciences is to be found in Galileo's effort to understand the motions of objects such as rocks and corks in air and water. Rather than requiring four separate special laws (for rocks in water, rocks in air, corks in water, and corks in air), he was able to explain their motions as arising from the interaction of three independent forces (gravity in a downward direction, buoyancy in an upward direction, and the resistance of the medium contrary to the direction in which the object was moving). This modular, nonunitary way of looking at the motion of rocks and and corks moving through air and water had the virtue of great simplicity and generality, and extended automatically to situations involving other objects and other media. Modular accounts are sought in current syntactic theory for the same reason that they have long been sought in the physical sciences: because they often allow us to explain a large and varied collection of complex phenomena by appealing to combinations of simple, fundamental principles.

RELATIONAL GRAMMAR AND LEXICAL-FUNCTIONAL GRAMMAR

Two additional syntactic theories, both of which originated in the 1970s, also adopt more restrictive views of possible syntactic rules. These two theories are noteworthy for the decidedly different tack that they take in their treatment of what kinds of concepts are important in defining various kinds of grammatical processes. These theories are *Relational Grammar,* first put forth by David Perlmutter and Paul Postal, and *Lexical-Functional Grammar,* first put forth by Joan Bresnan and Ron Kaplan.[14]

Both theories attribute a much greater significance than does Chomsky's theory to what are often referred to in the syntactic literature as "grammatical relations" such as subject and object, as opposed to "grammatical categories" such as noun phrase and verb phrase. One English construction with respect to which the difference in approach can be seen with particular clarity is the passive construction. The standard transformational rule creates the passive construction by associating two structures in which *the noun phrase after the verb* in the first structure is moved to *the position before the verb* in the new structure. On the other hand, the corresponding rule in Relational Grammar associates two structures in which the noun phrase that serves as the *direct object* in the first structure serves as *the subject* in the second structure. The passive operation assumed in Lexical-Functional Grammar is also couched in terms of subjects and objects, but it applies within the lexicon instead of as part of the syntax. The Lexical-Functional Grammar passive operation has roughly the effect of giving each transitive verb a new complement rule for passive structures calculated on the basis of its complement rule for active structures. For every transitive verb in the English lexicon, the semantic role assigned to the object in the active entry is assigned to the subject in the passive entry.

Like Chomsky's theory, Relational Grammar and Lexical-Functional Grammar also yield a treatment of the English passive construction that is distinctly modular. A central part of the account, of course, is a relation-changing rule, which changes the associations between the semantic roles called for by a verb and the grammatical relations used to express them. Also involved are rules of a different kind, which state how subjects, objects, and so on, are to be "realized" in the language in question. This second sort of rule is not limited to passive structures, but applies in the formation of active structures as well. The English passive construction is then seen as the result of the interaction between rules of these distinctly different types, as summarized in (32).

(32) a. Relation-changing rule (passivization): The argument that is expressed by the object in active structures comes to be expressed instead by the subject.

b. Syntactic realization rule: In English, the subject is realized by a noun phrase that joins with a verb phrase to make a sentence, the object by a noun phrase that joins with the verb in the formation of the verb phrase.

Although this last rule is quite different in conception from the Structure-Preservation Constraint cited in (30a), it has very much the same result: by both constraints, the noun phrase that joins with the verb to make a verb phrase in an active structure will join with a verb phrase to make a sentence in the corresponding passive structure. In the former theory, this will be so because the noun phrase must be moved to a position where noun phrases are legal, whereas in the latter theory, this will be so because the noun phrase becomes a subject and therefore must appear where subjects generally appear in English.

More generally, proponents of Lexical-Functional Grammar have argued for the usefulness of functional concepts in accounting for a great many other grammatical phenomena. For example, they have argued in favor of redefining certain island constraints in terms of functional concepts such as *complement* and *modifier* instead of in terms of various purely categorial concepts. They have also brought to light examples from various languages of situations where grammatical categories and grammatical functions do not coincide perfectly.[15] The overall vision of Lexical-Functional Grammar is one in which the grammars of languages associate each human-language sentence with structures of quite distinct types: on the one hand, a *constituent structure* defined in terms of syntactic categories, word order, and case marking, and on the other hand, an *argument structure* defined in terms of functions of various kinds.

GENERALIZED PHRASE-STRUCTURE GRAMMAR

One more theory that originated in roughly the same period seeks to put yet a different restriction on possible rules of grammar. This theory, known as *Generalized Phrase-Structure Grammar* (*GPSG* for short), originated in work circulated in the late 1970s and published in the early 1980s by Gerald Gazdar.[16] It directly challenges Chomsky's 1957 thesis that phrase-structure rules are insufficient for describing human languages in an illuminating way. Gazdar claims instead that the versatility of phrase-structure grammars has been underestimated and that the best way to put meaningful restrictions on transformational rules is to eliminate their use altogether.

Something of the character of GPSG can be seen in the treatment that it gives to those constructions described in transformational terms by rules such as *Wh* Movement. As noted previously, the theories that derive their treatment of these constructions from Chomsky 1973 assume that

Wh Movement is accomplished not in one long jump, but in a series of successive-cyclic jumps of the kind shown in (26). For GPSG, the connections that eventually link a *wh* phrase with the position where it is understood necessarily have to be even more numerous and more "local." Because of the self-imposed requirement of doing everything with phrase-structure rules, the necessity of a missing phrase farther down the tree cannot just be marked at the top (as has been done informally in the present textbook), but instead must be kept track of in every intermediate phrase. The sort of structure that GPSG requires for the bracketed indirect question in (33a) is shown in (33b).

(33) a. I wonder [which letters Alice let Susan see ____].

b.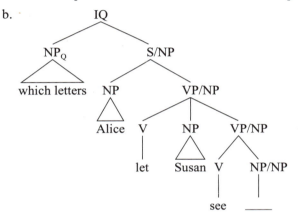

In effect, we can see at each step of the way down through the tree that the structure still owes us a missing noun phrase. The S/NP is assigned the responsibility of coming up with a missing noun phrase, a burden that it shifts onto its daughter verb phrase, which in turn shifts the burden onto *its* daughter verb phrase, which finally manages to have a missing noun phrase as its own daughter.

Although this treatment of missing-phrase constructions is dictated by the theoretical decision to rely entirely on phrase-structure rules, an interesting positive argument has been put forth for it. The argument is based on what was perhaps the oddest of Ross's island constraints, the Coordinate-Structure Constraint. This constraint bars the extraction of any element from one conjunct of a conjoined structure, thus ruling out examples like those in (34).

(34) a. *I don't know *which book* Bill [bought ____ from Shirley] and
       [sold *War and Peace* to Fred].
     b. *How many books did John decide to [remove some papers
       from his office] and [take ____ to Margaret's house]?

What is odd about this phenomenon is that when extractions are carried
out from both conjuncts instead of just one, the result is not worse, but
much better (in fact, perfectly normal).

(35) a. I don't know *which book* Bill [bought ____ from Shirley] and
       [sold ____ to Fred].
     b. How many books did John decide to [remove ____ from his
       office] and [take ____ to Margaret's house]?

Examples of this type led Ross to replace his Coordinate-Structure Constraint by what he called the Across-the-Board Constraint, stating that an
element can be extracted from one conjunct only if an identical element is
extracted from every other conjunct as well.

Gazdar argues that this particular phenomenon constitutes evidence in
favor of the GPSG treatment of *wh* constructions, if one simply assumes
in addition the basic idea about conjoined structures presented in chapter
16, to the effect that two or more structures can be conjoined only if they
are structures of the same type. The only structure that GPSG would
allow for the unacceptable indirect question in (34a) would be that shown
in (36).

(36)

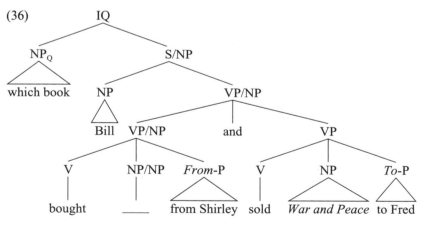

If a verb phrase with a missing noun phrase counts as a different sort of structure from a verb phrase without a missing noun phrase, then this structure accounts for the unacceptability of (34a), because it involves a conjunction of unlike structures, a possibility barred by the basic rule given in chapter 16 for conjoined structures. The crucial malformed portion of (36) is the conjoined structure isolated in (37).

(37)

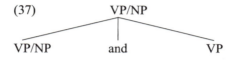

By contrast, the GPSG structure for the acceptable sentence in (35a) contains a conjunction of two structures of the same type, both verb phrases with missing noun phrases, as shown in (38).

(38)

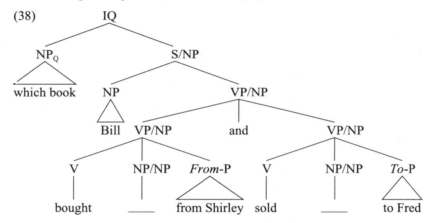

Here the conjunction joins two phrases of the same type, as seen in (39).

(39)

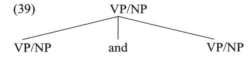

Exactly the same account can be given for the contrast between (34b) and (35b). Gazdar's argument, then, is that Ross's Across-the-Board Constraint follows as an automatic consequence of the GPSG analysis of *wh* constructions, rather than having to be stated as a separate condition, as in non-GPSG analyses of these constructions.

THE LARGER THEORETICAL PICTURE

In the preceding portion of this appendix, a number of different theories have been described and briefly illustrated—several distinct stages of Chomsky's theory, as well as Relational Grammar, Lexical-Functional Grammar, and Generalized Phrase-Structure Grammar. Despite the differences that have been brought out here among these theories, it should be noted that there are many specific points on which two or more of them share common ground. By the same token, it needs to be noted that the theories as described above are not really uniform and monolithic; for instance, there was a good deal of diversity of opinion on specific theoretical issues among syntacticians of the 1980s who would have considered themselves adherents of the Government-Binding Theory.[17] One final cautionary note is that these are far from being the only theories currently under development and consideration, or the only ones worthy of notice.[18] In fact, a wide variety of different theoretical approaches are being vigorously pursued. Moreover, at different times in the history of the discipline, ideas or research topics that have lain dormant for years or decades sometimes take on new interest, thanks to changing conditions in the field that make them relevant. The fact that many different detectives are following many different theories is not surprising, given the immense scope and complexity of the mystery that they are trying to solve.

AN ISSUE FOR THE FUTURE: PRINCIPLES AND PARAMETERS AND THE CORE-PERIPHERY DISTINCTION

One particular long-range vision of the 1980s and 1990s deserves special mention at the conclusion of this brief history, for its interest as an idea about the way in which English grammar and universal grammar are related. This idea, which often goes under the name *Principles-and-Parameters Theory,* is that universal grammar consists of a small finite set of principles, at least some of which are not entirely fixed, but which instead offer choices that the language-learner must make on the basis of evidence from the linguistic environment. These choice-points are called *parameters,* and a particular choice is sometimes described as a *parameter value* or a *parameter setting.* For instance, one such principle in universal grammar might initially take the form shown in (40), prior to a language-learner's exposure to evidence from his or her native language.

(40) Head words go $\left\{\begin{array}{l} \underline{\hspace{1em}} \text{ before} \\ \underline{\hspace{1em}} \text{ after} \end{array}\right\}$ their complements.

Learners growing up in an English-speaking environment would immediately find ample evidence to make the first of the two choices listed, so that the form that this universal principle would have when it becomes part of the grammar of English would be that shown in (41).

(41) Head words go $\left\{\begin{array}{l} \underline{\hspace{1em}\checkmark} \text{ before} \\ \underline{\hspace{1em}} \text{ after} \end{array}\right\}$ their complements.

By contrast, learners growing up in a Japanese-speaking environment would find ample evidence for the opposite choice, thus guaranteeing that the final form of (40) in their grammar would be (42).

(42) Head words go $\left\{\begin{array}{l} \underline{\hspace{1em}} \text{ before} \\ \underline{\checkmark\hspace{1em}} \text{ after} \end{array}\right\}$ their complements.

Starting with Chomsky 1981a and 1981b, that portion of the grammar of a language that consists of fleshed-out principles of universal grammar is called a *core grammar*. It is also proposed in these works that the grammar of a language contains a *periphery,* a residue of constructions that are irreducibly and idiosyncratically language-specific. For example, at least some aspects of the peculiar two-clause comparative structure in (6) might lie outside of core grammar and thus have peripheral status.

The principles-and-parameters vision takes a particularly ambitious form in several recent works by Chomsky and others (e.g., Chomsky 1991). In these works, it is hypothesized that the grammar of any specific language consists simply of the set of principles found in universal grammar, with particular choices selected in places where parametric options are available. According to this view, what are traditionally seen as particular syntactic rules and constructions in individual languages do not have any basic reality of their own, but instead are the result of specific parameter settings in the principles given by universal grammar. Thus, apart from knowledge of English words and their individual syntactic properties, knowledge of English syntax comes to amount to little more than knowledge of where English puts the check marks in the principles given by universal grammar. On this view, then, core grammar covers so much territory that peripheral grammar eventually disappears.

At the present time, advocates of this particular vision still have far to go in constructing a specific theory that will provide accounts of every construction in any single language in terms of principles and parameters of universal grammar. For English in particular, no theory of principles and parameters yet exists from which we could derive an account of all of the syntactic facts covered in this textbook, to say nothing of all of the facts about English that have not been covered. In addition, at least some other linguists have argued that certain syntactic phenomena are irreducibly peripheral. For instance, Fillmore, Kay, and O'Connor (1988) mention several English constructions that they believe must be accounted for in terms of construction-specific rules, including in particular the *let alone* construction illustrated in (43).

(43) I barely got up in time to eat lunch, let alone cook breakfast.[19]

Despite the large amount of work that remains to be done in fleshing it out, and despite the criticisms that have already been raised against it, this aggressive vision of core grammar is likely to prove very useful for generative syntactic theory in the future, in light of the extent to which it constantly focuses the attention of those working in the field on the question of what aspects of a fluent speaker's capacity for syntax are innate and what aspects are environmentally determined and thus specific to a particular language. There may indeed be a special benefit in the long run for those with a primary interest in the special field covered by this textbook —namely, a much sharper and clearer idea than we have at present about exactly what it is that is "English" in English syntax.

Notes

1. For a detailed history of generative linguistic theory to the middle 1980s, see Newmeyer 1986.

2. Elementary discussions of the learning problem that the young child faces and the role of innate linguistic principles in solving this problem can be found in Baker 1978, chapter 17, in Baker 1979, and in Hornstein and Lightfoot 1981, chapter 1.

3. For textbook discussions of early transformational grammar, see Akmajian and Heny 1975 and Baker 1978.

4. Details on verbal inflection are omitted here and also in the discussion of the passive transformation below.

5. Baker 1978, chapters 5 and 7, gives a more detailed account of what constitutes a legitimate transformational derivation.

6. In a later version of this theory (one inspired in part by an article of Luigi Rizzi's that eventually appeared as part II of Rizzi 1982), the bounding nodes for English were taken to be sentences and noun phrases instead of clauses and noun

phrases. One could deduce from the new theory, as from the original one, that the indirect question in (20) would be unacceptable.

7. The French argument is presented in Kayne and Pollock 1978, the Irish argument in McCloskey 1979.

8. One was the Fixed-Subject Constraint of Bresnan 1972. Another was the Empty Category Principle of Chomsky 1981a.

9. The suggestions on this topic include, among others, the single-clause restriction of Lees and Klima 1963, the Specified-Subject Condition of Chomsky 1973, and Principle A of the binding theory of Chomsky 1981a.

10. This theory originated in Chomsky 1970. It has been the topic of many works since that time, including a major monograph by Ray Jackendoff (Jackendoff 1977).

11. In Chomsky 1981a it was assumed that active verbs license following noun phrases by assigning abstract Case to them (abstract in the sense of possibly not being marked overtly in the words of the language). The supposition then is that passive verbs are distinguished by the loss of this capacity to assign Case to a following noun phrase, thus forcing the noun phrase to move to a position where Case can be assigned to it in some other way.

12. Several textbooks have been devoted to Chomsky's theory as it developed during the 1970s and 1980s, including Radford 1981, Van Riemsdijk and Williams 1986, and Haegeman 1991. See also Sells 1985, chapter 2.

13. A very modest example of modular thinking was given in subsection 3.5.4, where it was shown that complicated phrases can best be understood as resulting from the interaction of several simple rules.

14. Perlmutter 1983 collects a number of influential papers on Relational Grammar, and Blake 1990 gives a systematic exposition of the theory. Lexical-Functional Grammar was foreshadowed in Bresnan 1978, and the most basic collection of papers on this theory is Bresnan 1982. See also the discussion of Lexical-Functional Grammar in Sells 1985, chapter 4.

15. See, for instance, Kaplan and Zaenen 1989 on islands, and see Bresnan 1994 on relations between grammatical categories and grammatical functions in "locative-inversion" constructions.

16. See in particular Gazdar 1981, 1982; also Gazdar et al. 1985 and Sells 1985, chapter 3.

17. McCloskey 1988 contains an illuminating comparison of the four theories discussed above, noting several issues on which one finds more basic agreement across standard theoretical boundaries than within them.

18. For a collection of papers with remarks on a variety of different theoretical approaches that were being actively pursued in the late 1970s, see Moravcsik and Wirth 1980.

19. Another defense of peripheral grammar is given in Baker 1991, where it is suggested that a better theory of universal grammar will result if accounting for

the position of English auxiliary verbs and *not* is made the responsibility of peripheral grammar.

References

Akmajian, Adrian, and Frank Heny. 1975. *An introduction to the principles of transformational syntax.* Cambridge, Mass.: MIT Press.

Baker, C. L. 1978. *Introduction to generative-transformational syntax.* Englewood Cliffs, N.J.: Prentice-Hall.

Baker, C. L. 1979. Syntactic theory and the projection problem. *Linguistic Inquiry* 10, 533–581.

Baker, C. L. 1991. The syntax of English *not:* The limits of core grammar. *Linguistic Inquiry* 22, 387–429.

Blake, Barry. 1990. *Relational grammar.* Routledge: London.

Bresnan, Joan. 1972. On complementizers: Toward a syntactic theory of complement types. *Foundations of Language* 6, 297–321.

Bresnan, Joan. 1973. Syntax of the comparative clause construction in English. *Linguistic Inquiry* 4, 275–343.

Bresnan, Joan. 1978. A realistic transformational grammar. In *Linguistic theory and psychological reality,* ed. Morris Halle, Joan Bresnan, and George A. Miller, 1–59. Cambridge, Mass.: MIT Press.

Bresnan, Joan, ed. 1982. *The mental representation of grammatical relations.* Cambridge, Mass.: MIT Press.

Bresnan, Joan. 1994. Locative inversion and the architecture of universal grammar. *Language* 70, 1–52.

Chomsky, Noam. 1957. *Syntactic structures.* The Hague: Mouton.

Chomsky, Noam. 1959. Review of B. F. Skinner, *Verbal behavior* (New York: Appleton-Century-Crofts, 1957). *Language* 35, 26–58. Reprinted in Fodor and Katz 1964, 547–578.

Chomsky, Noam. 1962a. The logical basis of linguistic theory. In *Proceedings of the Ninth International Congress of Linguists, Cambridge, Mass., August 27–31, 1962,* ed. Horace G. Lunt, 914–978. The Hague: Mouton.

Chomsky, Noam. 1962b. A transformational approach to syntax. In *Proceedings of the Third Texas Conference on Problems of Linguistic Analysis of English, 1958,* ed. Archibald A. Hill, 124–158. Austin, Tex.: University of Texas Press. Reprinted in Fodor and Katz 1964, 211–245.

Chomsky, Noam. 1964. *Current issues in linguistic theory.* The Hague: Mouton.

Chomsky, Noam. 1965. *Aspects of the theory of syntax.* Cambridge, Mass.: MIT Press.

Chomsky, Noam. 1970. Remarks on nominalization. In *Readings in English transformational grammar,* ed. Roderick A. Jacobs and Peter S. Rosenbaum, 184–221. Waltham, Mass.: Ginn.

Chomsky, Noam. 1973. Conditions on transformations. In *A festschrift for Morris Halle,* ed. Stephen Anderson and Paul Kiparsky, 232–286. New York: Holt, Rinehart and Winston.

Chomsky, Noam. 1976. Conditions on rules of grammar. *Linguistic Analysis* 4, 303–351.

Chomsky, Noam. 1981a. *Lectures on government and binding.* Dordrecht: Foris.

Chomsky, Noam. 1981b. Principles and parameters in syntactic theory. In Hornstein and Lightfoot 1981, 32–75.

Chomsky, Noam. 1991. Some notes on economy of derivation and representation. In *Principles and parameters in comparative grammar,* ed. Robert Freidin, 417–454. Cambridge, Mass.: MIT Press.

Emonds, Joseph. 1970. Root and structure-preserving transformations. Doctoral dissertation, MIT.

Emonds, Joseph. 1976. *A transformational approach to English syntax.* New York: Academic Press.

Fillmore, Charles J., Paul Kay, and Mary Catherine O'Connor. 1988. Regularity and idiomaticity in grammatical constructions: The case of *let alone. Language* 64, 501–538.

Fodor, Jerry A., and Jerrold J. Katz, eds. 1964. *The structure of language.* Englewood Cliffs, NJ: Prentice-Hall.

Gazdar, Gerald. 1981. Unbounded dependencies and coordinate structure. *Linguistic Inquiry* 12, 155–184.

Gazdar, Gerald. 1982. Phrase structure grammar. In *The nature of syntactic representation,* ed. Pauline Jacobson and Geoffrey K. Pullum, 131–186. Dordrecht: D. Reidel.

Gazdar, Gerald, Ewan Klein, Geoffrey Pullum, and Ivan Sag. 1985. *Generalized Phrase Structure Grammar.* Cambridge, Mass.: Harvard University Press.

Haegeman, Liliane. 1991. *Introduction to Government and Binding Theory.* Oxford: Blackwell.

Hornstein, Norbert, and David Lightfoot, eds. 1981. *Explanation in linguistics: The logical problem of language acquisition.* London: Longman.

Jackendoff, Ray. 1977. $\overline{X}$ *syntax.* Cambridge, Mass.: MIT Press.

Kaplan, Ronald, and Annie Zaenen. 1989. Long-distance dependencies, constituent structure, and functional uncertainty. In *Alternative conceptions of phrase structure,* ed. Mark R. Baltin and Anthony S. Kroch, 17–42. Chicago: University of Chicago Press.

Kayne, Richard, and Jean-Yves Pollock. 1978. Stylistic Inversion, successive cyclicity, and Move NP in French. *Linguistic Inquiry* 9, 595–621.

Klima, Edward S. 1964. Negation in English. In Fodor and Katz 1964, 246–323.

Lees, Robert B., and Edward Klima. 1963. Rules for English pronominalization. *Language* 39, 17–29.

McCloskey, James. 1979. *Transformational syntax and model theoretic semantics: A case study in Modern Irish*. Dordrecht: D. Reidel.

McCloskey, James. 1988. Syntactic theory. In *Linguistics: The Cambridge survey*, vol. 1, ed. Frederick J. Newmeyer, 18–59. Cambridge: Cambridge University Press.

Moravcsik, Edith, and Jessica Wirth, eds. 1980. *Current approaches to syntax.* Syntax and semantics, vol. 13. New York: Academic Press.

Newmeyer, Frederick J. 1986. *Linguistic theory in America,* 2d ed. Orlando, Fla.: Academic Press.

Perlmutter, David, ed. 1983. *Studies in Relational Grammar 1.* Chicago: The University of Chicago Press.

Radford, Andrew. 1981. *Transformational syntax: A student's guide to Chomsky's Extended Standard Theory.* Cambridge: Cambridge University Press.

Riemsdijk, Henk van, and Edwin Williams. 1986. *Introduction to the theory of grammar.* Cambridge, Mass.: MIT Press.

Rizzi, Luigi, 1982. *Issues in Italian syntax.* Dordrecht: Foris.

Rosenbaum, Peter S. 1967. *The grammar of English predicate complement constructions.* Cambridge, Mass.: MIT Press.

Ross, John Robert. 1967. Constraints on variables in syntax. Doctoral dissertation, MIT.

Sells, Peter. 1985. *Lectures on contemporary syntactic theories: An introduction to Government-Binding Theory, Generalized Phrase-Structure Grammar, and Lexical-Functional Grammar.* Stanford, Calif.: Center for the Study of Language and Information. Distributed by University of Chicago Press.

Stockwell, Robert P., Paul Schachter, and Barbara H. Partee. 1973. *The major syntactic structures of English.* New York: Holt, Rinehart and Winston.

Appendix B

Summary of Basic Syntactic Structures

The purpose of this appendix is to gather in one place all of the basic structures introduced in the text. Each of these basic structures corresponds to a specific syntactic rule, and each can be thought of as one of the "tree pieces" from which larger syntactic units are constructed. The structures are organized by the chapter in which they first appear in tree form.

CHAPTER 3

3-1 The most basic structures for simple sentences

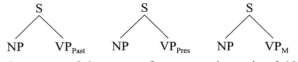

Structures of these types first appear in section 3.10.

3-2 Structure for infinitival phrases

3-3 Verb-phrase structures for intransitive verbs

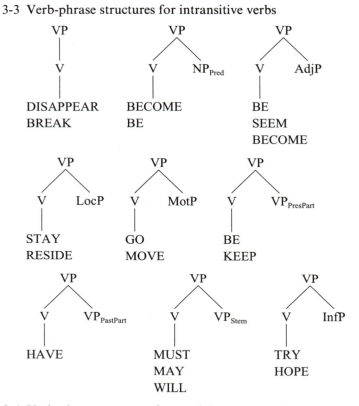

3-4 Verb-phrase structure for special-purpose DO

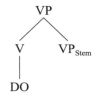

3-5 Verb-phrase structures for transitive verbs

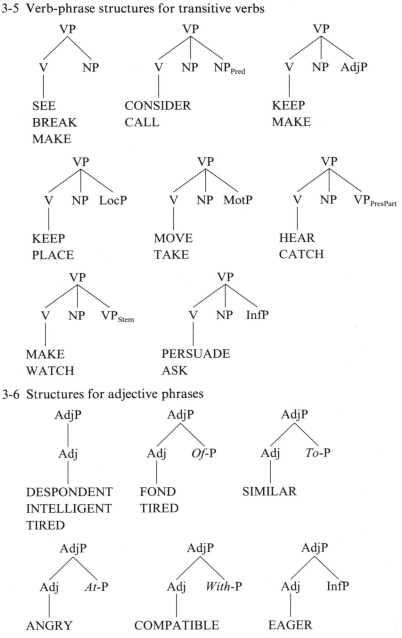

3-6 Structures for adjective phrases

A modified structure for EAGER is given in 4-7.

3-7 Structures for common-noun phrases

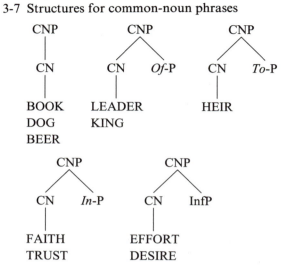

CHAPTER 4

4-1 Structures for two varieties of sentences, based on whether the verb phrase is headed by a finite verb (a past-tense verb, a present-tense verb, or a modal) or by a bare-stem verb

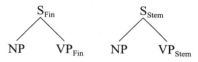

4-2 Structures for two varieties of *that* clauses, finite and bare-stem

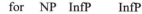

4-3 Structures for infinitival clauses

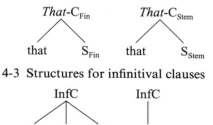

4-4 Structures for indirect questions

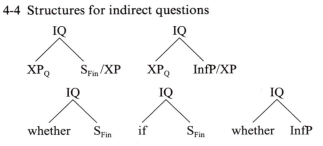

4-5 Verb-phrase structures for intransitive verbs that take clauses as complements

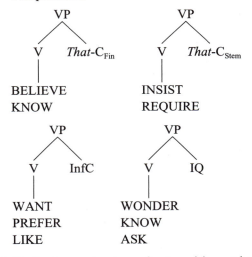

4-6 Verb-phrase structures for transitive verbs that take clauses as complements

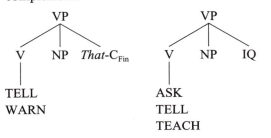

4-7 Adjective-phrase structures for adjectives that take clauses as complements

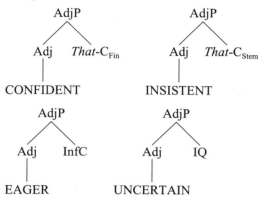

4-8 A common-noun structure for a noun that takes infinitival clauses

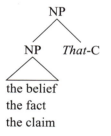

4-9 A special structure for noun phrases containing *that* clauses

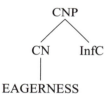

4-10 Additional structures for sentences, to provide for sentences that have clauses as subjects

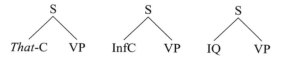

4-11 Sample structures with substitute-subject *it*

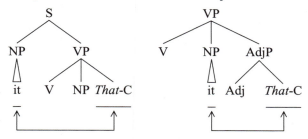

CHAPTER 5

5-1 Structure for genitive construction

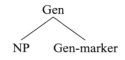

5-2 Structures for elementary noun phrases

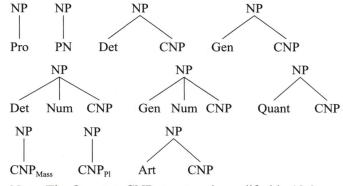

Note: The Quant + CNP structure is modified in 12-3.

5-3 Structure for partitive noun phrases (modified in 12-3)

5-4 Structure for noun phrases consisting of gerundive phrases

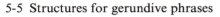

NP
|
Gerundive

5-5 Structures for gerundive phrases

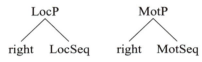

Gerundive   Gerundive

Gen   VP_{PresPart}   VP_{PresPart}

CHAPTER 6

6-1 Structures for locative phrases and motion phrases

LocP   MotP

right   LocSeq   right   MotSeq

6-2 Structures for locative sequences and motion sequences (all elements
are optional, except that at least one must be chosen)

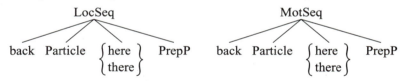

LocSeq   MotSeq

back Particle { here } PrepP   back Particle { here } PrepP
                { there }   { there }

6-3 Structures for (i) normal order of direct object and particle;
(ii) shifted order

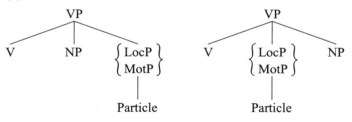

VP   VP

V   NP   { LocP }   V   { LocP }   NP
           { MotP }   { MotP }

Particle   Particle

CHAPTER 7

7-1 Basic tree pieces for four kinds of definite free relatives

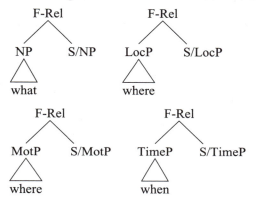

7-2 How the category membership of free relatives is determined on the basis of the category membership of their introducing phrases. (The last is a general schema that represents all of the more specific diagrams.)

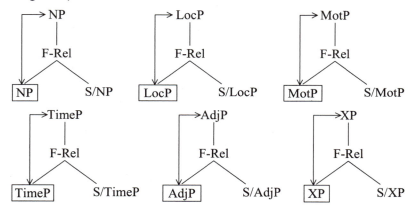

CHAPTER 9

9-1 Typical structures for passive phrases (past-participal verb phrases with missing first noun phrases)

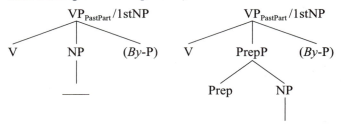

9-2 Larger verb-phrase structures involving passive phrases as complements

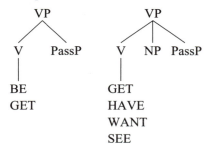

9-3 Adjective-phrase structures involving *easy* adjectives

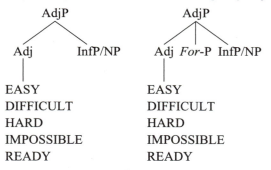

Note: READY also appears in the structure shown for EAGER in 4-7.

CHAPTER 10

10-1 Rules involved in the construction of finite bound relatives

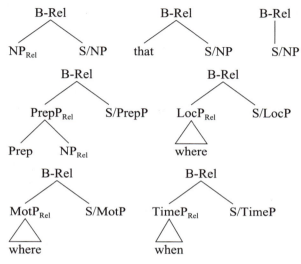

10-2 Rules involved in the construction of infinitival bound relatives

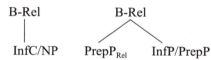

10-3 Rules combining bound relatives and other postnominal modifiers
to CNPs

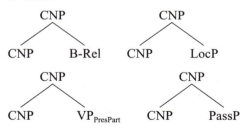

10-4 Rules constructing *with* phrases

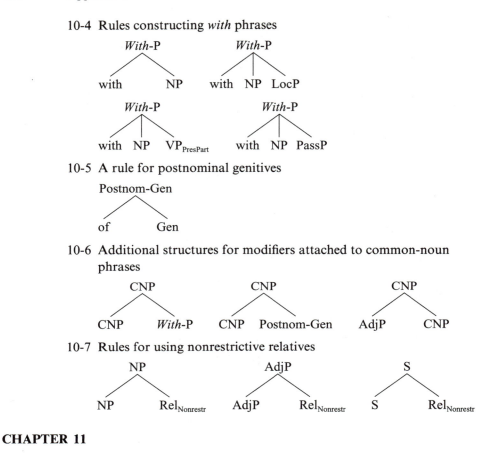

10-5 A rule for postnominal genitives

10-6 Additional structures for modifiers attached to common-noun phrases

10-7 Rules for using nonrestrictive relatives

CHAPTER 11

11-1 Basic rules for verbal and sentential modifiers

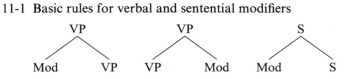

11-2 Tree illustrating special movement rule for unstressed "small" verbs

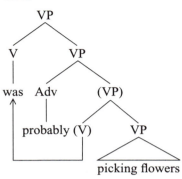

11-3 Trees illustrating special movement rule of special-purpose heads across *not*

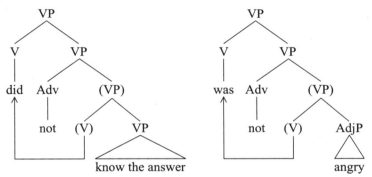

CHAPTER 12

12-1 Trees for degree elements, including a tree illustrating the special effect of *enough* on an adjectival (or adverbial) head

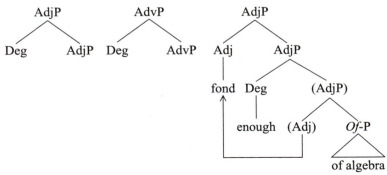

12-2 Tree illustrating the structure of comparative adjective phrases
      where the adjective ends in *-er*

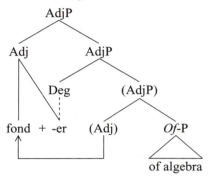

12-3 Revised rules involving quantity words and quantity phrases
      (earlier versions in 5-2 and 5-3)

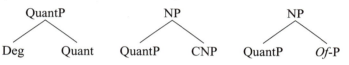

12-4 Special structures involving suppressed *much* and *many* with *more*
      and *enough*

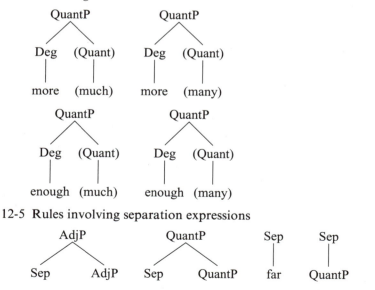

12-5 Rules involving separation expressions

12-6 A rule for using a quantity phrase as a verbal modifier

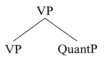

12-7 Two rules for comparative clauses

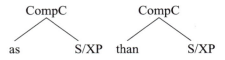

(Here XP can be any phrase that can serve as a compared phrase, including noun phrases, quantity phrases, adjective phrases, and many different kinds of adverbial phrases.)

12-8 Rules for positioning of clauses associated with degree words

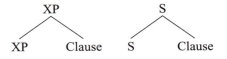

CHAPTER 13

13-1 The verb-phrase configuration for existential *there*, with *there* being understood as a subject, whether it is very near to BE, or else separated by a number of "transparent" verbs

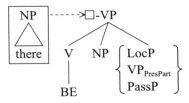

(The dashed arrow indicates that the identification may be indirect.)

13-2 An illustration of the kind of tree diagram that is appropriate for existential sentences when *there* and BE are separated by several transparent words

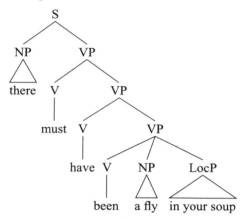

13-3 The verb-phrase configuration for cleft *it*, with *it* being understood as a subject, whether it is very near to BE, or else separated by a number of "transparent" verbs

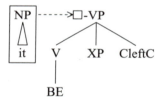

(Here XP can be a number of different kinds of phrases, listed in detail in subsection 13.3.2. The dashed arrow indicates that the identification may be indirect.)

13-4 An illustration of the kind of tree diagram that is appropriate for cleft constructions when *it* and BE are separated by several transparent words

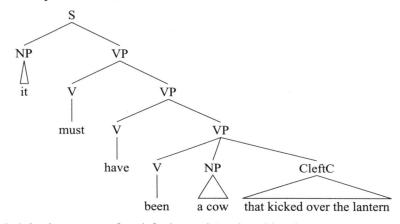
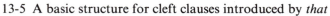
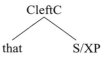

13-5 A basic structure for cleft clauses introduced by *that*

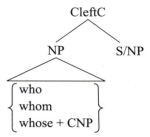

13-6 A structure for cleft clauses introduced by *wh* noun phrases

13-7 A rule for cleft clauses introduced by prepositional phrases

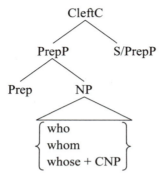

CHAPTER 14

14-1 Two trees illustrating how inverted sentences are formed

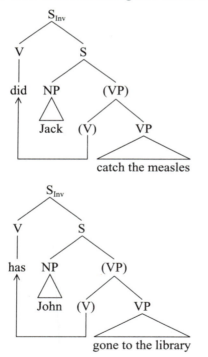

14-2 Structures for direct yes-no questions, direct alternative questions, direct phrasal questions where a nonsubject is questioned, and direct phrasal questions where the subject is questioned

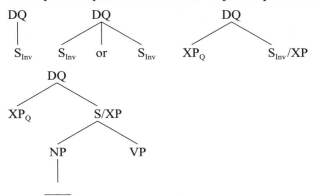

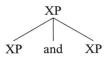

For the very complex structure found in a negative question, see (23) in subsection 14.1.2.

CHAPTER 16

16-1 General schema for conjoined structures, where XP is any kind of phrase or clause

```
        XP
      / | \
    XP and XP
```

See also (6), subsection 16.1.1, for other conjunction possibilities (*both* XP *and* XP, XP *or* XP, etc.).

16-2 Right Extraction

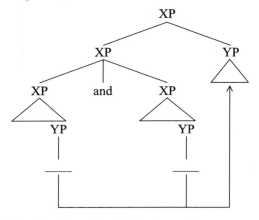

16-3 Sample alternative indirect question

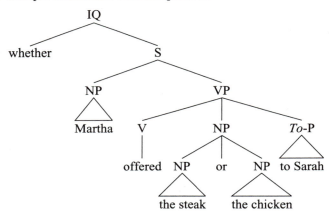

Index